AI DATA CENTER NETWORK DESIGN AND TECHNOLOGIES

AI DATA CENTER NETWORK DESIGN AND TECHNOLOGIES

Mahesh Subramaniam, Michal Styszynski,
Himanshu Tambakuwala

◆ Addison-Wesley

Hoboken, New Jersey

Many of the designations used by manufacturers and sellers to distinguish their products are claimed as trademarks. Where those designations appear in this book, and the publisher was aware of a trademark claim, the designations have been printed with initial capital letters or in all capitals.

The authors and publisher have taken care in the preparation of this book, but make no expressed or implied warranty of any kind and assume no responsibility for errors or omissions. No liability is assumed for incidental or consequential damages in connection with or arising out of the use of the information or programs contained herein.

Visit us on the Web: informit.com/aw

Library of Congress Control Number: 2025949447

Copyright © 2026 Pearson Education, Inc.

All rights reserved. This publication is protected by copyright, and permission must be obtained from the publisher prior to any prohibited reproduction, storage in a retrieval system, or transmission in any form or by any means, electronic, mechanical, photocopying, recording, or likewise. For information regarding permissions, request forms, and the appropriate contacts within the Pearson Education Global Rights & Permissions Department, please visit www.pearson.com/global-permission-granting.html.

No patent liability is assumed with respect to the use of the information contained herein. Although every precaution has been taken in the preparation of this book, the publisher and author assume no responsibility for errors or omissions. Nor is any liability assumed for damages resulting from the use of the information contained herein.

Please contact us with concerns about any potential bias at https://www.pearson.com/report-bias.html.

ISBN-13: 978-0-13-543628-8
ISBN-10: 0-13-543628-1

3 2026

Head of Enterprise Content and Training, Enterprise Learning and Skills
Julie Phifer

Executive Editor
James Manly

Development Editor
Ellie C. Bru

Managing Editor
Sandra Schroeder

Senior Project Editor
Mandie Frank

Copy Editor
Kitty Wilson

Indexer
Timothy Wright

Proofreader
Donna E. Mulder

Technical Reviewer
Tanveer Dandiana

Designer
Chuti Prasertsith

Compositor
codeMantra

To my brother, Rajesh, who taught me the meaning of connection—long before I ever studied networks. "Your absence echoes in every page, a quiet hum between the lines.... A bright star in my sky, the legacy I live and build for....You are the architecture of my soul—my reason to dream, my need to create, my home in every connection."

I also want to dedicate this book to my parents, Sarasu and Subramaniam, my wife, Ramya, and my sons, Rithvik and Rithish. They are my steady roots beneath every life storm, the strength that holds the ground I walk upon. Their love is my unwavering light; that light is the one and only thing which makes me stand.

—Mahesh

I want to dedicate this book to my wife, Kasia, and my sons, Ernest and Marcel, for their love, patience, and understanding. Their encouragement, and joy for life inspire me every day and have helped me complete this book.

—Michal

To the ones I owe it all: Neha, Rachit, Aanvi, and my parents, Prakash and Indu. Thank you for every late night and every quiet sacrifice you made.

—Himanshu

Contents

Foreword xv
Preface xvii
Acknowledgments xix
About the Authors xxi

1   Wonders in the Workload 1
    What's New in AI Data Center Workloads 1
    The Life Cycle of an AI Model 2
    Training an AI Model 3
    Parallelism 4
        Data Parallelism 4
        Model Parallelism 5
    Job Completion Time (JCT) 6
    Tail Latency 7
        Understanding Traffic and RDMA 8
        RDMA Transport Types 9
        RoCEv2 11
    Summary 16
    Test Your Knowledge 17

2   "The Common-Man View" of AI Data Center Fabrics 19
    Training vs. Inference AI Data Centers 19
        AI Training Data Centers 19
        AI Inference Data Centers 20
    InfiniBand vs. Ethernet for AI Training Data Centers 21
        Advantages of InfiniBand in AI Training Clusters 21
        Advantages of Ethernet in AI Training Clusters 22
    Ethernet Hardware Switches and Advanced Software Features 22
    Handling Elephant Flows 24

Load-Balancing Techniques 25

Congestion Management and Mitigation Techniques 26

Summary 28

Test Your Knowledge 29

3 Network Design Considerations 31

Background Introduction 31

Training Data Center Architecture 33

Rail-Optimized Design (ROD) 34

Rail-Unified Design (RUD) 42

Rack Design 45

    Top-of-Rack 45

    Middle-of-Row 47

    End-of-Row 47

    Design Comparison 48

Scheduled Fabric 49

Topologies 50

    Dragonfly Topology 50

    Torus Topology 53

Inference Data Center Architecture 56

Multi-Planar Scale-Out Architectures 56

Summary 63

Test Your Knowledge 64

References 66

4 Optics and Cable Management 67

Scaling Optics for AI Clusters 67

Challenges in Optical Innovation 70

Packet Flow 70

    Demultiplexers and Multiplexers 71

    Digital Signal Processors (DSPs) 71

Transmission Modes 73

Contents ix

   Multi-Mode Fiber (MMF) 74

   Single-Mode Fiber (SMF) 75

   Dense Wavelength Division Multiplexing (DWDM) 75

   AI Server Connectivity Options 75

  Transceiver Types 76

  Cable and Connector Types 78

  Standards 79

   High-Bandwidth Optics 80

  Further Innovations in Optics 82

  Summary 83

  Test Your Knowledge 85

  References 86

5 Thermal and Power Efficiency Considerations 87

  Thermal Footprints in AI Data Centers 87

  Airflow Options 88

   Front-to-Back Airflow 88

   Back-to-Front Airflow 88

   Bidirectional Fans 89

   Choosing the Fan Direction 89

  Liquid Cooling 89

   Immersion Liquid Cooling 90

   Cold Plate Liquid Cooling 91

   Rear-Door Heat Exchanger Liquid Cooling 92

   Sprayed Liquid Cooling 93

  Summary 93

  Test Your Knowledge 94

  References 95

6 Efficient Load Balancing 97

  Per-Flow Load Balancing 99

   Static Load Balancing 100

Contents

    Dynamic Load Balancing 103

    Global Load Balancing 106

    Traffic Engineering–Based Load Balancing 110

Per-Packet Load Balancing 115

    Random Spray 116

    DLB Per-Packet Mode 116

    Selective Packet Spraying 116

Load-Balancing Mechanism Comparison 117

Summary 118

Test Your Knowledge 119

7 RoCEv2 Transport and Congestion Management 123

Congestion Points 123

Explicit Congestion Notification (ECN) 127

    Priority Flow Control (PFC) 130

Data Center Quantized Congestion Notification (DCQCN) 134

Source Flow Control (SFC) 136

Congestion Signaling 137

Summary 139

Test Your Knowledge 140

8 IP Routing for AI/ML Fabrics 143

Dynamic IP Routing Options 144

eBGP Underlay for Three-Stage/Five-Stage Fabric for an AI Data Center 145

    eBGP Underlay and BGP Unnumbered 145

    BGP ASN Allocation 149

    BGP Advanced Capabilities 151

    BGP DPF for AI Data Center Path Diversity 155

    Traffic-to-Fabric Color Mapping 161

Interior Gateway Protocols for AI Data Center Fabric 162

    IS-IS for IP Fabric: Flood Reduction and Flex Algo 168

Multi-tenancy for an AI/ML Cluster Data Center Network 171
    Network-Level Multi-tenancy 171
    Server-Level Multi-tenancy 173
    Combining Server- and Network-Level Multi-tenancy
    for AI/ML Clusters 175
Microsegmentation and Multi-tenancy for an AI/ML Data Center 177
Extending IP Routing to the Server 177
Traffic Engineering in the AI Data Center Fabric 178
Segment Routing and SRv6 for AI/ML Fabrics 179
    SRv6-Based Traffic Engineering 182
    SRv6 Compressed SID 183
    Segment Routing for AI/ML Clusters 183
Summary 184
Test Your Knowledge 185
References 187

9 Storage Network Design and Technologies 189

The AI Data Center Life Cycle and Storage Networks 191
Storage Network Design Types 193
Block, Object, and File Storage Systems 198
NVMe-oF for Block-Level Access 199
    NVMe-o-TCP State Machine 201
NVMe-o-RDMA/RoCEv2 State Machine 206
High-Performance File Systems 208
GPUDirect Storage 211
    InfiniBand for Storage 213
    Typical InfiniBand Designs 214
    LID: InfiniBand Addressing and Frame Formats 215
    InfiniBand QoS Support 216
Summary 217
Test Your Knowledge 218
References 219

10 AI Network Performance KPIs 221
Significance of Performance Benchmarking 221
MLCommons for AI Data Centers 223
MLCommons Initiatives 224
MLCommons Benchmarking Suites 224
Benchmarking a Data Center for Machine Learning 225
Summary 226
Test Your Knowledge 227
References 228

11 Monitoring and Telemetry 229
Exploring Monitoring Options 229
Network Monitoring in an AI/ML Data Center Network 231
In-Band Flow Analyzer (IFA) 234
Corrective Actions 237
Summary 238
Reference 238

12 Ultra Ethernet Consortium (UEC) 239
UEC Developments and Working Groups 241
Link Layer Working Group 242
Transport Working Group 242
Software Working Group 243
Other Working Groups 243
UEC Key Terminology 244
The UEC and Network Architectures 246
UEC and the Existing Ethernet 246
A New Protocol Stack 247
Data Plan: Packet Forwarding Options 252
UDP-Based Encapsulation for UET 252
UET over IP: The New Entropy Field 255
Packet Delivery Modes 257

　　　　Reliable Ordered Delivery (ROD)... 259

　　　　Reliable Unordered Delivery (RUD)... 259

　　　　Reliable Unordered Delivery Idempotent (RUDI)............................. 259

　　　　Unreliable Unordered Delivery (UUD).. 260

　　　　UEC Delivery Modes Comparison... 260

　　Congestion Management (CM) in the UEC Specification........................ 261

　　　　Network Signal Congestion Control (NSCC)................................... 261

　　　　Receiver Credit Congestion Control (RCCC).................................... 262

　　　　Credit-Based Flow Control (CBFC).. 263

　　Packet Trimming and Fast Retransmissions.. 264

　　Link Layer Reliability (LLR) Mechanism.. 265

　　In-Network Collectives (INC) and xCCL... 266

　　Management and Orchestration.. 268

　　Interoperability and Backward Compatibility...................................... 269

　　Compliance and Certification.. 269

　　UEC Challenges and Future Directions... 269

　　Comparing UEC to InfiniBand and RoCEv2... 270

　　Summary... 271

　　Test Your Knowledge.. 272

　　References.. 273

13　Scale-Up Systems... 275

　　Key Building Blocks of Scale-Up Systems... 278

　　Scale-Up Ethernet Transport (SUE-T).. 281

　　Ultra Accelerator Link (UALink)... 286

　　Memory Coherence in Scale-Up Systems.. 291

　　Scale-Up Systems: Key Differences and Similarities............................. 292

　　Summary... 294

　　Test Your Knowledge.. 295

　　References.. 297

14	**Conclusion**	**299**
	DC Network Role for AI	299
	Caveats and Challenges	300
	Future Developments	302
	Final Remarks	304
	References	305

Appendix A Questions and Answers **307**

Appendix B Acronyms **329**

Index **335**

Foreword

If you've picked up this book, you're likely not someone who has bought into the media hysterics around AI or who thinks that it's a danger to humanity. Those folks have watched too many *Matrix* or *Terminator* movies. Don't get me wrong, as there are reasons to be concerned about AI and reasons there should be intelligent regulations around some of it. But AI is a tool, nothing more. Like any tool it can be used or misused.

Like it or not, AI is integrated into our everyday lives, often in ways that we don't even notice. Arguably, the first widespread use of AI was in spam filters. When you buy spam detection software, you buy a *database* of patterns common to most spam email and an algorithm (*model*) that watches for characteristics in your email that match those patterns. When it thinks it recognizes (*infers*) spam, it moves the email to an isolated mailbox. You actively *train* your spam filter by periodically reviewing your spam mailbox, identifying email that is not spam, so that the app can better infer spam from new data.

There are some fundamental AI/ML concepts in what I just described: a curated reference database, a pattern-matching model, training, and inference based on new data.

Want another example? The first "smart" doorbell I purchased was little more than a camera, a button, and some motion detection capabilities. The one I have now can differentiate a person from random motion. It can tell me if that person dropped off or picked up a package. With a little training (there's that word again), it can identify friends and family members who come to the door. Through my Wi-Fi network, it connects to a database and a pattern recognition model.

And, of course, there's your smartphone with AI apps from face ID and voice commands, to music and entertainment apps that learn your preferences and make recommendations, to targeted advertisements in your social media, to the ability to "Google" (the company name has become a verb) an answer to almost any question you might have. Your new television likely has AI and maybe your new refrigerator as well. Your new car is swimming with it, giving you directions and keeping you in your lane and telling you if you're following too closely. And as I type this foreword, Microsoft Word follows what I'm typing, suggests sentence completion, and catches spelling and grammatical errors.

Then there are the AI apps that are not quietly hiding in your refrigerator or word processor: generative AI that can create images and music, write academic papers or code, or generate designs; predictive AI that can make forecasts based on analysis of historical data (note that predictive AI can make some embarrassingly bad predictions when analyzing particularly chaotic systems, such as human behavior); and natural language models that allow you to communicate naturally with AI systems and receive human-sounding answers.

And, of course, self-driving automobiles utilize a variety of AI models to operate safely on the road. I personally believe self-driving automobiles are not quite ready for prime time, but I also believe they are our future. There could well be a not-so-distant future in which manually driving a car is considered illegally dangerous.

Finally, as network nerds we've all heard the term "autonomous networks." Networks tend to be highly predictable systems, and with machine learning and analytics we are moving closer to network autonomy and further away from the one factor that accounts for most network outages: humans touching the network.

AI, in its many subgroups, can be simple enough for you to create and run programs right on your laptop. But processing massive databases can be hugely expensive in infrastructure, power, and cooling costs. Massive databases require massive, quickly accessible storage infrastructure. Processing that data within reasonable job completion times requires powerful servers running GPU/TPU/DPU clusters in parallel, sometimes requiring tens of thousands of processors running the same model. In the largest-scale cases the storage, processing backends, and inference frontends can involve not just separate types of data centers but also physically separate data centers. Reliably distributing and collecting data among these processors calls for new kinds of data center networking because storage, processing (training), and inference all have different requirements.

That's where this first-of-its-kind book comes in. My friends Mahesh, Himanshu, and Michal have among them a vast level of experience designing AI data centers. They explain in great detail the unique requirements of AI data centers and the technologies created to address these problems. Many of these technologies are already finding their way into high-performance compute (HPC) data centers and will eventually find their way into normal cloud data centers. So even if you are not an AIDC specialist, it behooves you to become familiar with the technologies and design principles covered here.

–Jeff Doyle

Preface

AI Data Center Network Design and Technologies is a comprehensive, practical guide for network engineers, architects, and technology leaders who are building, scaling, or optimizing the infrastructure that supports artificial intelligence. This book bridges the gap between theory and practice, providing an in-depth look at the design, deployment, and management of high-performance AI data centers—where scale-out and scale-up networking, xPU-based computing, storage, and operations work together.

Register your copy of *AI Data Center Network Design and Technologies* on the InformIT site for convenient access to updates and/or corrections as they become available. To start the registration process, go to informit.com/register and log in or create an account. Enter the product ISBN (9780135436288) and click Submit. Look on the Registered Products tab for an Access Bonus Content link next to this product, and follow that link to access any available bonus materials. If you would like to be notified of exclusive offers on new editions and updates, please check the box to receive email from us.

Acknowledgments

We take this opportunity to sincerely acknowledge those individuals who have provided insightful meets and encouragement from the very start of our careers, helping us lay a strong foundation for the advancements in networking technologies we see today:

Manish Prakash, Shivam Srivastava, Raghu Subramanian, Gouthaman Guna, Tim McCarthy, Rajesh Sunkara, Ansuha P, John Steele, Jim Lowe, Ken D, Varun Arya, Rob Nath, Jim Hurd, Mathias Kokot, Sanjeev Ugalkar, Kaushal Agrawal, Karthik Vugane, Vinod Subramaniam (Vinod), Praful Lalchandani, Mike Bushong, Praveen Jain, A.E. Natarajan, Mansour Karam, Murali Vemula, Kiran K.L., Raj Yavatkar, T. Sridhar, Jay Ramalingam, Arun Viswanathan, Jasmeet Sawhney, Yogesh Kumar, Chirag Kachalia, Rajesh Dhople, Dharshan Ravichandran, Ashwin Balaji Sundaresan, Kumuthini Ratnasingham, Francis Guiller, Jeff Doyle, Amit Sanyal, Arun Gandhi, Ben Baker, Himansu Sahu, Mallikarjun Tallapragada, Suryanarayana MNV, Suraj Kumar, Harisankar Ramalingam, Rajashekhar Reddy, Parthipan T.S., Balaji Palanisami, Rajesh Venmanad, Manoj Kulandaivel, Sureshkumar Chinnappan, Pavan Kurapati, Dilip Sundarraj, Murugan Kanniappan, Russ White, Amogh Vijayakumar, Vince Loschiavo, Gilbert Montanez, Gustavo Castellanos, Nishal Singh, Kevin Oriet, Vinay Kakkar, Praveen Shetty, Sivakumar Gnanasundram, Shankar Nagaraj, Murali Chandran, Santha Kumar, Shahid Ali Khan, Abey Rajan, and Senthilnathan Ramasubbu.

We also extend our sincere appreciation to:

Nipun Chawla, Rahul Mehta, Aroshi Handa, Rajat Setia, Shaleen Vashisht, Mike Albano, Ramesh Kandula, Manish Gupta, Tamas Mondal, Kevin Wang, Antoni Przygienda, Wen Lin, Ajay Gaonkar, Selvakumar Sivaraj, Aquin Mathai, Vrishab Sikand, Kishore Tiruveedhula, Thorbjoern Zieger, Zacharias El Banna, Lars Axeland, Elisabeth Rodrigues, Washid Lootfun, Adrien Desportes, Krzysztof Szarkowicz, Riccardo Belli, Zuhair Makawa, Krishnamachari KR, Ridha Hamidi, Grzegorz Koscian, Piotr Czechowicz, Fathi Ben Zaied, Vikram Nagarajan, Jonathan Scherman, Rene Triana, Danny He, Chris Hackett, Muzamil Khan, Jeff Haas, Andy McCarthy, Pawel Rabiej, Pawel Kocimowski, Ahmed Bilal Khan, Slawomir Karas, Soumyodeep Joarder, and Jeffrey Zhang.

About the Authors

Mahesh Subramaniam is a proven leader in AI data centers and next-generation networking technologies. He played a key role in defining the advanced software roadmap for AI fabrics, which are now deployed in production networks across various AI data centers worldwide. As the Senior Director of Product Management for AI Data Centers at HPE Juniper Networks, he leads cutting-edge innovations in AI infrastructure and cloud-scale solutions, optimized for both scale-up and scale-out architectures. Mahesh is also an inventor with several technology patents and a recognized speaker at global forums, including the UEC Summit, OCP, and Tokyo MPLS forum. His work has earned him accolades, including the CEO Excellence Award, the Record High Business Award, and the Star Award for the Cloud DC Reference Architecture. With a remarkable history in the networking industry, Mahesh has a strong track record of leading products and managing technical and business strategies across cross-functional teams.

Michal Styszynski is a Product Management Director in the Data Center Networks Business Unit (DC BU) at HPE Juniper Networking. Michal has been with Juniper Networks for more than 13 years. Before his current role, he was a Technical Marketing Engineer (TME) in the DC BU and a Technical Solution Consultant at Juniper. In these roles, he handled data center projects for large-scale enterprises and federal networks and worked closely with Tier 2 cloud and telco-cloud service providers. Before joining Juniper, he spent around 10 years working at Orange, FT R&D, and TPSA Polpak engineering. Michal graduated from the Electronics & Telecommunications department at Wroclaw University of Science & Technology with a master's degree in engineering. He also holds an MBA from Paris Sorbonne Business School and is a JNCIE-DC#523, as well as PEC, PLC, and PMC certified from the Product School in San Francisco.

Himanshu Tambakuwala is a highly accomplished networking expert and certified technical architect whose experience spans the entire product lifecycle—from hands-on engineering to product strategy. He is a JNCIE holder in Data Center and Service Provider technologies and an inventor with four granted technology patents and two additional patents currently filed. As a Product Manager at Juniper Networks, Himanshu was instrumental in defining the feature roadmap for network fabrics that power cutting-edge AI/ML data centers.

What You'll Find Inside

Chapter 1: Wonders in the Workload

Start your journey by examining the complete lifecycle of AI/ML workloads. This chapter explains how raw data is collected, labeled, and preprocessed before being routed into distributed training pipelines. You will understand the fundamentals of forward and backward propagation, gradient descent, and iterative optimization—and see how these processes scale across thousands of GPUs through data, pipeline, and tensor parallelism. The chapter introduces job completion time (JCT) and tail latency as key metrics and discusses how RDMA (in RoCEv2) facilitates the low-latency, high-throughput transfers needed for modern AI. The technical groundwork clarifies why lossless, high-radix, dynamically balanced fabrics are crucial.

Chapter 2: "The Common-Man View" of AI Data Center Fabrics

This chapter examines the different requirements for AI training and inference data centers. It provides a technical comparison of InfiniBand and Ethernet fabrics, emphasizing their trade-offs in latency, scalability, cost, and ecosystem support. The section discusses AI-specific traffic patterns, such as low-entropy flows, elephant bursts, and synchronization-induced congestion, and explains how advanced load-balancing techniques (static, dynamic, and global) and congestion management methods (ECN, PFC, and DCQCN) are used to maintain fabric efficiency and resilience.

Chapter 3: Network Design Considerations

In this chapter, the book becomes a practical blueprint for building scalable AI clusters. It introduces rail-optimized design and rail-unified design (aka non-rail-optimized design), explaining how each approach affects latency, scalability, and fault tolerance. You'll get hands-on guidance for rack layouts (ToR, MoR, and EoR), cable management, and power/cooling planning. The text then expands to advanced topologies—Clos, Dragonfly, and Torus—showing how to scale from a few racks to tens of thousands of GPUs and how to adapt these principles for inference-centric data centers.

Chapter 4: Optics and Cable Management

Dive into the physical layer with a technical tour of optics and cabling. This chapter covers the evolution from 10 Gbps to 400 Gbps/800 Gbps/1.6 Tbps, the role of DSPs, advanced modulation (PAM4 and QAM), and FEC. It compares transceiver types (QSFP, OSFP, and CFP), connectors (MTP/MPO and LC), and cable options (DAC, AEC, AOC, MMF, SMF, and DWDM). The chapter also explores the latest in pluggable, co-packaged, and linear-drive optics, emphasizing the importance of power and thermal management in high-density environments. We have not addressed the upcoming CPO and LRO/LPO optics technologies in this book as they are subject to ongoing architectural development and discussions with multiple vendors regarding power-efficient rack solutions.

Chapter 5: Thermal and Power Efficiency Considerations

AI clusters push power and cooling to their limits. This chapter addresses the engineering required to keep them running. You'll learn about airflow management (front-to-back, back-to-front, and bidirectional), advanced liquid cooling (immersion, cold plate, rear-door heat exchangers, and spray cooling), and the impact of high-density servers and optics on rack design. Real-world examples from hyperscalers illustrate how next-generation clusters are redefining what's possible in data center thermal management.

Chapter 6: Efficient Load Balancing

This chapter is the technical heart of the networking discussion. It starts with the limitations of traditional ECMP and hash-based load balancing and then introduces a suite of modern technologies: static load balancing, dynamic load balancing (DLB), global load balancing (GLB), flowlet-based rebalancing, per-packet spraying, and selective spraying for RDMA. You'll see how each method works, where it excels, and how to tune it for AI/ML traffic patterns, ensuring optimal utilization and minimal congestion.

Chapter 7: RoCEv2 Transport and Congestion Management

This chapter provides an in-depth technical overview of RoCEv2, the primary transport protocol for AI clusters. The chapter details every potential congestion point and explains the mechanisms—including ECN, PFC, DCQCN, SFC, and CSIG—that can be used to manage them. You'll learn how to tune these controls for different environments, how to prevent PFC storms, and how to use emerging techniques for even more precise congestion management.

Chapter 8: IP Routing for AI/ML Fabrics

Routing is the silent backbone of AI performance. This chapter explores BGP, OSPF, IS-IS, and RIFT in the context of AI data centers, detailing advanced features such as BGP unnumbered, add-path, bandwidth communities, and deterministic path forwarding. You'll learn how to design for multi-tenancy, overlay networks, and server-level routing, as well as how to integrate telemetry and controllers for adaptive, performance-aware routing.

Chapter 9: Storage Network Design and Technologies

Training is fundamentally an I/O challenge. This chapter reviews storage technologies—block, file, and object storage; NVMe-oF; parallel file systems; and GPUDirect Storage—and explains the protocols, state machines, and design patterns that enable high-performance, scalable, and resilient storage networks. The chapter provides practical advice on integrating on-premises and cloud storage, as well as on designing for both hot and cold data paths.

Chapter 10: AI Network Performance KPIs

This chapter outlines the key KPIs—throughput, latency, accuracy, power, efficiency, and scalability—and presents the MLCommons/MLPerf benchmarking suite. You'll learn how to create and analyze benchmarks for both training and inference, ensuring that your performance claims are meaningful, reproducible, and actionable.

Chapter 11: Monitoring and Telemetry

Operations is where design meets reality. This chapter covers the tools and techniques for monitoring and telemetry, from SNMP and syslog to streaming telemetry and in-band flow analyzers. You'll see how to combine real-time and historical data, leverage AI-driven analytics, and automate corrective actions to keep your fabric healthy and performant.

Chapter 12: Ultra Ethernet Consortium (UEC)

This chapter introduces the Ultra Ethernet Consortium and its new protocol stack, which is designed for million-node AI clusters. You'll learn about technical innovations in transport (UET), congestion management (NSCC, RCCC, and CBFC), and packet delivery (ROD, RUD, RUDI, and UUD) and see how UEC compares to InfiniBand and RoCEv2. The chapter offers practical guidance for transitioning to UEC-ready fabrics and highlights the challenges and opportunities ahead.

Chapter 13: Scale-Up Systems

The emergence of scale-up systems represents a significant development in AI data center infrastructure. This chapter details advanced integrated high-performance computing platforms for AI data centers, referred to as super-accelerators. These platforms employ more than eight XPUs (accelerators) within a single system rack, interconnected via next-generation technologies such as UALink, which is a viable alternative to Nvidia NVLink. The chapter presents an overview of encapsulation formats and their key characteristics. It also discusses the placement of these new scale-up systems within the data center network and their integration with scale-out backend solutions, including ESUN (Ethernet for Scale-Up Networking), as proposed at a high level by the Open Compute Project Foundation (OCP).

Credits

Cover: BAIVECTOR/Shutterstock

Figures 4.2.1 Dell'Oro Group

Wonders in the Workload

What's New in AI Data Center Workloads

Right now, we are in the era of generative AI, which means that AI is being used for generating new content based on inputs. The input could be in different formats—like images, conversations, audio, or video—and the system needs to be able to understand the input correctly. Then it needs to generate accurate output. The content being generated can be of any type: text, audio, image, video, or animation.

Different AI models are used to generate different content or different results. These models use algorithms that look at patterns in existing data sets to generate content. Hence, data is crucial for generative AI applications, such as large language models (LLMs), image classification, or protein design. Raw data is collected from various places, like specific database sources, Wikipedia, and even other Internet sites. Data scientists or engineers preprocess this raw data, which includes historical data and usage patterns labeling or tokenizing each piece of data. The tokens need to be trained to produce the desired result.

For example, you might use a large language model to get relevant answers for a query. To do that, you need a model that has been trained on a relevant data set. This training involves feeding huge amounts of data (petabytes) into a training cluster. The more relevant data that is used for training, the more robust the model will be.

The Life Cycle of an AI Model

Figure 1-1 illustrates the different stages of AI workloads, which are detailed in the following list:

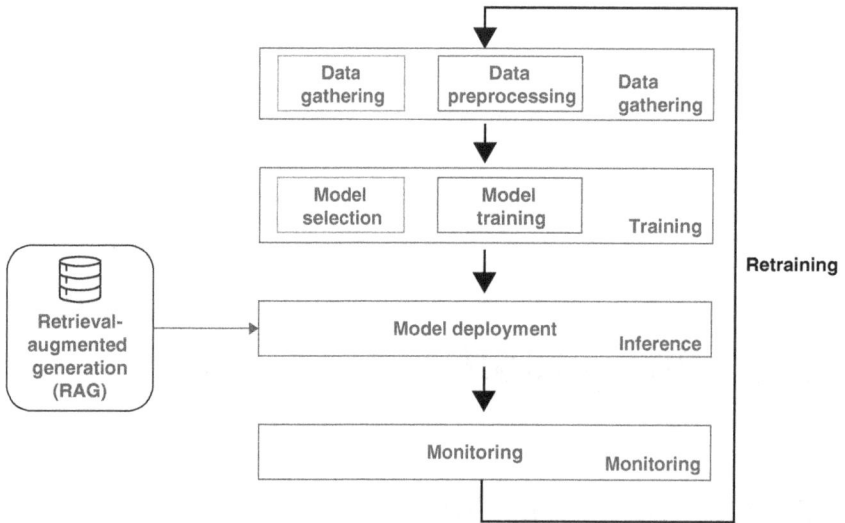

Figure 1-1
Stages of processing AI/ML workloads

- **Data gathering:** Data gathering involves collecting data from various sources. Currently, the companies that have the most data have a clear advantage. The quality of data is also important. Using data that is not relevant to the required use case can impact the accuracy of the model. In general, data needs to be processed to remove noise and duplication, and it should be tagged. Tagging makes it possible to get the right data set for the specific business problem the model aims to solve.

- **Training:** Training involves selecting an algorithm, often referred to as a model, and a set of parameters, which are variables to be used by the algorithm. The model is run across various data sets. It is run iteratively on the curated data. The result of the iteration is checked to validate the accuracy based on the existing inputs and corresponding expected output. The results of each iteration show the accuracy of the model, parameters chosen, and the gradient derived, which represents the changes required to the parameters. The parameters are adjusted on each iteration to achieve better accuracy. The model then goes through retraining to get the next set of results. This iterative process continues until the model with the desired accuracy is derived. Training yields the model and parameters that give the most accurate results. There are different ways of machine learning:

    - **Supervised:** The model trains on labeled data which includes input and expected output. Model learns to learn how to map inputs to outputs.

    - **Reinforced:** System is trained by trial and error; receives rewards or penalties for its actions to maximize success.

- **Unsupervised:** The model trains on unlabeled data which is provided as input. It must find hidden patterns in the data on its own to reach corrected output.
- **Inference:** Inference involves deploying the trained model for real-world use and monetization. The AI applications that we interact with in our day-to-day life—like ChatGPT from OpenAI and Gemini from Google—use inference.
- **Retrieval-augmented generation (RAG)/Model Context Protocol (MCP):** Using RAG or MCP with inference enables the model to retrieve the latest up-to-date data from a large database and provide more appropriate answers. After retrieving the necessary recent information, the model generates a response or output based on that new information.
- **Monitoring:** The deployed model is monitored for accuracy and periodically retrained on newer data sets.

Training an AI Model

Training is a critical phase that enables the AI and machine learning (ML) to make correct predictions or decisions using data. During this stage, the model processes input data, performs calculations, and generates output. In AI/ML Training, forward propagation is the mechanism by which the model produces an initial prediction. And then, the predicted value is compared with the actual value.

Simple Steps:

1. Input Data: Provide the model with a picture, number, or sentence.
2. Calculations: Each layer multiplies input by a weight, adds a bias, and applies an activation function in sequence.
3. Output: The model returns a prediction, such as "This is a pen" or "The price will be $380."

This is the first iteration.

In the second iteration, the output is compared with the expected output to check the accuracy. If the accuracy is not found to reach the expected level, changes in the weights, or *gradients*, are suggested. The gradients are then applied to parts of the input. This process is referred as backward propagation. The data is again passed through the function of interest, which investigates the parts of the input and weights and generates output. The iterations continue until the desired level of accuracy is achieved.

In this example, we have discussed the steps involved for one set of data. For a model to be scalable, it needs to be robust enough for many sets of data. The same process needs to be repeated for a very large set of data to fine-tune the parameters based on the use cases. The amount of data can range up to petabytes, which means running this process on a single CPU or GPU core in serialized fashion is practically impossible. This is where parallel processing enters the picture. The idea is to include as many processor cores as possible to perform operations simultaneously. The more cores that are used, the less time it takes to train the model. In general, GPUs are preferred for this processing because they can support higher numbers of cores and are easier and cheaper to scale out. A challenge with parallel processing is the synchronization of results. To address it, collective communication libraries (xCCLs) are used. xCCLs can be used for multiple cores within a node as well as across nodes.

Table 1-1 describes the various training stages.

Table 1-1 Training Stages

Training Stage	Description
Training	The data is broken into multiple batches, and the model is trained using a process called forward propagation.
Forward propagation	The model processes the data through different layers, performing advanced math such as matrix multiplication.
Error calculation	At the end of the forward pass, errors are calculated from the real result that the model should have presented.
Backward propagation	The errors are fed back in a backward propagation through the model, where a lot of calculus is done.
Use of local gradients	Local gradients are calculated and used to tweak or learn from the model's parameters.
Collective communication	Collective communication libraries (xCCLs) enable communication among multiple nodes, which is essential for the data transfer that is required with parallel processing. xCCLs ensure fast and efficient communication among multiple GPUs and networking devices across different machines. Some examples of CCLs are the NVIDIA Collective Communication Library (NCCL) from Nvidia, the ROCm Communication Collectives Library (RCCL) from AMD, Gloo from Meta, and UCC from OpenUCX.
Iteration	All of the stages just described are done iteratively for the whole batch of data to train the model and improve at every iterative step.

Parallelism

The training of an AI/ML model can take anywhere from hours to several weeks or even months, depending on the model's size and the data sets being trained. When the data set used for training is very large, the training time required is also high. As we have discussed, it is possible to speed up the training process by dividing the data and processing it on multiple GPUs simultaneously. This process, known as parallelism, involves breaking the data of the model into batches and sharing those batches with multiple GPUs to speed up the training (see Figure 1-2). All the GPUs synchronize their respective batch training results (gradients) using various parallelism techniques, all of which aim to reduce the communication overhead and speed up the training.

To reduce the training time, parallel processing has become the de facto standard. Parallelism can be achieved by using various techniques, including data parallelism and model parallelism (which includes both pipeline parallelism and tensor parallelism). These techniques can be combined to achieve maximum parallelization and speed up the training process.

Data Parallelism

Data parallelism can significantly speed up the training process for AI models. With data parallelism, all GPUs run the same model across different data sets. The results of one GPU need to be shared with all the GPUs. So, all GPUs store the results of all the other GPUs. There are three methods of sharing results: *all-reduce*, *all-gather*, and *all-to-all*.

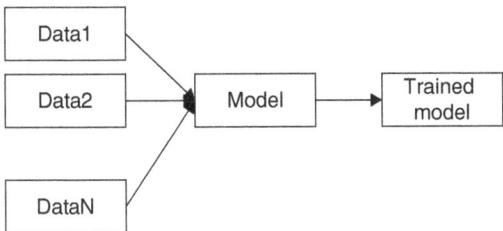

Figure 1-2
Data parallelism

Model Parallelism

Model parallelism, illustrated in Figure 1-3, is a technique in which a model is broken down and processed on multiple GPUs. It is used when a model is large and cannot be executed using a single GPU. Model parallelism involves the ring-reduce operation, in which all GPUs run the same data sets across different model layers. The result of the first GPU running the first layer of the model is passed to the second GPU, where it is coupled with the result of the second layer of the model. This combined result is then passed on to the third GPU, and so on.

Model parallelism can be further classified into two types of parallelism: pipeline parallelism and tensor parallelism.

With pipeline parallelism, a neural network or model is broken into layers, and each layer is run on a different GPU or subset of GPUs.

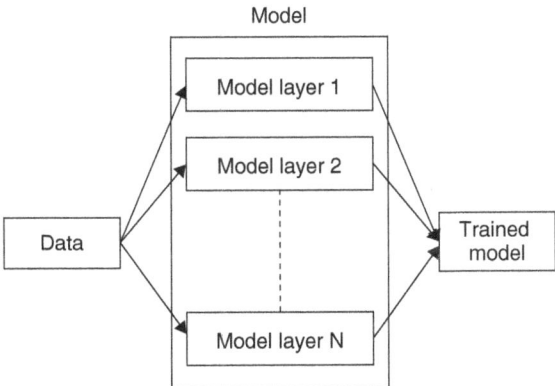

Figure 1-3
Model parallelism

With tensor parallelism, operations such as matrix multiplication are broken down and distributed across multiple GPUs within a single server. The layers within the model are further broken into smaller chunks. This process of allowing the operations to be processed simultaneously on different GPUs can significantly speed up the training process for an AI model.

Job Completion Time (JCT)

Job completion time (JCT) is a common term for training clusters in ML fabric. But what does it mean?

When we're talking about JCT, a *job* is an algorithm that helps train a large ML model to get a particular result. Usually, a job is split into multiple tasks, threads are created for each task, and the threads run across different GPUs in parallel to get the result faster. Each thread takes some time to run; this is called the *thread execution time*. Also, each thread needs to communicate its results with other GPUs through the fabric. So, inter-GPU communication is essential to get results.

JCT is a metric that measures the amount of time between the start and end of a job. For example, say that a job is divided into 100 threads, as illustrated in Figure 1-4. Out of 100 threads, 99 threads finish on time, but 1 thread takes a long time at the end due to fabric congestion or tail latency. This delay affects the whole job completion process, causing a delay in getting the result and moving to the next phase of the job. Therefore, overall system performance is directly proportional to the worst-performing thread.

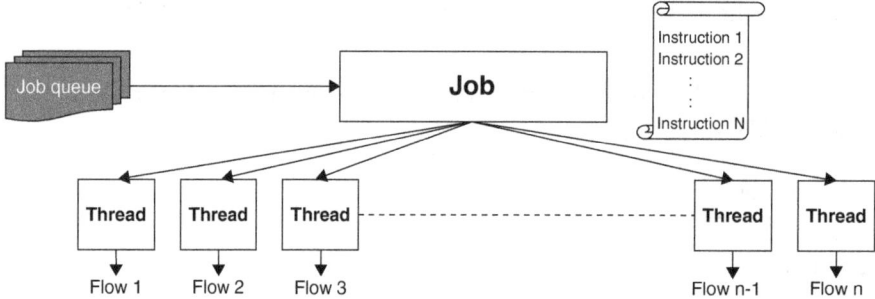

Figure 1-4
Job completion time

JCT is a critical KPI in AI/ML networks. To achieve a low JCT, a data center must have a fabric that is free of congestion, that efficiently uses load balancing, and that has low tail latency.

So, ultra-high-throughput switches with high-radix ports are required for AI/ML networks. But with those switches, intensive computation needs to be completed on time, which is the job completion time. To complete a job within a given time, the tail latency needs to be reduced on the fabric. To reduce the tail latency on the fabric, the high-radix switches must have powerful software features, such as dynamic load balancing and optimized lossless fabric using RDMA over Converged Ethernet version 2 (RoCEv2). (In the following chapters, we will talk more about the hardware and software involved and the basic definition of job completion time.)

Tail Latency

Tail latency is high-percentile latency—that is, high latency with a response time longer than the majority of all requests handled by a service or application. For example, out of 100 processes, if just 1% of processing requests observe latency in seconds, and the remaining 99% of the processing requests are less than 100 ms, the tail latency will be calculated as seconds.

The impact of tail latency is very critical in serial and parallel job tasks. For example, Figure 1-5 illustrates a situation with *n* tasks of a job, running serially. All the tasks are performed in 1 ms, except for one of the tasks, taskX, which is executed in 1 second. So, the overall job completion time is 1 second + (*n* x 1 ms). For example, if *n*=10, with 10 tasks, the result would be 1.010 seconds. The JCT increased a lot in this case due to the high latency of a single job.

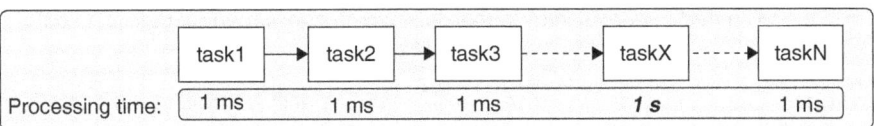

Figure 1-5
Tail latency with task serialization

Figure 1-6 illustrates that *n* tasks of a job are running in parallel. All the tasks are performed in 1 ms, except for one of them, taskX, which is executed in 1 second. So, the job has to wait 999 ms for this thread to complete while the rest of the tasks are completed. The overall job completion time is 1 second. The JCT increased a lot due to the high latency of a single job.

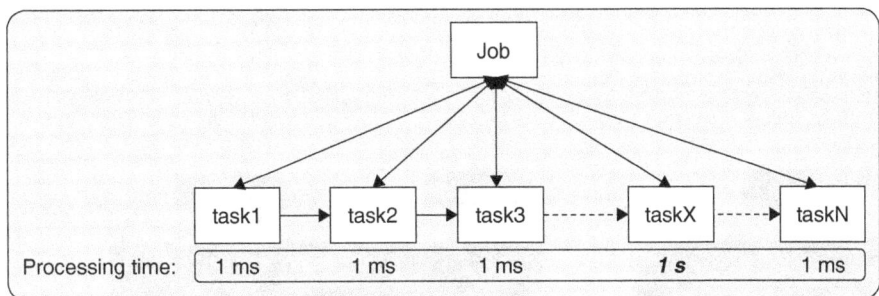

Figure 1-6
Tail latency with task parallelization

Think of it in this way: We build a system that performs badly 1 in a million times. It is definitely a very good system. Now, let's say we have to perform a job that has a million tasks to be performed. This means the system is going to perform badly for the job every time. This is the case with AI/ML data centers; they need to perform a very high number of tasks, and tail latency can bring down the overall performance.

In an AI/ML data center, tail latency can impact both the backend, or training clusters, as well as the frontend, or inference clusters. In training data centers, tail latency impacts the overall job completion times, whereas in inference clusters, it impacts the user experience in specific cases.

Understanding Traffic and RDMA

AI/ML workloads use remote direct memory access (RDMA) for data transfer, bypassing the CPU to make the data transfer faster. With RDMA, a network interface card (NIC) directly accesses the remote hosts' memory, bypassing the CPU and kernel. Consequently, an application running on a GPU can directly access memory on a remote host. The many benefits of RDMA include the following:

- Low CPU utilization
- High throughput
- Lower latency due to limited data copy requirements between application memory and data buffers
- Synchronous operations as multiple copies are transferred in parallel with the use of multiple GPU cores

RDMA is a popular data transfer technology for AI/ML training workloads that perform parallel processing in GPUs across multiple servers, resulting in a lot of data transfer.

Figure 1-7 illustrates how the RDMA transfers bypass the kernel networking stack on both hosts. It reduces data copy operations and CPU or kernel bottleneck issues.

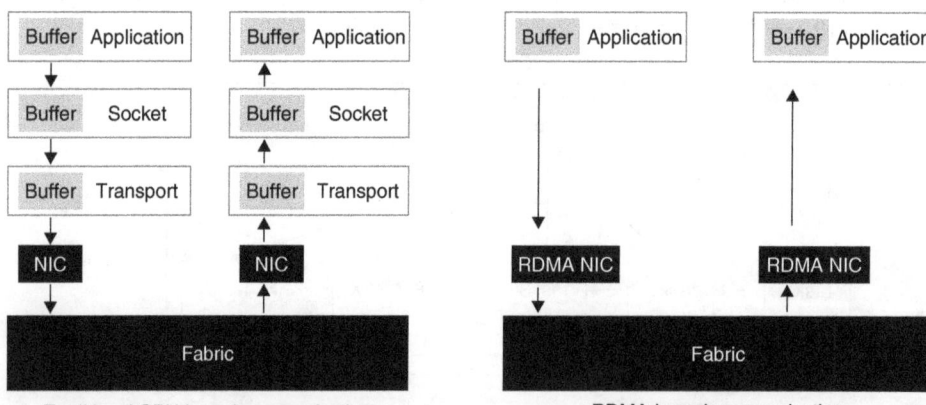

Figure 1-7
CPU-based versus RDMA-based communication

With RDMA, an application issues a job using a work queue element (WQE) or a work request. A WQE is a struct with a pointer to a buffer. The RDMA driver manages the following three queues:

- **Send queue:** Used for data to be sent to a remote host
- **Receive queue:** Used for data received from a remote host
- **Completion queue:** Used to put the WQE in the completion queue once the work request is complete

RDMA supports two types of data transfer:

- **Unidirectional:** For RDMA read, write, and atomic operations
- **Bidirectional:** For RDMA send and receive operations

Figure 1-8 illustrates the RDMA layers within a node. In this case, an application that requires RDMA transfer posts the work requests to the queue. The Verbs API services the application requests. The RDMA driver manages the work queues and address translation, and the RDMA NIC handles transport and reliability of the frames.

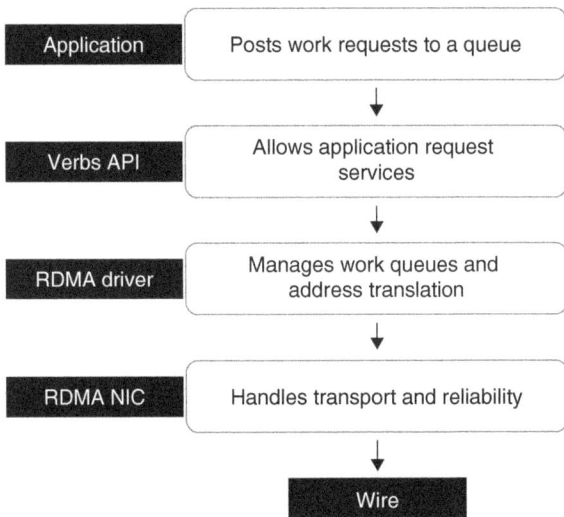

Figure 1-8
RDMA layers within a node

RDMA Transport Types

When RDMA must be transported over a network, it needs a transport mechanism. There are three networking protocols that can be used as transport for RDMA:

- **InfiniBand (IB):** IB is governed by the InfiniBand Trade Association (IBTA).
- **RDMA over Converged Ethernet (RoCE):** RoCE is also governed by IBTA. There are two versions of RoCE. The first version introduced Ethernet as the link layer and kept the IB network

layer and payload. The second version, RoCEv2, replaced the IB network layer and preserved the InfiniBand Base Transport Header (IB BTH) header and IB Payload header, with IP and UDP as the outer headers.

- **Internet Wide Area RDMA Protocol (iWARP):** This is a competing solution to IB but not as popular.

Figure 1-9 illustrates the differences between InfiniBand, RoCE, and RoCEv2.

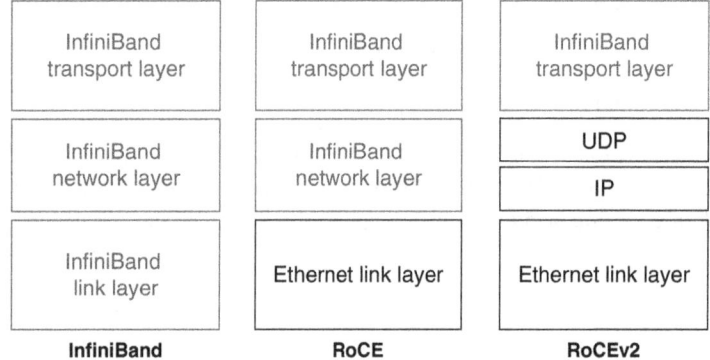

Figure 1-9
Differences between InfiniBand, RoCE, and RoCEv2

Figure 1-10 illustrates the differences in the headers for the transport options for RDMA traffic. InfiniBand is a channel-based transport that enables faster communications between endpoints. Ethernet is a traditional standards-based technology for connecting endpoints.

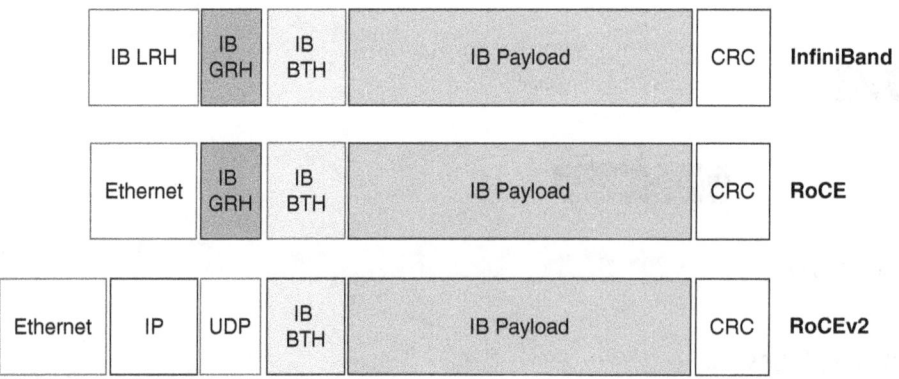

Figure 1-10
Transport headers for InfiniBand, RoCE, and RoCEv2

RoCEv2

The RoCEv2 header has IP or IPv6 as the Layer 3 protocol and UDP as the Layer 4 protocol. The UDP destination port is set to 4791, and InfiniBand BTH is the next header. The UDP source port is derived based on the queue pair (QP), which is a combination of send and receive queue ports. Figure 1-11 illustrates the RoCEv2 header.

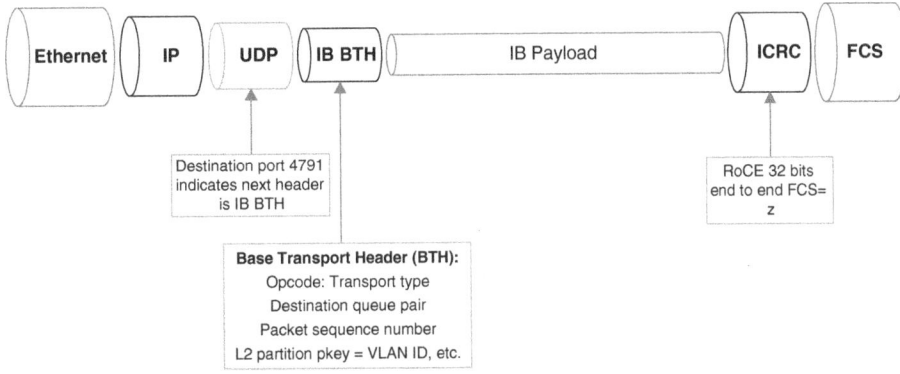

Figure 1-11
RoCEv2 header

IB BTH has the opcode to indicate RDMA operations like read, write, send, receive, and more. It also carries the QP information of the destination. Because RoCEv2 uses UDP as the transport, RDMA uses the packet sequence number for reliability. The packet sequence number tracks the delivery sequence of packets.

Figures 1-12 and 1-13 illustrate how a session is formed using RDMA message exchange for read and write operations. First, a three-way handshake is initiated, during which the QP information and sequence number are exchanged between both the server and the client. After the session is established, memory-related information is exchanged based on the type of communication. Subsequently, the data is exchanged. When the data exchange is complete, the session is terminated.

The RDMA read request message contains the remote address, key, and size information. The RDMA read response message includes data from the server. Also, notice the acknowledgement request flag in the message, which indicates that the recipient has received the request. This flag enables selective acknowledgement. Figures 1-14 and 1-15 show the RDMA read request and response packets.

12 Chapter 1 Wonders in the Workload

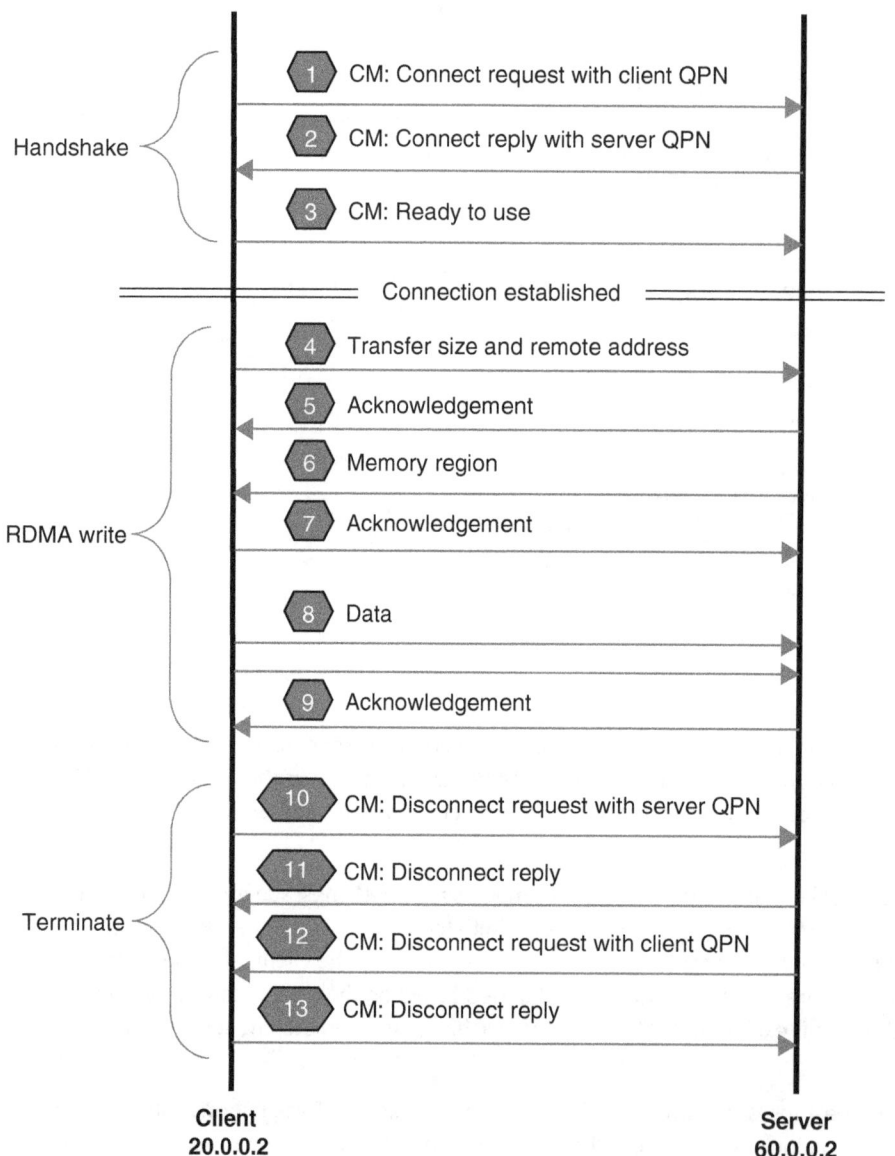

Figure 1-12
RDMA write message exchange

Tail Latency 13

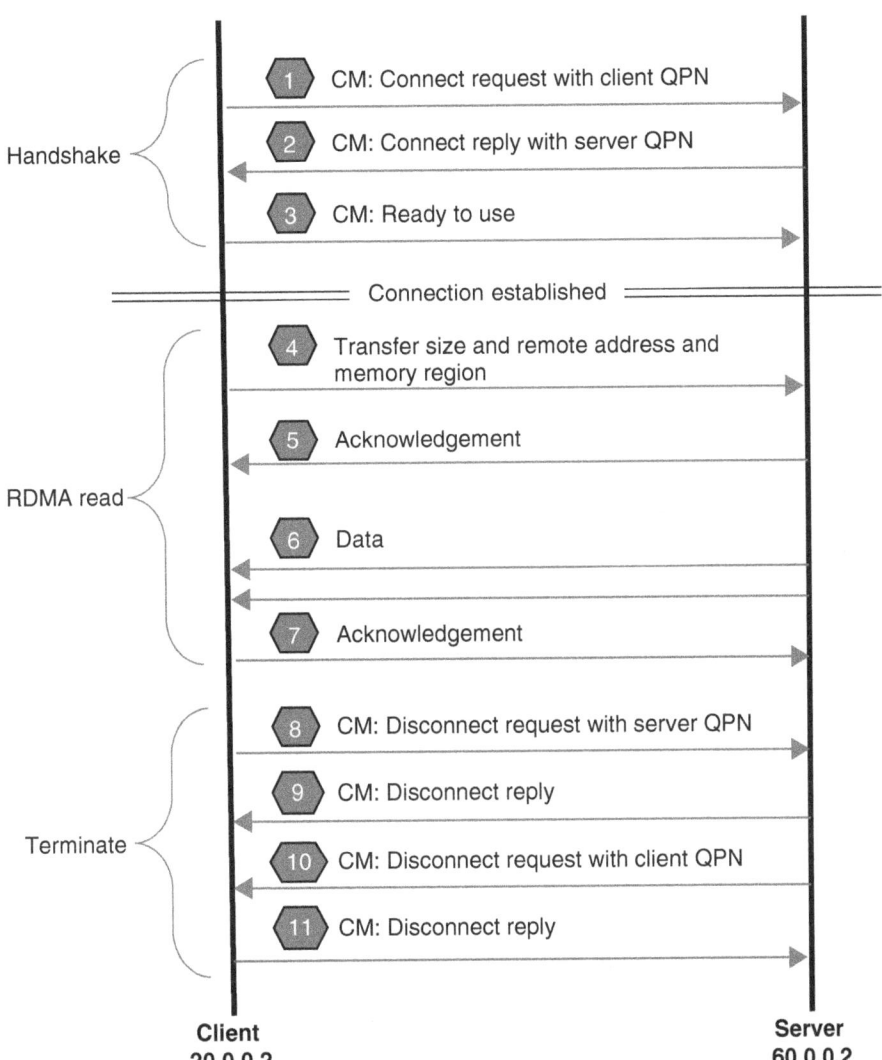

Figure 1-13
RDMA read message exchange

```
InfiniBand
    Base Transport Header
        Opcode: Reliable Connection (RC) - RDMA READ Request (12)
        0... .... = Solicited Event: False
        .1.. .... = MigReq: True
        ..00 .... = Pad Count: 0
        .... 0000 = Header Version: 0
        Partition Key: 65535
        Reserved: 00
        Destination Queue Pair: 0x0000fe
        1... .... = Acknowledge Request: True
        .000 0000 = Reserved (7 bits): 0
        Packet Sequence Number: 16548361
    RETH - RDMA Extended Transport Header
        Virtual Address: 0x00007ff9de5f4000
        Remote Key: 0x00207100
        DMA Length: 65536 (0x00010000)
    Invariant CRC: 0xb87e1cbc
```

Figure 1-14

RDMA read request

```
InfiniBand
    Base Transport Header
        Opcode: Reliable Connection (RC) - RDMA READ response Middle (14)
        0... .... = Solicited Event: False
        .1.. .... = MigReq: True
        ..00 .... = Pad Count: 0
        .... 0000 = Header Version: 0
        Partition Key: 65535
        Reserved: 00
        Destination Queue Pair: 0x00007b
        0... .... = Acknowledge Request: False
        .000 0000 = Reserved (7 bits): 0
        Packet Sequence Number: 16543980
    Invariant CRC: 0x5b522360
Data (1024 bytes)
    Data [...]: a704e5c62354894e95d13fc222a7dfbc6c35f3dfc4b58293c18a13093293cc
    [Length: 1024]
```

Figure 1-15

RDMA read response

Figure 1-16 shows the acknowledgement packet that contains the IB BTH header with the destination QP information as well as the packet sequence number for which it is sending acknowledgement. Above the IB BTH header is the Acknowledge Extended Transport Header (AETH) header, which contains the info to indicate whether it is an acknowledgement (ACK) packet or a not acknowledgement (NACK) packet. The message sequence number (MSN) in the AETH header contains the acknowledgement sequence number of the last message completed at the receiver. This helps in detecting any missed acknowledgment.

```
InfiniBand
    Base Transport Header
        Opcode: Reliable Connection (RC) - Acknowledge (17)
        0... .... = Solicited Event: False
        .1.. .... = MigReq: True
        ..00 .... = Pad Count: 0
        .... 0000 = Header Version: 0
        Partition Key: 65535
        Reserved: 00
        Destination Queue Pair: 0x000123
        0... .... = Acknowledge Request: False
        .000 0000 = Reserved (7 bits): 0
        Packet Sequence Number: 2592248
    AETH - ACK Extended Transport Header
        Syndrome: 0, Ack
            0... .... = Reserved: 0
            .00. .... = OpCode: Ack (0)
            ...0 0000 = Credit Count: 0
        Message Sequence Number: 1
    Invariant CRC: 0x33e6e2af
```

Figure 1-16
Acknowledgement packet

Table 1-2 shows the differences between Ethernet and InfiniBand.

Table 1-2   InfiniBand and Ethernet Comparison

Characteristic	InfiniBand	Ethernet
Transmission speed	IB supports SDR (Single Data Rate), DDR (Double Data Rate), QDR (Quad Data Rate), FDR (Fourteen Data Rate), EDR (Enhanced Data Rate), HDR (Hundred Gigabit Data Rate), and NDR (Next Data Rate). Slower than Ethernet.	Ethernet supports 10 Mbps, 100 Mbps, 1 Gbps, 10 Gbps, 25 Gbps, 100 Gbps, 200 Gbps, 400 Gbps, 800 Gbps, and 1.6 Tbps
Latency	Lower latency	Higher latency
Reliability	Greater reliability as it is designed for lossless	Inherently a lossy protocol. TCP is reliable, and DCQCN adds reliability to UDP.
Power consumption	Low power consumption	Comparatively higher power consumption
Scalability	Limitations beyond a certain cluster size	Highly scalable
Standardization	Controlled by IBTA and requires vendor lock-in	Open standards enable multi-vendor networks

Characteristic	InfiniBand	Ethernet
Cost	Higher cost and lead times	Lower cost and lead times
Versatility	Suitable for certain types of fabrics, like storage, HPC, and AI/ML	Most widely deployed technology and can run in any environment if appropriate protocols are enabled

Summary

As you have seen in this chapter, there are many nuances in an AI/ML workload, mainly on the training side. This is why we titled this chapter "Wonders in the Workload." Novel ingredients—from the training model to inference, job completion time, parallelism, tail latency, and RDMA transport types, including RoCEv2—are interconnected. To get these ingredients to work together, AI data center fabric for GPU cluster interconnectivity is essential. The critical point is that the data center fabric needs to be lossless; it requires high-radix switches with powerful software features, such as dynamic load balancing, selective routing, and RoCEv2. The next chapter discusses key requirements in AI data center fabrics.

Test Your Knowledge

Chapter Review

The following questions are designed to test your understanding of the content covered in Chapter 1. Following the questions, answers are provided so you can verify your conclusions.

Questions

1. How does the data life cycle influence AI model performance in data centers?
2. Explain the iterative process of training an AI model, including the roles of forward and backward propagation.
3. What are the main types of parallelism in AI training, and how do they address scalability challenges?
4. Define job completion time (JCT) and discuss its significance in AI/ML clusters.
5. How does tail latency affect distributed AI training, and what architectural features help mitigate it?
6. Describe the function and benefits of RDMA in AI/ML data center networks.
7. Compare InfiniBand, RoCEv2, and iWARP as RDMA transport protocols for AI/ML workloads.
8. What are the key requirements for AI data center fabrics to support efficient AI/ML workloads?

Answers

1. The data life cycle—spanning collection, cleaning, labeling, and tokenization—directly impacts model accuracy and robustness. High-quality, relevant, and well-labeled data enables models to learn meaningful patterns, while poor data can introduce bias or reduce generalization. The robustness of a model is proportional to the diversity and volume of the training data, which is why petabyte-scale data sets are often used in modern AI/ML workloads.
2. Training involves feeding input data through the model (forward propagation) to generate predictions, comparing these predictions to expected outputs, and then adjusting model parameters using gradients (backward propagation). This process is repeated over many iterations (epochs) and across large batches of data, gradually improving model accuracy.
3. Data parallelism involves splitting data across multiple GPUs, each running the same model; model parallelism involves splitting the model itself across GPUs; pipeline parallelism involves dividing model layers into stages that are processed in sequence; and tensor parallelism involves splitting tensor operations. These approaches enable simultaneous computation, reducing training time and overcoming the limitations of single-processor systems.

4. JCT is the elapsed time from the start of a training job to the end of the job. It is a critical KPI because AI/ML workloads are often split into many parallel tasks, and the slowest task (due to tail latency or congestion) determines the overall JCT. Optimizing JCT is essential for efficient resource utilization and faster model iteration.

5. Tail latency refers to the slowest responses among many parallel tasks. In distributed AI training, high tail latency can delay job completion, as all tasks must finish before the job can proceed. Architectural features such as use of high-radix switches, dynamic load balancing, and lossless fabrics (for example, RoCEv2) help reduce tail latency by minimizing congestion and ensuring even traffic distribution.

6. RDMA (remote direct memory access) enables direct memory access between servers, bypassing the CPU and kernel, which reduces latency, increases throughput, and lowers CPU utilization. It is especially beneficial for AI/ML workloads that require frequent, high-volume data transfers between GPUs across nodes.

7. InfiniBand offers low latency and lossless transport but is less scalable and more expensive. RoCEv2 runs RDMA over Ethernet using UDP/IP, providing scalability and compatibility with existing Ethernet infrastructure, but it requires careful congestion management. iWARP is less popular, offering RDMA over TCP/IP, but with higher latency and less adoption in AI/ML clusters.

8. AI data center fabrics must be lossless, support high throughput and low latency, provide dynamic load balancing, and be capable of handling large-scale parallelism. Features like high-radix 400 Gbps/800 Gbps Ethernet switches, RoCEv2 support, and advanced congestion management—such as DCQCN, including PFC and ECN—are essential for optimally maximizing performance in the AI data center. The design should allow for the integration of a higher number of servers with GPUs; it should help to move, for example, from a three-stage topology to a five-stage topology when the number of AI workloads is increasing over time.

2

"The Common-Man View" of AI Data Center Fabrics

Training vs. Inference AI Data Centers

AI applications rely on large amounts of data to train and test their models, as well as to provide inputs and outputs for their operations. Data centers are facilities that house computing, storage, and networking equipment to enable the processing and distribution of data. There are two main types of data centers that support AI/ML applications: AI training data centers and AI inference data centers.

AI Training Data Centers

AI training data centers are data centers that are designed to perform the training of AI models. Training is the process of teaching an AI model to perform a specific task by providing it with labeled data, such as images, text, or speech, and adjusting its parameters based on the feedback it receives. Training can take from hours to weeks or months, depending on the task's complexity, the data's size, and the computing power available. It typically requires high-performance computing (HPC) systems that can handle large-scale parallel processing, massive memory bandwidth, and fast interconnects.

AI training data centers are data centers that specialize in training AI models using large amounts of data—in petabytes or exabytes—and they need to be able to store and manage the training data.

Training AI models involves applying various learning algorithms, such as supervised, unsupervised, or reinforcement learning, to optimize the parameters of the models based on the data and the desired outcomes. A lot of computing power, memory, storage, bandwidth, and energy are required to perform the complex and iterative calculations needed for training AI models. AI training data centers also need to be able to handle the challenges of data quality, diversity, and availability, as well as the security and privacy of the data and the models.

AI Inference Data Centers

AI inference is the process of feeding live data to trained AI models and getting the outputs. AI inference data centers are specialized facilities that run the AI models that have been trained. They provide the computing resources and infrastructure needed to use the models for inference or prediction. AI inference data centers can support various domains and applications, such as image recognition, speech synthesis, natural language generation, or recommender systems. These data centers are built to do the inference of AI models.

Inference involves using an AI model on new data, such as user queries, sensor readings, or video streams, and generating outputs, such as answers, recommendations, or actions. Inference can last from milliseconds to seconds, depending on the speed requirements of the application, token count, the size of the model, time to the first token, and the amount of data.

AI inference data centers usually need low-power computing systems that can handle fast and timely processing, such as edge devices, servers, or cloud platforms. They also need to store and manage the inference data, which can be terabytes or petabytes. The key network and server requirements related to AI inference are summarized in Figure 2-1.

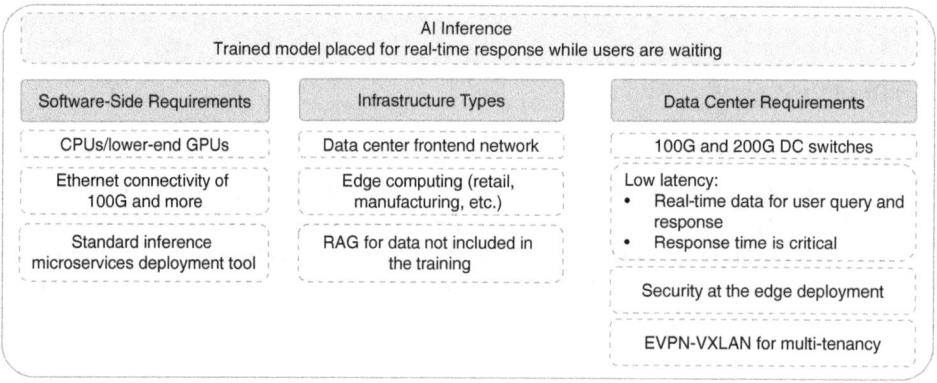

Figure 2-1
AI inference requirements

InfiniBand vs. Ethernet for AI Training Data Centers

For many, InfiniBand runs the show on HPC infrastructure, and nowadays it is one key solution for specific GPU vendors. But nowadays customers are looking for many AI Data centers Infrastructure from low-mid-large even hyper scale deployments. With that in minds, customer and architect are looking common open solution like ethernet instead vendor specific solution for AI fabric for wider expertise, ease operations and open unified tooling systems starting front-end to backend.

InfiniBand is widely used in HPC infrastructure and has traditionally been a key solution for specific GPU vendors. However, as AI data centers scale from small to medium to hyperscale deployments, customers are increasingly seeking open infrastructure options that range from low- to high-capacity clusters. In response, both customers and architects are considering common open designs, such as Ethernet, rather than vendor-specific InfiniBand fabric for AI workloads, aiming for broader expertise, simplified operations, and open standard integrated tooling from frontend to backend systems.

Advantages of InfiniBand in AI Training Clusters

InfiniBand is a network technology that enables fast, low-latency, and dependable data transfer among nodes in a cluster. It is suited for parallel and distributed computing, such as AI training, where multiple nodes have to exchange and coordinate large amounts of data. InfiniBand uses a switched fabric architecture, where nodes are linked by switches that route packets according to their destination address. Each node has a network adapter, called a host channel adapter (HCA), that connects to the switch via a cable. The HCA takes care of sending and receiving the data, as well as the network protocol and memory management.

InfiniBand supports various transport services, such as reliable or unreliable connection-oriented or connectionless communication, as well as remote direct memory access (RDMA), which allows one node to access the memory of another node without involving the operating system or the CPU. This reduces the overhead and latency of data transfer and allows higher throughput and scalability.

InfiniBand offers the following advantages for AI training clusters:

- **Low latency:** InfiniBand can achieve sub-microsecond latency for data transfer, which is much lower than other network technologies, such as Ethernet or TCP/IP. This reduces the communication delay and improves the convergence speed of AI training.

- **RDMA:** InfiniBand supports RDMA, which enables direct memory access between nodes without involving the operating system or the CPU. This reduces CPU utilization and memory consumption and increases the performance and efficiency of AI training.

- **Scalability:** InfiniBand can scale up to thousands of nodes in a cluster, and it supports multiple parallel connections between nodes. It therefore enables larger and more complex AI models to be trained on more data and resources.

Advantages of Ethernet in AI Training Clusters

Ethernet offers the following advantages for AI training clusters:

- **Cost-effectiveness:** AI data center Ethernet fabric uses commodity switches and cables that are widely available and cheaper than InfiniBand hardware. Ethernet fabric also reduces the need for expensive gateways or adapters to connect different network technologies, as Ethernet is compatible with most devices and platforms.

- **Simplicity:** Ethernet fabric simplifies network management and configuration by using standard Ethernet protocols and tools. Data center Ethernet fabric also eliminates the need for specialized skills and knowledge to operate and maintain InfiniBand networks, which require proprietary software and drivers.

- **Compatibility:** Ethernet fabric enables seamless integration and interoperability with existing Ethernet networks and devices, such as storage systems, servers, and cloud services. Ethernet fabric also supports various workload applications and frameworks that run on top of Ethernet by default, such as Kubernetes, TensorFlow, and PyTorch, without requiring any modifications or adaptations.

- **Flexibility:** Ethernet fabric allows for dynamic and adaptive network provisioning and optimization, based on the workload and performance requirements. Ethernet fabric can leverage features such as load balancing, congestion control, quality of service, and multipathing to improve network efficiency and reliability. Ethernet fabric can also support different network topologies and architectures, such as leaf–spine or mesh, depending on the needs and preferences of the AI data center.

As you can see, Ethernet fabric is a strong alternative to InfiniBand in AI data centers, as it provides a more cost-effective, simple, compatible, and flexible network solution that can meet the demands and challenges of AI training and inference. Ethernet fabric can deliver high-speed, low-latency, and reliable data transfer between nodes in a cluster, while also offering lower operational costs, easier management, and greater scalability.

Ethernet Hardware Switches and Advanced Software Features

As we consider the workload characteristics in Chapter 1, "Wonders in the Workload," we notice a few clear challenges with the RDMA over Converged Ethernet version 2 (RoCEv2) transport:

- **Low entropy at the network layer:** At the network layer, most of the IP headers are likely to be the same for RoCEv2 except for the source address and destination address. If the traffic is flowing from one source GPU to multiple destination GPUs (1:N), we expect to see good entropy based on the destination headers. However, with AI/ML fabrics, there is a high chance of traffic flows between one source GPU and one destination GPU (1:1) or a very small number of GPUs. This means low entropy at the network layer is likely.

- **Low entropy at the transport layer:** As discussed in Chapter 1, the UDP header used in RoCEv2 transport has the destination port 4791, which indicates that the next header is the IB BTH header. Even if this header is derived from a queue pair, we do not have enough data showing the efficiency of this approach to handling entropy. Hence, the UDP headers of all the RoCEv2 packets are likely to be similar. This means there is very low entropy at the transport layer, and we can use efficient load balancing to mitigate the low-entropy problem.

- **Flowlets:** Because there is low entropy between the flows, switches may treat different low-entropy flows as part of the same flow. These individual low-entropy flows are referred to as *flowlets*. Flowlets can be of two types:

    - **Simultaneous flows with low entropy:** There may be simultaneous flows between a pair of GPUs where the entropy is only at the queue pair and sequence number part of BTH header in the RoCEv2 transport. Because a switch does not look into this header, it may treat the header as part of the same flow.

    - **Sequential flows with low entropy:** There are scenarios where a flow corresponding to a job completes between a pair of GPUs and another flow starts for a different job. However, because there is low entropy between these flows, the switch may continue to treat them as part of the same flow. This results in long-lived flow from a switch perspective. The resources assigned to the flow may need to be rebalanced over a period of time.

- **High-bandwidth flows:** Much like storage data centers, AI/ML data centers involve a lot of data transfer. The data read and write speed within the server has become very fast, thanks to the evolution of storage devices and RDMA technology. To increase the speed of the data transfer between two nodes, nodes may try to use the full capacity of the network interface card (NIC). A job scheduler with a server tries to schedule the jobs so that they are completed in the least possible time; in doing so, it tries to consume the full pipe bandwidth of the interfaces connected to the NIC.

- **Burstiness:** As we discussed in Chapter 1, the concept of gradients with parallelization implies that there are instances when the gradients are synchronized across the GPUs. When this happens, data transfer across the GPUs is bound to increase. Hence, a regular flow of data transfer can peak at the time of synchronization and then reduce back to the normal level once synchronization is complete to continue with the next level of processing. This results in bursts of traffic through the fabric.

Based on the understanding of AI/ML workloads covered in Chapter 1 and the challenges discussed previously, let's investigate the requirements from a network design perspective:

- **High-radix with high-bandwidth links:** Large AI/ML clusters are being designed with 32,000 and 64,000 GPUs and beyond. Each GPU has a NIC with high link capacity compared to traditional 25Gbps or 100Gbps server NICs. So, for a 32K GPU cluster, 32K server-facing ports are required on the leaf, or top-of-rack (ToR), switches, along with ports for connectivity to spine switches and beyond.

- **Oversubscription ratio:** As we have discussed, JCT is the most important requirement for AI/ML data centers. Congestion in the fabric can impact the JCT (Job Completion Time), and so we need to make the fabric congestion free. To achieve that, we need to avoid oversubscription in the fabric wherever we expect to have traffic reaching the line rate.

- **Optimized design:** A GPU server that is used for AI/ML fabrics contains multiple GPUs. Usually there are 8 GPUs in a server. There is an internal switch within the server that is used for the transfer between GPUs within the server. The traffic goes out from the switch for communication across different servers. This provides an opportunity to design the network in an optimized way to suit the AI/ML clusters. Rail-optimized design (ROD) is one of the most discussed designs for these environments. Another option, rail-unified design (RUD), can also be considered.

These design options are discussed in detail in Chapter 3, "Network Design Considerations."

Handling Elephant Flows

As we discussed the challenges of AI/ML data center workloads from a network perspective, we talked about the issue of low-entropy and high-bandwidth flows. Traffic flows with these characteristics are referred to as *elephant flows*.

The evolution of software around large language models and other domain-specific training models has led to the use of parallel computing power at different server nodes and continuous synchronization of their states before they finish their job. For some jobs, this translates to enormous east–west data exchange across the data center backend fabric on an Ethernet network. So, we need to ensure that the fabric bandwidth utilization is efficient and works well even in elephant flow situations. It is therefore important for a backend AI/ML data center network to guarantee the following characteristics:

- **Efficient use of IP ECMP load balancing (LB):** With multiple high-capacity (for example, 400Gbps, 800Gbps, or 1.6Tbps) links between leaf and spine, concurrent massive data chunks are being exchanged east–west between the server's GPU, and all the fabric bandwidth must be efficiently used to quickly synchronize all the data—with no frame loss. This is considered a proactive method of congestion management where, based on flow count and/or flow characteristics, the best outgoing interfaces and best paths are selected.

- **Congestion management and mitigation techniques:** PFC-DSCP (Priority Flow Control) and ECN (Explicit Congestion Notifications) are both coordinated through DCQCN. Both PFC-DSCP and ECN are categorized as reactive methods for congestion management: When switch buffer thresholds are reached, the rate of the workload at the origin is reduced.

Figure 2-2 provides a summary of proactive and reactive congestion-handling techniques.

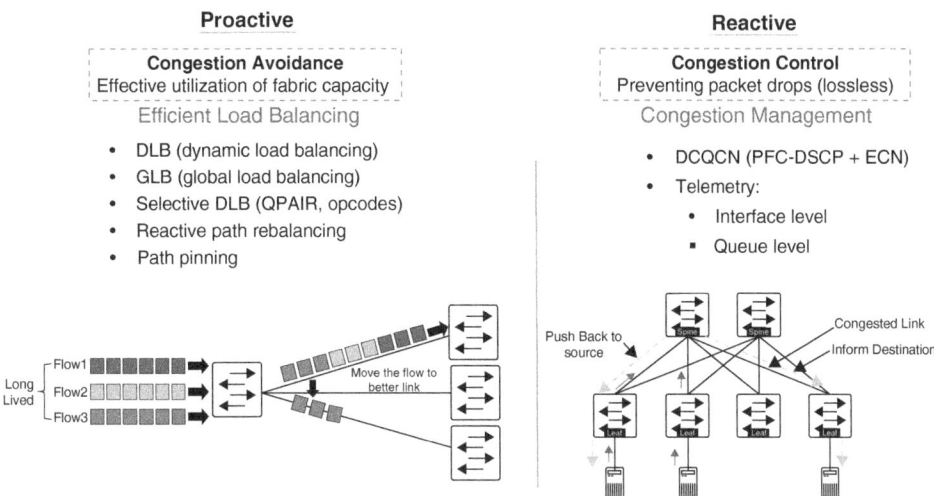

Figure 2-2
Proactive versus reactive mechanism for congestion management

With the proper implementation, advanced load balancing (which is proactive) should be sufficient in most cases to minimize the occurrence of reactive congestion management techniques, such as ECN and PFC.

Load-Balancing Techniques

In this section, let's focus on efficient load-balancing techniques in the AI data center fabric. There are different ways to improve the efficiency of load balancing. Some techniques use only local node–level awareness of the link quality, and others use a combination of local link and remote node quality performance to select the best path. We can categorize these techniques into four ways of doing load balancing, as shown in Figure 2-3:

- **Static load balancing (SLB):** SLB, which is the traditional load-balancing technique, is not efficient in the context of AI/ML fabric because it only considers the packet format and packet entropy characteristics instead of evaluating the real-time utilization of the equal-cost links and buffers.

- **Dynamic load balancing (DLB):** DLB considers the local-link bandwidth utilization and buffer utilization of equal-cost links. This helps in selecting a healthy link to pin the flow.

- **Global load balancing (GLB):** With GLB, besides including the link-local bandwidth and queue sizes, the path selection algorithm includes the next-to-next-hop (NNH) information on the link quality. It considers the quality of links on the local leaf and also the spine links to select the best member link to use for new or existing flows.

SLB

- Static load balancing (SLB) is a five-tuple lookup.
- With SLB, hashing is solely based on the packet contents (for example, source IP address, destination IP address).
- The biggest advantage of SLB is that packet ordering is guaranteed because all packets of a given flow take the same path.

GLB

- Global load balancing (GLB) extends DLB by modulating the local path selection using path quality perceived at downstream switches.
- GLB allows an upstream switch to avoid downstream congestion hotspots and select a better end-to-end path.

DLB

- Dynamic load balancing (DLB) considers the bandwidth and queue utilization of the local member link.
- DLB considers the state of the member links for new and existing flows. Existing flows can be re-assigned to another aggregate member link based on real-time changes in the quality of member links.

sDLB

- sDLB also incorporate the ROCEv2 specific BTH header read/write option information for use in selecting the correct IP ECMP link member.
- It is used to identify elephant flows for better spraying.

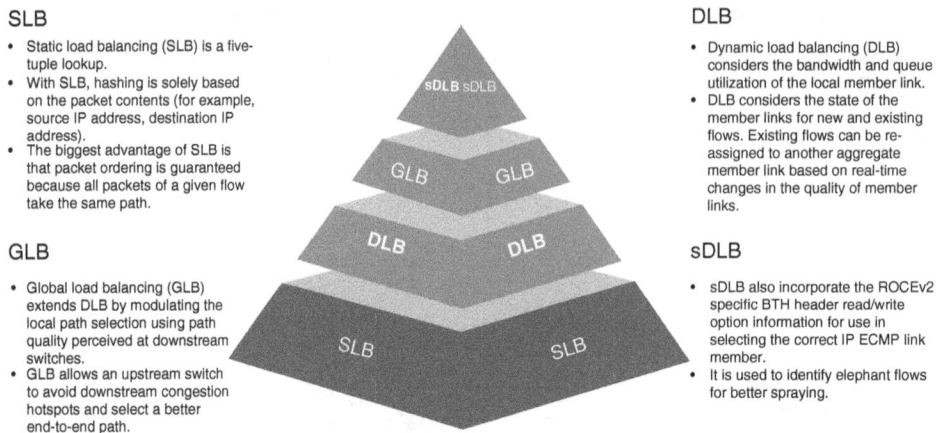

Figure 2-3
Different ways of load balancing

- **Selective DLB (sDLB):** sDLB identifies the flow and spray packets for specific flows. sDLB uses opcode matching, based on the base transport header, to detect elephant flows and then enable per-packet load balancing.

- With an additional option, flow pinning, the flows are pinned (mapped) at the switch outgoing paths/interfaces in a round-robin fashion, based on their characteristics and based on the state of the paths/interfaces.

These options are discussed in detail in Chapter 6, "Efficient Load Balancing."

Congestion Management and Mitigation Techniques

We need congestion management in AI/ML fabrics for several reasons:

- Load balancing is not always perfect unless we use per-packet load balancing, which has the challenge of reordering at the destination NIC. With elephant flows, the chance of in-cast congestion is high.
- Load balancing may not handle bursts of traffic in an efficient manner.
- When both storage and compute are connected to the same leaf switch, communication can happen locally from one port to another within the same switch. In-cast congestion can also happen in this case.

Figure 2-4 illustrates an example of fabric congestion where the spines are connecting multiple Ethernet switch rails. A switch rail is a collection of switches connected to GPU-enabled AI/ML servers—typically eight switches per rail. In the figure, the spine1 link connected to leaf switches from Rail2 is experiencing congestion. However, frame loss will not occur as long as spine1 is enabled with the lossless fabric features ECN and PFC.

Congestion Management and Mitigation Techniques

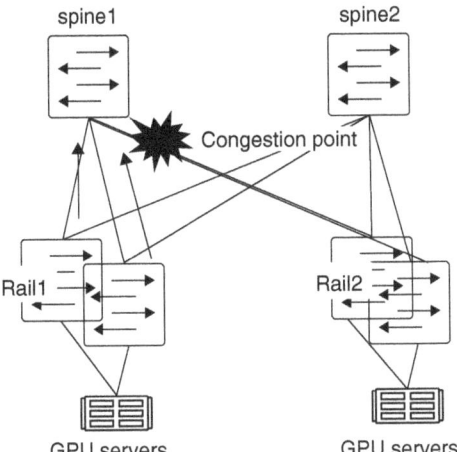

Figure 2-4
Congestion management at the spine

In AI data center fabric, we can handle congestion management on RoCEv2 transport by using DCQCN (Data Center Quantized Congestion Notification), which is an end-to-end congestion control protocol designed for use in large IP-routed data center networks. It allows for the deployment of RDMA in these networks by combining two key techniques:

- **Explicit Congestion Notification (ECN):** This mechanism allows network switches to notify end hosts of impending congestion, allowing them to reduce their transmission rates before packet loss occurs.

- **Priority Flow Control (PFC):** PFC is a link-level flow control mechanism that can pause the transmission of specific traffic classes to prevent packet loss.

- In Figure 2-5, ECN Side:
    - 1 and 2- Shows the flow comes from GPU server and reaches leaf and spine.
    - 3- Node on detecting congestion sets the ECN bit to the packets.
    - 4- Destination finds ECN is set and sends a congestion notification packet to the source server.
    - 5- Source server slows down the traffic based on local NIC card setting.
- In the PFC Side:
    - 1 and 2- Shows the flow comes from GPU server and reaches leaf and spine.
    - 3- The node detects congestion and sends a PFC pause frame toward the previous node on a specific queue number.

- 4- Previous node slows down the traffic in that queue and sends an update to the last node toward the source.
- 5- The source server slows down the traffic based on the quanta values received.

Figure 2-5 illustrates these congestion management techniques.

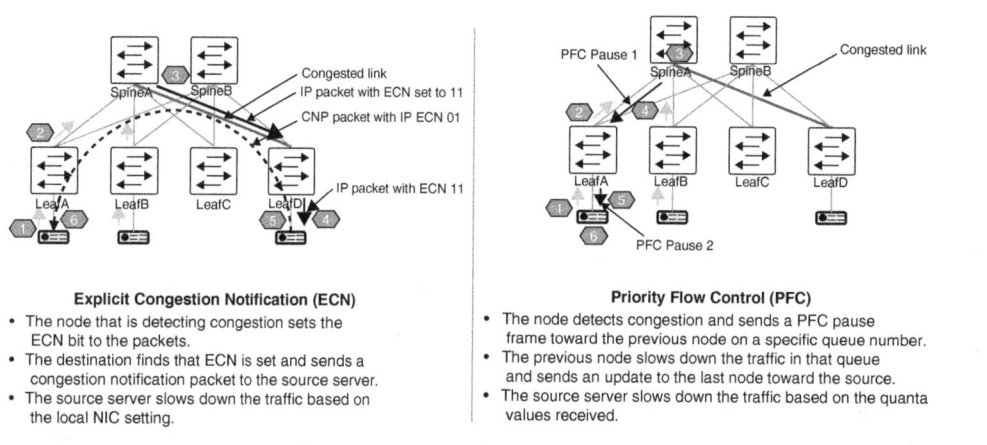

Explicit Congestion Notification (ECN)
- The node that is detecting congestion sets the ECN bit to the packets.
- The destination finds that ECN is set and sends a congestion notification packet to the source server.
- The source server slows down the traffic based on the local NIC setting.

Priority Flow Control (PFC)
- The node detects congestion and sends a PFC pause frame toward the previous node on a specific queue number.
- The previous node slows down the traffic in that queue and sends an update to the last node toward the source.
- The source server slows down the traffic based on the quanta values received.

Figure 2-5
Congestion management techniques

DCQCN helps to reduce the congestion with ECN and PFC by adding end-to-end congestion control at a per-flow granularity. This means that individual flows can back off and reduce their transmission rates before congestion spreads, preventing packet loss and improving overall network performance. DCQCN requires only standard RED (random early detection) and ECN support from data center switches, and the rest of the protocol functionality is implemented on the end host NICs.

Summary

In this chapter, we have briefly covered the requirements of AI/ML fabrics. We began by looking at the traditional load balancing used inside data centers for many years. Traditional load-balancing methods are not suitable for newer AI/ML backend data center networks mainly because of the high application diversity in a typical data center and the larger number of flows entering the same switch, as well as the mixed east–west and north–south communications. In the case of AI/ML cluster switching infrastructure, the typical communication pattern is east–west, and the number of applications running in the backend Ethernet is relatively low, so RoCEv2 transport is typically used. This is one reason recent developments in DCQCN, buffer management techniques, DLB, and GLB are helpful in Ethernet-based AI data center fabric. Of course, we will continue to see more advanced capabilities in the coming years. In subsequent chapters, we will further investigate the requirements for AI/ML data center fabrics.

Test Your Knowledge

Chapter Review

The following questions are designed to test your understanding of the content covered in Chapter 2. Following the questions, answers are provided so you can verify your conclusions.

Questions

1. How do the requirements of AI training data centers differ from those of inference data centers?
2. What are the technical trade-offs between InfiniBand and Ethernet for AI training cluster deployments?
3. Explain the concept of low entropy in AI/ML network traffic and its impact on load balancing.
4. What are elephant flows, and why do they pose a challenge in AI/ML fabrics?
5. Describe the proactive and reactive congestion management techniques used in AI/ML fabrics.
6. How does RoCEv2 address the need for lossless transport in Ethernet-based AI data centers?
7. What are the main load-balancing techniques used for AI/ML fabrics, and how do they differ?
8. Why is oversubscription ratio a critical design parameter in AI/ML data center fabrics?

Answers

1. Training data centers require high-performance computing, massive memory bandwidth, and fast interconnects to process large data sets over long periods. Inference data centers prioritize low-latency, real-time responses and typically use smaller, more effective multi-tenant systems.
2. InfiniBand offers sub-microsecond latency, native RDMA, and high reliability but at higher cost and with vendor lock-in. Ethernet is more cost-effective, widely compatible, and easier to manage, but it requires enhancements (such as RoCEv2 and advanced load balancing) to match InfiniBand's performance for AI workloads.
3. Low entropy means that many packet headers are similar, making it difficult for switches to distinguish flows and distribute them evenly. This can lead to inefficient load balancing, congestion, and underutilization of network resources, especially in one-to-one or small-group GPU communications.

4. Elephant flows are large, sustained data transfers and are typical in AI/ML clusters. They can monopolize bandwidth, cause congestion, and require specialized load-balancing and congestion management techniques to prevent performance degradation.

5. Proactive techniques include dynamic and global load balancing to prevent congestion before it occurs. Reactive techniques, such as ECN (Explicit Congestion Notification) and PFC (Priority Flow Control), respond to congestion events by signaling endpoints to slow down or pause traffic.

6. RoCEv2 uses UDP/IP encapsulation and relies on lossless Ethernet features (such as PFC and ECN) to provide RDMA capabilities over standard Ethernet, enabling the high-throughput, low-latency data transfers required for AI/ML workloads.

7. Static load balancing (SLB) uses fixed rules, dynamic load balancing (DLB) adapts to real-time link and buffer utilization, global load balancing (GLB) incorporates remote link quality, and per-packet spraying distributes packets across all paths. Each technique offers different trade-offs in complexity and efficiency.

8. The oversubscription ratio determines how much aggregate server bandwidth exceeds the available network bandwidth. High oversubscription can cause congestion and increase JCT, so AI/ML fabrics aim for low or no oversubscription to ensure predictable, high-performance communication. In rare cases, an undersubscription type of design is used (with more links to the spines and fewer to the servers) to include better packet spraying from leaf to spine and also get more dedicated egress buffers in a shallow buffer switch deployment.

3

Network Design Considerations

Background Introduction

As we discussed in Chapter 1, "Wonders in the Workload," processing AI/ML workloads involves three stages: data gathering and preprocessing, model selection and training, and deployment and monitoring.

Figure 3-1 illustrates the different stages of processing AI/ML workloads. Initially, data is gathered from various sources. In inference, the quality of data is directly proportional to the quality of the results. (You have probably seen instances in social media where AI model results are way off from the expectation—sometimes in a humorous way.) In the preprocessing phase, any data that contains errors, missing values, or inconsistencies is either corrected or removed. The data is then identified and tagged with labels. Now the data is ready to be used for model training.

The next step is to select models (algorithms) that apply to the prepared data set. A model is trained with the prepared data set to determine its efficiency. The training is run iteratively with different model parameters until the model gives consistent results with high accuracy. Training can be supervised—with the involvement of experts or reinforced.

Once the trained model is determined to be accurate, it is deployed in production systems for external inference requests. It is monitored for inaccuracies and unexpected behavior. Models are trained periodically with newer data sets for fine-tuning and improved accuracy.

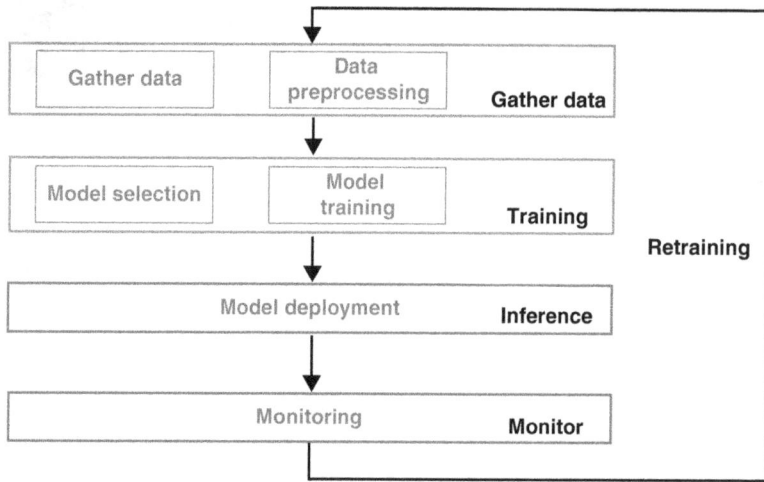

Figure 3-1
Stages of processing AI/ML workloads

Figure 3-2 illustrates different network fabrics connecting to a server. Storage fabric can either be distributed or dedicated to data centers. Inference fabric acts as frontend and is used for user interactions. Training fabric acts as a backend and is used for training or learning purposes.

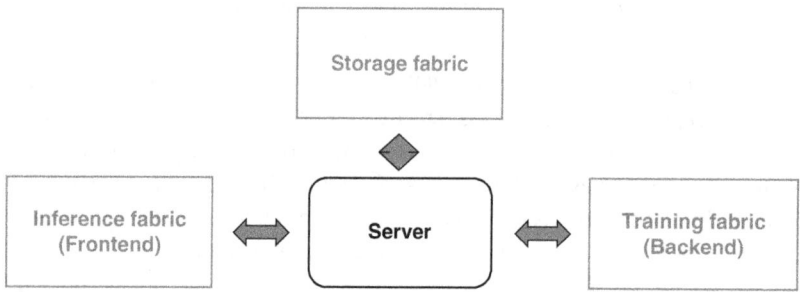

Figure 3-2
Network associations with a server

The following data centers are connected to the server in Figure 3-2:

- **Storage data center:** This data center stores all the gathered data. While smaller data volumes may be stored in the training cluster, large data volumes typically use storage data centers. These data centers have existed for a long time and have continued to evolve. The primary consideration for a storage data center fabric is a low-latency, lossless network. Currently, InfiniBand and Ethernet are the two options for storage. The InfiniBand technology offers superior performance while supporting lossless, low-latency networks. Ethernet is implemented with a three-stage or five-stage Clos network with RDMA over Converged Ethernet version 2 (RoCEv2) features to make it a lossless fabric.

- **Training data center:** Training clusters that are built for research have clusters of GPUs to accommodate large data sets. They work on a comprehensive list of models to derive a focused list of trained models. These models are used by various applications to provide results to the user. In contrast, the GPU clusters in an enterprise data center are much smaller and run focused models and data sets.

  Training data centers, also called backend data centers, have similar considerations to storage data centers. We cover training data center fabric design in this chapter.

- **Inference data center:** The inference data center is the production data center, where the trained model is deployed for external inference requests. The architecture of this type of data center is similar to the architecture of an enterprise, cloud, or telco data center. In most cases, it is similar to a collapsed three-stage or five-stage Clos network.

In this chapter, we investigate the various options for training, or backend, cluster architecture in detail.

Training Data Center Architecture

The network design for AI/ML workloads requires a balance between performance, cost-efficiency, reliability, and scalability. An organization needs a durable network that can cope with the challenging nature of AI/ML calculations while staying flexible to future expansion and technological improvements. This can be achieved by applying optimized topologies, weighing cost trade-offs, and using strong failover strategies.

AI/ML workloads have demanding networking requirements that necessitate high-speed connections between server and leaf switches—typically between 200 Gbps and 400 Gbps. The network design therefore must include specialized switches, high-bandwidth cabling, and topology adjustments to ensure optimal performance and throughput.

Servers such as the Nvidia A100 or H100 are equipped with 8 GPUs, and each GPU may be linked to one or two NICs. While multiple NICs per GPU is feasible, cost considerations around optics, NICs, and server port scalability often favor the implementation of a single NIC per GPU. This approach reduces expenses and eliminates port-level redundancy, removing the requirement for multi-homing on the server side.

The GPU-to-leaf connectivity options include multiple GPUs connected to a single leaf or a one-to-one GPU-to-leaf configuration. For example, for a server housing 8 GPUs, it is essential to have 8 leaf connections, forming what is commonly referred to as a rail-optimized topology. This topology choice is preferred because of its efficiency in handling high-throughput AI/ML workloads; it offers enhanced data transfer capabilities and optimized performance.

There are two design options for GPU-to-leaf connectivity:

- One-to-one GPU-to-leaf configuration, referred to in this book as rail-optimized design (ROD). (There is a similar-sounding concept, rail-only design, where there is no communication between the different rails. We discuss this design in subsequent sections on the network fabric.)

- Multiple GPUs connected to a single leaf, referred to in this book as rail-unified design (RUD).

Figure 3-3 shows the different network ports found on GPU-based servers. GPUs use specific ports on a server to communicate to other GPUs across servers. These servers are mainly used for training in training networks. Certain ports within a server are used for CPU communication across servers or for northbound connections. These ports are mainly used for inference and are part of frontend networks. In addition, some ports are used for Non-Volatile Memory Express (NVMe) communication for fast data transfer.

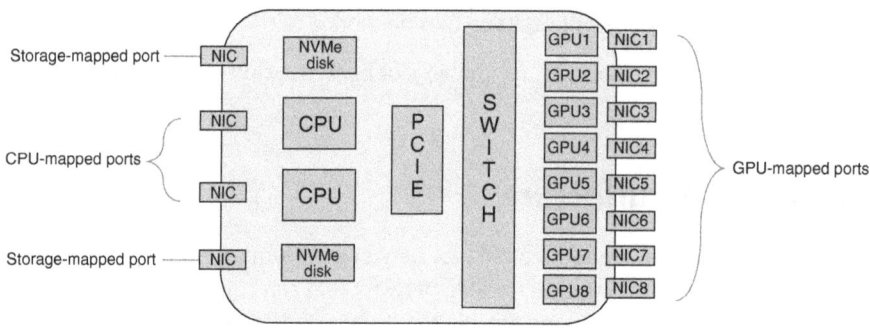

Figure 3-3
NICs in a GPU-based server

Rail-Optimized Design (ROD)

Servers used in AI data centers, for example, DGX series, HGX series from Nvidia, SuperMicro GPU Super server series, MI series from AMD, and so on; each have an internal switch that connects the GPUs. This internal switch is used for any communication within the server, and it is faster and provides higher performance compared to an external switch. However, when the workload processing requires more than 8 GPUs, the load is shared across servers, resulting in east–west traffic. While the GPUs within a server communicate via the internal switch, the NICs mapped to the GPUs can be connected to multiple leaf switches for low latency, with one-hop communication between servers.

Each GPU in a server is considered to be part of a different rail. Across servers, a GPU number is mapped to a rail of the same number. Figure 3-4 displays the mapping of GPUs to a rail.

To keep the latency within a rail to a minimum, each GPU is connected to a leaf switch; this is referred to as rail-optimized topology. Eight leaf nodes connecting to 8 different GPUs is referred to as a row, or a stripe. Each leaf switch can establish connections with several servers. For instance, a 64 × 400 Gbps switch with a 1:1 oversubscription ratio can have 32 × 400 Gbps links toward the servers and an additional 32 × 400 Gbps links toward the spine, as illustrated in Figure 3-5.

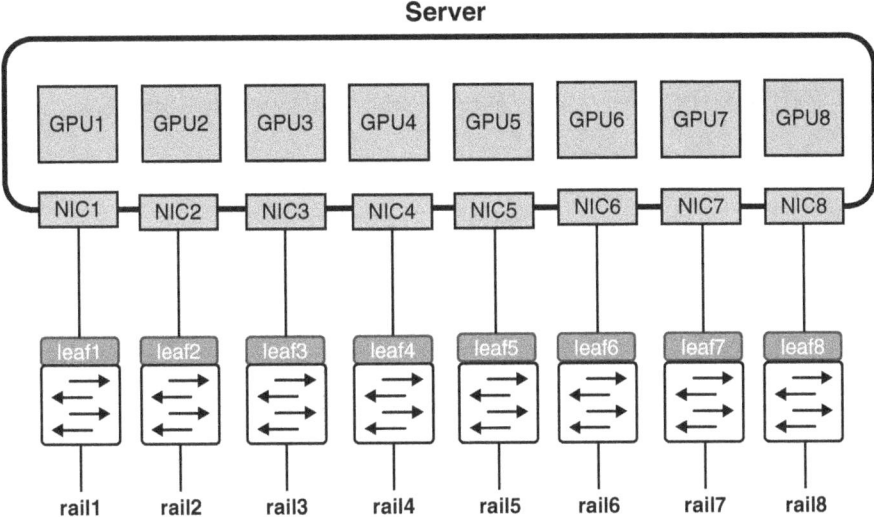

Figure 3-4
Rail-optimized topology

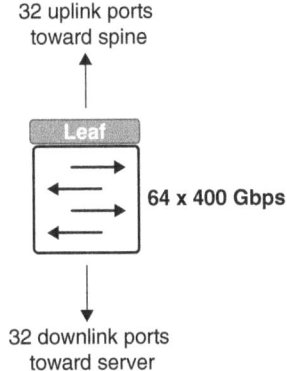

Figure 3-5
Leaf switch with 32 uplinks and 32 downlinks

A cluster of 256 GPUs (32 servers × 8 GPUs per server) can be built using 8 leaf switches with 32 × 400 Gbps downlinks per switch. Alternatively, using 8 leaf switches with 64 × 400 Gbps downlinks per switch can enable the creation of a larger cluster, accommodating up to 512 GPUs (64 servers × 8 GPUs per server). For a cluster of this size, the infrastructure can operate efficiently without the spine layer, as shown in Figure 3-6.

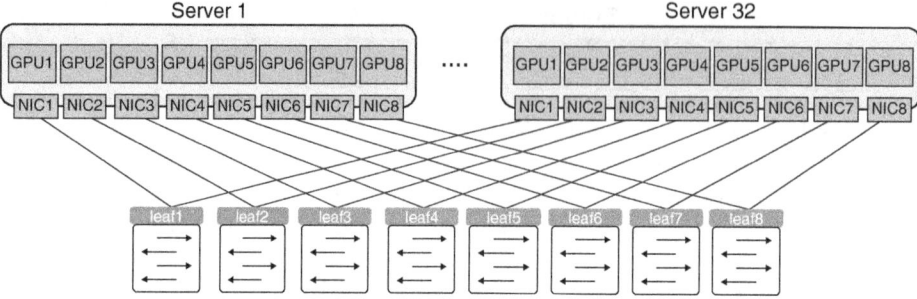

Figure 3-6
Rail connections with multiple servers

Note that this topology enables switching only within the same rail—in other words, on the same GPU number on all the servers through the leaf; this is called intra-rail communication. There is minimal latency within a rail. For communication between different GPUs across rails, the traffic needs to flow via the spine layer, as shown in Figure 3-7. This is called inter-rail communication, and its latency is doubled compared to the latency in intra-rail communication.

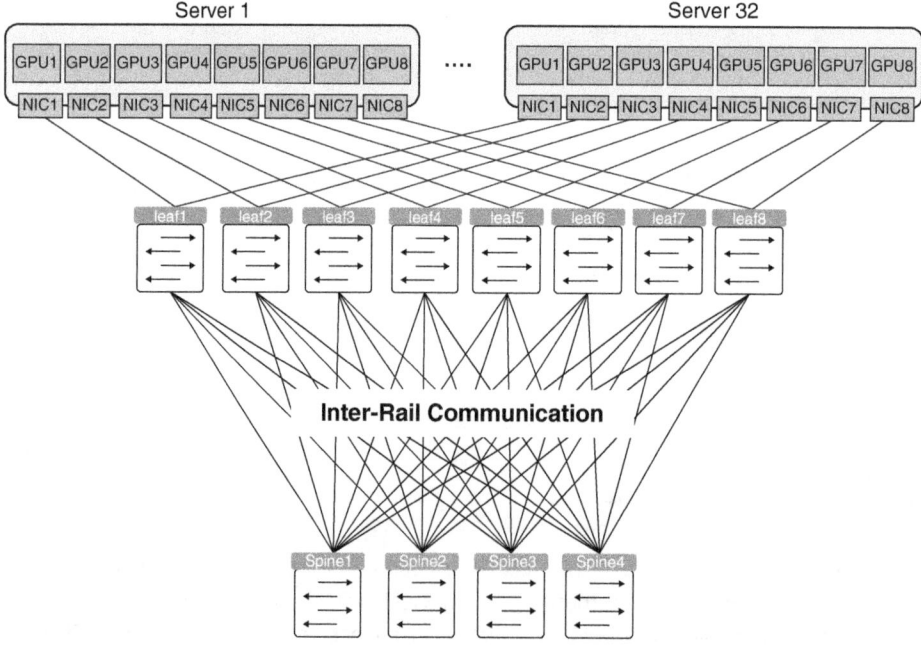

Figure 3-7
Inter-rail communication

With 8 leaf switches and 4 spine switches, each 64 × 400 Gbps, the cluster can be scaled to 32 servers (or 256 GPUs). To scale additional servers or GPUs, further rows of leaf and spine switches must be added. With two such rows of leaf switches—that is, 16 leaf switches—and 8 spine switches, the cluster can scale to 64 servers (or 512 GPUs), as shown in Figure 3-8.

Rail-Optimized Design (ROD)

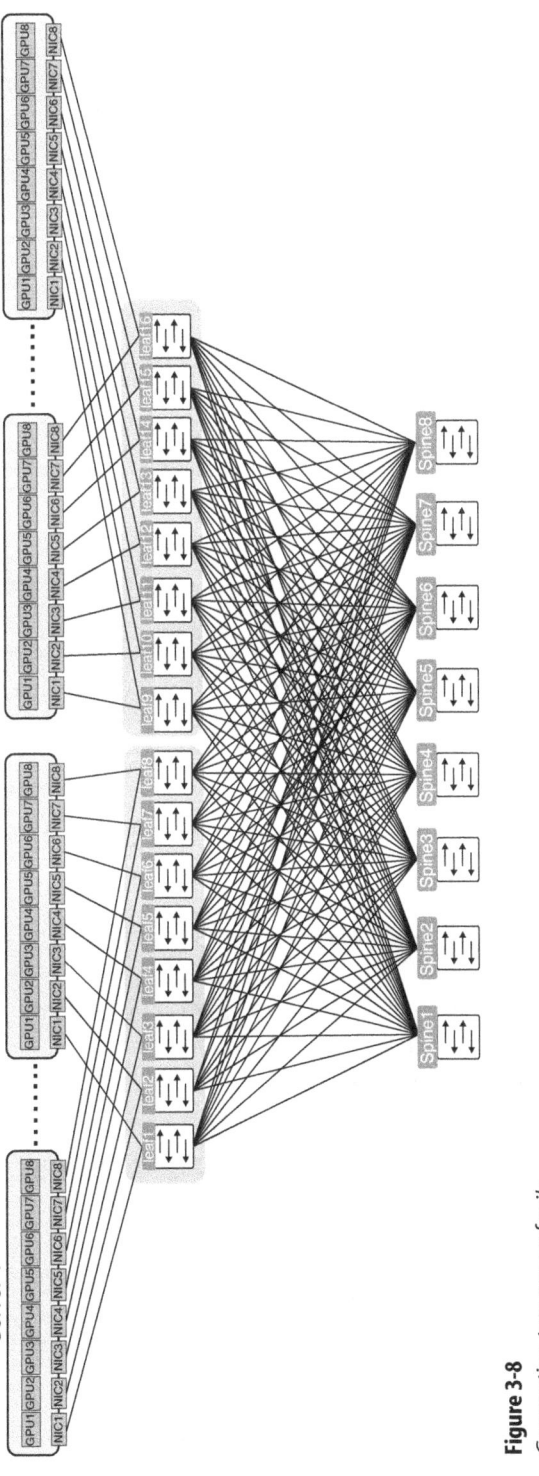

Figure 3-8
Connecting two rows of rails

To scale further, either the number of spines needs to increase or a chassis-based spine must be used. However, increasing the number of spines will create load-balancing and management challenges. Figure 3-9 illustrates the GPU scale supported with a three-stage Clos fabric. It uses 64 × 400 Gbps switches at each layer.

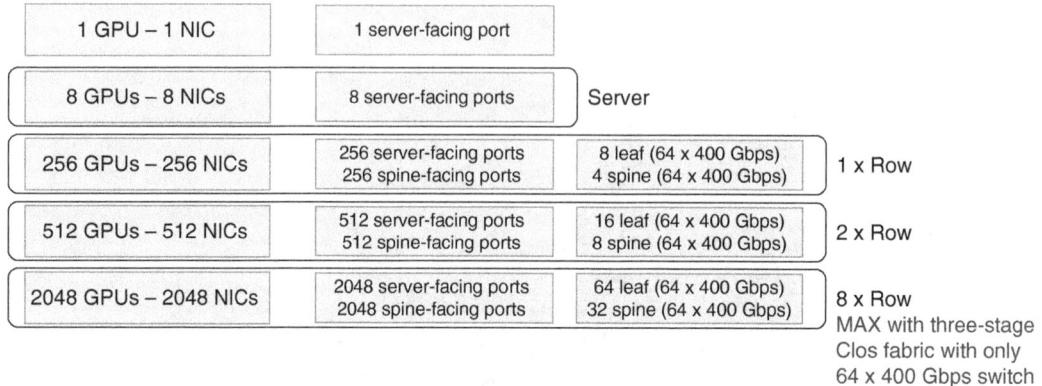

Figure 3-9
GPU scale supportability with three-stage Clos fabric

Now, if the spine is a chassis-based system with, let's say, 256 × 400 Gbps, the number of spines needed will be reduced to one-fourth compared to 64 × 400 Gbps spines, as illustrated in Figure 3-10.

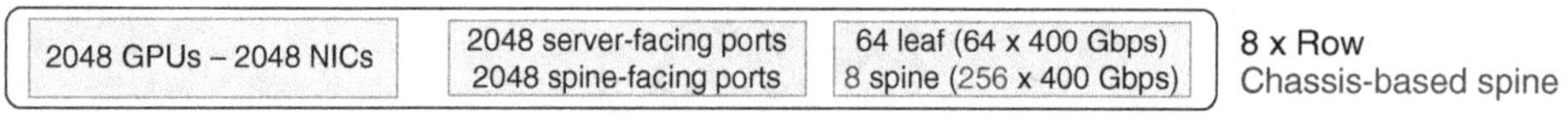

Figure 3-10
GPU scale supportability with a chassis-based spine

Often, large AI/ML clusters can scale up to 32K, 64K, or 128K GPUs. To achieve such a cluster size, you may need to deploy 8K, 16K, or 32K leaf switches. This requires a multistage Clos architecture such as a five-stage or seven-stage Clos fabric.

A combination of spine-connected rows is called a block, or brick. The blocks, or bricks, are interconnected via a super spine. In addition, the communication between blocks may not be 1:1 oversubscribed, if correctly controlled via server applications.

There are several ways to scale up to 32K, 64K, or 128K GPUs:

- Use five-stage or seven-stage Clos architecture.
- Use chassis systems with high port density at the spine and super spine layers.
- Apply oversubscription at the super spine layer.

Figure 3-11 illustrates the block, or brick, for a five-stage Clos fabric with enough ports for super spine connectivity.

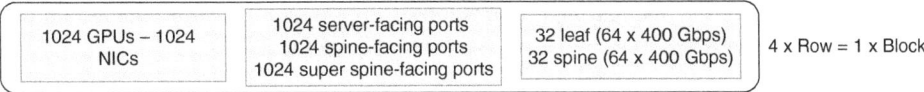

Figure 3-11
GPU scale supportability per block with five-stage Clos fabric

With 1K GPUs per block, we need 32 blocks to make a cluster of 32K GPUs. Figure 3-12 illustrates how cluster sizes are incremented with different oversubscription ratios at the super spine layer. Note that the number of super spines is consistent.

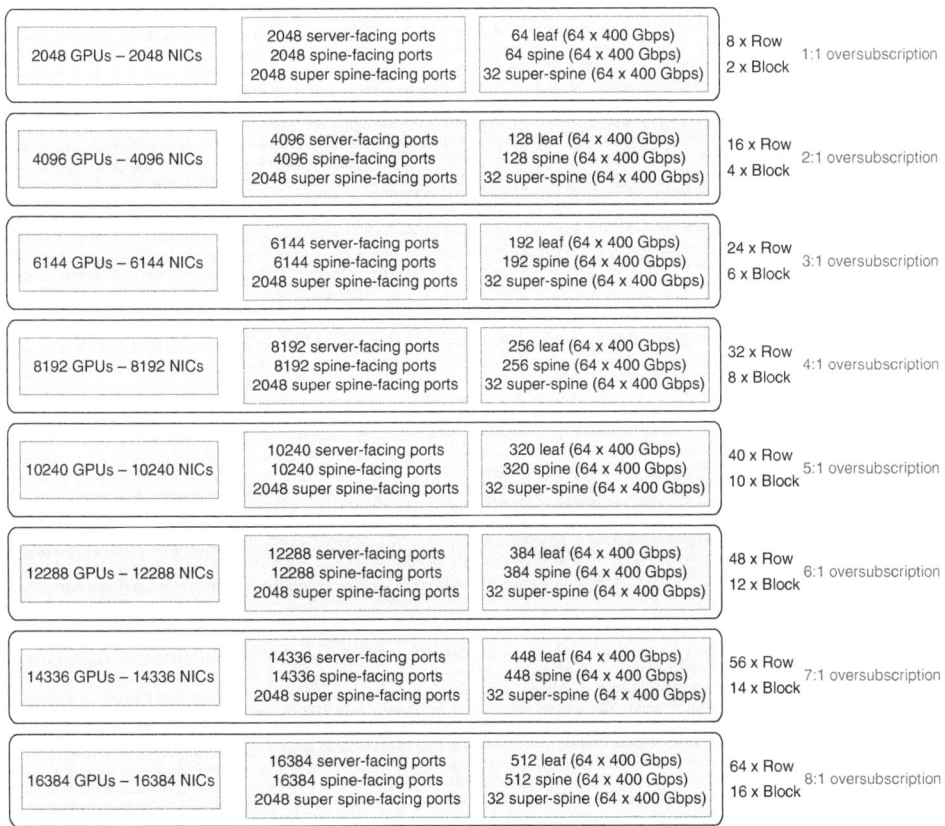

Figure 3-12
GPU scale supportability with different oversubscription ratios

Currently, some companies are evaluating use of an oversubscription ratio up to 7:1 at the super spine layer. The challenge with higher oversubscription ratios is that the likelihood of congestion at the super spine layer also increases. This congestion requires implementation of Data Center Quantized Congestion Notification (DCQCN)—a congestion control mechanism for RoCEv2, as discussed in Chapter 7, "RoCEv2 Transport and Congestion Management."

It is also possible to create large clusters by using a chassis-based system for the super spine layer. With super spine switches of higher port capacity, it is possible to create a 16K cluster without increasing the number of super spines, as shown in Figure 3-13.

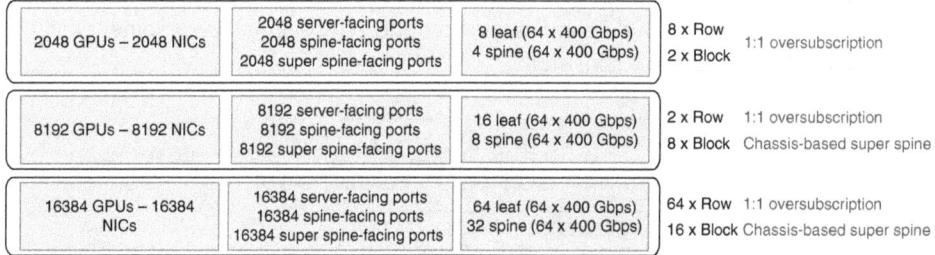

Figure 3-13
GPU scale supportability with five-stage Clos fabric and a chassis-based super spine

We already discussed inter-rail traffic. Companies are trying to evaluate the requirement of inter-rail traffic in the training clusters. With inter-rail traffic, each of the GPU servers has 8 GPUs and an internal high-bandwidth switch for communication between the GPUs within the server. The idea is that if inter-rail traffic can be handled via the switch internal to the server, we do not need inter-rail connections in the fabric. This design, referred to as rail-only design, reduces the budget of an AI/ML data center, as illustrated in Figure 3-14.

Rail-only design can also be used in extending the rails across the stripe. In this case, the spine layer will be used to connect different stripes. The spine-to-leaf connectivity needs to be 32 × 400 Gbps for 1:1 oversubscription ratios. The scaling constraints remain the same as those discussed previously, but the spine also follows the rail connectivity. This kind of topology can make the topology simpler in cases where there is no communication between the rails. Troubleshooting is also often simpler because the faults in one rail do not impact the other rails.

The benefits and adoption of rail-only topology are still to be determined at the time of writing of this book.

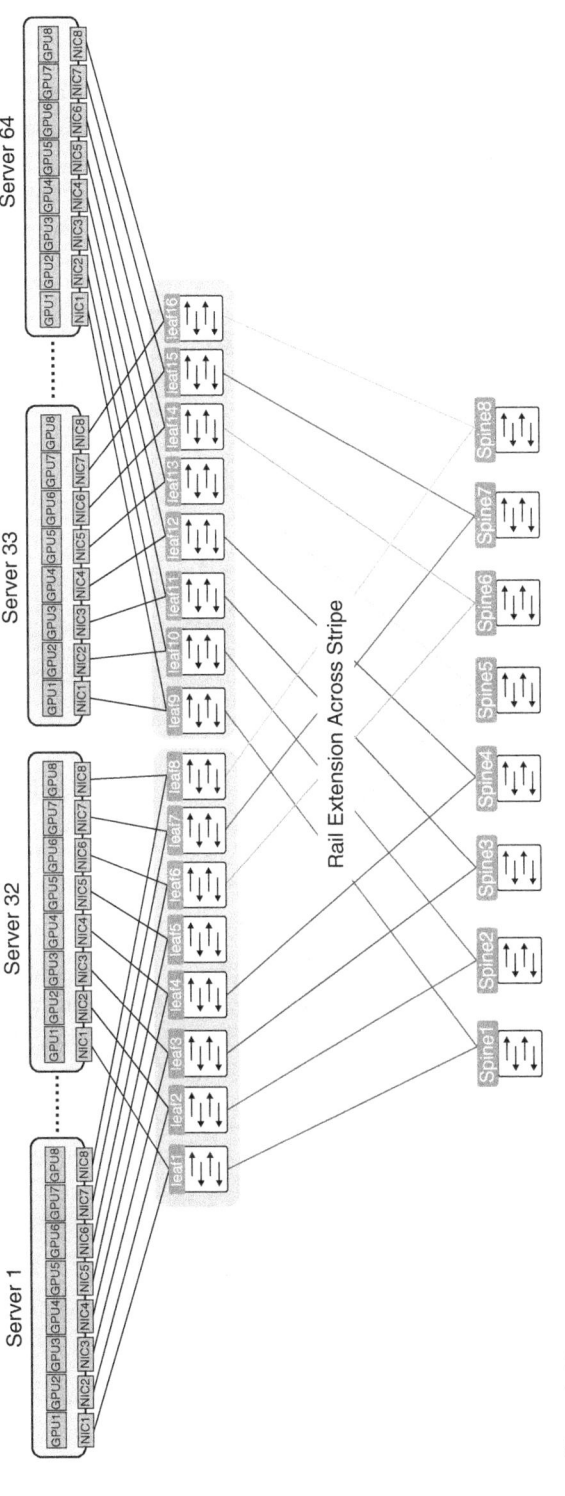

Figure 3-14
Rail-only design

Rail-Unified Design (RUD)

Another design option is to connect multiple GPUs in a server to a single leaf. You can connect all 8 GPUs of a server to one leaf switch, you can connect 4 GPUs to two leaf switches, and so on, as illustrated in Figure 3-15. The advantage of this topology, called rail-unified design (RUD), is simplified cabling, easier scaling, and well-established architecture. The challenge is that if the single leaf goes down, the server is completely isolated.

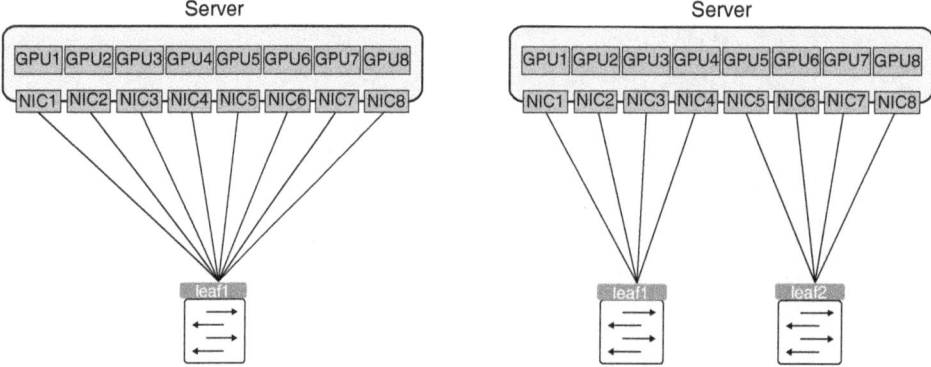

Figure 3-15
Rail-unified design

As discussed earlier, the GPUs within a server communicate via the internal switch. Therefore, local GPU traffic does not use the links from the leaf toward the server. Four servers connected to the same leaf will have the least latency. Intra-rail and inter-rail communication with up to 4 servers has one-hop latency. Traffic from the GPUs on servers other than these four servers passes through the spine, with a latency of two hops, as shown in Figure 3-16.

Because each leaf has multiple rails in this topology, it must be able to segregate rail traffic. This requires additional features such as deterministic path forwarding, as shown in Figure 3-17, where the green-colored highlight represents a rail. (If you are reading a printed copy of this book, you will see a shade of gray here, but you can still see the highlighted rails.)

The rail-unified design topology can be quite attractive to customers who do not plan to use the internal switch for GPU communication within a server and instead use a higher-throughput switch. For example, the Nvidia NVSwitch offers fast throughput, at 900 Gbps, for GPU-to-GPU connectivity. However, this topology comes at a cost compared to an external data center switch. Figure 3-18 illustrates using a leaf switch for GPU communication within the same server.

Rail-Unified Design (RUD) 43

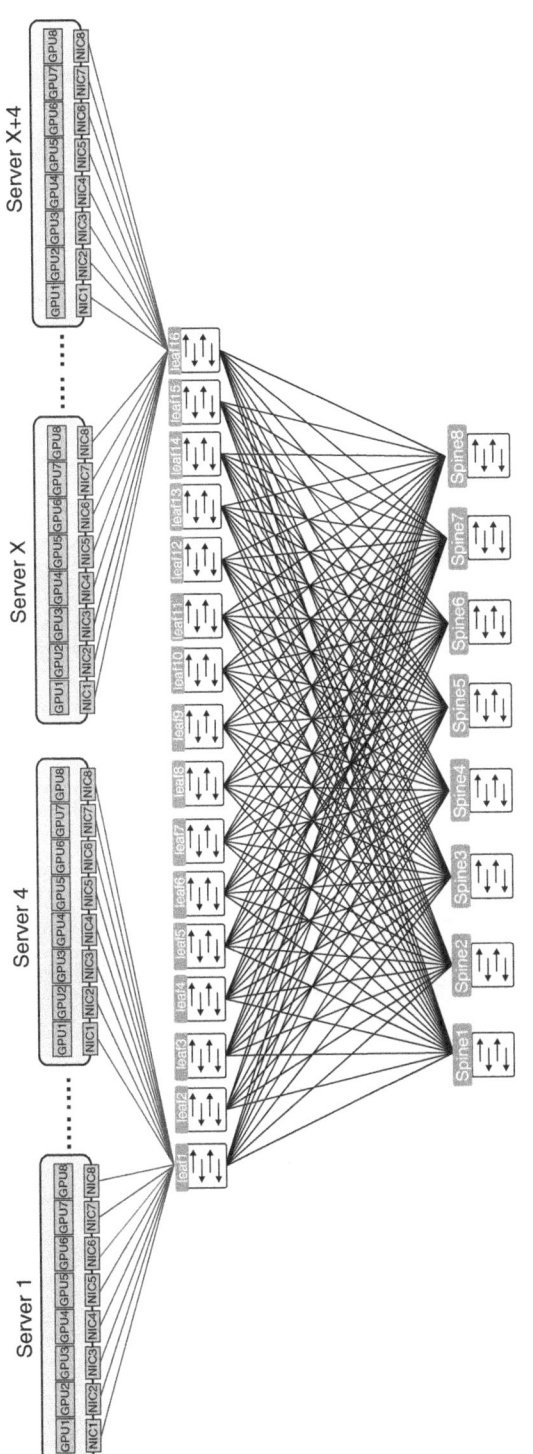

Figure 3-16
Rail-unified design with multiple servers

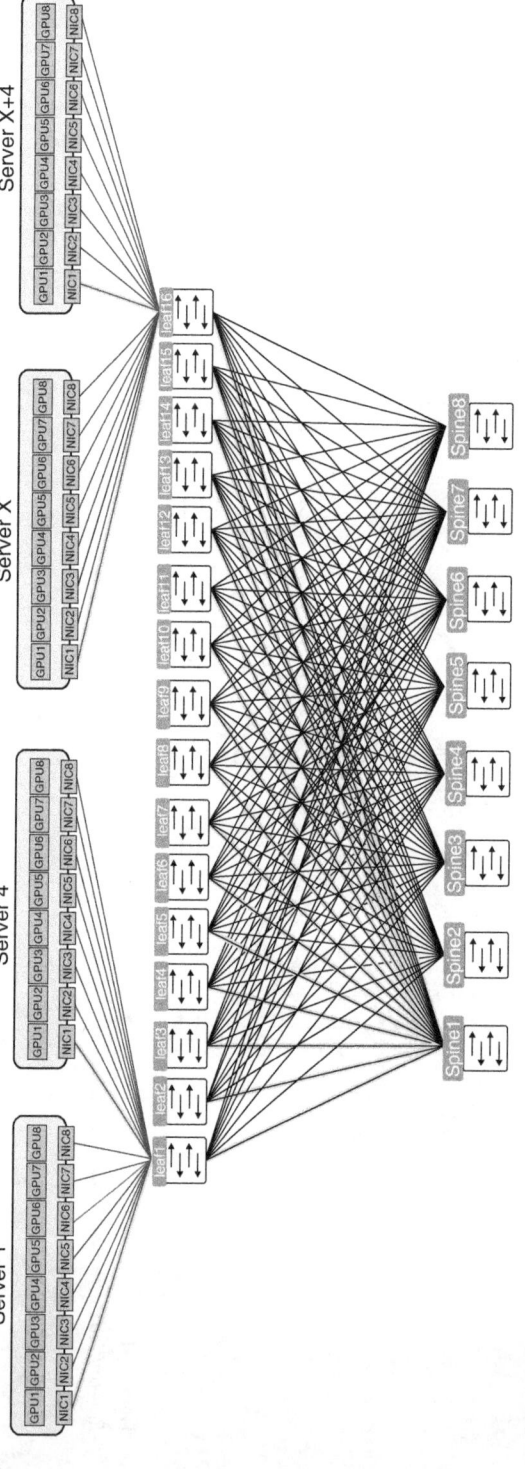

Figure 3-17
Rail-unified design with deterministic path forwarding

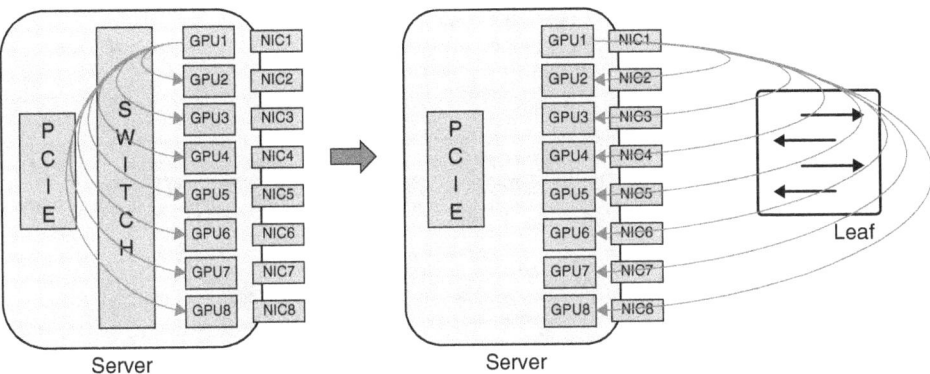

Figure 3-18
Intra-GPU communication options

Rack Design

When designing a data center rack, various factors must be considered, including the following:

- Rack capacity
- Power budget of the rack
- Cooling requirements
- Cabling requirements

A typical rack in a data center is 19 inches wide, 36 inches deep, and 42U tall. The Nvidia DGX H100 server is 19 inches wide, 35.3 inches deep, and 8U tall, whereas the DGX A100 is 6U tall. A single rack can host four or five DGX H100 servers and a leaf switch, requiring a power budget between 48 kW and 60 kW. This is very high compared to the average power budget of 20 kW to 25 kW in current data centers. We cover power and thermal management in Chapter 5, "Thermal and Power Efficiency Considerations."

There are three data center designs for the position of leaf switches:

- Top-of-rack
- Middle-of-row
- End-of-row

In addition, for rail-optimized design, one server needs to connect to 8 different leaf switches.

Top-of-Rack

In the top-of-rack (ToR) design, the switch is installed at the top in each rack. Figure 3-19 illustrates a ToR design that has a row of 8 racks, where a rack has 4 servers and 1 leaf switch. This makes a cluster of 32 servers and 256 GPUs.

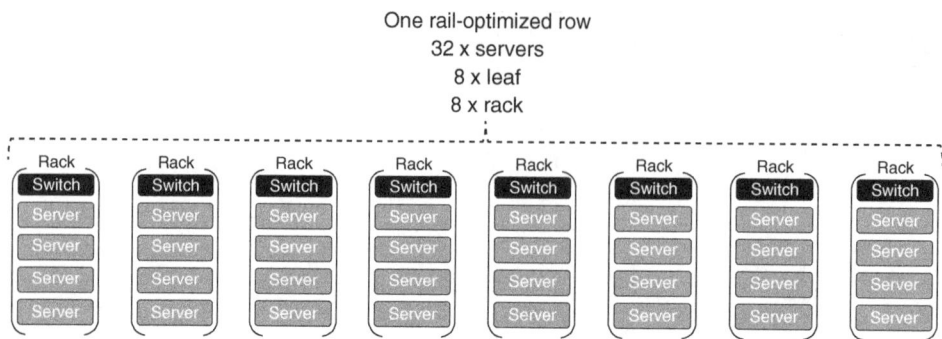

Figure 3-19
Top-of-rack design

With this design, the spine can be installed either in a separate rack or in the same rack. A spine in the same rack can be used with the block, or brick, design. Figure 3-20 illustrates a ToR design with the spines in separate racks. Keep in mind that the number of spines and racks depends on the design requirements.

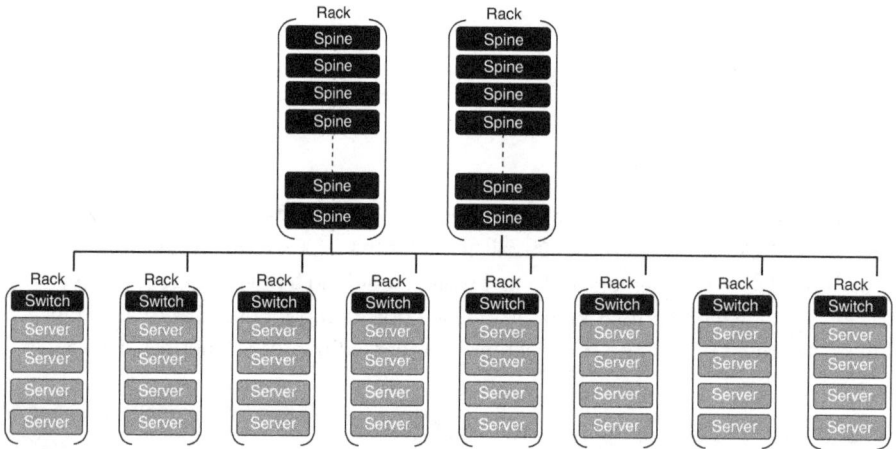

Figure 3-20
Top-of-rack design with the spines in separate racks

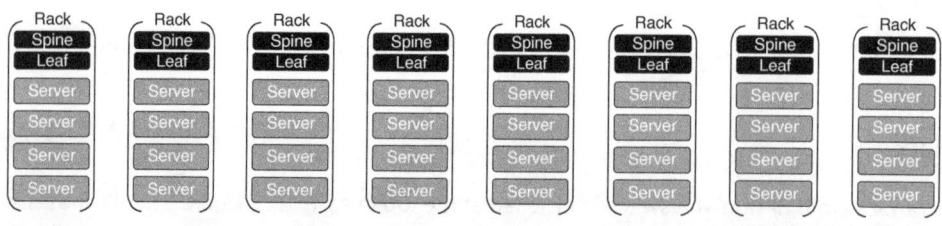

Figure 3-21
Top-of-rack design with the spine in the same rack

The topology illustrated in Figure 3-21 has an equal number of spine and leaf switches. However, it is possible for only a few racks to have spines based on cluster size and oversubscription requirements. This topology requires cable lengths to run within the rack as well as across the 8 racks. The power budget and cooling requirement of the rack increase with switches on the same rack. This type of topology is advantageous for an RUD design, though. The cabling is easier, and copper-based Direct Attach Copper (DAC) or Active Electrical Cable (AEC) cables can be used for cost benefit.

Middle-of-Row

In the middle-of-row design, a switch is installed in the middle rack, between the server racks, as shown in Figure 3-22. The design in this figure has a row of 8 server racks, each rack with 4 servers. It makes a cluster of 32 servers and 256 GPUs. Each server connects to 8 leaf switches, which are installed in their own racks in the middle of the row. The leaf switches can be in one rack or more than one rack for better failure handling. Spine switches can be installed on the same rack as the leaf switches or on a separate rack.

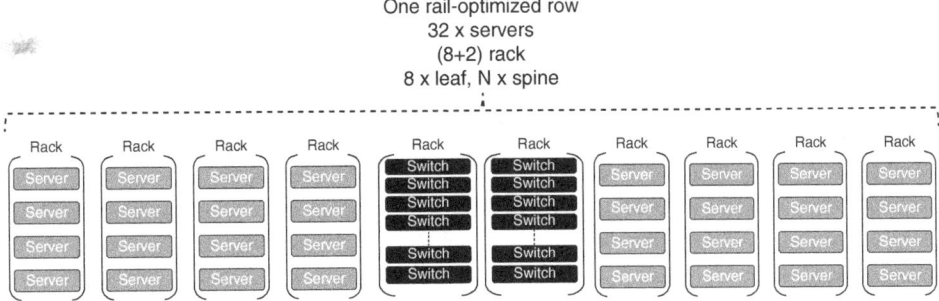

Figure 3-22
Middle-of-row design

This topology requires the cable lengths to run from servers to leaf switches across a maximum of five or six racks. The power requirement of a switch does not add to the power budget of the rack. However, this topology requires more rack space, especially when spines are installed in their own racks, separate from the leaf switches.

End-of-Row

In the end-of-row design, the leaf switches are installed in a rack at the end of the row, as shown in Figure 3-23. This figure shows a row of 8 server racks, each rack with 4 servers. It makes a cluster of 32 servers and 256 GPUs. Each server connects to 8 leaf switches, which are installed in separate racks at the end of the row. The leaf switches can be in one rack or more than one rack for better failure handling. Spine switches can be installed on the same rack as the leaf switches or on a separate rack.

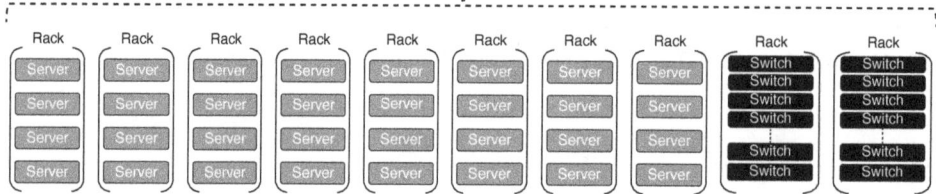

Figure 3-23
End-of-row design

This topology requires cable lengths to run from server to leaf across a maximum of 10 racks. The power requirement of a switch does not add to the power budget of the server rack. However, it requires more rack space, especially when spines are installed in their own racks, separate from the leaf switches.

Design Comparison

Table 3-1 provides a comparative summary of the rack design options for rail-optimized design.

Table 3-1 Leaf Placement Comparison

	Top-of-Rack	Middle-of-Row	End-of-Row
Rack space requirement	Less	More	More
Power requirement per rack	More	Less	Less
Cooling requirement per rack	More	Less	Less
Cabling requirements within the rack	Varying size connecting servers to leaf switches in each rack	No cabling within a rack	No cabling within a rack
Cabling requirements across the racks	Each server connects to a leaf switch in each rack that is part of a row.	Varying sizes are used from different racks, based on the distance from the network rack. Each server in the rack needs cable of the same size to reach the leaf switch.	Varying sizes are used from different racks, based on the distance from the network rack. Each server in the rack needs cable of the same size to reach the leaf switch.
Maximum cable length	To span 8 racks	To span 6 racks	To span 10 racks

When deploying the rail-unified design, the top-of-rack design is ideal because of the low rack requirements and low cabling requirement. Further, copper-based DAC or AEC cables can be used for cost benefits.

Scheduled Fabric

Scheduled fabric is yet another architecture that Cisco is developing with Silicon One and that Broadcom is developing with Jericho3-AI and Ramon3. This architecture expands the chassis cell-based packet handling to the fabric. As illustrated in Figure 3-24, each leaf switch acts as a line card, and each spine switch acts as a backplane. The packets arriving at the leaf are split into smaller cells of 64, 128, or 256 bytes, much like a switch or a router. The cells assemble to the spine that acts as the backplane. Finally, the cells are assembled to the egress leaf, and the packet is forwarded to the destination server.

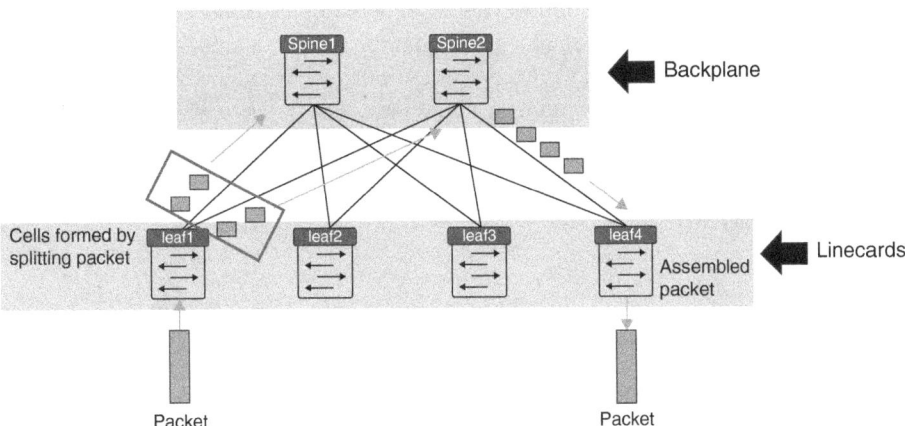

Figure 3-24
Scheduled fabric

This architecture has a number of advantages, including the following:

- **Better congestion handling:** This architecture implements a virtual output queue across the fabric.
- **Better utilization of fabric links:** This architecture sprays cells across multiple links.
- **Improvements with latency:** As the cells are transmitted over the fabric, cells split and assembly is happening only once in the fabric instead of each node doing it separately.

However, this is a new architecture and must be evaluated against the following constraints:

- Scaling constraints
- Link or node failure handling

- Latency with congestion
- Vendor lock-in for a block or brick (or pod)

Virtual output queueing (VOQ) is a technique used to address head-of-line blocking in switching devices. With VOQ, the buffer at each input port maintains a separate virtual queue for each egress port. Consequently, congestion on an egress port does not affect traffic toward other egress ports. This is achieved using a scheduling algorithm. VOQ has been used in chassis-based switch architecture. Extending it to the fabric provides better congestion handling compared to the DCQCN measures.

Topologies

In a data center, Clos is the most commonly used topology. It exists as a three-stage leaf-spine fabric, five-stage leaf-spine-super spine fabric, and so on. Clos topology, also referred to as fat-tree topology, provides a non-blocking architecture that fits the data center requirements. However, in the case of high-performance computing (HPC) clusters and AI clusters, where the cluster size is considerably large, the Clos topology with its multiple stages introduces latency with every additional hop. Topologies that reduce the number of hops, such as Dragonfly (DF and DF+) topology and Torus topology, may be considered.

Dragonfly Topology

Dragonfly is a hierarchical topology in which multiple blocks, or bricks (or groups, or pods), connect with each other in a full mesh. Any topology can be implemented within the block. This topology reduces the number of hops compared to the five-stage Clos topology with a super spine and reduces the link requirements for a full mesh within the block. Eventually, it reduces the diameter, latency, and cost of multi-stage networks.

These are some of the benefits of the Dragonfly topology:

- **Scalability:** The Dragonfly topology is designed to be modular and highly scalable. It can be expanded by adding more compute node groups, so it allows straightforward growth to accommodate larger clusters.
- **Low latency:** Dragonfly is known for its low latency. Communication between nodes within the same group is extremely fast and experiences minimal latency. This makes Dragonfly topology suitable for applications that require real-time or near-real-time communication.
- **Fault tolerance:** The modular nature of Dragonfly topology enables fault tolerance. If a particular group or network component fails, the network can still function, although with reduced capacity.

Also, adaptive routing can help dynamically adjust to network conditions to optimize the data traffic and reduce congestion, as discussed in Chapter 8, "IP Routing for AI/ML Fabrics."

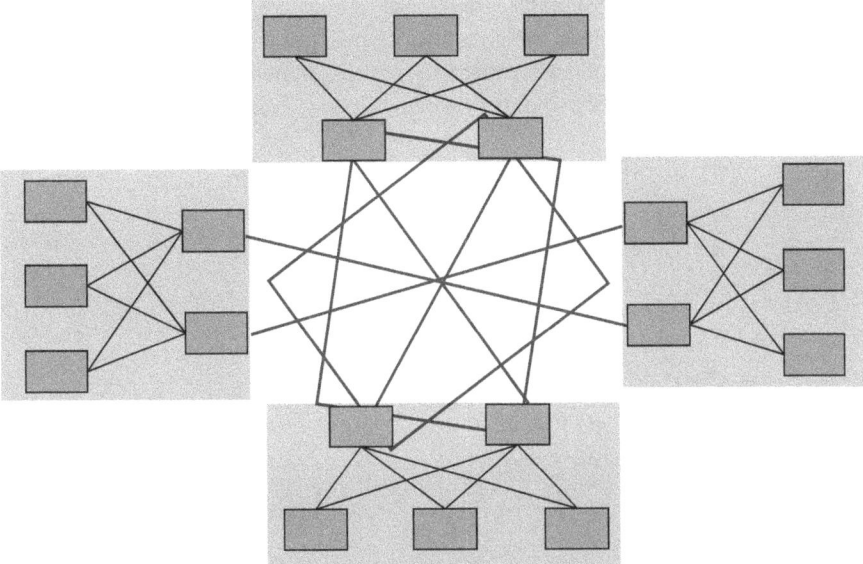

Figure 3-25
Dragonfly topology

Figure 3-25 illustrates Dragonfly topology with four blocks of three-stage Clos fabric connected with each other via a full mesh. In this topology, each spine in a block has mesh connections to all other spines, and each block is a full mesh to other blocks in two planes, as shown in Figure 3-26.

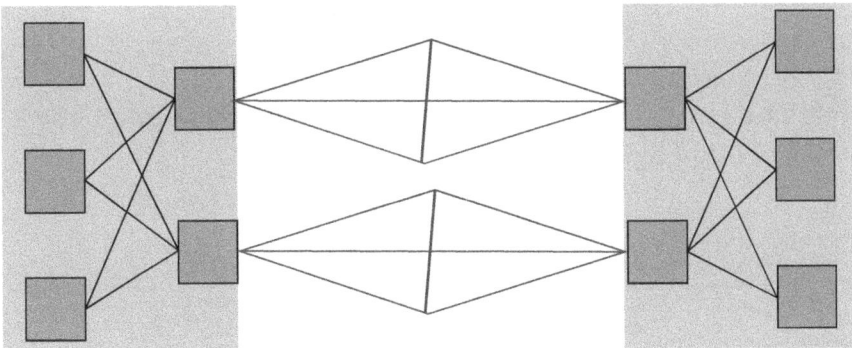

Figure 3-26
Dragonfly topology planes view

This topology is helpful for building large clusters with more GPUs for AI/ML fabrics.

Dragonfly supports multiple topologies within a group, or block. Of the different flavors of Dragonfly topologies, the following two topologies are worth mentioning:

- **Inter-group topology:** In this topology, which is also referred to as full-graph topology, all nodes within the group connect with each other in a mesh, as shown in Figure 3-27. The topology can be one dimensional or two dimensional.

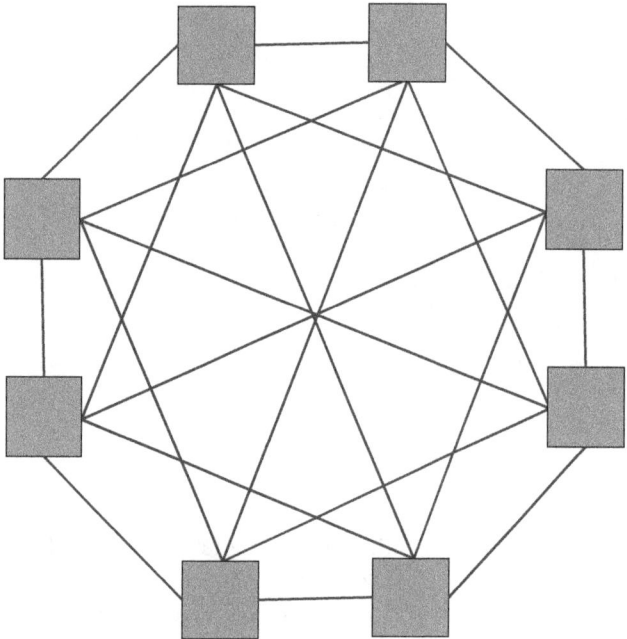

Figure 3-27
Inter-group topology

- **Clos topology:** This is a typical Clos fabric within a group, as shown in Figure 3-28. It is also referred to as Butterfly+ or full bipartite topology.

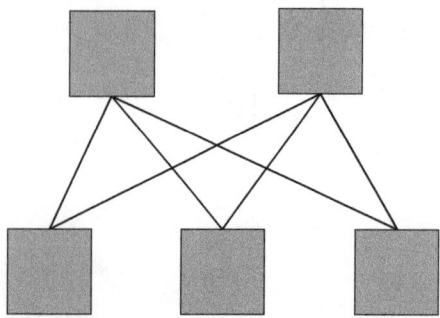

Figure 3-28
Clos intra-group topology

Torus Topology

A torus is a geometric shape that is generated by revolving a circle in a three-dimensional space. A doughnut is a good example of a torus shape. A torus network topology is interconnected, with nodes connecting to their neighboring nodes.

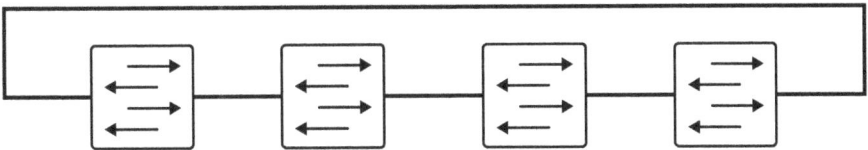

Figure 3-29
One-dimensional torus topology

Figure 3-29 illustrates a one-dimensional torus topology. In this topology, each node is connected to its neighbor on either side, as shown in Figure 3-30. The edge nodes are also connected to each other, and it looks like a ring topology. In one-dimensional torus topology, each node has two connections.

Figure 3-30
One-dimensional node-level connectivity

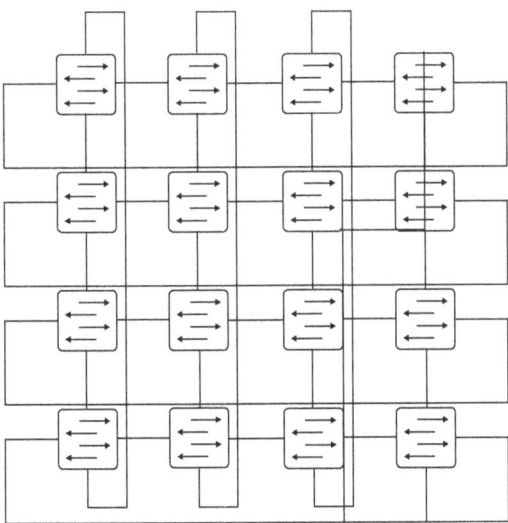

Figure 3-31
Two-dimensional torus topology

Figure 3-31 illustrates a two-dimensional torus topology. Each node is connected to its neighbor on either side, both horizontally and vertically, as shown in Figure 3-32. The edge nodes are also connected to each other in horizontal and vertical directions. In a two-dimensional torus topology, each node has four connections.

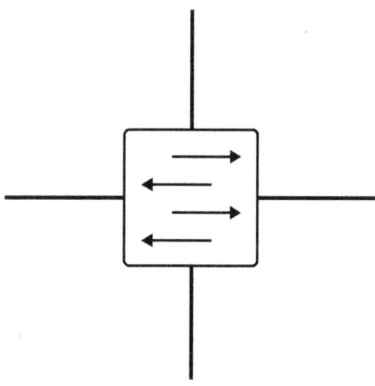

Figure 3-32
Two-dimensional node-level connectivity

Figure 3-33 illustrates a three-dimensional torus topology.

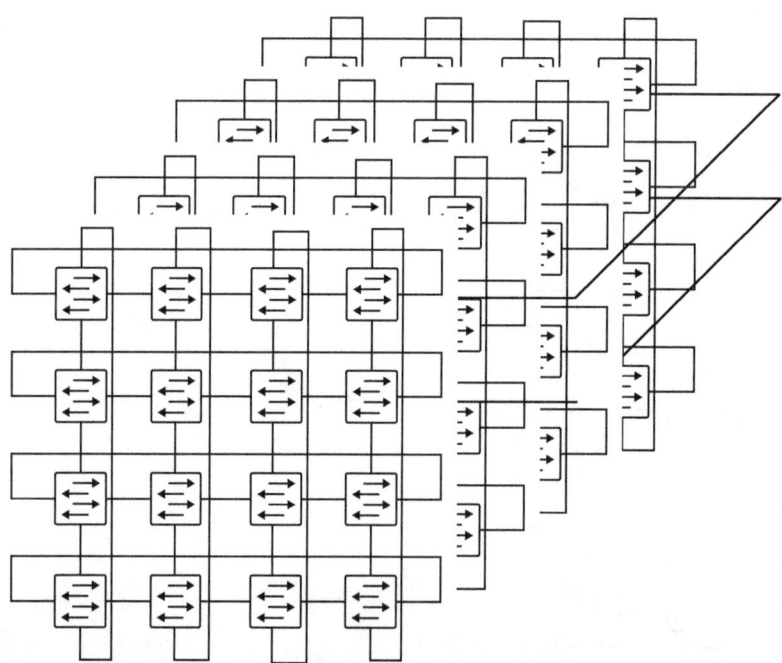

Figure 3-33
Three-dimensional torus topology

Each node is connected to its neighbor on either side along the x-axis, y-axis, and z-axis, as shown in Figure 3-34. The edge nodes are also connected to each other in the x-axis, y-axis, and z-axis. In the three-dimensional torus topology, each node has six connections.

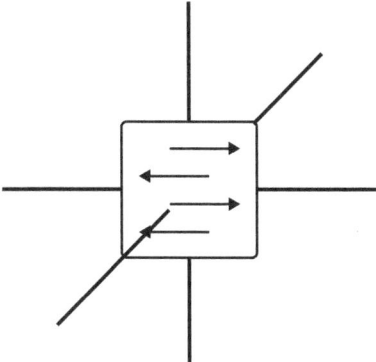

Figure 3-34
Three-dimensional node-level connectivity

As shown in Figure 3-35, it is possible to build a rail topology with a one-dimensional torus topology. Instead of spine connectivity, the connections between the leafs enable inter-rail communication. For connecting multiple rails, a two-dimensional torus or three-dimensional torus topology can be used.

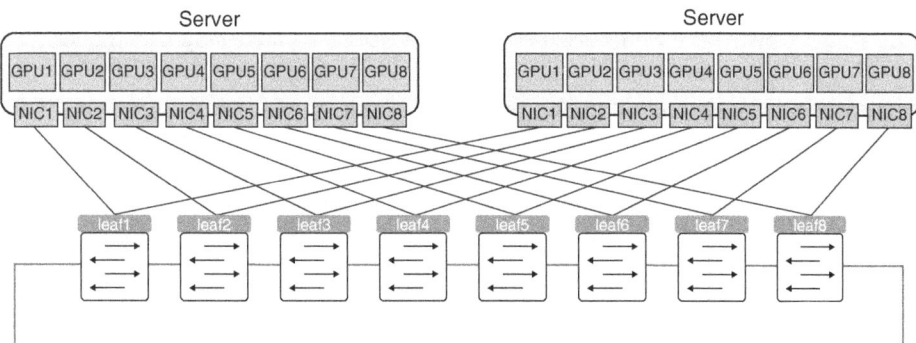

Figure 3-35
Rail topology with a one-dimensional torus

The torus topology offers many benefits:

- It is cost-effective at high scale due to the lower port requirement.
- It is relatively easy to scale out the topology.
- It offers the best performance when applications use nearest nodes.

Inference Data Center Architecture

Inference, as we have said, is a way of using a trained model and input data to get the required results. The deployment of inference data center architecture depends on the model size being used and the number of simultaneous users. There are a number of locations where inference models can be deployed:

- On a mobile device like a phone or a laptop for use by a single user
- In edge computing locations for multiple users, manufacturing units, retail, and so on
- In enterprise data centers
- In cloud data centers
- Co-located with training data centers

In most data centers, rail alignment is not required for inference data centers as the model can be run on a GPU or a small set of GPUs. Traffic in these cases may or may not use RDMA. The design follows Clos and typical data center design. However, the server side includes specialized GPUs and server connects.

Multi-node inference is not a common scenario and is required only in very special cases. Traffic in these cases is RDMA, and designers must determine whether to use the Clos or rail-based designs.

Multi-Planar Scale-Out Architectures

The rapid, exponential growth of AI workloads, particularly those driving large language models (LLMs), has brought traditional cloud networking to its scalability limits. The massive models require clusters spanning hundreds of thousands of GPUs, pushing conventional three-tier network architectures beyond their sustainable limits for efficiency and reliability. Traditional data center networking relies on the Clos topology, typically implemented in three tiers, which scales well for general-purpose workloads. However, as cluster size increases, the three-tier design presents several drawbacks that can be addressed by adding multi-planar as an extension. The multi-planar network architecture has been developed to address the extreme challenges of scale, performance, and reliability of cloud AI infrastructures. A few of the advantages of multi-planar architecture:

- In a single, unified control plane of a massive three-tier network, any node or link failure could affect the entire fabric. In the multi-planar topology, there's a disjoint network control plane and data plane, so there's always a path to the server GPU, even if its capacity can be temporarily reduced.

- In a 5-stage single-plane topology, there is an additional hop between the second and third tiers. This can negatively impact the performance of latency-sensitive AI workloads or larger inference deployments, especially when GPU servers are used. For very large deployments of over 100K GPUs, specific jobs may still be scheduled across the 5-stage topology. Still, for most of them in a multi-planar design, they will be contained within leaf-and-spine or rail leaf nodes for smaller LLM training deployments.

To overcome the limitations of reliability and latency, the multi-planar network architecture can be used, where the main idea is to replace the single three-tier backend network with multiple independent two-tier network planes, leveraging also more intelligent packet spraying at the server Network Interface Card (NIC). Instead of connecting to a single switch from the GPU server, the NIC now breaks out and connects simultaneously to two or four independent planes, while still giving at the application level an impression of having a single flow based on more efficient packet ordering done by the NIC. Even if packets for the given workloads arrive through different active network planes, they are seen from the application level as a single workload. An example multi-planar topology is shown in Figure 3.36, where each server NIC is connected not to a single 400G or 800G link in a rail-optimized topology, but to four different planes via breakout cables.

Figure 3.36 illustrates GPU server 1 connecting to a multi-planar design with four Fabric Planes (FP)—FP1, FP2, FP3, and FP4—using breakout cables. For example, for the 800G server NIC cards can be break out into 4x200G each connecting to a FP. It also means that the given plane can now offer a higher number of GPU connections per leaf switch. For example, a ToR (Top of Rack) switch with 64 ports at 800G will offer 128 * 200G connections to the GPU servers and keep 64 * 400G ports or 32 * 800G ports for the spines. From the software perspective, the application assumes that 800 GB of capacity is still available because only at the lower level will unordered packet delivery be handled.

The architecture presented in Figure 3.36 also introduces more sophisticated traffic management, handled by the NIC's firmware and at the host-based software libraries. An efficient packet spraying for a single application flow (or Q-pair) is used across all planes simultaneously, while coalescing on the receive side. The target NIC collects all the packets coming from different planes and coalesces them before presenting them to the application layers. Because packets may arrive out of order due to traversing different paths and independent planes, the NIC or its associated host software manages reassembly, delaying completion until all data is received in sequence to ensure in-order delivery, which is mandatory for most RDMA (Remote Direct Memory Access) applications.

The server bridging on the host side must also be handled correctly to ensure there are no Ethernet loops in the network fabric. It can use technologies like any form of overlay EVPN-VXLAN MAC-VRF bridging on top of the IP Fabric underlay. This is why, in cases of multi-tenancy with additional requirements, it's sometimes easier to consider only the pure IP Fabric underlays for the multi-planar and manage tenants with a combination of dynamic ACLs and RADIUS server tenant profiles.

When each plane has multiple rails, the spines within the plane may also be used. Figure 3.37 illustrates such an example where two planes of IP Clos fabric design are used to improve the reliability and improve the latency. Within the given plane, the server communication will still happen sometimes across the spines when two servers of the same plane are part of the same collective.

In the design example shown in Figure 3.37, when server4 GPU1 needs to reach server2 GPU1, it would not use spine devices. However, to reach server1 GPU1 (in Rail A), it will forward the packets across the Fabric Plane 1 spine devices.

58 Chapter 3 Network Design Considerations

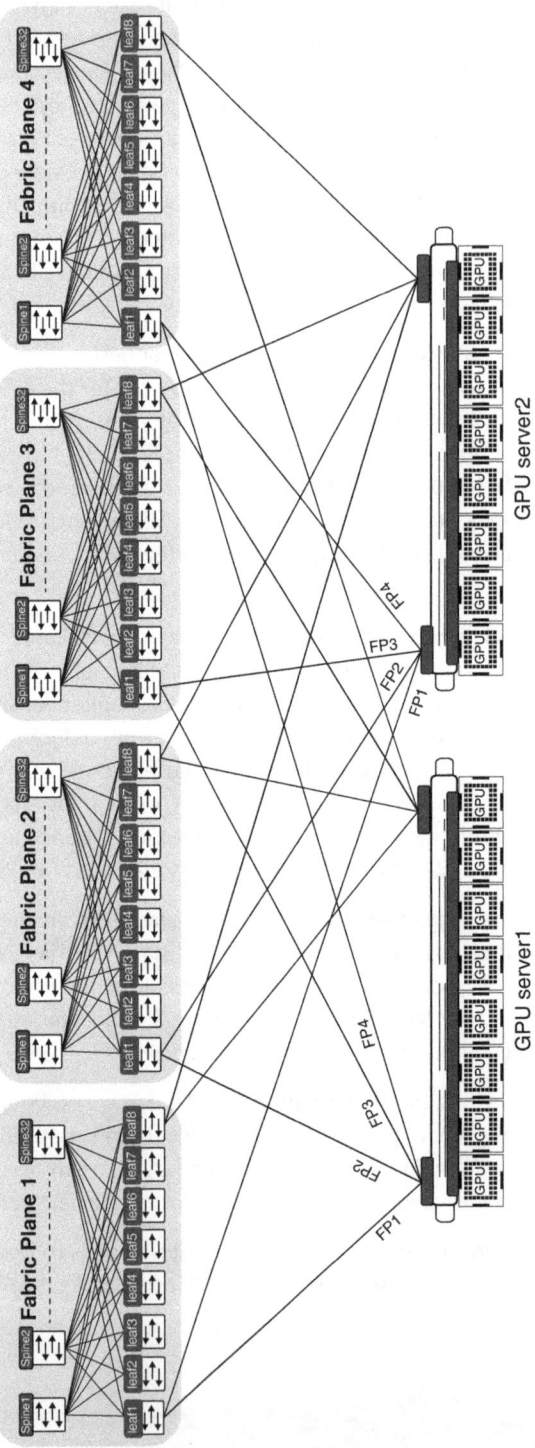

Figure 3-36
Scale-out AI/DC multi-planar architecture

Multi-Planar Scale-Out Architectures

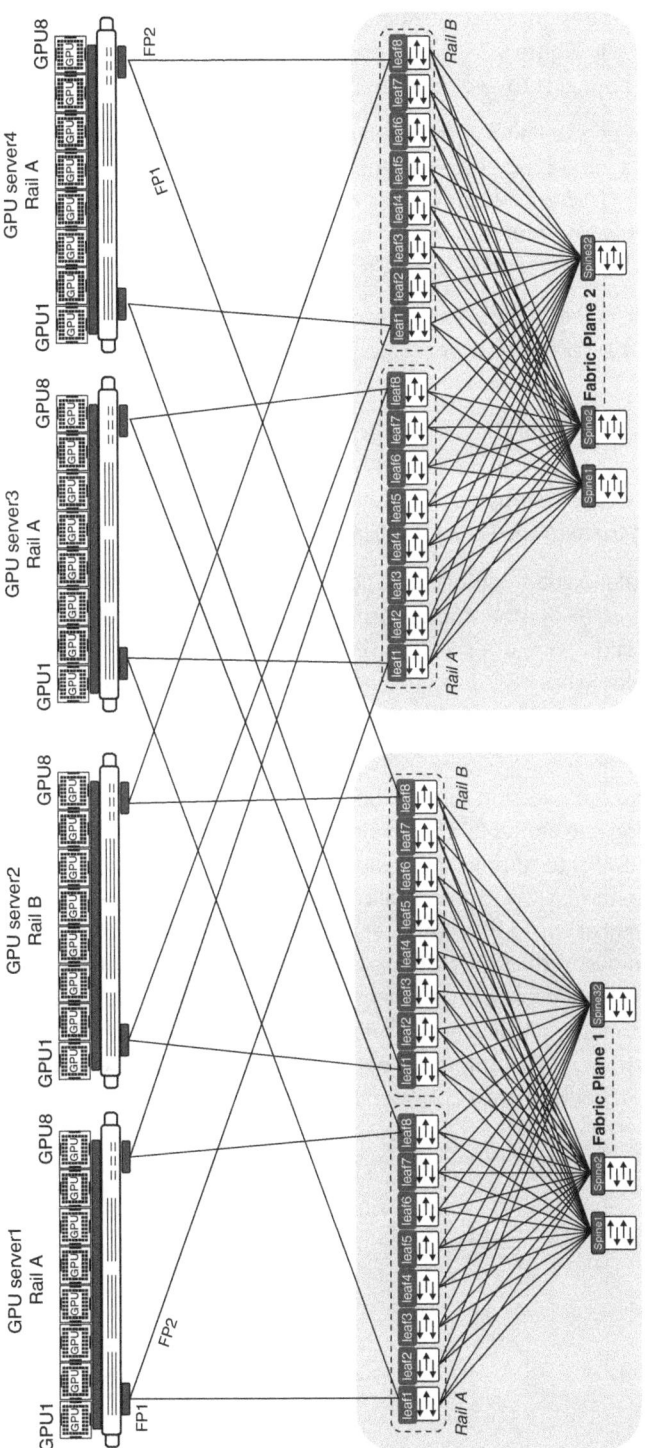

Figure 3-37
Multi-planar design—two planes and two rails per plane

In a larger-scale GPU cluster design the super spines may still have to interconnect two different sets of multi-planar fabrics. In Figure 3.38, a dual-planar design is shown, with two rails per plane, and each GPU server NIC connects to two different planes.

For example, server4 connects to Rail B in Fabric Plane 1a and Fabric Plane 2a, and server1 connects to Rail A in Fabric Plane 1a and Fabric Plane 2a. When these two servers have to communicate, they won't use the super spines; however, when server4 must reach server8, it will cross the super-spine layer. When such a collective communication is scheduled, the latency may not be observed, while the reliability of each GPU still increases.

The Fabric Plane 1a/Fabric Plane 2a represents one domain, and the Fabric Plane 1b/Fabric Plane 2b represents another multi-planar domain, which are interconnected using a high radix super-spine layer.

The same type of multi-planar, multi-domain design is shown in Figure 3.39, where four different planes are used. GPU server1 will spray the packets across all four planes, and the spines, as well as the super spines, will have to efficiently deliver them to target server8, which will reassemble all the packets before delivering them to the RDMA application layer.

When comparing single-plane and multi-plane designs, the traditional cabling infrastructure may become more complex, with 4x or more cables coming out of each host and from every port on the ToR switch side. To address this, one option is to use shuffle cables. These are consolidated cabling solutions that bundle multiple fibers and shuffle links internally, maintaining the randomized connectivity required by the network while vastly simplifying the installation and management of large clusters.

This type of cabling design optimization can also be combined with power optimizations in the optics, such as Linear Pluggable Optics (LPO) and Linear Receive Optics (LRO). Traditional optics use Digital Signal Processors (DSPs) to re-time and clean up signals, a process that consumes significant power. Due to improvements in NIC and switch silicon (SERDES), some of the DSP functionality can now be moved to the host chip. LPO eliminates both DSPs on a link, and LRO eliminates one, resulting in a significant power reduction. Optics is covered in detail in Chapter 4. This power savings extends beyond the optic itself, since less heat is dissipated and less cooling is required, allowing the switch fans to run more slowly and further reducing total power draw, ultimately freeing up that power for customer GPU compute capacity. Thermal and power efficiency is covered in Chapter 5, "Thermal and Power Efficiency Considerations."

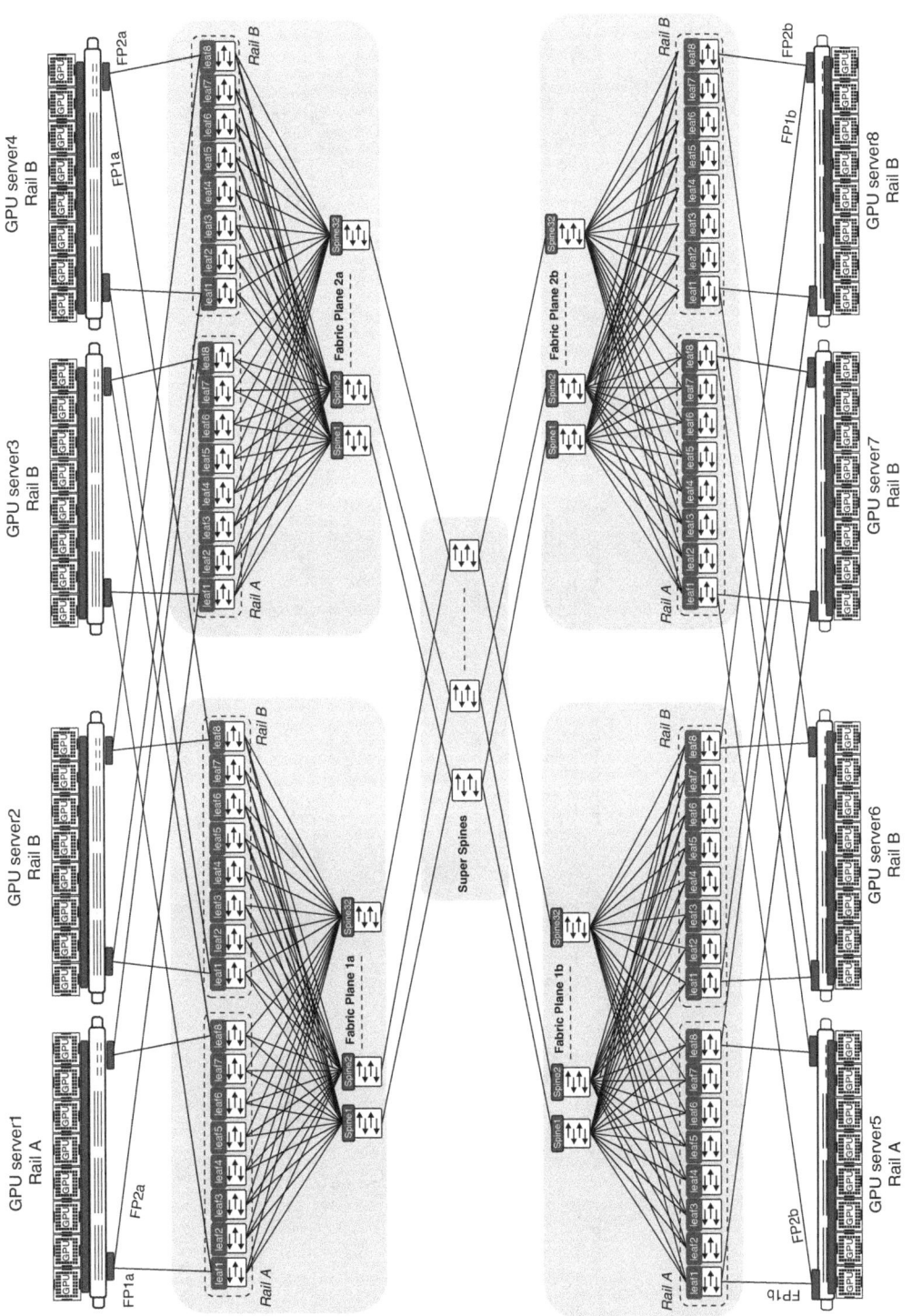

Figure 3-38
Dual-planar fabrics interconnected by super-spines

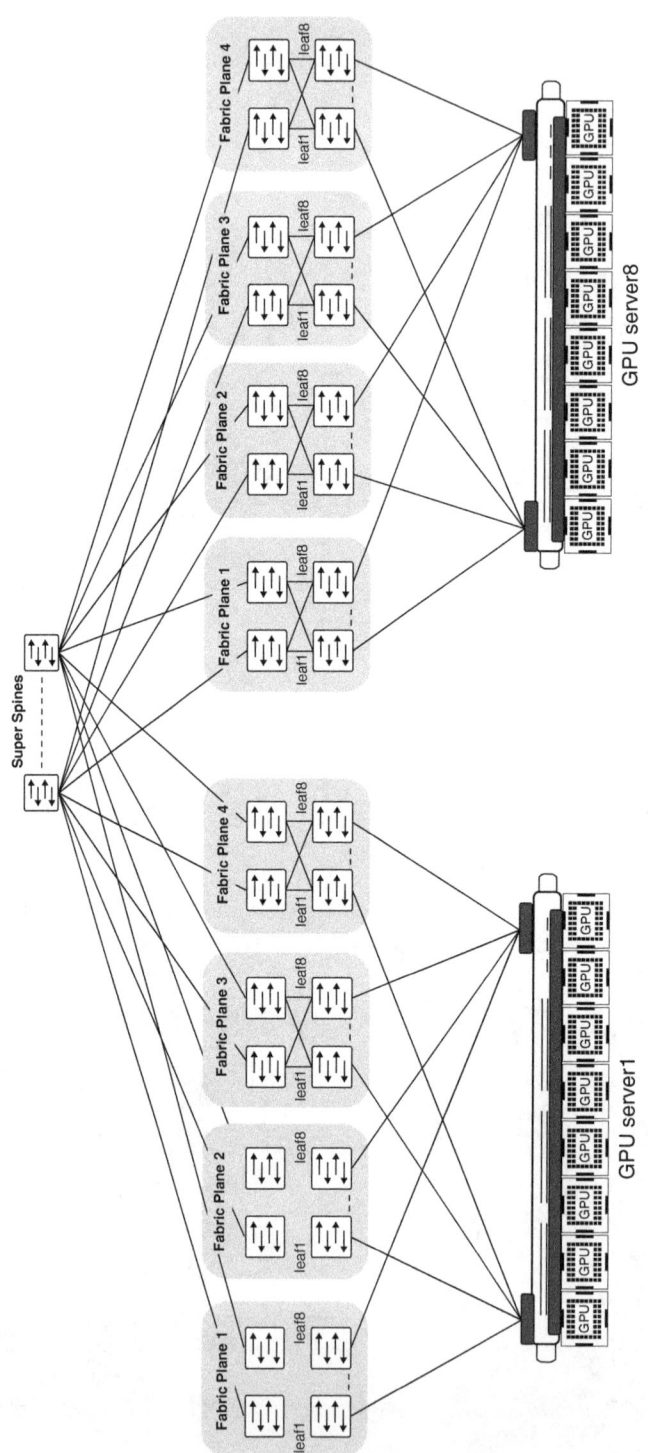

Figure 3-39
Four-plane designs interconnected by super-spines

Summary

In this chapter, we have investigated different fabric design options and topologies for AI/ML workloads. Various options are being considered now, and eventually the most effective designs may be determined. In later chapters, we will discuss the routing options, optics, and thermal management for these topologies.

Test Your Knowledge

Chapter Review

The following questions are designed to test your understanding of the content covered in Chapter 3. Following the questions, answers are provided so you can verify your conclusions.

Questions

1. What are the main architectural stages in AI/ML workload processing, and how do they influence network design?
2. How do rail-optimized design (ROD) and rail-unified design (RUD) differ in terms of GPU-to-leaf connectivity, and what are the implications for scalability and fault tolerance?
3. What are the key considerations and trade-offs in rack design (top of rack, middle of row, end of row) for AI/ML data centers?
4. How does the Clos (fat-tree) topology enable scalable, non-blocking AI/ML fabrics, and what are the challenges at extreme scale (for example, 32,000+ GPUs)?
5. What are the benefits and limitations of alternative topologies like Dragonfly and torus for AI/ML clusters?
6. How do scheduled fabric architectures (for example, cell-based switching, VOQ) improve congestion management and link utilization in AI/ML data centers?
7. What are the power and cooling implications of high-density AI/ML racks, and how do they influence network and facility design?
8. How do deterministic path forwarding and traffic engineering support performance and reliability in large-scale AI/ML fabrics?

Answers

1. AI/ML workload processing typically follows three main stages:
   - Data gathering and preprocessing: Data is collected from diverse sources and cleaned, labeled, and tagged. This stage requires high-throughput storage networks and efficient data pipelines to ensure that large data sets can be ingested and prepared without bottlenecks.
   - Model selection and training: The curated data is used to train models, often requiring clusters of GPUs interconnected with high-bandwidth, low-latency fabrics. The network must support massive east–west traffic, parallel data transfers, and collective communication operations.
   - Deployment and monitoring: Trained models are deployed for inference, and their performance is monitored. This stage may involve both backend (training) and frontend (inference) networks, each with different latency, bandwidth, and reliability requirements.

2. These are the differences between ROD and RUD:

    - ROD: Each GPU in a server is connected to a separate leaf switch, forming "rails." This design minimizes intra-rail latency and maximizes bandwidth, as each GPU has a dedicated path to the network. It allows for efficient scaling by adding more rails (leaf switches) and supports high GPU counts per cluster. Faults are isolated to individual rails, limiting the impact of a switch failure.

    - RUD: Multiple GPUs from a server connect to the same leaf switch. This simplifies cabling and can reduce costs, but it increases the risk that a single leaf switch failure will isolate all GPUs in a server. Scaling is easier in terms of cabling but less optimal for performance and fault isolation compared to ROD.

    ROD is preferred for large-scale, high-performance clusters where minimizing latency and maximizing parallelism are critical. RUD may be chosen for smaller deployments or where cost and cabling simplicity are prioritized and when larger chassis-based systems are used (for example, a higher-end, multi-linecard Ethernet switch instead of a 1RU ToR).

3. These are the key trade-offs:

    - Top of rack (ToR): Switches are placed at the top of each rack, minimizing intra-rack cable lengths and simplifying management. However, this design increases per-rack power and cooling requirements.

    - Middle of row (MoR): Switches are centralized in the middle of a row, reducing the number of switches but increasing cable lengths and complexity.

    - End of row (EoR): Switches are placed at the end of a row, further centralizing switching but requiring the longest cables and careful planning for airflow and power.

    - ToR is best for high-density, high-performance clusters where minimizing latency and maximizing manageability are key. MoR and EoR can reduce switch count and cost but may complicate cabling and cooling. The choice depends on cluster size, density, and operational priorities.

4. The Clos topology uses multiple stages (leaf, spine, super spine) to create a non-blocking, highly parallel network. Each leaf connects to every spine, ensuring multiple equal-cost paths between any two endpoints. Clos can scale to tens of thousands of endpoints with the addition of more stages and higher-radix switches. At extreme scale, challenges include managing oversubscription, cabling complexity, and power/cooling and maintaining low-latency paths. As the number of GPUs increases, the number of required switch ports and interconnects grows rapidly. Multi-stage Clos (three-stage, five-stage, seven-stage) and chassis-based spines/super spines are used to manage this, but careful planning is needed to avoid bottlenecks and ensure efficient load balancing.

5. Dragonfly connects groups of switches in a mesh, reducing the number of hops and the network diameter. It offers lower latency and better scalability for certain traffic patterns but requires more complex routing and fault management.

Torus connects nodes in a ring (1D), grid (2D), or cube (3D), providing multiple paths and high bisection bandwidth for nearest-neighbor communication. It is cost-effective and easy to scale but can suffer from higher average latency and less flexibility for arbitrary traffic patterns.

Both topologies can complicate routing, require specialized hardware/software support, and may not be as flexible as Clos for mixed or unpredictable workloads.

6. Scheduled fabric splits packets into fixed-size cells, uses virtual output queueing (VOQ) to prevent head-of-line blocking, and schedules cell transmission across the fabric. This approach allows for fine-grained congestion management, efficient spraying of traffic across multiple links, and improved fairness.

    The key benefits of scheduled fabric are reducing latency, maximizing link utilization, and preventing congestion hot spots. Scheduled fabric is particularly effective for bursty, synchronized AI/ML workloads, where traditional packet-based switching may struggle. Scheduled fabric requires advanced switch hardware and careful configuration, and it may introduce additional complexity in troubleshooting and monitoring, as well as higher costs compared to a distributed lossless Ethernet fabric with shallow buffers.

7. Modern AI/ML servers (for example, DGX H100) can require up to 15 kW per server, with racks exceeding 60 kW. This necessitates advanced power distribution, redundant supplies, and high-capacity cooling (liquid, immersion, or advanced airflow). High-density racks may require distributed switches (for example, ToR) to minimize cable lengths and manage heat. Facility design must ensure adequate power delivery, cooling capacity, and airflow management to prevent hot spots and ensure reliability. Power and cooling are primary constraints in scaling AI/ML clusters, influencing rack placement, switch location, and overall data center architecture.

8. Deterministic path forwarding ensures that specific flows (for example, between GPUs in the same rail) follow predictable, optimized paths, reducing contention and improving performance. This is achieved through careful network configuration, use of deterministic routing protocols, and sometimes explicit path pinning.

    Traffic engineering involves dynamically adjusting routing and load balancing based on real-time network conditions, workload requirements, and failure scenarios. Techniques include ECMP, flowlet-based balancing, and policy-based routing. Such an approach improves reliability, reduces tail latency, and ensures that critical AI/ML jobs meet performance SLAs even as the network scales and workloads fluctuate.

References

https://www.advancedclustering.com/wp-content/uploads/2022/03/gtc22-whitepaper-hopper.pdf

https://images.nvidia.com/aem-dam/en-zz/Solutions/data-center/nvidia-ampere-architecture-whitepaper.pdf

https://en.wikipedia.org/wiki/Torus_interconnect

4

Optics and Cable Management

Scaling Optics for AI Clusters

In Chapter 3, "Network Design Considerations," we discussed design concepts involved in building an AI/ML data center. Optics and cables are important components of any data center, so requirements of an AI/ML data center.

With AI/ML clusters, the ports on a server currently support 200 Gbps and 400 Gbps throughput and are moving toward 800 Gbps and 1.6 Tbps throughput. Nvidia is the top vendor for the GPU server supplies for AI/ML clusters. It has multiple generations of GPUs—Volta, Ampere, Hopper, and Blackwell. Nvidia currently has A100 (Ampere) and H100 (Hopper) on the market and is moving toward H200 and further versions of GPU based on Blackwell.

From the GPU, Nvidia uses NVLink to connect to the NVSwitch, which is used within the server to communicate between the GPUs that are internal to the server. Each NVLink is 300 Gbps for the Volta generation, 600 Gbps for the Ampere generation, and 900 Gbps for the Hopper generation, moving toward 1800 Gbps for the Blackwell generation. Other vendors have similar solutions; for example, AMD has Infinity Fabric, and Intel has CXL (Compute Express Link), UCIe (Universal Chiplet Interconnect Express), and PCIe (Peripheral Component Interconnect Express) switches.

Figure 4-1 illustrates the system topology of a server with 8 GPUs, where an internal switch helps with communication across the GPUs in the server.

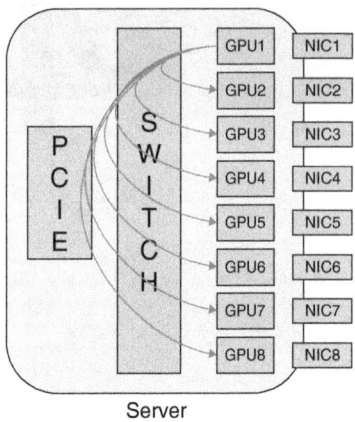

Figure 4-1
System topology

In addition to the NVSwitch for internal communication, there are different NICs that are used for external connectivity between the GPUs across multiple servers. In either case of NVIDIA or AMD-based GPU servers for the scale-out DC use-case, each GPU is connected to a dedicated NIC card, and then each NIC card from the same server connects to different top-of-rack Ethernet or InfiniBand switches. It means for local intra-server communication, the NV switch will be used, and for any server-to-server communication, the external switch is used. GPU-to-NIC card connections are 400 Gbps or 800 Gbps Ethernet or IB. This means a top-of-rack switch is also typically a high-port-density 400Gbps/800Gbps and 1.6Tbps switch. From the AI DC server perspective, besides the GPU-connected NIC cards, there are also storage NIC cards (NVMe-o-F, for example) and out-of-band connections. They are all interconnected via PCIe generation 5 and newer to offer even higher local server interconnects to memory blocks or the CPU.

Figure 4-2 shows a chart from a Dell'Oro report on market adoption of optics for AI clusters from 2020 to 2027. This chart indicates that optics adoption is going to move toward 1.6 Tbps. With the requirement of high-bandwidth optics, there is also a need for high-radix switches that can support a large number of ports per rack unit (RU). In addition, optics need to be power-efficient to reduce the power and thermal budget of a rack. These needs are driving the enhancement of small-form-factor optics, modulation, connectors, and cables.

Figure 4-2.1 shows a 2025 study from Dell'Oro showcasing the adoption of 800 Gbps in 2025 and growing demand for 3.2 Tbps optics by 2029.

Scaling Optics for AI Clusters   69

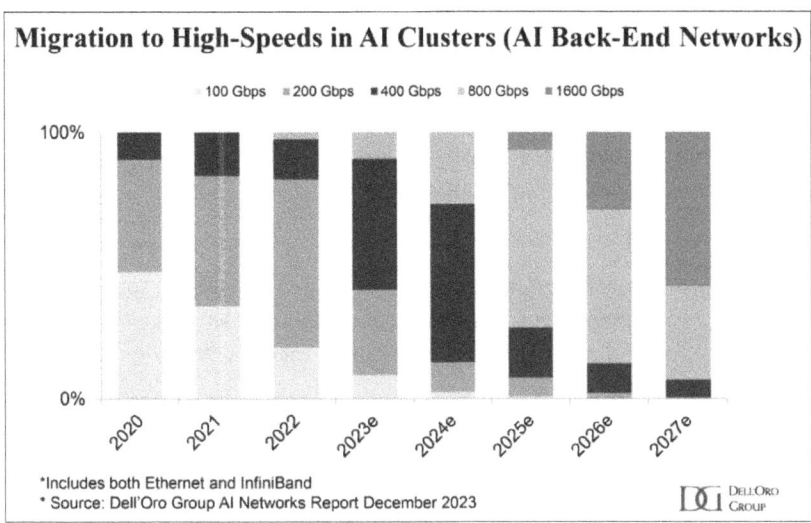

Figure 4-2
Dell'Oro chart on optics evolution

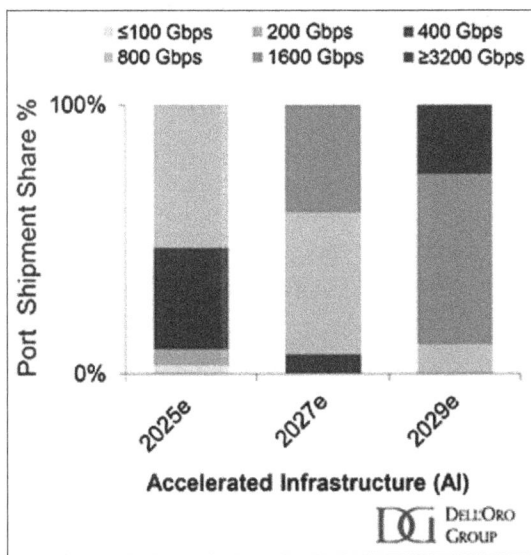

Figure 4-2.1
Dell'Oro chart report on optics evolution 2025

The throughput requirement from server to leaf is expanding to 200 Gbps/400 Gbps/800 Gbps/1.6 Tbps, which is leading vendors to focus on optics to support high-bandwidth connections.

Challenges in Optical Innovation

The optics industry has rapidly advanced from 10 Gbps to 100 Gbps and now to 800 Gbps and beyond. This growth is outpacing traditional models, driven by the need for more bandwidth and faster innovation. Although optical technology doesn't directly follow Moore's Law, it is propelled by data center demands, powerful processors, and expanding data volumes.

These are some of the challenges related to optics technology:

- **Signal quality:** Maintaining signal integrity gets harder as data rates rise. Higher speeds mean more attenuation, dispersion, and noise from crosstalk, all of which can harm signal quality. To tackle these challenges, advanced modulation schemes and error correction are required.

- **Signal conditioning:** At elevated speeds, a signal may experience more severe impairments. To preserve signal integrity, sophisticated methods like digital signal processing and equalization are required.

- **Power consumption and cooling requirements:** Higher-speed optics usually require more power, which can create significant challenges in data centers, where energy efficiency is vital. In addition, increased power usage results in high heat dissipation and requires cooling.

- **Availability and cost:** As AI/ML data centers are demanding higher-speed optics, different organizations are working toward coming up with standards for high-speed optics. Optics technology is lagging, and challenges include availability and cost of high-speed optics units.

Packet Flow

Whenever a network device receives data, it is in the form of either electrical signals or optical signals. A signal goes through multiple stages before it reaches the packet-forwarding engine. Similarly, a packet goes through multiple stages before it is transmitted out. Figure 4-3 illustrates the major components related to the optics in a switch.

In the following sections, we'll discuss packet flow for the newer 400 Gbps and onward optics.

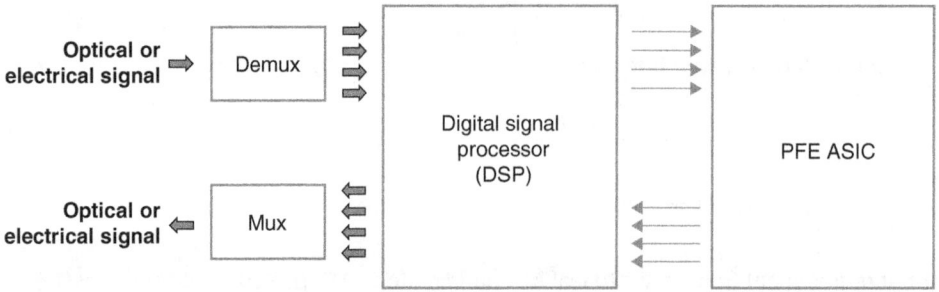

Figure 4-3
Packet flow from optics toward the PFE ASIC

Demultiplexers and Multiplexers

As shown in Figure 4-4, when a signal—either in electrical form when using copper cables or optical form when using optical fiber—reaches the pluggable optics, it goes through a demultiplexer (demux) function that splits the signals.

Figure 4-4
Demultiplexer

The PFE ASIC has multiple SerDes (serializer/deserializers), which form a high-speed interface used to convert data streams received between serial and parallel forms. As the PFE ASIC processes packets serially, the SerDes performs the job of serializing the data received from multiple SerDes links in parallel. If the PFE ASIC supports ~50 Gbps SerDes, a demux could perform the demultiplexing to 8 × 50 Gbps from 400 Gbps optics. If the PFE ASIC supports ~100 Gbps SerDes, a demux could perform the demultiplexing to 4 × 100 Gbps from 400 Gbps optics or 8 × 100 Gbps from 800 Gbps optics.

After the PFE ASIC processes the data, the SerDes again parallelizes the data into separate streams. Either single or multiple SerDes can be mapped to a single optics unit to achieve the required rate. This process is used for creating N:1 conversion of signals, and it is achieved with the help of multiplexing, as illustrated in Figure 4-5.

Figure 4-5
Multiplexer

With AI/ML requirements of 400 Gbps, 800 Gbps, and beyond, the SerDes links are now at 200 Gbps and moving toward higher speeds. Further improvements in the mux and demux are required to be able to achieve higher speeds.

Digital Signal Processors (DSPs)

The signals from the demultiplexer are passed to the digital signal processor (DSP), which carries out several functions. Let's investigate each of them in detail.

Modulation and Demodulation

DSPs are responsible for dealing with sophisticated modulation methods in high-speed optical communications, as illustrated in Figure 4-6. They encode digital data onto the optical carrier wave by converting it into diverse amplitude and phase states. On the receiving side, DSPs decode the optical signal by interpreting the detected changes in amplitude and phase to retrieve the original data.

Modulation is the process of converting data or information to electrical or optical signals. Modulation is required from the ASIC to the electrical signals and then later from electrical signals to optical signals. The modulation at each layer may be different. NRZ, also known as PAM-2, is a traditional modulation technique that does not support higher-bandwidth requirements. PAM-4 and above are being used for newer optics to support the higher-bandwidth requirements of AI/ML data centers.

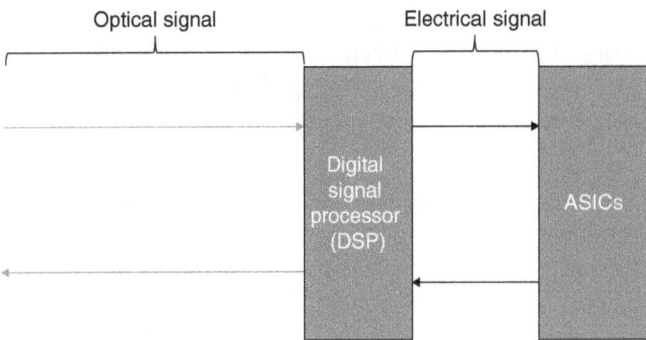

Figure 4-6
Conversion of optical to electrical signals and vice versa

The following modulations are used in different types of network connectivity:

- **NRZ:** Non-Return-to-Zero (NRZ), which used to be a widely used scheme, has two voltage levels to represent 0 and 1. It is commonly used in the 28 GHz range and for some 56 GHz channels.

- **PAM-4:** Pulse Amplitude Modulation with four levels (PAM-4) is a signal-encoding technique that uses four distinct signal levels (that is, voltage levels) to represent four combinations of two-bit logic (00, 01, 10, and 11). PAM-4 modules double the bandwidth of a connection, with each signal level representing 2 bits of logic information. PAM-4 is used for some 56 GHz channels and all 112 GHz channels.

- **Higher-order modulation:** For greater speeds, modulation schemes such as PAM-8 or QAM (quadrature amplitude modulation) are considered. These methods boost data rates by using additional signal levels or combining various amplitude and phase states.

- **DWDM (dense wavelength division multiplexing):** Coherent DWDM technology uses amplitude, phase, and polarization of light. It supports much higher bit rates on a single wavelength when DSPs are used. DWDM is used for transmitting multiple data channels over a single fiber, expanding data capacity in high-speed connections between data centers. 400G ZR modules have ushered in a new era of DWDM technology marked by open, standards-based, and pluggable DWDM optics, enabling true IP-over-DWDM. 400G ZR modules are used for connectivity between data centers (up to 80 km).

To achieve higher data transmission rates, the industry is trying out different modulation methods that make it possible to transmit more data at a time. We can compare it to adding more seats to carry a larger number of passengers on a flight, where the downside is that privacy is reduced. Similarly, transmitting more data at a time results in more noise to the signals and creates a need for more sophisticated mechanisms to deal with it.

Error Detection and Correction

DSPs are responsible for error detection and handling retransmission or correction of received packets to maintain data accuracy. They use forward error correction (FEC) algorithms to rectify errors that occur during transmission. Methods like low-density parity-check (LDPC) codes and Bose-Chaudhuri-Hocquenghem (BCH) codes are often used to enhance data integrity and reliability. At 400 Gbps and above, FEC is needed for reliability, although it introduces latency.

Clock Data Recovery

DSPs play a critical role in synchronizing the transmitter and receiver to maintain data integrity and minimize errors. A DSP extracts clock signals from the incoming data, which is vital for precise data sampling and decoding. This function becomes especially important at high data rates, where accurate timing is essential.

Equalization

DSPs use equalization to improve the signal-to-noise ratio (SNR). Equalization is a signal processing technique that restores the shape of a signal waveform in optics. Equalization algorithms include feed-forward equalization (FFE) and decision-feedback equalization (DFE).

Transmission Modes

Beyond the DSP and mux/demux, we move more toward optics. Two decades ago, most network gear, including switches and routers, relied on copper cables for data transmission. But these cables are limited in terms of how fast data can move. As data speeds picked up, these cables couldn't keep up, as they only reached about 3 meters for 100 Gbps Ethernet links. They were good for connections in the same rack, though, such as connecting servers to the top of rack (TOR) switch.

Today, we have high-performance switches, routers, and SmartNICs that can handle speeds of 200 Gbps, 400 Gbps, and even 800 Gbps. To handle these speeds, fiber-optic cables have taken over from copper ones. Instead of using electrical signals, optical fiber uses light to send data.

The advantage in fiber-optic cables is that they can go much farther—up to 80 km or even 120 km—without losing signal strength. They're also much more reliable than copper because they use total internal reflection to carry light and therefore aren't affected by electromagnetic interference. In addition, fiber-optic cables handle changes in temperature and pressure well.

The following sections detail the different cable options available for connectivity in data center fabrics.

Multi-Mode Fiber (MMF)

MMF is optical fiber that is designed for the transmission of multiple rays of light at a time (see Figure 4-7). Normally, the core diameter of MMF is 50 μm (micrometers) and 62.5 μm. It propagates 850 nm (nanometers) and 1300 nm wavelengths from low-cost light sources like LEDs or VCSELs and has more attenuation. MMF is used for short-to medium-range connections, as well as for connecting devices within the same rack or in nearby racks.

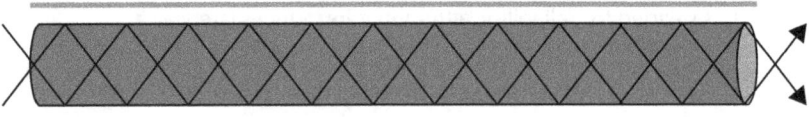

Figure 4-7
Multi-mode fiber

There are five different grades of MMF:

- **OM1:** OM1 supports 1 Gbps speeds up to a distance of 300 m and 10 Gbps speeds up to 33 m.
- **OM2:** OM2 supports 1 Gbps speeds up to a distance of 550 m and 10 Gbps speeds up to 82 m.
- **OM3:** OM3 supports 40 Gbps speeds up to a distance of 240 m and 100 Gbps to 400 Gbps speeds up to a distance of 100 m.
- **OM4:** OM4 supports speeds of 100 Gbps to 400 Gbps up to a distance of 150 m.
- **OM5:** OM5 supports speeds of 100 Gbps to 400 Gbps up to a distance of 150 m. It can accomplish 400 Gbps with just four transmit and receive cables and wavelength division multiplexing (WDM) technology. OM5 uses the wavelength 953 nm along with the wavelength of 850 (OM4).

OM1 has a glass core diameter of 62.5 μm. The other grades of MMF have a glass core diameter of 50 μm.

Single-Mode Fiber (SMF)

SMF is an optical fiber that is designed for the transmission of a single ray of light at a time, eliminating distortion from overlapping light pulses (see Figure 4-8). Normally, SMF has a core diameter of 8 μm to 10 μm, which can propagate higher wavelengths of 1310 nm and 1550 nm from the laser. It is an expensive type of cable that is used for long-distance data transmission between different buildings or data centers.

Figure 4-8
Single-Mode Fiber

Dense Wavelength Division Multiplexing (DWDM)

DWDM enables dense wavelength multiplexing by multiplexing multiple electrical signals to a single optical lane, as illustrated in Figure 4-9. DWDM technology helps in transmitting data over long distances, as described earlier in this chapter. This is specially required in case of data center interconnects.

Figure 4-9
DWDM

AI Server Connectivity Options

On the switch side, the connection could be either single-mode or multi-mode fiber and optics, depending on the distance. Since the server ports an OSFP transceiver with 800 Gbps, the switch side must be a 800 Gbps port or two 400 Gbps ports with the use of breakout cables. Figure 4-10 illustrates both of these connectivity options. For rail-optimized design (ROD), another option is able to connect 8 GPUs to 8 different switches.

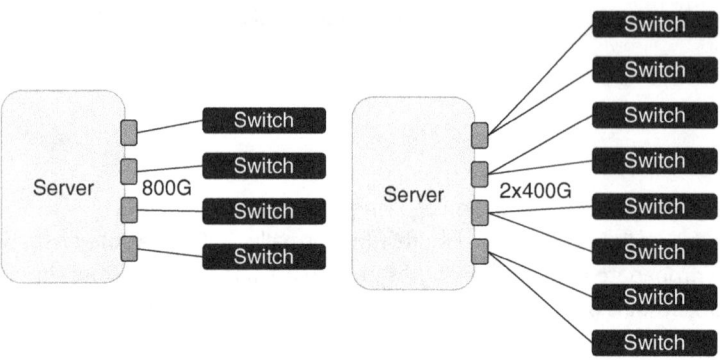

Figure 4-10
Connection options with the Nvidia H100

Figure 4-11 illustrates the connectivity option with the A100 server. There are 8 ports on the server that can connect to 8 different switches in ROD.

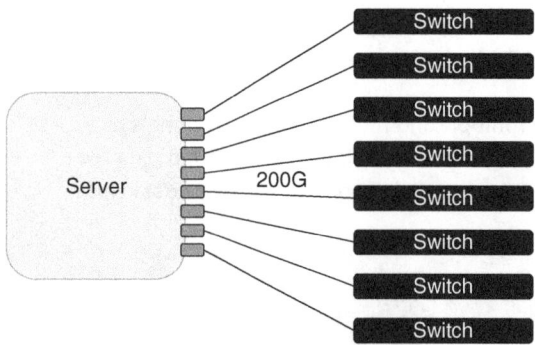

Figure 4-11
Connection option with the Nvidia A100

Transceiver Types

The choice of optics is based on the connectivity distance between two nodes. In general, optics meant for smaller distances are cheaper than those meant for longer distances. Each type of optical fiber has a suffix to denote the reach and optical lanes. For example, in 400G-SR8, SR stands for *short reach*, which is up to 100 m, and 8 denotes the number of optical lanes; 400G-SR8 can have 8 optical lanes of 53 Gbps each, which are multiplexed to support 400 Gbps bandwidth.

Table 4-1 lists the transceiver types and the reach and mode of optical fiber with which it can be used.

Table 4-1 Transceiver Types

Transceiver	Full Form	Reach	Mode
VR	Very short reach	50 m	MMF
SR	Short reach	100 m	MMF
DR	Data center reach	500 m	SMF
FR	Far reach	2 km	SMF
LR	Long reach	10 km	SMF
ZR	Extended reach	>80 km	DWDM
CR	Copper	Up to 7 m for passive Direct Attach Cable (DAC) type	
		Up to 10 m for active Direct Attach Cable (DAC) type	

The length of the cable and type of optics needed are determined based on the design option chosen—for example, top-of-rack, middle-of-row, or end-of-row. Within a rack, copper-based Active Electrical Cable (AEC) has good potential. Across racks, Active Optical Cable (AOC) has good potential. Very short reach (VR) optics support is being added currently and may be suitable in AI/ML clusters.

Figure 4-12 illustrates an example of top-of-rack server-to-leaf connectivity and leaf-to-spine connectivity in the rail-optimized design. This topology requires cables of varying length within the rack.

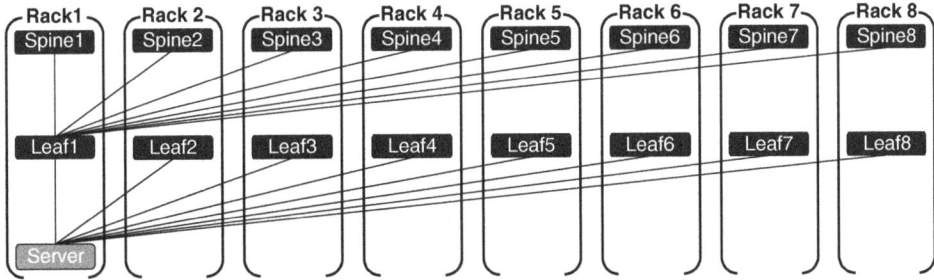

Figure 4-12
Cable connections with ToR design in Rail Optimized Design (ROD)

Figure 4-13 illustrates an example of middle-of-row and end-of-row design server-to-leaf connectivity and leaf-to-spine connectivity in the rail-optimized design. This topology requires cables of similar lengths from a rack, but across the rack, the cable length varies.

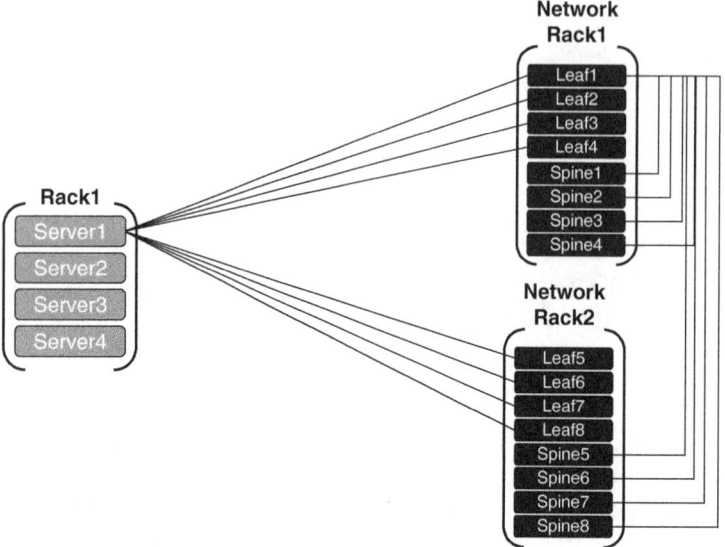

Figure 4-13
Cable connections with end-of row/middle-of-row design in Rail Optimized Design (ROD)

Cable and Connector Types

A connector connects to the transceiver and has cable connected to it. The optical signal from the transceiver is sent to the cable via connectors. As the bandwidth increases, innovation in connectors is required to support the growth. These are the most commonly used connectors:

- **LC:** This is a commonly used connector that can carry single-mode or multi-mode fiber. Earlier versions of this connector type, which are now legacy components, were SC, FC, and ST. LC (which stands for Lucent Connector) is used with single-mode fiber for longer distances. For example, QSFP-DD-FR4 would be used with 2 km SMF and dual LCs.

- **MPO:** These connectors are used for breakout cables. MPO stands for multi-fiber push on, and MTP is a brand name of MPO cable. MPO fiber-optic cable assemblies support 400 Gbps transmission, and MPO trunking systems are available in 8-, 12-, and 24-fiber variants. The assemblies are offered in single-row 16-fiber and two-row (2×16) 32-fiber configurations to achieve the highest-density physical contact for multi-fiber connectors in the market. For example, QSFP-DD-SR8 would be used with 100 m MMF and MPO-16 (with 8 fibers for transmission and 8 fibers for receipt), and QSFP-DD-DR4 would be used with 500 m SMF and MPO-12 (with the first 4 fibers for transmission and last 4 fibers for receipt).

- **Direct attach copper (DAC):** These short-distance cables are normally used for connectivity within a rack and are not expensive. They are copper-based cables with connectors on both ends and used with QSFP and OSFP (discussed later in this chapter). DAC cable can be either passive or active. Passive DAC cable contains no electrical components. It consumes minimal power (<0.15 W), and its distance is limited to 7 m. Passive DAC is used for quick connections within or between racks in data centers. Active DAC cable contains electrical components in the connectors that can boost signal levels, allowing greater distances (>5 m) and consuming more power. DAC cables are mostly used within the rack connections in data centers. They are less expensive than optical cables.

- **Active electrical cables (AEC):** These copper-based cables have added electronics that can remove noise and improve signal quality. AEC can reach up to 7 m for higher data rates up to 800 Gbps. It is cost-effective and offers faster data transmission within the rack compared to AOC.
- **Active optical cables (AOC):** These fiber-optic cables have built-in transceivers. They are multimode fibers and can reach up to 100 m and can be used for connecting devices to the top of the rack, middle of the row, or end of the row within data center racks. AOC cables are thinner and have a smaller bend radius compared to other optical cables; they also cost less than other optical cables.

Standards

Up to this point, we have discussed high-bandwidth optics like 400 Gbps, 800 Gbps, 1.6 Tbps, and beyond. In the current industry landscape, companies are looking to use standardized solutions to avoid getting tied to proprietary solutions. Different standards bodies are trying to innovate to meet the requirements. Let's investigate the different standards that define optics today:

- **IEEE 802.3bm**
    - **QSFP28:** This transceiver is small, versatile, and widely used for 100 Gbps rates in data centers. It uses NRZ/PAM4 technology, supports 4 lanes, and has two variants: SR4 and LR4.

        A QSFP28 typically consumes around 3 to 4 W per module. Cooling requirements vary based on the deployment density and environmental conditions. QSFP56 has been developed to support 200 Gbps rates. As of now, there is no support for 400 Gbps and above.
- **IEEE 802.3bs**
    - **DD-QSFP:** This transceiver was developed for increased port density and specialized use cases. It uses PAM4 technology, supports 8 lanes of 50 Gbps traffic, and typically consumes around 3 to 4 W per module. QSFP-DD has three types of cages: Type 1, Type 2, and Type 2A. Type 2A has a heat sink on top of the optics to deal with the heat and is likely to become popular.
- **OIF-OSFP-01.0**
    - **OSFP:** This transceiver, which is designed for higher speeds and densities, is emerging in some applications. It uses PAM4 technology and supports 8 lanes. It has only the LR4 variant, where LR stands for *long range* (typically up to 10 km over SMF). Its power consumption is typically rather high and comparable to that of the CFP2.

- **ITU-T G.959.1**

    - **CFP:** This transceiver, which was the initial 100 Gbps form factor, is larger than newer options and is becoming less common. It is based on NRZ technology and supports 10 lanes. It has only the LR4 variant. Its power consumption is typically rather high due to its larger size.

    - **CFP2:** This transceiver, which is larger than the QSFP28, is used for longer-distance 100 Gbps connections, such as CFP2 LR4. It is based on NRZ technology and supports 10 lanes. It has only the LR4 variant. Its power consumption varies but is typically higher than that of the QSFP28.

    - **CFP4:** This transceiver has a compact size. Its capabilities are similar to those of the CFP2 but in a smaller form factor. It is based on NRZ technology and supports 4 lanes. It has only the LR4 variant. It consumes less power compared to a CFP2.

In addition, CPAK is Cisco's proprietary form factor, for use with Cisco devices. Its use is limited in the industry.

In the next section, we'll look more closely at the IEEE-based QSFP options in detail and compare them with OSFP.

High-Bandwidth Optics

QSFP (Quad Small Form-factor Pluggable) optics came into existence for 40 Gbps bandwidth. It then evolved to QSFP28 to support 100 Gbps. QSFP56 is an enhancement to support 200 Gbps. QSFP-DD (Double Density) doubles the number of channels to support 200 Gbps and 400 Gbps. Table 4-2 summarizes the differences between these form factors.

Table 4-2   QSFP28, QSFP-DD, and QSFP56

Feature	QSFP28	QSFP-DD	QSFP56
Data rate	100 Gbps	200–400 Gbps	200 Gbps
Channel count	4 channels	8 channels	4 channels
Per-channel data rate	25 Gbps	25/50 Gbps	50 Gbps
Connector types	MPO	MPO	MPO
	LC	LC	LC
		CS	CS
Backward compatibility	QSFP+	QSFP+	QSFP+
		QSFP28	QSFP28
		QSFP56	

On the modulation front, QSFP28 and QSFP-DD200 support NRZ, whereas QSFP56 and QSFP-DD400 support PAM4.

Now let's investigate 200 Gbps, 400 Gbps, and 800 Gbps supportability:

- **QSFP:** While QSFP28 primarily supports 100 Gbps, variations like QSFP-DD have been developed to support 200 Gbps and 400 Gbps, using a higher number of lanes and advanced modulation techniques. There might be future variations, such as QSFP-DD800, intended for 800 Gbps support. The QSFP-DD form factor has the advantages of small size, high density, and backward compatibility, enabling easier migration to 400 Gbps Ethernet. It is expected that the QSFP-DD form factor will become the most appropriate form factor for 400 Gbps Ethernet applications.

    As noted earlier, there are four types of QSFP-DD optics: Type 1, Type 2, Type 2A, and Type 2B.

    Type 1 is similar to the QSFP28 in size

    Type 2 has longer back cage to provide more room for design

    Type 2A has a heat sink packaged in the optics

    Type 2B has heat sink higher to make room for internal connector and port separation

- **OSFP:** The OSFP form factor was specifically designed to support higher speeds, including 200 Gbps and 400 Gbps. Developments for further evolutions are ongoing, and OSFP may potentially support 800 Gbps, with increased lanes and advanced modulation techniques.

- **CFP:** CFP2 and CFP4 form factors were initially designed for 100 Gbps, but newer revisions such as CFP8 have been introduced to support higher speeds like 200 Gbps and 400 Gbps by utilizing more lanes and updated modulation schemes. CFP enables only 16 ports per rack unit compared to 36 ports per rack unit available with QSFP-DD and OSFP.

Among the listed form factors, QSFP-DD, CFP8, OSFP, and future advancements in DD-QSFP are the primary form factors intended or being developed to support higher data rates like 200 Gbps, 400 Gbps, and possibly 800 Gbps. These form factors achieve higher speeds through increased lane counts, advanced modulation techniques (such as PAM4), and improved signal processing capabilities.

Table 4-3 compares QSFP-DD and OSFP, which are the most discussed options for AI/ML data centers.

Table 4-3 QSFP and OSFP Comparison

Feature	QSFP-DD	OSFP
Size	Compact	Larger and denser
Lane configuration	Typically supports 8 or 16 lanes	Supports 8 lanes
Speeds supported	Designed for higher speeds (e.g., 200 Gbps, 400 Gbps)	Primarily for higher speeds (e.g., 200 Gbps, 400 Gbps, 800 Gbps)
Power consumption	Moderate power consumption	Higher power consumption

Feature	QSFP-DD	OSFP
Cable compatibility	Supports copper and fiber-optic cables (SMF and MMF)	Primarily supports fiber-optic cables (SMF and MMF)
Modulation techniques	Supports advanced modulation techniques like PAM4	Supports advanced modulation techniques like PAM4
Heat dissipation	Efficient heat dissipation with compact size	May require robust cooling due to higher power consumption
Application	Evolving for higher-speed networks	Targeted for next-gen high-speed networking
Cost	Generally lower cost due to smaller size and standardized manufacturing	Relatively higher cost due to larger size and advanced capabilities

Further Innovations in Optics

Pluggable optics have been in use since the beginning of fiber optics and provide maximum flexibility. The industry is now observing innovations such as co-packaged optics (CPO), linear-drive pluggable optics (LPO), and linear receive optics (LRO) technologies, which aim to add more ports to switches with lower power requirements. These innovations come at a cost, such as less flexibility.

Figure 4-14 illustrates pluggable optics that contain both the optical module and digital signal processor (DSP) on the transceiver. This is the most commonly used technology as it provides the most flexibility and can be changed based on the environment and cost.

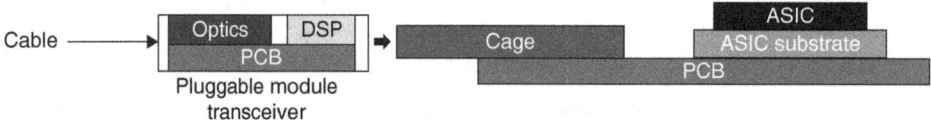

Figure 4-14
Pluggable optics

In pluggable optics, the DSP is normally 20% to 40% of the Bill of Materials (BOM) of the optics, and it consumes about 50% of the power of the transceiver. Moving the DSP functionality to the ASIC, as illustrated in Figure 4-15, helps reduce costs as well as power requirements. This is achieved through the LPO technology.

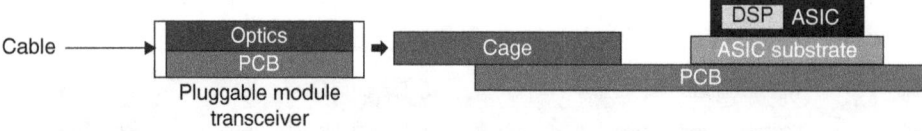

Figure 4-15
Linear-drive pluggable optics (LPO)

With LPO, the pluggable module is smaller because the DSP is moved out of the module. LPO also reduces the cooling requirements. The DSP on the PFE ASIC can be cooled using the same cooling technology used for the PFE ASIC. LPO completely removes the DSP from the transceiver and relies on the PFE ASIC to perform most of the DSP operations. While this solution reduces the cost and power requirements, it creates challenges in interoperability, network robustness, and volume deployments, significantly increasing operating expenses (opex), time to market, and overall risk.

LRO removes the DSP from the module receive path only and maintains the DSP in the module transmit path. The LRO implementation achieves an optimal balance of standards compliance, interoperability, network reliability, ease of deployment, and power efficiency.

Another option that has been attracting a lot of attention in the market is CPO, which meets the demand for high port density. With this option, the optics module is integrated with the switch, as illustrated in Figure 4-16. This results in higher port density, lower power consumption, and lower cost. However, it also means that the switch will be more expensive initially, as it includes the cost of all optics. If there are problems with the optics module, the switch will need to be checked and changed. CPO technologies are emerging and will develop over time.

Figure 4-16
Co-packaged optics (CPO)

LPO and CPO are technologies that will benefit PFE and switch vendors, whereas LRO is more beneficial for optics vendors. These technologies are developing right now, and what will work best for customers is yet to be determined.

Summary

Development of optics technology has accelerated at each layer to be able to meet the requirements of AI/ML data centers. OSFP is becoming popular for connectivity with the Nvidia servers, and QSFP-DD is being considered. DR optics have become popular for rail-optimized design for server-to-leaf connectivity. In rail-optimized design, because the leaf and spines are near one another, AOC and AEC can be considered. Figure 4-17 illustrates a summary of the optics landscape with respect to 100 Gbps and 400 Gbps.

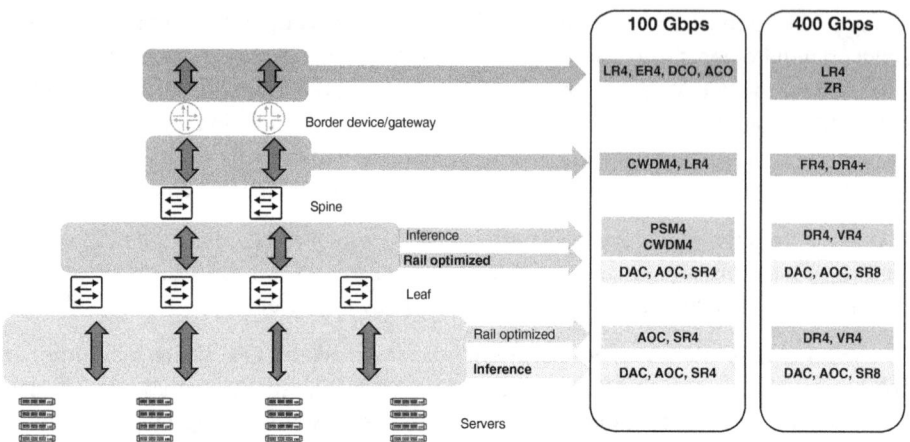

Figure 4-17
Optics landscape in AI data centers

Test Your Knowledge

The following questions are designed to test your understanding of the content covered in Chapter 4. Following the questions, answers are provided so you can verify your conclusions.

Questions

1. Why are high-speed optics (200 Gbps/400 Gbps/800 Gbps/1.6 Tbps) critical for AI/ML data centers?
2. Explain the function of digital signal processors (DSPs) in optical transceivers.
3. Compare the use cases for multi-mode fiber (MMF) and single-mode fiber (SMF) in data centers.
4. What are the technical differences between the QSFP28, QSFP56, and QSFP-DD form factors?
5. How do modulation schemes like PAM4 enable higher bandwidth in optical links?
6. Describe the role and selection criteria for optical connectors (for example, LC, MPO/MTP) in high-density AI clusters.
7. What are the advantages and trade-offs of pluggable, linear-drive, and co-packaged optics?
8. How does cable management impact signal integrity and operational efficiency in AI data centers?

Answers

1. AI/ML clusters require massive bandwidth to move data between GPUs and servers. High-speed optics enable these data rates, reducing training time and supporting large-scale parallelism.
2. DSPs handle signal modulation, error correction, and equalization, compensating for signal degradation over long distances and enabling higher data rates with advanced modulation schemes like PAM4.
3. MMF is used for short-range connections within racks or rows (up to 150 m), while SMF supports long-range connections between buildings or data centers (up to 10 km or more). MMF and SMF require different transceivers and connectors.
4. QSFP28 supports 100 Gbps (4x25 Gbps), QSFP56 supports 200 Gbps (4x50G, PAM4), and QSFP-DD supports 400 Gbps/800 Gbps (8x50 Gbps/100 Gbps, PAM4), with increasing channel counts and backward compatibility for migration.

5. PAM4 encodes 2 bits per symbol (four amplitude levels), doubling the data rate per channel compared to NRZ (1 bit per symbol), enabling higher aggregate bandwidth over the same fiber.

6. LC connectors are used for single-mode, duplex connections; MPO/MTP connectors support multi-fiber, high-density connections (8, 12, 16, or 24 fibers), enabling efficient cabling for large-scale deployments.

7. Pluggable optics offer flexibility and easy replacement. Linear-drive optics reduce power and cost by moving DSP functions to the switch ASIC. Co-packaged optics integrate optics with the switch, increasing port density and efficiency but reducing flexibility.

8. Proper cable management minimizes signal loss, reduces crosstalk, and ensures efficient airflow for cooling. Poor management can lead to increased errors, downtime, and maintenance complexity.

References

"Exploring the Data Center Switch and AI Networks Markets Landscape in 2024" https://www.delloro.com/exploring-the-data-center-switch-and-ai-networks-markets-landscape-in-2024/

"Challenges in Operating Large Scale AI Clusters"
https://www.delloro.com/beyond-the-gpu-arms-race-the-potential-role-of-oxc-in-building-next-gen-ai-infrastructure/

Nvidia A100, H100 and H200 Server
https://docs.nvidia.com/dgx/dgxh100-user-guide/introduction-to-dgxh100.html
https://docs.nvidia.com/dgx/dgxa100-user-guide/introduction-to-dgxa100.html

5

Thermal and Power Efficiency Considerations

Thermal Footprints in AI Data Centers

Current estimates indicate that the power consumption of data centers is around 2% of global power consumption. This is huge, and data center power consumption will continue to grow. AI/ML data centers are designed for maximum computation, using cutting-edge devices, including servers, storage devices, and switches. The latest devices do more in less space, making it possible to build bigger clusters—but these devices also need more power and emit more heat in less space. Accounting for these factors is an important aspect of designing AI/ML clusters.

The power budget per rack in a data center is normally in the range 10 kW to 25 kW, with most data centers having rack power consumption around 16 kW to 18 kW. The power consumption of the latest multi-GPU servers is huge. For instance, a DGX H100 system has a balanced distribution of power load across multiple power supplies. It has six power supplies, at 3.3 kW each. In addition, it has 4 + 2 redundancy, which means it consumes 4×3.3 kW =13.2 kW.

A switch with 64×400 Gbps has its own power requirements. For instance, the QFX5230 switch from Juniper has a 3 kW power supply. In optics, a QSFP56-DD has max power consumption of 12 W, and an OSFP has max power consumption of 15 W, which is very high compared to 3.2 W for a QSFP28.

With all these parameters, you can begin to see the challenges involved in designing racks for next-generation AI/ML data centers. In addition to energy considerations, there are thermal management considerations because all the components emit heat. So, thermal management has become a big talking point with AI/ML data centers. Cooling systems in data centers are the second largest consumers of electricity. According to various reports, in a data center, data center IT equipment accounts for 40% to 45% of the power consumption, the cooling system accounts for 35% to 40%, and the electrical power distribution, UPS, lighting, and other uses account for the rest.

Efficiency of a cooling system is defined by the power usage effectiveness (PUE), which is a measure of the efficiency with which a data center consumes power. It is the ratio of the total DC power consumption to the computing-equipment power consumption. The ideal PUE is 1.0.

Airflow Options

The goal is to cool a data center effectively with the least possible power consumption. Currently, fans are the most widely used means of cooling data center equipment. Different types of fans can be used in a data center design, based on direction of airflow, as detailed in the following sections.

Front-to-Back Airflow

With front-to-back airflow, air comes in from the front panel and is emitted out the back panel (see Figure 5-1). Because the front panel of the switches houses the ports, front-to-back airflow is most helpful for cooling optics because the air is first passed through the optics and then through the rest of the board. The racks need to be designed to support front-to-back airflow, and all the other equipment, such as the server, storage, and networking equipment, needs to be aligned with this design.

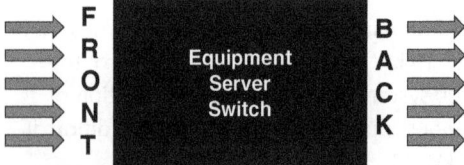

Figure 5-1
Front-to-back airflow

Back-to-Front Airflow

With back-to-front airflow, air comes in from the back panel and is emitted out the front panel (see Figure 5-2). This method cools the power supply units first. Because the air reaches optics modules last, this method may require extra heat sinks on the optics. The racks need to be designed to support back-to-front airflow, and all the other equipment, such as the server, storage, and networking equipment, needs to be aligned with this design.

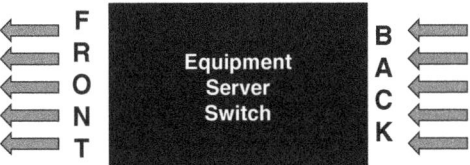

Figure 5-2
Back-to-front airflow

Bidirectional Fans

Bidirectional fans can be configured to support both front-to-back airflow and back-to-front airflow, depending on the requirements. They offer flexibility as the direction of airflow can be changed in real time, based on the heat sensors. This flexibility comes at a high cost because the switch or server needs to be designed to work with both modes. Bidirectional fans provide flexibility because it's not necessary to specify the airflow direction at the time of initial design and equipment order; however, the cost is usually prohibitive.

Choosing the Fan Direction

Once a data center rack is designed, the airflow direction is usually clear. Most customers prefer front-to-back airflow. For AI/ML clusters, customers need fans that are able to cool down the equipment. Newer and faster fans are constantly being developed for use with servers, storage devices, and switches. So, it's important to choose the fan direction before building the data center infrastructure.

In addition to fans, a data center requires huge-capacity air conditioners. Data centers are hitting their power limits and need more efficient cooling systems.

Liquid Cooling

One alternative to airflow systems is liquid-based cooling systems. Liquid cooling solutions offer greater heat removal capabilities that make power-efficient data centers operate at a lower cost. They have the potential to significantly reduce a data center's power consumption by about 70% and optimize the PUE of the data center.

In addition, liquid cooling solutions can significantly improve processor performance. According to a research report by Global Market Insights, Inc., the data center liquid cooling industry is expected to surpass USD$3 billion by 2026.

In the following sections, we'll examine these liquid cooling technologies:

- Immersion liquid cooling

- Cold plate liquid cooling
- Rear-door heat exchanger liquid cooling
- Sprayed liquid cooling

Immersion Liquid Cooling

With immersion liquid cooling, the equipment is immersed in liquid, which is typically a coolant. The liquid goes over the whole system and the boards inside it. The whole data center needs to be designed in a way that supports liquid cooling, and all the equipment in the data center needs to support liquid cooling.

There are two types of immersion cooling:

- Single-phase immersion cooling (see Figure 5-3)
- Two-phase immersion cooling (see Figure 5-4)

Single-Phase Immersion Cooling

In single-phase immersion cooling, electronic components are placed in a sealed tank of fluid, and the heat they generate is efficiently absorbed by the fluid. Pumps are used to make the coolant flow from the tank to a heat exchanger outside the tank. The heat exchanger then causes the coolant to pass through tubes that are surrounded by the water, which absorbs the heat from the coolant. The cooled coolant is then cycled back into the tank that contains the equipment. The hot/evaporated water in the heat exchanger is then taken outside the heat exchanger, and cold water is pushed to the heat exchanger. This cycle keeps repeating.

Figure 5-3 illustrates a single-phase liquid cooling system. Note that the whole rack is submerged in the coolant inside the tank.

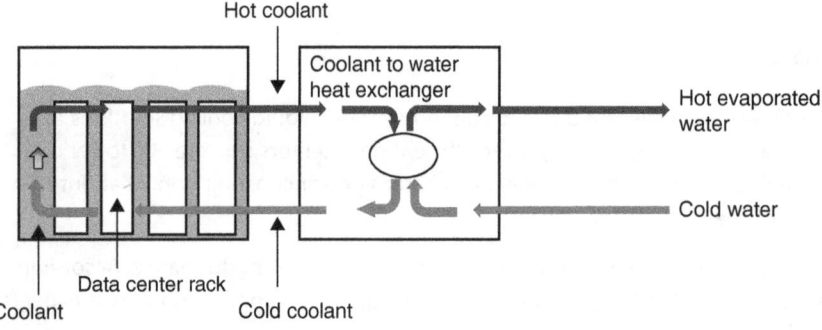

Figure 5-3
Single-phase liquid cooling

Two-Phase Immersion Cooling

With two-phase immersion cooling, the fluid that is used has a boiling point that is lower than the temperature of the heat-emitting components. As the fluid is heated and moves up in the tank, it transitions from liquid to gas. There is a tube toward the top of the tank that continuously runs cold water. The temperature of the rising gas inside the tank is reduced as it moves up and passes over the tube that contains cold water. The liquid condenses and transforms back to a liquid in the form of tiny droplets, which fall back into the liquid pool, and the process starts all over again. In this design, there is no need for a separate heat exchanger; both the phases happen inside the tank itself.

Figure 5-4 illustrates a two-phase liquid cooling system. Note that the whole rack is submerged in the coolant inside the tank. The choice of liquid is very important.

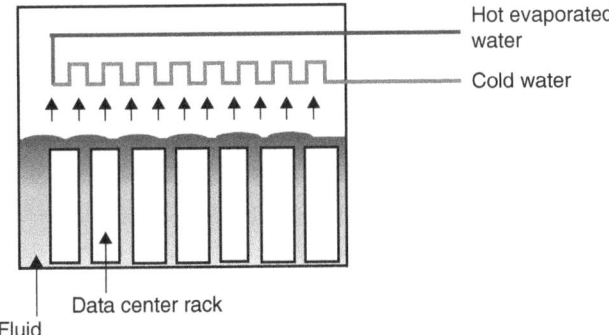

Figure 5-4
Two-phase liquid cooling

Cold Plate Liquid Cooling

With cold plate liquid cooling, the cooling system is integrated directly into the server/switch chassis. With this method, the rack and equipment do not need to be submerged in the liquid. Cold liquid is passed with the help of pipes to cold plates or heat sinks that sit directly next to components such as CPUs, GPUs, or memory cards. Small tubes carry the cool liquid to each plate, where the liquid draws off the heat from the underlying components. The warm liquid is then circulated to a cooling device or heat exchanger. After it's been cooled, the liquid is then circulated back to the cold plates. This method is sometimes referred to as *direct-to-chip liquid cooling*.

Figure 5-5 illustrates the relationship of the board, the CPU, and heat sink. The liquid is passed through pipes to the heat sink to absorb the heat, as illustrated in Figure 5-6. The liquid is then passed to the heat exchange to be cooled down and stored in a container. Then a pump pushes the liquid to the heat sink again.

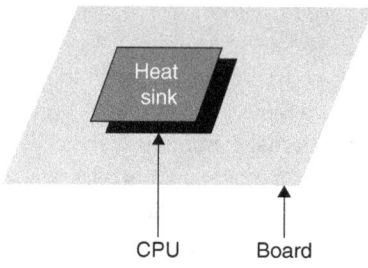

Figure 5-5
Board, CPU, and heat sink

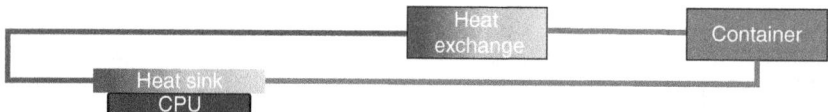

Figure 5-6
Cold plate liquid cooling

This method makes the data center design cool down with a lower price. It also provides flexibility in that all the equipment need not support this type of cooling. Because the board is not completely submerged in the liquid, the cost of the equipment is lower than the cost of equipment used with immersion cooling.

Rear-Door Heat Exchanger Liquid Cooling

The rear-door heat exchanger liquid cooling method is ideal for supporting high-density data centers. It can cool a 20 kW rack at standard chilled water design temperatures.

With this method, radiator-like doors are mounted at the back of the racks. The servers, storage, and networking equipment exhaust hot air, which the radiator doors push back toward the heat exchanger. The heat exchanger has a pipe that carries cold liquid and absorbs the heat from the air, reducing the temperature of the air. The heated liquid then travels to cooling towers that are linked to an external chilled water system. This system cools the air in the data center space.

In the rear-door heat exchanger liquid cooling method, also called air-assisted liquid chromatography (AALC), all the equipment needs to be air cooled, preferably using front-to-back airflow. It does not require any change to the equipment, but it does require a particular data center design.

Figure 5-7 illustrates the rear-door heat exchanger cooling method. This is the simplest liquid cooling method, but it is less efficient than immersion cooling and cold plate liquid cooling.

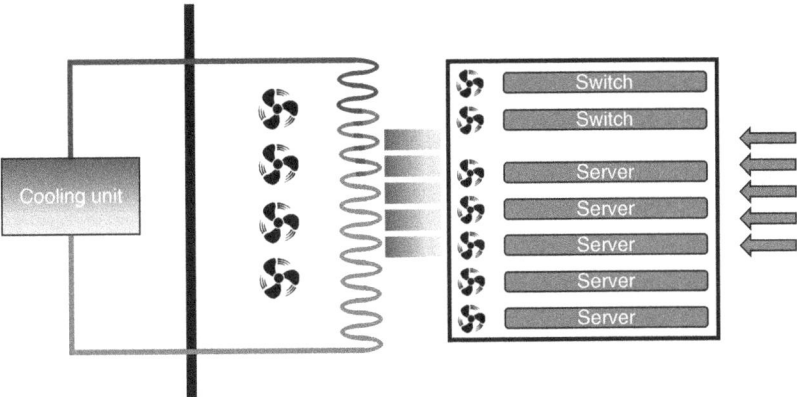

Figure 5-7
Rear-door heat exchanger liquid cooling

Sprayed Liquid Cooling

With sprayed liquid cooling, equipment needs to be modified in order to deploy the corresponding spray device. With this liquid cooling method, coolant is sprayed through a nozzle onto the surface of the heating element to absorb heat. Sprayed liquid cooling is a targeted cooling technology that uses less coolant than the other liquid cooling methods, and so it is more economical. The total energy consumption of data centers that use sprayed liquid cooling can be reduced by 25.8% compared with air-cooled data centers.

Figure 5-8 illustrates sprayed liquid cooling. This cooling method is similar to cold plate liquid cooling, but in the spray method, liquid is sprayed on the component.

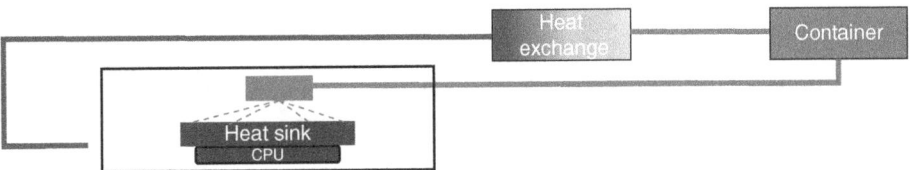

Figure 5-8
Sprayed liquid cooling

Summary

Cooling systems are an important area of exploration in data center design. Different cloud providers have made different choices. For example, Microsoft has deployed two-phase immersion cooling in a production environment. Google has used liquid cooling similar to cold plate liquid cooling for TPU (Tensor Processing Unit). Meta is planning to embrace rear-door heat exchanger liquid cooling and cold plate liquid cooling. Various server vendors and switch vendors have started to qualify their devices for liquid cooling. These technologies are becoming more interesting as the needs of power-hungry devices in data centers grow.

Test Your Knowledge

Chapter Review

The following questions are designed to test your understanding of the content covered in Chapter 5. Following the questions, answers are provided so you can verify your conclusions.

Questions

1. Why do AI/ML data centers have higher power and cooling requirements than traditional data centers?
2. What is power usage effectiveness (PUE), and how is it calculated?
3. Compare front-to-back, back-to-front, and bidirectional airflow cooling methods.
4. How does immersion cooling work, and what are its benefits and limitations?
5. Describe the cold plate liquid cooling method and its application in AI data centers.
6. What are the trade-offs between air and liquid cooling in high-density AI clusters?
7. How does rack design (height, width, and power budget) influence cooling strategy?
8. What is the impact of cooling system efficiency on overall data center sustainability?

Answers

1. AI/ML clusters use high-density GPU servers and high-speed switches, each consuming significant power and generating more heat per rack, necessitating advanced cooling and power distribution systems.
2. PUE = Total Facility Power / IT Equipment Power. A lower PUE indicates more efficient use of power for computing rather than cooling or overhead.
3. Front-to-back airflow cools optics first, and back-to-front airflow cools power supplies first. Bidirectional fans can be configured for either direction, offering flexibility but with higher cost and complexity.
4. Immersion cooling involves submerging equipment in a dielectric fluid, providing efficient heat removal and supporting higher power densities. It requires specialized equipment and facility design and may complicate maintenance.
5. Cold plate cooling involves circulating liquid directly to heat sinks attached to CPUs/GPUs, efficiently removing heat without submerging the entire system. It offers targeted cooling but requires custom plumbing and careful design.

6. Air cooling is simpler and less expensive but less effective at high densities. Liquid cooling (immersion, cold plate, spray) is more efficient but requires specialized infrastructure and higher upfront investment.

7. Rack dimensions and power density determine airflow requirements, cooling capacity, and the feasibility of different cooling methods. High-density racks may require liquid cooling or enhanced airflow management.

8. Efficient cooling reduces energy consumption, lowers operational costs, and minimizes environmental impact, contributing to more sustainable AI data center operations.

References

https://docs.nvidia.com/dgx/dgxh100-user-guide/introduction-to-dgxh100.html
https://www.iea.org/reports/energy-and-ai/energy-demand-from-ai
https://www.datacenterknowledge.com/energy-power-supply/power-shortages-will-restrict-40-of-ai-data-centers-by-2027-gartner

6

Efficient Load Balancing

As we discussed in Chapter 1, "Wonders in the Workload," AI/ML clusters use different kinds of models, such as large language models (LLM) with both natural language understanding (NLU) and natural language generation (NLG) components. The models are trained at the same time, across multiple GPUs. As a part of the training, GPUs need to synchronize massive amounts of data across nodes, which leads to enormous east–west traffic in the data center. Typically, the number of applications generating traffic in a cluster is low, most of the traffic is RDMA over Converged Ethernet (RoCEv2) traffic, and there is low entropy at the transport layer. Also, in many cases, the traffic in an AI/ML fabric is between source/destination pairs. This results in low entropy at the network layer, and high-bandwidth flows end up consuming network port bandwidth between switches. In this chapter, we will discuss how proactively implementing efficient load-balancing mechanisms can help achieve better fabric utilization and reduce the chances of congestion.

Equal-cost multipathing (ECMP) is an important concept to understand before we look into various load-balancing options for AI/ML fabrics. Consider the Clos fabric illustrated by Figure 6-1.

You can see in Figure 6-1 that GPU1 is connected to LeafA, and GPU2 is connected to LeafB. LeafA and LeafB are connected to three spines: SpineA, SpineB, and SpineC. From LeafA, there are three paths to reach LeafB, via each of the three spines. When using an IGP routing protocol such as IS-IS or OSPFv2/v3 with equal-cost links or multipathing with BGP (a more common IP routing option in the case of IP fabrics), the GPU2 IP address will be reachable via all three paths from LeafA's perspective. This is referred to as ECMP. The routing plane will show the route to GPU2 (the destination IP address) as:

- ASIC ECMP nh-id123
    - Unicast_nh1—SpineA

- Unicast_nh2—SpineB
- Unicast_nh3—SpineC

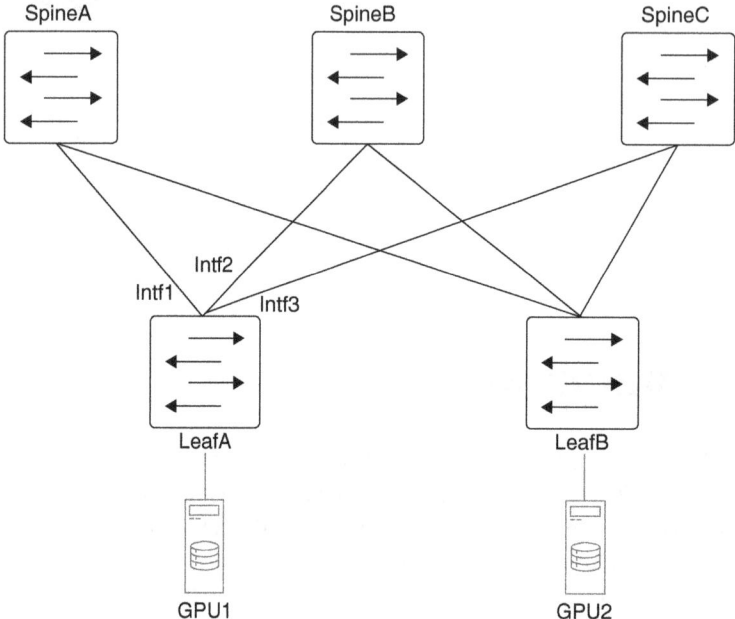

Figure 6-1
Equal-cost multipathing (ECMP)

First, the switch analyzes the information available from the IP routing control plane. For example, the LeafA switch gets reachability information for the IP subnet of the destination GPU2 through the BGP routing protocol. LeafB advertises the GPU2 IP address to the three spines: SpineA, SpineB, and SpineC. The spines further advertise the GPU2 IP address to LeafA with the BGP protocol next hop IP routing attribute as self. Consequently, LeafA has three routes for the same destination IP address but different next hops. Because the BGP attributes are the same, LeafA considers the three paths to be equal.

The control plane sends a request to the ASIC to install an IP prefix with an ECMP next hop. In this example, the three spines represent three next hops from the ToR switch perspective. However, in real-world deployments of AI/ML clusters, the spine count is usually much higher than in traditional data center networks; there may be, for example, 32 or 64 spines for large-scale deployments.

Additional destinations reachable via the same ECMP path use the same ECMP next hop, which usually helps to optimize the scale of the next-hop tables at the Ethernet switch level. In a Clos fabric, all leaf switches connect to all spine switches. Hence, in most cases, the same ECMP next hop is used to forward traffic to all destinations connected to other leaf switches. There could be multiple flows from one ingress leaf to destinations connected to one or more egress leaf switches. This is where load balancing becomes relevant. Even if for each destination IP address all three next-hop spines are available, the leaf switch will typically select one of the next-hop addresses based on the flow characteristics (source/destination UDP/IP or using the RoCEv2 BTH header information, such as QPAIRs). This selection is performed at the ASIC level directly, and the IP routing control plane is not involved at this stage.

As we will discuss in this chapter, there are various load-balancing techniques. Flow-based load balancing is just one option for load balancing within the AI/ML fabric. Flow entropy is not always very high in the RoCEv2 AI/ML context; a single massive flow is sent from the GPU server with the same source/destination IP/UDP. Therefore, the packet-spraying technique known as per-packet load balancing can be used as an alternative load-balancing technique.

When the destination GPU2 is reachable via overlay EVPN-VXLAN (in case of the multi-tenancy), the ECMP nh-id is related to the loopback IP address used by the VXLAN tunnel termination, as advertised for the given MAC-VRF or RT5 routing instances, in which the given GPU server switch port is connected.

Per-Flow Load Balancing

Before we investigate flow-based load-balancing techniques, let us first look at how a switch classifies packets into different flows.

When a packet arrives at the ingress port of a switch, it goes through a pipeline of processing stages in the packet forwarding engine (PFE). One of the stages of the pipeline is to create a unique value referred to as a hash, based on the fields of the packet header. Typically, a 5-tuple is used for the hash computation, which includes the source and destination IP addresses, the source and destination port numbers, and the protocol type. This is the default computation in most deployments, though it can be changed if required. In the context of AI/ML data center fabrics, the additional fields from the RoCEv2 BTH header can also be considered to improve the entropy level.

The computed unique hash identifies whether the packets belong to the same flow. The flow table maintains mapping of various flows and the assigned outgoing interface for each of them. The PFE validates whether the computed hash for a packet exists in the flow table. If a match is found, the PFE forwards the packet out the assigned outgoing interface. If the computed hash does not exist in the flow table, it is considered a new flow. The ASIC makes an entry of the new hash in the flow table and assigns an outgoing interface to the flow.

Let us now look at the different methods of flow-based load balancing that can be used in a data center, each of which offers a unique level of efficiency:

- **Static load balancing (SLB):** SLB is a traditional load-balancing technique. Although it is the most commonly deployed technique, it is typically not sufficient with AI/ML fabric because it only considers the entropy in the packet header.
- **Dynamic load balancing (DLB):** DLB checks the quality of the local switch links in term of the queue depth and bandwidth load. Broadcom coined the term DLB, and there are alternative similar mechanisms from other vendors, such as adaptive load balancing (ALB).

- **Global load balancing (GLB):** GLB uses the local link quality, queue depth, and neighboring switch (for example, spine quality information) to calculate the best end-to-end path. Broadcom coined the term GLB, and at this point, there are no similar alternative solutions.
- **Traffic engineering–based load balancing (TELB):** Using RoCEv2 or UET flow characteristics, workloads are pushed through diverse paths across the three-stage or five-stage fabric using lightweight traffic engineering.

Static Load Balancing

SLB is the most popular load-balancing technique in Ethernet switching and routing. In traditional server deployments that utilize a variety of applications, SLB is an effective method for distributing flows across fabric links to achieve optimal bandwidth utilization. In an SLB implementation, the switch selects the outgoing interface for a flow based on the ECMP interface with the least number of flows assigned to it. However, the SLB mechanism does not consider the link bandwidth utilization when assigning flows, which may result in ineffective load balancing. Let us look at a few scenarios.

Figure 6-2 illustrates SLB-optimized flow distribution across ECMP interfaces with flows carrying different traffic rates.

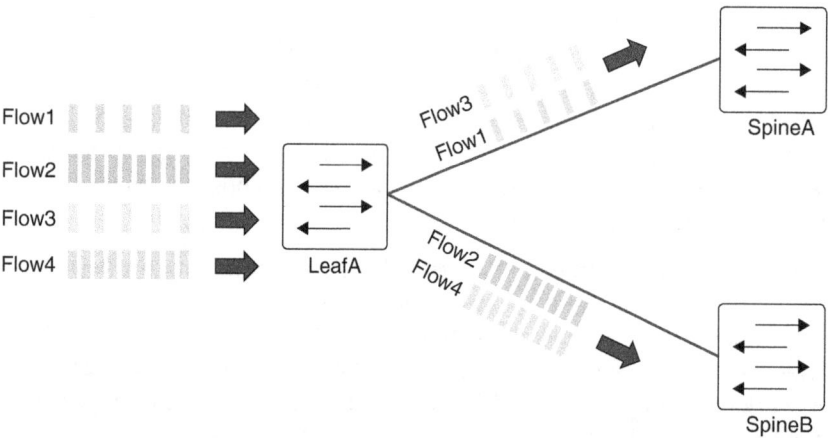

Figure 6-2
Static load balancing

An equal number of flows is assigned to each ECMP interface. Flow1 and Flow3 are assigned to the interface between LeafA and SpineA, while Flow2 and Flow4 are assigned to the interface between LeafA and SpineB. Now suppose Flow1 and Flow3 each carry 50 Gbps traffic, and Flow2 and Flow4 each carry 100 Gbps traffic. If the leaf-to-spine interface bandwidth is 200 Gbps, the LeafA-to-SpineB interface is 100% utilized, while the LeafA-to-SpineA interface is only 50% utilized. This is because in SLB, the outgoing interface bandwidth utilization and the switch buffer queue depth are not included in the hash key calculation, and the load-balancing decision is only made based on the flow characteristics.

In the context of load balancing, the hash key is a numeric result of the hash function (e.g., CRC32 over the 5-tuple), and N is the number of active members in the IP ECMP group. The result of the outgoing interface index will, in this case, be a function of the hash key. The hash key value itself comes from the CRC32 computation mathematical binary algorithm over the 5-tuple characteristics of the given flow coming from the server, for example, the source/destination UDP port numbers. If the CRC32 computation over the 5-tuple results in the value 10, then for the 5 member IP ECMP the outgoing interface will be with the index 0 and for the hash key = 11 ⊠11 mod 5 will give the interface index 1. The CRC32 function itself, which refers to the cyclic redundancy check, is used as a mixing function. So, in a 5-tuple scenario, the switch ASIC runs those bits through a CRC32 generator and outputs the hash key.

For example, say that the source IP address is 192.168.1.20 (hex C0A80114), the destination IP address is 192.168.2.10 (hex C0A8020A), the IP protocol is 17 for UDP (11 in hexadecimal), the source UDP port is 1024 (0400 in hexadecimal), and the destination UDP port is 4791 (12B7 in hexadecimal). In this case, the numeric string of C0A80114 C0A8020A 11040012 B7 will then go through the CRC32 function and produce the hash key value of 0x8BDA7C2D (2346351661 in decimal). This value will then be used to calculate the outgoing interface in the IP ECMP scenario. Using the raw modulo 0x8BDA7C2D % 5 will result in the interface index 1, and if the number of member links/next hops is increased to 8, the result of the raw modulo function will yield the outgoing interface index 5.

In the example we just looked at, we can see the drawbacks of simple static load balancing: The number of links that are part of the IP ECMP group may impact the selection of the outgoing interface for the given flow, so that if we increase the number of leaf-to-spine links from five to eight, the modulo function, which uses the IP ECMP member count, will always result in a different interface index for the given flow when the links go up and down. This is also why in many cases resilient hashing is used in the context of SLD (Static Load Balancing), where instead of the N number of IP ECMP links, a fixed bucket table size is used (with 512 or 1024 buckets), and only buckets that point to the link that went down are reassigned to the new outgoing interface instead of all the flows, as when using the ECMP link count in the mod function.

As an example, we can take a simplified bucket size of 8 and map different buckets to five different interfaces to form the IP ECMP group:

    bucket 0 to interface_0

    bucket 1 to interface_1

    bucket 2 to interface_2

    bucket 3 to interface_3

    bucket 4 to interface_4

    bucket 5 to interface_0

bucket 6 to interface_1

bucket 7 to interface_2

In this scenario, if the hash key is equal to 10, then the mod % 8 function (because 8 is the bucket size) will result in bucket 2, which is mapped to interface 2; so in this case, when interface 2 goes down, only the flows from bucket 7 and bucket 2 will be affected instead of all of the flows. When the bucket size is high, the churn level is highly reduced compared to in traditional member link count-based SLB.

Besides resilient hashing, SLB may require symmetric hashing, where flows in opposite directions (A⊠B and B⊠A) hash to the same member link or ECMP path. Instead of having the same pair of IP addresses and the same UDP port number, two different hash keys and different outgoing interfaces are used, and a normalized or XOR function is added to calculate the CRC32 or CRC16 hash key. This guarantees that the same bucket (or the same interface) is used in both directions of the given bidirectional flow. In the data center environment, it may help, for example, when traffic is sent to firewalls. With the symmetric hashing, the reverse flows land on the same path and same interface.

Weighted ECMP may sometimes be included in static hashing. Weighted ECMP uses the same CRC32 or CRC16 hash machinery to identify a flow, but instead of mapping evenly, the bucket indirection table is filled in proportion to configured weights. This way, some next hops get bigger shares of flows than others. Instead of assuming that all next hops are equal in the IP ECMP group, weighted ECMP deliberately biases the distribution of flows toward some next hops more than others.

At first glance, it might seem that load balancing with a 5-tuple hash key value with resiliency, symmetric, or weighted enhancements should be sufficient. However, with very low entropy between the flows and with a very small number of flows entering a switch, the switch may end up using the same outgoing interface when using SLB. Figure 6-3 shows Flow1 and Flow2 taking the same interface (that is, the same hash key value) due to low entropy. Still, in some cases, the ingress interface where the GPU server is connected generates just one large fat stream; therefore, if each interface gets a similar stream, there is an increased probability of getting a hash calculation that results in the same outgoing interface. If Flow1 and Flow2 are the fat flows occupying 100% of the bandwidth at the LeafA-to-SpineB link level, then any other flow hashed to that link will create a congestion point.

This is exactly what may happen in an AI/ML cluster network, where implementing SLB may lead to the following challenges:

- Poor bandwidth utilization between leaf and spine or spine and super spine links
- Elephant flows completely utilizing the interface bandwidth, resulting in a drop in mice flows, which are short-lived flows that send only a small amount of data

This is why modern and more advanced load-balancing mechanisms, such as DLB, have been developed and are typically implemented in the context of AI/ML data center fabrics instead of the traditional SLB.

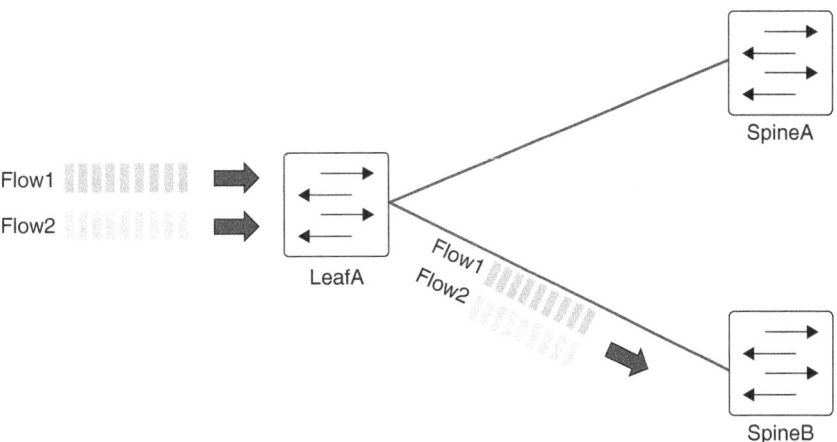

Figure 6-3
SLB with low entropy

Dynamic Load Balancing

DLB overcomes the limitations of SLB by considering link bandwidth and buffer utilization metrics, in addition to the 5-tuple mod function, for outgoing interface assignment. DLB implements an algorithm that generates a link quality band based on link utilization and buffer utilization as inputs. The link quality band is usually an integer that is derived for each ECMP interface and stored in the link quality table. The microkernel in the ASIC runs the algorithm in real time and updates the quality table locally, based on recent utilization of the interface and buffer. When assigning the outgoing interface to a flow, the switch looks in the link quality table to identify the best link.

Figure 6-4 illustrates DLB optimized flow distribution across ECMP interfaces with flows carrying different traffic rates. An equal number of flows are assigned to each ECMP interface.

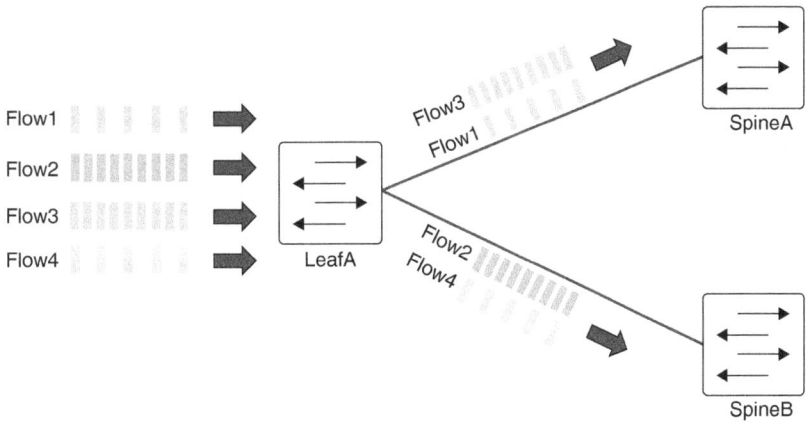

Figure 6-4
Dynamic load balancing

The rate of traffic for Flow2 and Flow4 is high compared to the rate of traffic for Flow1 and Flow3. DLB assigns Flow1 to the interface between LeafA and SpineA and Flow2 to the interface between LeafA and SpineB. At this time, the LeafA-to-SpineA link has better link quality due to lower utilization. Hence, DLB assigns Flow3 to the interface between LeafA and SpineA. Another time, the LeafA-to-SpineB might have better link quality, in which case DLB would assign Flow4 to the interface between LeafA and SpineB. Now suppose Flow1 and Flow3 each carry 50 Gbps traffic, and Flow2 and Flow4 each carry 100 Gbps traffic. If the interface bandwidth is 200 Gbps, then both interfaces are 75% utilized. This is how DLB helps with efficient load balancing compared to SLB, where one link to the spine was 100% utilized and the other was at 50% only.

Since DLB monitors the link utilization and buffer utilization in real time, it can also detect link failures faster by detecting them in the PFE. Receiving link updates via the control plane usually takes more time.

DLB has two main modes of operation, which we'll examine in the following sections:

- Assigned-flow mode
- Flowlet mode
- Per-packet mode

DLB Assigned-Flow Mode

In DLB assigned-flow mode, an active flow is assigned to an interface for its entire lifetime and is never rebalanced based on the flow characteristics. Interfaces assigned to traffic flows that remain active for a long period may deteriorate in quality, resulting in inefficient utilization of fabric bandwidth. Therefore, assigned-flow mode is not typically recommended for AI/ML cluster networks even if it helps to deliver the packets to the target server; however, it may be relevant for a traditional data center, where higher entropy of flows is available.

DLB Flowlet Mode

In DLB flowlet mode, when a flow is assigned to an interface, the ASIC monitors the flow for inactivity. If the flow is paused for a shorter time than the configured inactivity timer, the flow continues to use the assigned interface. If the flow is paused for longer than the configured inactivity timer, the flow is reassigned. This results in rebalancing of traffic flows.

When or why might a flow be paused? Consider a flow initiated between a pair of GPUs for a specific data transfer task. The task- or application-related data is present in the IB BTH header, above the UDP header when RoCEv2 transport is in use. When a new data transfer task is initiated between the same pair of GPUs, the switch does not differentiate between the flows. It continues to forward the packets through the assigned interface. The flow is considered paused when there is no data transfer between a pair of GPUs. Such flows remain active for long periods within the switch and result in deterioration of quality on the assigned interface. The flowlet mode addresses this problem by using an inactivity timer.

Figure 6-5 illustrates two flowlets between the same pair of GPUs. When the flow is paused for longer than the inactivity timer, the flowlets are assigned to different interfaces. In the flowlet mode, the ASIC builds quality tables with flowset identifiers mapped to the egress ports, based on the port load and port queue depth, which are also sampled at the ASIC level. Multiple micro-flows with the same flow characteristics can be mapped to the same macro-flow with the same flowset identifier. Some implementations of DLB also propose fine-tuning the size of the flowset table to increase the total number of macro-flows and achieve even better flow distribution.

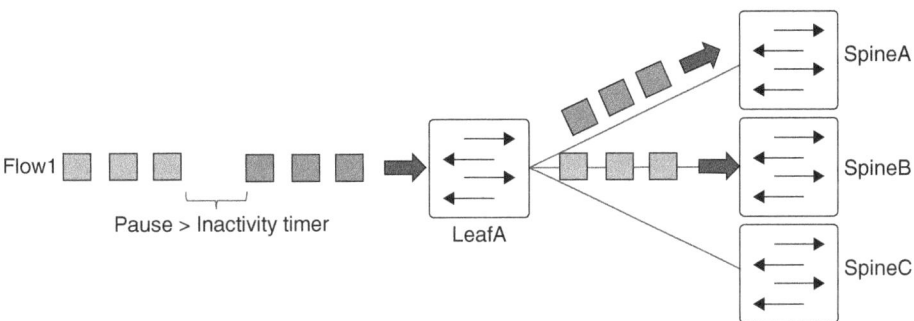

Figure 6-5
DLB flowlet mode with inactivity timer

For scenarios where all egress ports to the spines are assigned the same quality value (for example, quality 0 as the lowest quality with 7 as the highest priority), a random link selection will occur based on the flow characteristics.

In addition to using the inactivity timer, the DLB flowlet mode can also perform reactive load balancing. DLB can monitor the link assigned to the flow for degradation and compare it with the other available ECMP paths. If it finds an interface with better link quality, it rebalances traffic to that interface. This is useful when the flow is not paused for longer than the configured inactivity timer. However, it should be done only if the target server supports the packet reordering correctly because the rebalancing may result in short-term packet reordering at the server.

Figure 6-6 illustrates reactive path rebalancing using DLB flowlet mode.

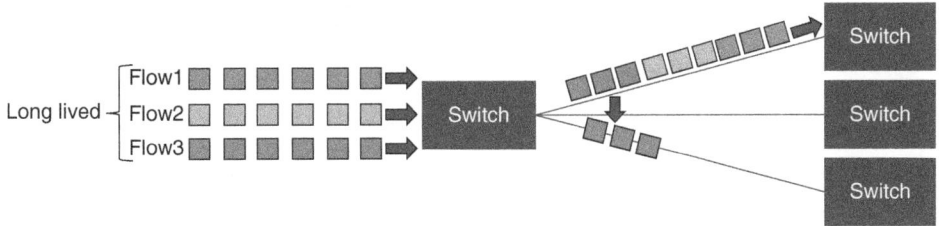

Figure 6-6
DLB reactive path rebalancing

Flow1, Flow2, and Flow3 are long-lived flows assigned to the interface between LeafA and SpineA based on link quality. However, over a period of time, the link quality may deteriorate, in which case the reactive-path load balancing can identify and rebalance one or more flows over the other available ECMP paths, such as the interface between LeafA and SpineC.

Global Load Balancing

DLB improves load balancing by using local link quality information to select the outgoing interface for a given flow. This significantly improves the fabric bandwidth utilization for data centers compared to the traditional static load balancing. However, DLB tracks the quality of local links only instead of tracking the quality of the whole path from the ingress node to egress node.

Figure 6-7 illustrates a scenario with congestion at the spine switch. In this case, assume that all interfaces in the fabric are of the same bandwidth. The servers connected to LeafA and LeafB initiate flow at the line rate toward the destination server connected to LeafD. Both ingress leaf switches independently choose the outgoing interface based on DLB. Now imagine that both of the flows send traffic via SpineA. Since SpineA has only one interface toward the egress LeafD, flow collisions occur on the spine, and congestion eventually results. Even though the ingress leaf used a load-balancing mechanism for interface assignment, the fabric could still observe congestion. Multiple simultaneous elephant flows are a common occurrence in AI/ML clusters, and this scenario illustrates an important problem that must be solved.

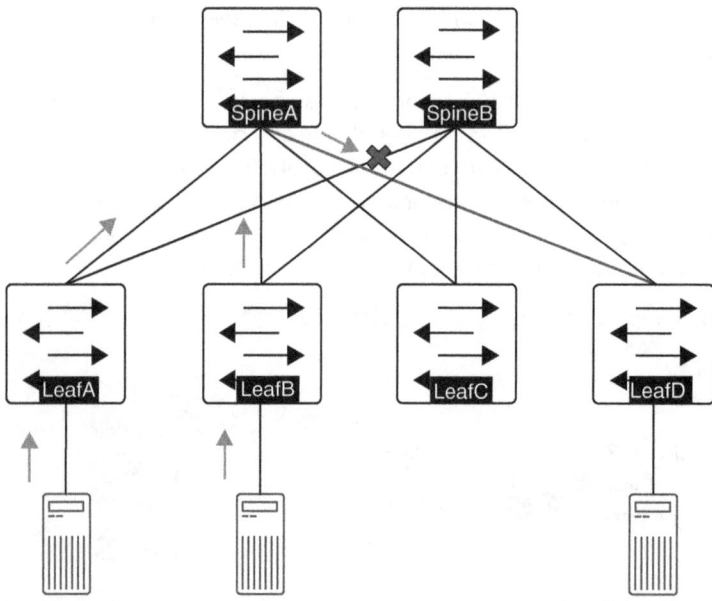

Figure 6-7
Congestion at the spine

GLB (global load balancing) is an effective solution to the problem just described. In a GLB implementation, the leaf switch also learns the link quality information from the spine to make a more informed decision. GLB, which is a new technology that is currently being developed by Broadcom, is useful because spines aggregate traffic from many leaf nodes and may, in fact, have a higher probability of degradation in link quality.

Figure 6-8 illustrates a scenario where every spine advertises link quality of all the interfaces to each leaf switch connected to it. A leaf uses this information to make more informed decisions. For example, LeafA has the local link quality information of interfaces A and B via DLB. SpineA sends the link quality for links connected to LeafB, LeafC, and LeafD to LeafA via GLB. Similarly, SpineB sends the link quality of links connected to LeafB, LeafC, and LeafD to LeafA.

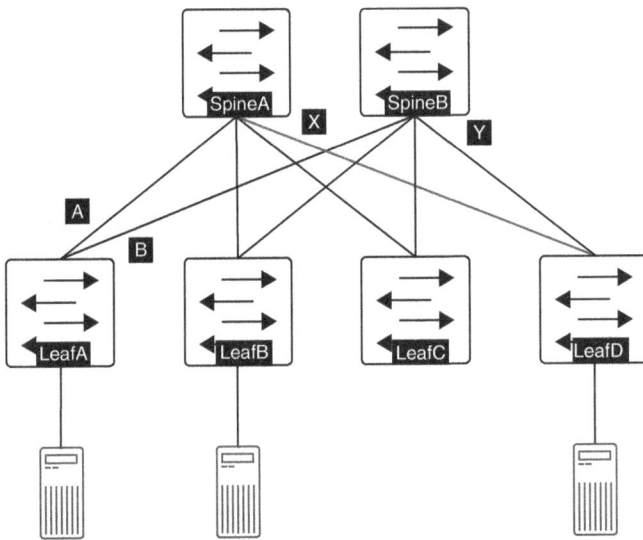

Figure 6-8
Global load balancing

To use the link quality information effectively, LeafA needs to know that its destination is connected to LeafD. It also needs to know that Interface X on SpineA and Interface Y on SpineB are connected to LeafD. While link state protocols such as IS-IS and OSPF have the complete topology information, the protocol most commonly used in data centers is BGP, which is not aware of the complete topology. Hence, BGP could be enhanced to support this functionality. There may be other protocols or technologies—such as Routing in Fat Tree (RIFT), Bidirectional Forwarding Detection (BFD), and Operations, Administration, and Maintenance (OAM)—that could be used for this purpose. Network vendors such as HPE/Juniper Networking and Nvidia are currently discussing this issue and may promote a standard in the future for the ASIC level GLB heartbeats and the Next-Next Hop Node (NNHN) new BGP attribute. This is referenced at the IETF standard organization internet draft level under the draft-wang-idr-next-next-hop-nodes document.

Once LeafA is aware of the egress node and the interfaces that connect to the node from the spine switches, it maps this topology information and the link quality information received from the spines. Because LeafA now knows the link quality of all its locally connected interfaces as well as remote interfaces connecting the spines toward the egress leaf, it can identify that interface X is congested and has poor link quality.

With this technology, the challenge is obviously the frequency of updates for topology as well as link quality information. Topology information updates may be limited to when there are changes in topology. Link quality updates could be done in real time or initiated by changes. Message propagation must be fast (microsecond level) to reduce the impact of change. However, the efficiency of GLB heartbeats during frequent microbursts may need to be fine-tuned during the initial phase of the GLB deployment.

GLB has the potential to reduce the number of Data Center Quantized Congestion Notification (DCQCN) triggers in the fabric at the spine level because GLB signalizes the quality information via the GLB heartbeats from the spine to the leaf at the microsecond level; in the event of degradations in the spine links, the leaf nodes move the new flows to other paths where there's a lower chance of running into the congestions. (DCQCN triggers are covered in Chapter 7, "RoCEv2 Transport and Congestion Management.") This means GLB would also reduce the probability of an avalanche of Priority Flow Control (PFC) frames in the fabric.

Because GLB uses real-time remote link utilization information, the leaf switches identify link failure at the spine layer much faster, which can result in faster recovery from link failures. Updates via the control plane usually take much more time.

GLB implementation is part of the cognitive routing umbrella of implementations that started with the Broadcom TomaHawk5 chipset. Other vendors are exploring alternative ways of implementing GLB, using a combination of the ASIC heartbeats and routing control plane.

BGP NNHN

From an implementation perspective, GLB has two parts:

- A control plane part to learn the topology information
- Heartbeats, with path quality information sent at the ASIC level

One way of implementing the control plane part has been published in draft-wang-idr-next-next-hop-nodes. This draft describes the new BGP next-next-hop nodes (NNHN) capability in the next-hop dependent capabilities attribute to signal all next-next-hop nodes of a given next hop (see Figure 6-9).

In the BGP capability information shown in Figure 6-9, we can find the following:

- **Next-hop BGP ID:** This is the 32-bit BGP identifier of the next-hop node.
- **Next-next-hop BGP IDs:** This is one or more 32-bit BGP identifiers, each representing a next-next-hop node used by the next-hop node for ECMP forwarding for the NLRI in the BGP update.

This IETF draft is used to implement the control plane part of GLB, which correlates the topology information with the heartbeat node information at the packet forwarding engine (PFE) level.

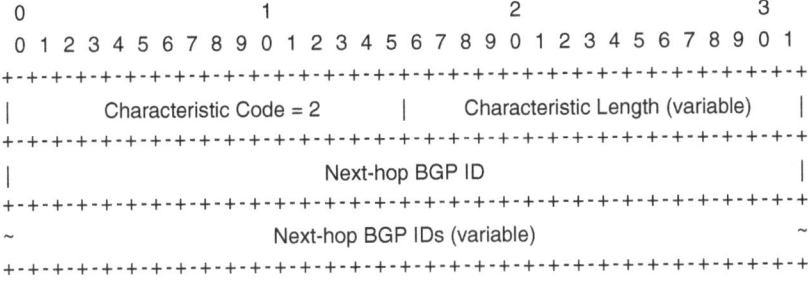

Figure 6-9
NNHN capability TLV format of the BGP update

The PFE sends heartbeats, which are the second part of GLB, at the interfaces on which BGP underlay peering is enabled between leaf and spine devices. This way, the GLB gets enabled only where it's needed and does not consider the heartbeat information coming through the links that are not part of the leaf-spine fabric topology. Each unique next-next-hop node generates a simple path quality profile for the Tomahawk 5 GLB app. All next hops sharing the same next-next-hop node are grouped together to form a GLB path. Two or more simple path quality profiles may be grouped into a compound path quality profile. If a route has only one next-next-hop node (as in three-stage Clos fabric), it will be programmed with a profile ID that corresponds to a simple path quality profile. A route with more than one next-next-hop node (as in five-stage Clos fabric) will be programmed with a profile ID that corresponds to a compound path quality profile.

Based on the path quality profile and the corresponding paths of a route, the GLB app knows the next-next hop of each next-hop leg. This allows the app to use the combined link quality of the next hop and next-next hops to make load-balancing decisions. When an EBGP session comes up, BGP sends a path monitor message to PFE, requesting the GLB app to start monitoring the quality of the link that the EBGP session is on. The GLB app floods the link quality to neighboring Ethernet switches so they can use the link quality for GLB purposes.

The frequency of the heartbeat is change-based, and it occurs every 20 ms.

In terms of packet forwarding decisions, once the path quality tables are created, the packets of the new flows are directed to the best-quality paths. When the calculated quality of the paths is the same, path selection follows the hash-based forwarding used for the flowlet mode.

GLB can be implemented in several different parts of a data center network:

- **Three-stage Clos fabric:** GLB can be implemented in a three-stage Clos fabric on all devices.
- **Within a pod or pods:** In a five-stage Clos architecture, GLB can be implemented within each pod or in a subset of pods based on feasibility and requirements. With this implementation, each pod is treated as a three-stage Clos GLB.
- **Spine or super spine layer:** In a five-stage Clos architecture, GLB can be implemented between spine and super spine layer if the user expects or observes load-balancing issues at this layer due to oversubscription.

- **All layers:** In a five-stage Clos architecture, GLB can also be implemented at all layers. However, it is important to be cognizant of the scaling limitations based on the entries required in the table to be able to achieve this.

Traffic Engineering–Based Load Balancing

Another approach to efficiently utilizing fabric bandwidth is to involve traffic engineering technologies and direct the AI/ML workloads in a more deterministic way across the fabric by pinning them to specific paths. Traffic engineering is a mature technology commonly used across service provider networks. It has multiple options for defining paths and controlling traffic behavior using different timers and knobs. MPLS Traffic Engineering (MPLS-TE) and Segment Routing MPLS (SR-MPLS), which are known for performing traffic engineering, are, however, too complex and too expensive to implement in the data center fabric environment. Upgrading 400 Gbps and 800 Gbps switches to offer support for traffic engineering can significantly increase the capital expenditures (capex) and operating expenses (opex) of a data center.

Furthermore, the operational costs of MPLS-TE and SR-MPLS are expensive compared to the costs of current data center technologies. Typically, MPLS requires a premium license, so data center network administrators may prefer to preserve MPLS only in the core network to establish clear demarcation points at the edge of the data center gateway. The telemetry support for MPLS/SRv6 is not always as good as in the case of raw IP fabric, especially when it comes to compatibility of MPLS/SRv6 with the mandatory lossless fabric DCQCN, which is also usually limited or incompatible. This is why pure IP fabrics are still a better choice for most AI/ML data center deployments.

However, a shared pool of fabric bandwidth resources, as illustrated in Figure 6-10, may not always be simple to manage, especially when multi-tenancy is used with multiple LLM trainings simultaneously; it may lead to performance degradation and inconsistency. This is where a lightweight dynamic and pure IP traffic engineering solution might help, offering path diversity within the Ethernet/IP fabric and better predictability of performance per tenant for each AI/ML job iteration.

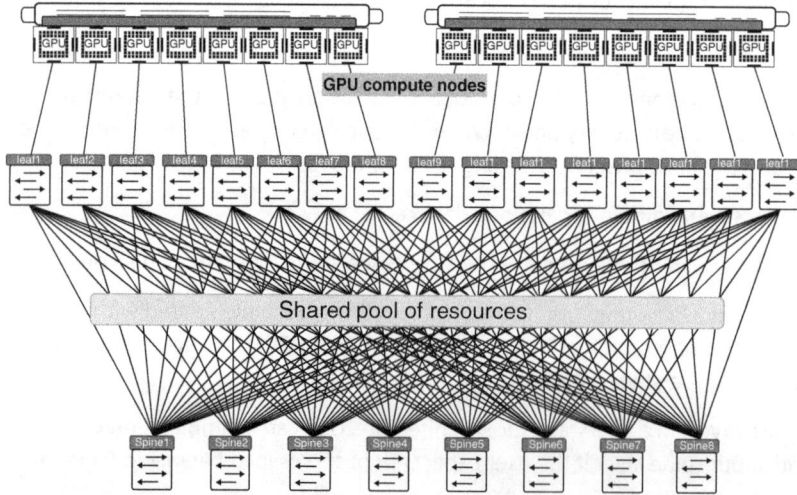

Figure 6-10
Rail-optimized design with a shared pool of resources

In three-stage Clos fabric, as shown in Figure 6-11, there's sometimes a requirement to slice the fabric and dedicate one or multiple spines to a specific tenant or specific AI/ML workloads.

In Figure 6-11, Tenant1 AI traffic is explicitly directed between the two rails over one spine, and Tenant2 to Tenant7 use all the rest of the paths based on the IP ECMP. In this example, only one spine is used, to guarantee in-order delivery of packets to the target end host; however, more spines can also be used. For example, in a fabric with eight spines, one set of tenants can use four spines, and the other set of tenants use the other four spines to guarantee that specific tenant traffic will never be forwarded across the fabric with the other tenants.

In the example shown in Figure 6-11, the given GPU ID is used by all seven tenants; however, selecting all the traffic from the given tenant through one spine or a minimal number of spines may lead, in some cases, to traffic congestion as well, especially when the given job execution generates bursty traffic. So, sometimes it's better to split the traffic from the given GPU to multiple QPAIRs and then direct each traffic stream through a different set of spines. This can be achieved through automated filter-based forwarding (FBF), also known as policy-based routing (PBR), where a range of QPAIRs or a range of source UDP ports is placed on the specific path ID or path color ID to efficiently balance the traffic load. This approach is possible if the fabric is connected to an orchestrator and knows which ranges of ports or which ranges of QPAIRs are allocated to the specific tenant.

The TELB (Traffic Engineering Load Balancing) mechanism described here must also handle link or node failure scenarios properly, so that in the event of reduced spine capacity or link failures, the right backup path ID is immediately selected at the ASIC level. BGP Deterministic Path Forwarding (BGP-DPF), covered in more detail in Chapter 8, "IP Routing for AI/ML Fabrics," aims to pin a specific QPAIR or GPU ID to a specific colored path throughout the fabric based on flow characteristics with a pre-installed backup path ID.

The same traffic engineering mechanism may also be useful when an AI/ML server with multiple GPUs is connected to the same switch (for example, a chassis-based switch with linecards), using the rail-unified design (RUD). In the case illustrated in Figure 6-12, each GPU/NIC generating elephant or mouse flows may push the flows to different logical fabric colors, efficiently use the bandwidth, and deliver the packets to the target server in order. Unlike with the TELB in the rail-optimized design (ROD), load balancing can be applied to the traffic based on the ingress interface as input, and each GPU from the given server can get a dedicated logical fabric with path diversity. This way, even if one GPU takes more bandwidth, it won't impact any other GPU jobs as the path diversity is maintained between GPU IDs from different servers.

Using a centralized controller is another design approach for TELB in AI/ML fabrics. When equipped with telemetry data collected from all nodes in the fabric, the controller may have a better understanding of the bandwidth utilization and congestion across multiple paths in the fabric. Figure 6-13 illustrates controller-based data center management where the controller can handle various tasks, such as configuration management, monitoring, alerting, and automated actions based on trigger events.

BGP-based deterministic path load balancing (discussed in Chapter 8) is just one way of delivering TELB. Some IGP protocols, such as IS-IS, can also be used to deliver Flex-Algo load control, which involves analyzing the KPI constraints before selecting the path for the given destination IP address. In addition to IP-based traffic engineering techniques, other well-known techniques from core IP MPLS could be used as well. However, they may be harder to implement or too expensive for data center deployment.

Chapter 6 Efficient Load Balancing

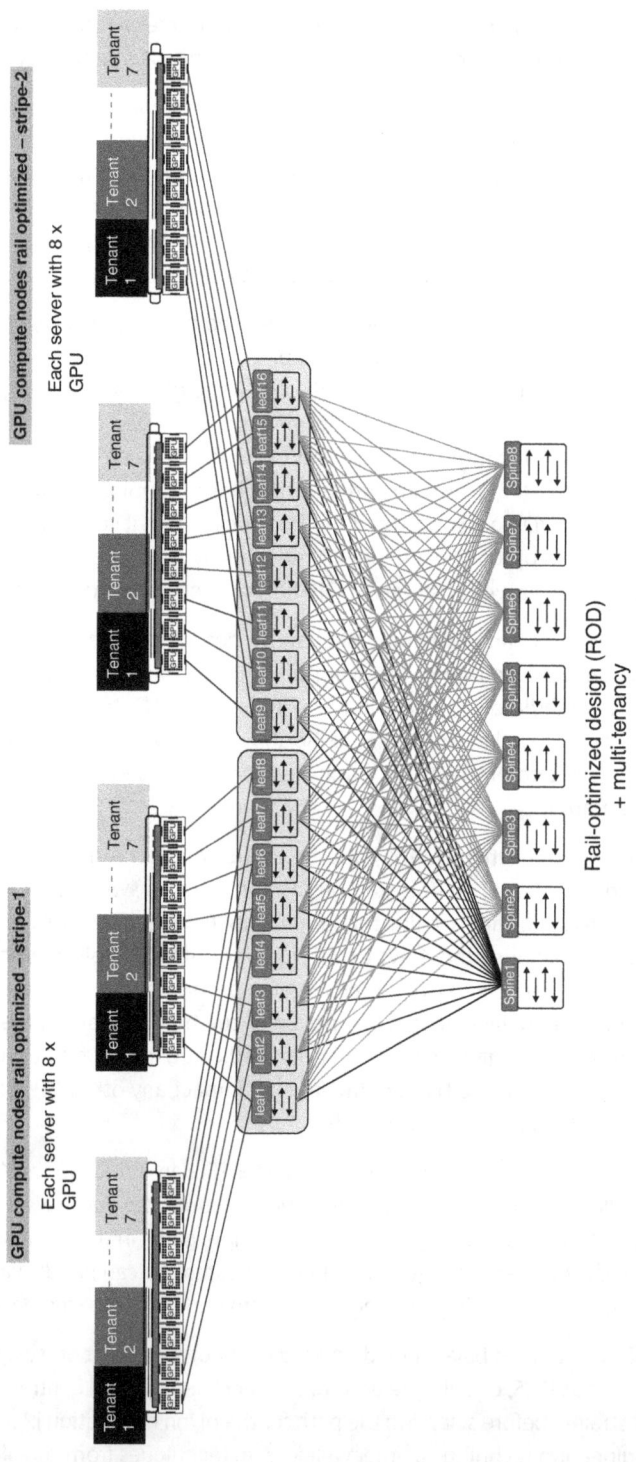

Figure 6-11
TELB: Multi-tenant use case

Per-Flow Load Balancing 113

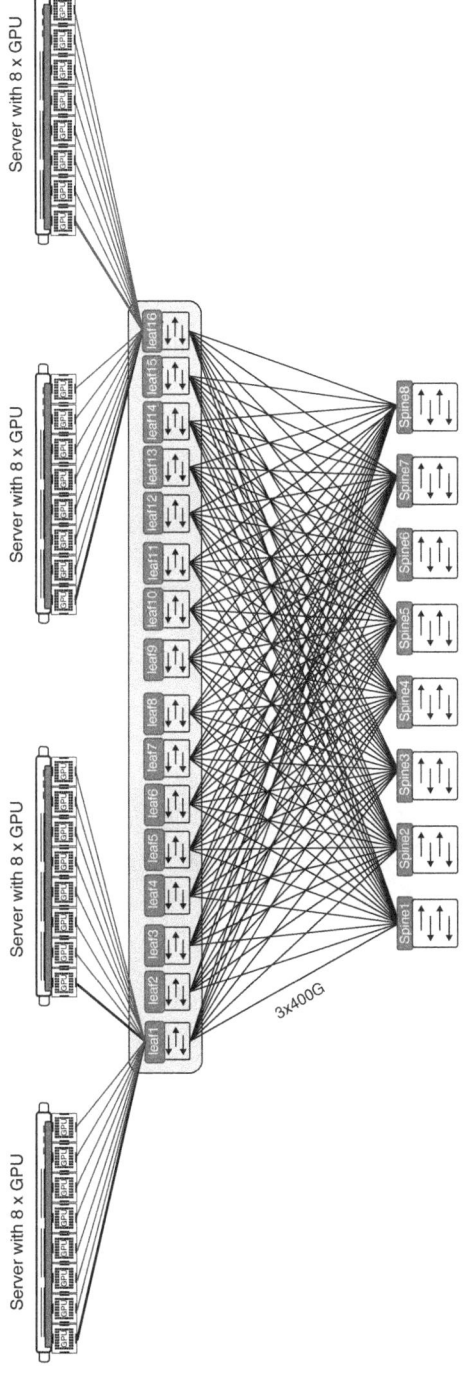

Figure 6-12
Traffic engineering–based load balancing in the rail-unified design

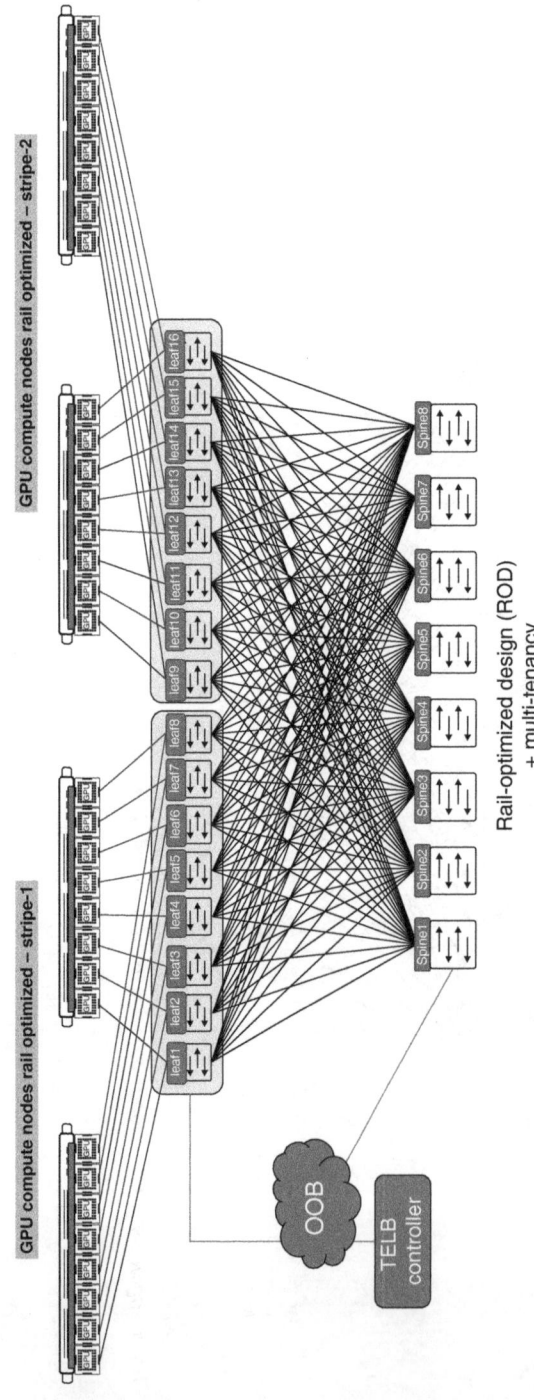

Figure 6-13
Controller-based traffic engineering load balancing

Per-Packet Load Balancing

With per-packet load balancing, the switch does not create a hash based on the packet header and does not maintain flow information. All ingress packets are treated as individual packets and forwarded out the best available outgoing interfaces. The advantage of this mechanism is that it helps in achieving efficient load balancing by better utilizing each available interface in the ECMP path.

Figure 6-14 illustrates per-packet load balancing. Imagine that there is a single stream with three datagrams of 1500 bytes each. Each packet will be sprayed on different interfaces of the available ECMP paths, such as Port-1, Port-2, and Port-3 in this topology. All three interfaces carry one datagram each. This results in nearly perfect load balancing across all ECMP members.

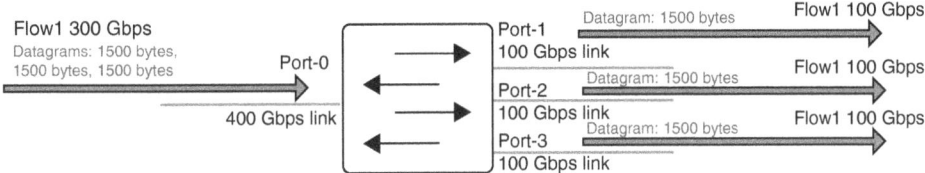

Figure 6-14
Per-packet load balancing

However, this mechanism faces a challenge: The receiver must reorder the unordered packets received (see Figure 6-15), so it is not a popular choice. Flow1 is an elephant flow that is sprayed over all outgoing interfaces of the available ECMP paths by Leaf1, but the interfaces are connected to different spine nodes. Each spine may process the packets at slightly different times. Even if the three 1500-byte datagrams—A, B, and C—all have the same prioritization on all nodes, the processing of packets inside the buffers of the intermediate spines may vary, resulting in the arrival of packets in a different order than the originally sending order. Here Datagram B arrived at time T1, followed by Datagrams A and C.

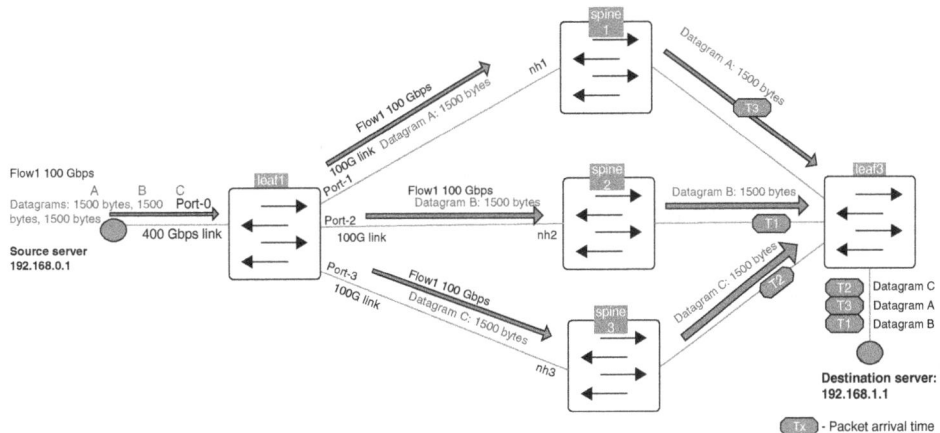

Figure 6-15
Unordered packets at the destination

The NICs must perform reordering of packets. Before they can order the packets, the packets must first be buffered. A code must run to find a packet in sequence and then forward it to the application. Handling a small number of unordered packets is possible with a manageable buffer, but when there is congestion on the switch, the number of unordered packets can be very high.

With recent advancements in NIC capabilities, many types of NICs are available that support reordering of packets. The extent of reordering that can be handled is yet to be evaluated. As a result of this advancement, the idea of per-packet load balancing has gained traction. Next, we'll take a look at the options available for per-packet load balancing:

- Random spray
- DLB per-packet mode
- Selective packet spraying

Random Spray

With random spray per-packet load balancing, the packets of a flow are sprayed across the ECMP members in a random or round-robin fashion. The switch does not validate the quality of the interface before sending the packets. Normally, if random spray is deployed for all the traffic through a switch, validating quality may not offer much advantage. However, if the flows carry packets of varying datagram sizes, it may be helpful to monitor link quality information before deciding on the outgoing interface.

DLB Per-Packet Mode

DLB also supports a per-packet mode, in which it simply takes the datagram packets of the same flow and sprays them across the members of the ECMP path based on the link quality information present in the quality table. It sprays more packets to the member interfaces with better link quality at any given time.

Selective Packet Spraying

Certain 400 Gbps NIC vendors claim to support packet reordering only for specific read or write operations of remote direct memory access (RDMA) traffic. It is therefore important to include the option to selectively enable per-packet load balancing based on packet characteristics for a flow for which NIC can handle reordering.

Figure 6-16 illustrates selective packet spraying. Flow1 does not match the defined filter criteria, so it uses the default load balancing. Flow2 matches the filter criteria, and so per-packet mode is applied to this flow.

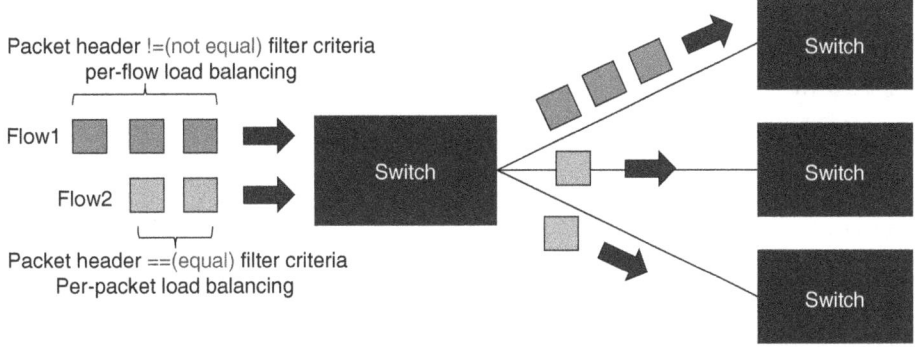

Figure 6-16
Selective packet spraying

In an AI/ML data center, the transport protocol is normally RoCEv2, carrying the RDMA traffic. Most of the elephant flows are for the write opcodes. Nvidia CX6 and CX7 NICs as well as Bluefield DPUs can handle reordering for write opcode traffic. Hence, a selective per-packet spraying mechanism has a lot of potential for AI/ML workloads.

It is good to have this option to allow different treatment, depending on the capabilities of the server. Selective packet spraying requires a good understanding of flow characteristics as well as some TCAM (Ternary Content-Addressable Memory is a special kind of high-speed memory used in network switches) space allocation to enable specific treatment of a packet based on the access lists enabled for ingress. The same rule can typically be applied for specific types of storage or data synchronization operations in the context of an AI/ML data center network where specific RoCEv2 opcode values can be selected and used as ACL matching criteria to enable one mode of load balancing or the other.

The Ethernet switch ASIC also must support the specific customizations of the load-balancing mode in function of the server-originated flow characteristics, and take the action from the ACL to enable a specific load-balancing mode.

Load-Balancing Mechanism Comparison

Table 6-1 summarizes the various load-balancing mechanisms and compares their capabilities. In some use cases, basic load-balancing mechanisms such as SLB may be good enough. On the other hand, in more complex deployments, such as in an AI/ML storage data center, the DLB and GLB mechanisms may be needed to provide efficient bandwidth utilization.

Table 6-1 AI/ML Data Center Fabric Load-Balancing Options

Feature	SLB	DLB	GLB	TELB
Load balancing based on packet characteristics	✓	✓	✓	
Includes local link bandwidth		✓	✓	✓
Uses queue size information		✓	✓	
Can use remote link quality			✓	✓
May have RoCEv2 BTH header included for load balancing	✓	✓	✓	✓
Can use fabric telemetry for load balancing				✓
Industry adoption level	High	Medium	Low	Low

There is also a possibility of applying different load-balancing mechanisms to different flows in the same fabric. This option gives users more control over the fabric utilization.

For IP Clos fabrics with 400 Gbps, 800 Gbps, or 1.6 Tbps interface deployments, poorly utilized interfaces result in poor return on investment. That is why the interface speed and how efficiently it is utilized are equally important. We will continue to observe more advanced capabilities in the market in the coming years.

Summary

Load-balancing technologies such as DLB and GLB enable the most efficient use of IP fabrics for AI/ML training clusters, even when the flow entropy on the server side is low or medium. With the DLB flowlet mode, most deployments will observe a significant improvement in load distribution and reduced risk of congestion. For most AI data center deployments, efficient load balancing and fast convergence are both important, and end-to-end path quality awareness is required; this is where GLB comes into play and may be considered an evolution of DLB. The interoperability of newer load-balancing technologies, such as GLB, can sometimes be challenging; therefore, the industry will undoubtedly evolve to support multi-vendor, end-to-end load-balancing technologies. In a multi-tenant environment, predictable AI flow pinning may also be required, and BGP-DPF selective traffic engineering can be used. When target servers are incapable of supporting packet reordering for some RoCEv2 operations or specific QPAIRs, the administrator must ensure that the correct type of load balancing is used. Therefore, flexibility in fine-tuning leaf and switch load balancing is crucial. More innovative load-balancing techniques will be proposed in the future to ensure that the upcoming UEC (Ultra Ethernet Consortium) workloads, covered in Chapter 12, "Ultra Ethernet Consortium (UEC)," can coexist with RoCEv2 on the same fabric and still offer predictable high performance.

Test Your Knowledge

Chapter Review

The following questions are designed to test your understanding of the content covered in Chapter 6. Following the questions, answers are provided so you can verify your conclusions.

Questions

1. What is the role of ECMP (equal-cost multipathing) in AI/ML data center fabrics, and how does it interact with flow hashing?
2. Why is static load balancing (SLB) often insufficient for AI/ML workloads, and what are its operational limitations?
3. Describe the operational modes of dynamic load balancing (DLB) and their impact on flow distribution.
4. How does flowlet-based load balancing address the challenges of bursty and synchronized AI/ML traffic?
5. What is global load balancing (GLB), and how does it enhance network-wide congestion management?
6. Explain the technical challenges and trade-offs of per-packet load balancing in RoCEv2-based AI fabrics.
7. How do load-balancing mechanisms interact with RoCEv2's low-entropy flow characteristics, and what enhancements are required?
8. Summarize the comparative strengths and weaknesses of SLB, DLB, GLB, and TE-LB (Traffic Engineering Load Balancing) in AI/ML data center networks.

Answers

1. ECMP enables the distribution of traffic across multiple network paths with equal cost, maximizing bandwidth utilization and redundancy. In AI/ML fabrics, ECMP relies on hash functions (typically using a 5-tuple: source/destination IP, source/destination port, protocol) to assign flows to specific paths. However, in RoCEv2-based AI clusters, low entropy in packet headers (due to similar source/destination pairs and UDP port 4791) can cause hash collisions, leading to uneven load distribution and potential congestion on certain links. Advanced ECMP implementations may incorporate additional fields (for example, RoCEv2 BTH QPAIR) to improve entropy and flow separation.
2. SLB assigns flows to paths based on a static hash, without considering real-time link utilization or flow size. In AI/ML clusters, where elephant flows dominate and flow entropy is low, SLB can result in persistent hot spots, underutilized links, and increased tail

latency. SLB also lacks adaptability to dynamic traffic patterns, making it unsuitable for environments with bursty or synchronized workloads, which are typical of distributed training.

3. DLB improves upon SLB by considering real-time link and buffer utilization. Its modes include:

    - Assigned-flow mode: Each flow is pinned to a path for its lifetime. This is suitable for high-entropy, short-lived flows but can cause persistent congestion for long-lived elephant flows.
    - Flowlet mode: Flows are divided into flowlets (bursts separated by idle periods). Flowlets can be reassigned to less congested paths to balance responsiveness and packet ordering.
    - Per-packet mode: Each packet is independently assigned to the best path based on current link quality, maximizing utilization but requiring advanced NICs and software to handle packet reordering at the destination.

4. Flowlet-based DLB detects natural pauses in traffic (flowlets) and uses them as opportunities to reassign subsequent bursts to less congested paths. This approach balances the need for dynamic load distribution with the requirement to minimize packet reordering, making it well suited for AI/ML workloads that exhibit bursty, synchronized communication patterns (for example, gradient synchronization in distributed training).

5. GLB extends DLB by incorporating remote link quality metrics (for example, spine-to-leaf utilization) into path selection. Switches share link quality information, enabling more informed decisions that prevent bottlenecks at aggregation points. GLB is particularly effective in Clos and multi-stage topologies, where congestion can occur at intermediate layers. It reduces the risk of multiple flows converging on the same congested link, improving end-to-end bandwidth utilization and reducing tail latency.

6. Per-packet load balancing achieves nearly perfect link utilization by distributing packets across all available paths. However, it introduces packet reordering, which can degrade RDMA performance and increase CPU overhead for reassembly. Modern NICs (for example, Nvidia CX6/CX7) and DPUs can handle limited reordering for specific RDMA operations (for example, write opcodes), but excessive reordering can still impact throughput and latency. Selective per-packet spraying, enabled via ACLs and flow classification, allows administrators to balance efficiency and reliability based on workload characteristics.

7. RoCEv2 traffic often exhibits low entropy due to fixed UDP ports and similar source/destination pairs, making traditional hash-based load balancing less effective. Enhancements include incorporating RoCEv2 BTH QPair fields into the hash, using flowlet or per-packet modes, and deploying GLB to leverage remote link quality. These techniques increase flow separation, reduce collisions, and improve overall network utilization in AI/ML fabrics.

8. Strengths and weaknesses are as follows:

    - SLB: Simple and widely supported but static and prone to hot spots in low-entropy environments.

    - DLB: Adaptive, considers local link/buffer utilization, and supports flowlet/per-packet modes but may require hardware support and careful tuning.

    - GLB: Incorporates remote link quality and prevents aggregation bottlenecks but increases control-plane complexity and requires protocol enhancements.

    - TE-LB: Enables deterministic path selection and tenant isolation via policy-based routing but is complex to configure and maintain and may reduce path diversity, if overused.

    The optimal choice depends on workload characteristics, hardware capabilities, and operational requirements.

7

RoCEv2 Transport and Congestion Management

RDMA over Converged Ethernet (RoCEv2) is the most popular transport protocol used to synchronize data chunks between application buffers on distributed GPU servers of an AI/ML cluster. It uses UDP, which does not require maintaining state on the GPU NIC, as the transport protocol. Because RoCEv2 does not engage the server CPU, it scales better than any other TCP-based data transport, such as Non-Volatile Memory Express over TCP (NVMe/TCP), a protocol that is often used for traditional storage data networks. However, despite offering better parallel session scalability, RoCEv2 has entropy characteristics that present networking challenges. The traffic originating from GPUs may cause either momentary or persistent traffic congestion inside the network, resulting in slower data synchronization between GPUs.

In the previous chapter, we discussed various load-balancing techniques to better utilize the fabric. However, even with the best load-balancing mechanisms, congestion may still occur, especially in the case of local switching at a leaf, where load-balancing mechanisms are not prevalent. Also, sudden bursts in a flow can result in congestion in an otherwise well-balanced fabric. Later in this chapter, we will discuss the various congestion management techniques for RoCEv2.

Congestion Points

Let's consider congestion points in detail. With no oversubscription in the fabric and line rate traffic from servers, there is a high chance of congestion at various links in the network:

- **Local leaf link congestion:** Assume that two servers and a storage device are connected to LeafA, as shown in Figure 7-1. Both servers are sending line rate traffic toward the locally connected storage server on the same link, resulting in congestion.

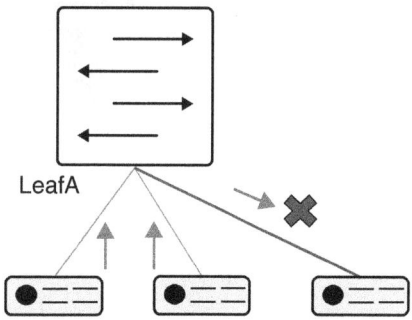

Figure 7-1
Incast congestion toward south-facing links

- **Leaf-to-spine link congestion:** Assume that two servers are connected to LeafA, as shown in Figure 7-2. Both servers are sending line rate traffic toward SpineA. The traffic is load balanced into the same link from LeafA toward SpineA, which can cause congestion in the leaf-to-spine link.

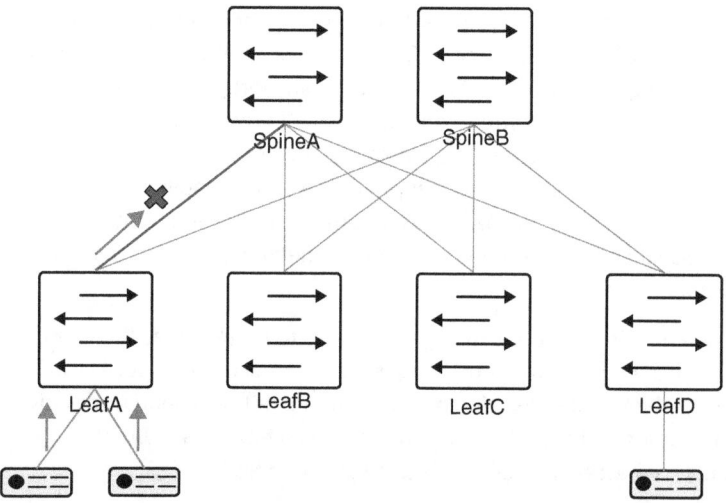

Figure 7-2
Incast congestion at an ingress leaf

- **Spine-to-leaf link congestion:** Assume that a server is connected to LeafA and another server is connected to LeafB, as shown in Figure 7-3. Both servers are sending line rate traffic. Traffic from LeafA and LeafB reaches SpineA without any congestion. However, when traffic is load balanced into the same link from SpineA toward LeafD, it can result in congestion in the spine-to-leaf link.

Congestion Points   **125**

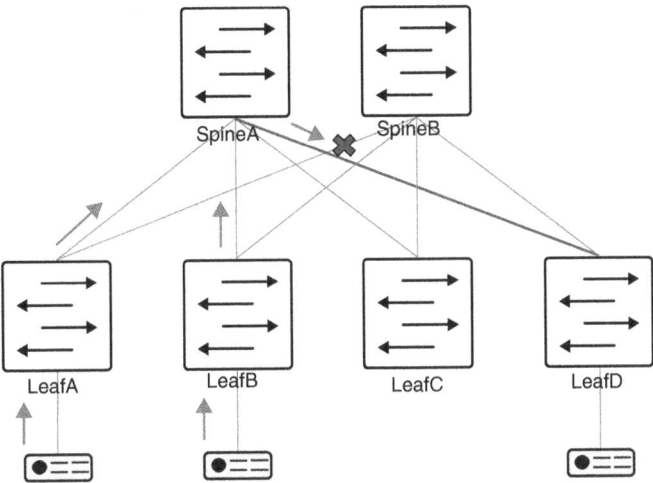

Figure 7-3
Incast congestion at a transit spine

- **Leaf-to-server link congestion:** Assume that a server is connected to LeafA and another server is connected to LeafB, as shown in Figure 7-4. Both servers are sending line rate traffic. The traffic is distributed between two spines, SpineA and SpineB, and it will reach LeafD without any congestion. However, if traffic volume is greater than the bandwidth of the link between LeafD and the server attached to it, there may be congestion in the leaf-to-server link.

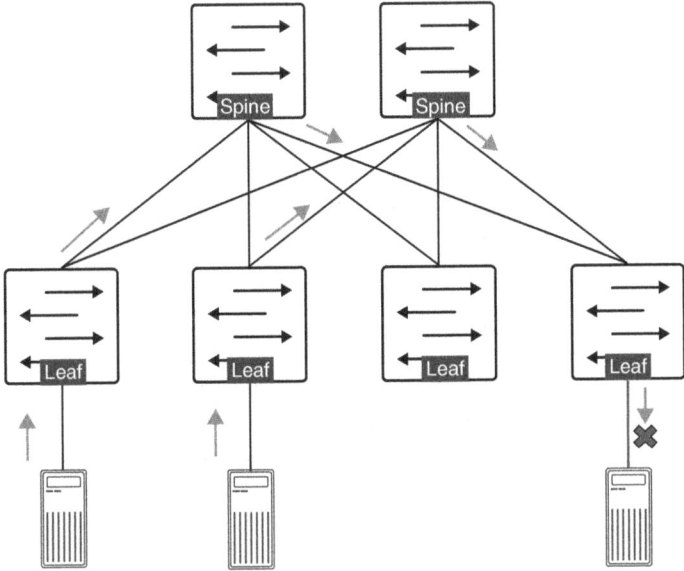

Figure 7-4
Incast congestion at an egress leaf

- **Spine-to-super spine link congestion:** Assume that a server is connected to LeafA and another server is connected to LeafB, as shown in Figure 7-5. Both servers are sending line rate traffic. Traffic from LeafA and LeafB reaches SpineA without any congestion. However, when traffic is load balanced into the same link from SpineA toward SuperSpineA, it can result in congestion in the spine-to-super spine link.

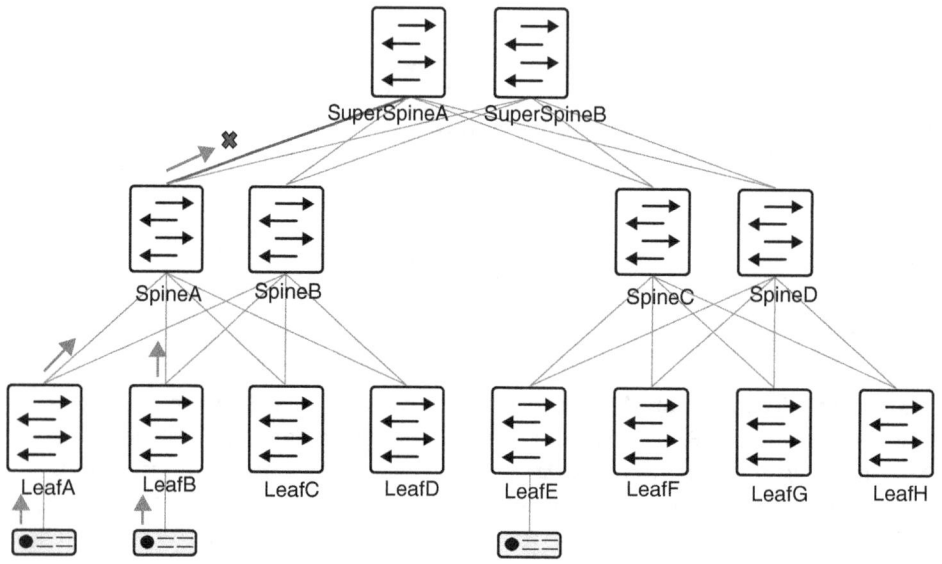

Figure 7-5
Incast congestion at the spine-to-super spine link

- **Super spine-to-spine link congestion:** Assume that a server is connected to LeafA and another server is connected to LeafB, as shown in Figure 7-6. Both servers are sending line rate traffic. Traffic from LeafA and LeafB reaches SpineA and SpineB without any congestion. Also, traffic is load balanced into the links toward SuperSpineA without congestion. However, when traffic is load balanced into the same link from SuperSpineA to SpineC, it can result in congestion in the super spine-to-spine link.

Storage networks that use RoCEv2 must be lossless. However, Ethernet is lossy. It supports two transport protocols: TCP and UDP. TCP is reliable because it uses acknowledgement to detect packet drops and retransmits lost packets. It also uses a windowing mechanism to reduce the drops in the network. UDP, on the other hand, is unreliable and more prone to losses. Therefore, Ethernet requires implementation of congestion management techniques, as we'll discuss next.

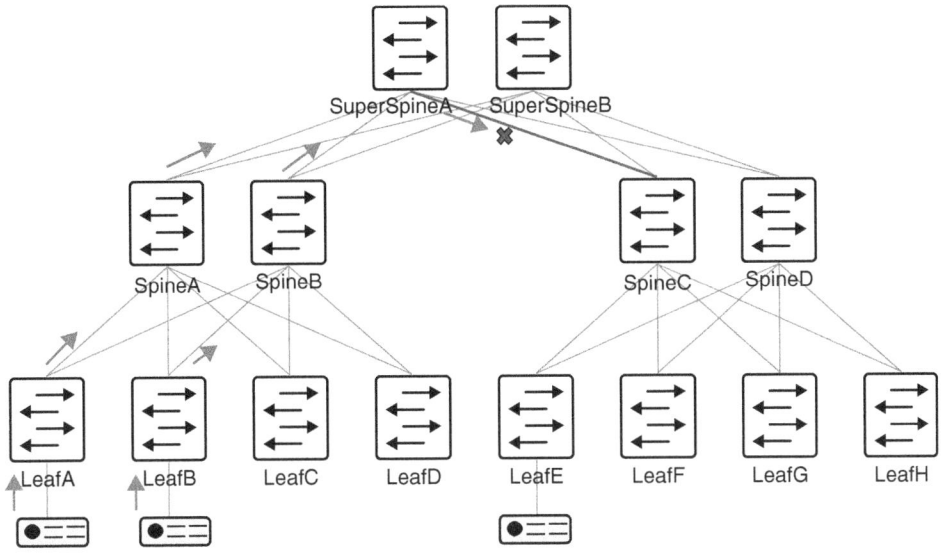

Figure 7-6
Incast congestion at the super spine-to-spine link

Explicit Congestion Notification (ECN)

Explicit Congestion Notification (ECN) enables end-to-end congestion notification between endpoints—that is, between a sender and a receiver. ECN must be enabled on both of the endpoints as well as on intermediate devices between them. The ECN threshold needs to be configured on the transit switches. Any device in the transmission path that does not have ECN enabled breaks the end-to-end ECN functionality.

ECN works with ECN bit marking and congestion notification packets (CNPs). In an IP header, there are 8 bits for Differentiated Services Code Point (DSCP). The first 6 bits are for Quality of Service (QoS) or Class of Service (CoS) marking. The last 2 bits are used for ECN marking. The first ECN bit signifies ECN-capable transport (ECT), identifying whether the transport is ECN capable. The second bit signifies congestion experienced (CE), identifying congestion on the link. Table 7-1 explains the ECN bit values.

Table 7-1 ECN Bits

ECT Bit	CE Bit	Description
0	0	The transport is not ECN capable. In the event of congestion, the packet will be dropped instead of being marked with the ECN bits.
0	1	The transport is ECN capable. This is set by the receiver toward the sender at the time the CNP is sent. ECN 01 and 10 were created as two different values for some experimental purpose. From a networking point of view, they are treated the same.

ECT Bit	CE Bit	Description
1	0	The transport ECN capability is enabled. In the event of congestion, the packet will be marked ECN instead of being dropped. This bit is set by the sender toward the receiver. It can be set by the receiver toward the sender at the time the CNP is sent.
1	1	Congestion has been experienced on the link. In the event of congestion, the router will mark the packet with the ECN bits and send it to the receiver.

The CNP is generated by the receiver or the destination server. It is a RoCEv2 frame with ECN bits set to 01. The IB BTH opcode is 129 (10000001). It contains the destination queue pair information, which helps the sender identify the flow under congestion and reduce the traffic rate for that specific flow.

Figure 7-7 illustrates the flow of packets between servers attached to LeafA and LeafD:

1. The server attached to LeafA initiates traffic flow.

2. LeafA forwards the traffic to SpineA.

3. Congestion is detected on the link between SpineA and LeafD. As a result, SpineA marks packets with the ECN bit set to 11.

4. When the ECN-marked packet reaches the receiver, it understands there is congestion along the path. It generates a CNP with the ECN bit set to 01 and sends it to the sender.

5. The sender receives the CNP, understands there is flow congestion, and reduces the rate of traffic.

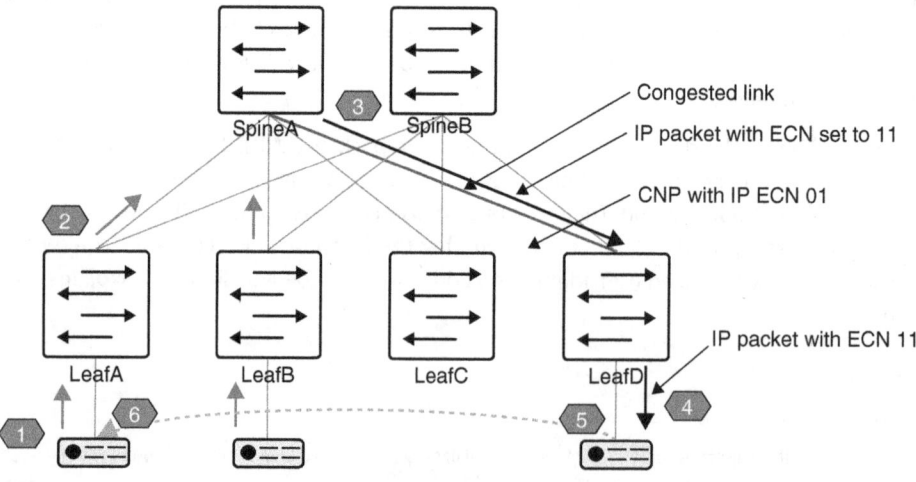

Figure 7-7
ECN behavior

Figure 7-8 shows the message flow between sender and receiver with ECN enabled.

Explicit Congestion Notification (ECN)

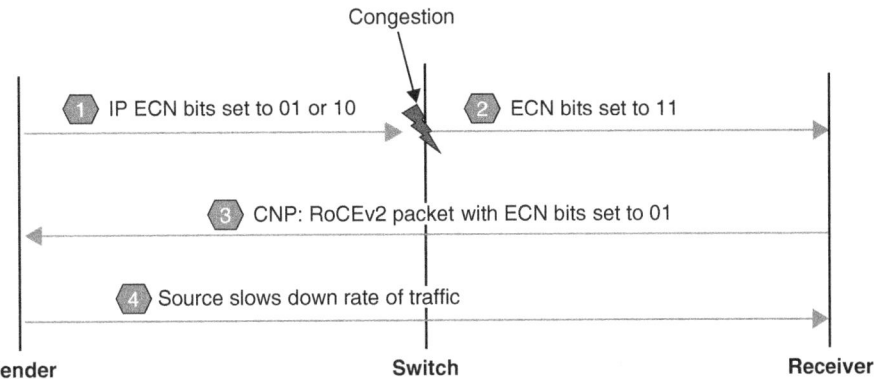

Figure 7-8
ECN-enabled data transfer

Congestion is detected based on the queue usage and an ECN threshold. Figure 7-9 illustrates the ECN threshold in a buffer. The ECN threshold is a static but configurable value. When the buffer utilization crosses this threshold, the switch marks ECN bits in the packet. The path of the packet remains the same. Beyond the threshold, the switch may apply weighted random early detection (WRED) and drop some packets, based on the buffer utilization. Operators are exploring ways to monitor ECN statistics and dynamically modify the threshold. It is possible for a number of flows to share the same queue, and ECN is evolving to support such scenarios.

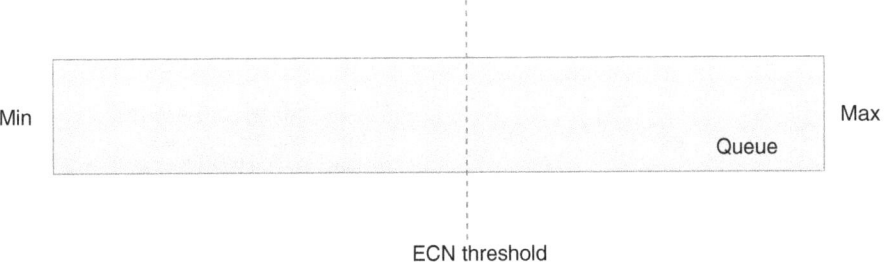

Figure 7-9
ECN threshold

While ECN is a popular congestion control mechanism, a problem with ECN is the time it takes to inform the source of the congestion. As discussed earlier, first the ECN-marked packet reaches the receiver, and then the receiver informs the source by sending a CNP. In the meantime, if the traffic continues to increase, packet drops may occur, which is not acceptable for AI/ML fabrics. Therefore, a queue with ECN enabled is referred to as a *lossy queue*.

Priority Flow Control (PFC)

Routers and switches use Priority Flow Control (PFC) in the transit path to inform the upstream hop about congestion for a traffic class. PFC uses pause frames, also referred to as XOFF frames, to control congestion. A network device generates a pause frame and sends it upstream, toward the source. The frame is generated for the class of traffic experiencing congestion such that the upstream devices stop forwarding traffic for the entire class of traffic—and not just for a flow. A queue on which PFC is configured is referred to as a *lossless queue*.

Figure 7-10 illustrates a PFC frame, which is a Layer 2 frame with the destination address set to unknown unicast. The source address is the address of the switch that generated the frame. Ether Type is set to 0x8808 to indicate a PFC frame. Priority Control Vector or class-enabled bits are used to specify which class or classes the PFC pause is requested for. Time is a 16-octet field with 2 octets for each class of traffic. It indicates the time duration for which traffic to the queue is paused. The value 0 indicates un-pause for the traffic class.

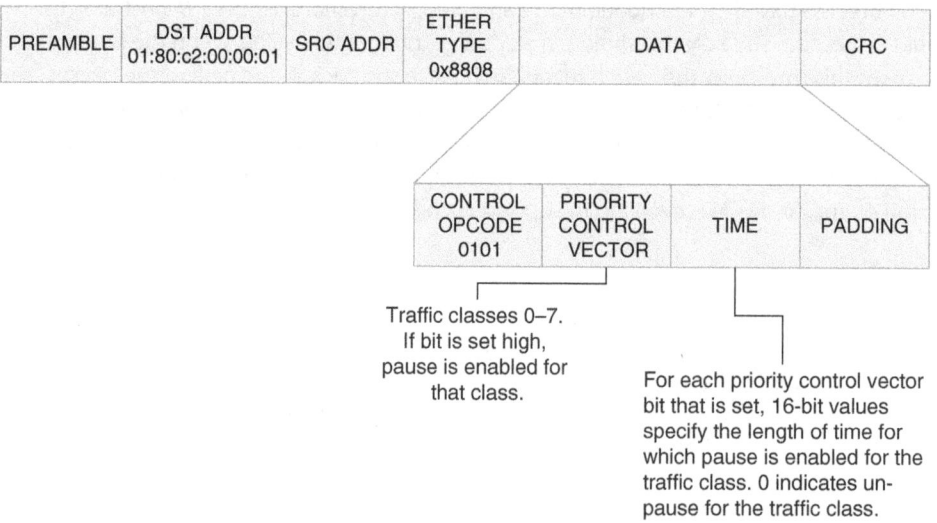

Figure 7-10
PFC frame

There are two buffer thresholds used with PFC: XOFF (Transmit Off) and XON (Transmit On). During congestion, the buffer starts to fill up due to congestion on the egress port. When buffer size crosses the XOFF threshold, a PFC pause frame is sent upstream to pause traffic associated with the class of traffic. Figure 7-11 illustrates the PFC pause, or XOFF, frame generated for the C3 class of traffic. The timer field in the frame is set to 65535 microseconds. If no further PFC pause frames are received, transmit will be turned on after this period. If new PFC pause frames are sent upstream, the timer will be reset to a new value.

```
Frame 1: 64 bytes on wire (512 bits), 64 bytes captured (512 bits) on interface \\.\pipe\view_capture_10-207-68-207_1_13_07122017_133437, id 0
Ethernet II, Src: JuniperNetwo_b7:a7:1b (10:0e:7e:b7:a7:1b), Dst: MAC-specific-ctrl-proto-01 (01:80:c2:00:00:01)
MAC Control
    Opcode: Class Based Flow Control [CBFC] Pause (0x0101)
    CBFC Class Enable Vector: 0x0008, C3
        .... .... .... ...0 = C0: False
        .... .... .... ..0. = C1: False
        .... .... .... .0.. = C2: False
        .... .... .... 1... = C3: True
        .... .... ...0 .... = C4: False
        .... .... ..0. .... = C5: False
        .... .... .0.. .... = C6: False
        .... .... 0... .... = C7: False
    CBFC Class Pause Times
        C0: 0
        C1: 0
        C2: 0
        C3: 65535
        C4: 0
        C5: 0
        C6: 0
        C7: 0
```

Figure 7-11
PFC pause, or XOFF, frame

When congestion is mitigated and buffer utilization falls below the XON threshold, an XON frame is generated and sent to the upstream switch. The switch starts the data transmission. Figure 7-12 illustrates a PFC XON frame generated for the C3 class of traffic. The frame also has the timer set to 0 microseconds, which indicates that data transmission can be resumed.

```
Frame 364: 64 bytes on wire (512 bits), 64 bytes captured (512 bits) on interface \\.\pipe\view_capture_10-207-68-207_1_13_07122017_133437, id 0
Ethernet II, Src: JuniperNetwo_b7:a7:1b (10:0e:7e:b7:a7:1b), Dst: MAC-specific-ctrl-proto-01 (01:80:c2:00:00:01)
MAC Control
    Opcode: Class Based Flow Control [CBFC] Pause (0x0101)
    CBFC Class Enable Vector: 0x0008, C3
        .... .... .... ...0 = C0: False
        .... .... .... ..0. = C1: False
        .... .... .... .0.. = C2: False
        .... .... .... 1... = C3: True
        .... .... ...0 .... = C4: False
        .... .... ..0. .... = C5: False
        .... .... .0.. .... = C6: False
        .... .... 0... .... = C7: False
    CBFC Class Pause Times
        C0: 0
        C1: 0
        C2: 0
        C3: 0
        C4: 0
        C5: 0
        C6: 0
        C7: 0
```

Figure 7-12
PFC XON frame

Figure 7-13 illustrates the flow of packets with PFC implemented:

1. The server attached to LeafA initiates the packet flow.

2. LeafA forwards the packets toward SpineA.

3. Congestion is detected in the link from SpineA to LeafD, based on the queue usage and PFC threshold.

4. SpineA sends a PFC pause, or XOFF, frame for the queue under congestion. For each packet that crosses the XOFF threshold, an XOFF frame is generated.

5. LeafA receives the PFC pause frame and pauses the class of traffic in the congested queue for the duration set for the timer field in the pause frame. Also, LeafA sends the PFC pause frame downstream toward the server.

6. Upon receiving the PFC pause frame, the server also pauses the flow for the duration set for the timer field in the pause frame.

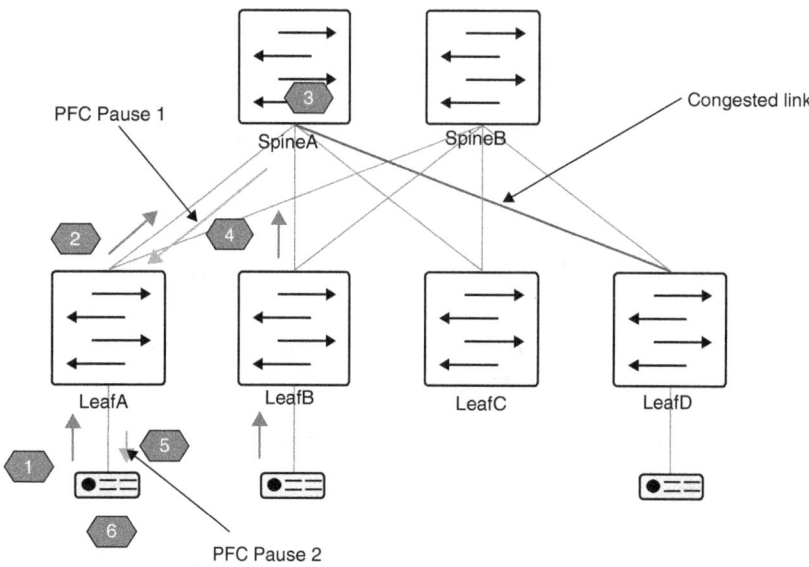

Figure 7-13
PFC behavior

Figure 7-14 illustrates threshold levels for XOFF and XON. The thresholds must be configured appropriately for an environment. XOFF should not be set to the maximum buffer size, or traffic drops may occur before congestion control activates. XOFF also should not be set too low, or PFC might pause the traffic for a class at lower queue utilization. The XON threshold should not be set to the minimum buffer size, as this setting may result in delayed traffic transmission once congestion is mitigated. It is a good idea to monitor the PFC statistics and adjust the thresholds. The XOFF value can either be configured directly or controlled via the alpha configuration, based on the chipsets.

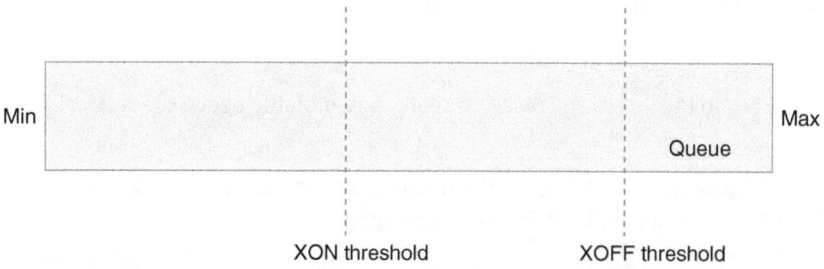

Figure 7-14
XOFF and XON thresholds

Explicit Congestion Notification (ECN)

There are a few issues with PFC, though. The first problem is that PFC is designed to stop the traffic for the entire class experiencing congestion and not just the flow; this results in unfairness and head-of-line blocking, and it eventually leads to poor application performance.

Second, in some instances, the switch may receive excessive PFC pause frames from the downstream switch. The switch in turn propagates these PFC pause frames to its upstream neighbors toward the source. This results in a back-pressure mechanism propagating to the whole network, stopping the network traffic, and causing congestion and packet loss. This situation is referred to as a *PFC storm* and must be mitigated.

PFC watchdog is a technology that detects and mitigates PFC storms. PFC watchdog monitors the PFC pause frames received for each port and triggers mitigation actions when a PFC storm is detected. PFC watchdog has three functional blocks: detection, mitigation, and restoration. Figure 7-15 illustrates a simplified topology where PFC watchdog optimization is implemented for an AI/ML data center fabric.

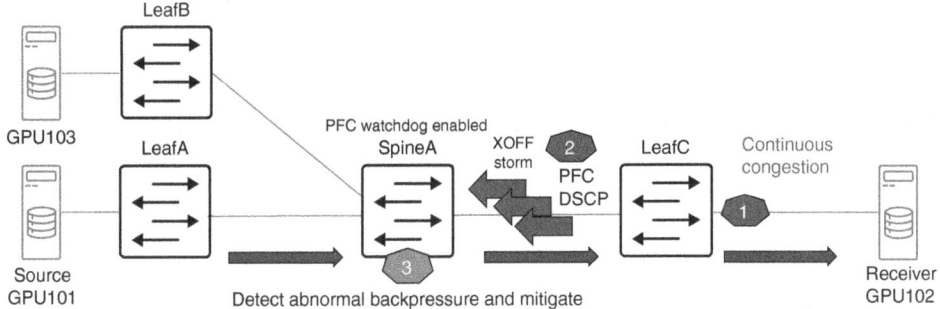

Figure 7-15
PFC watchdog

Figure 7-15 illustrates three steps:

1. **Detection:** SpineA receives PFC pause frames from LeafC, and as the queue continues to fill up, the pause frames get propagated. As LeafC continues to send PFC frames, SpineA continues to propagate them to all switches in the path toward the source (for example, LeafA). This results in a pause of traffic of the same class from LeafB. This, in turn, results in blockage conditions on all of the switches. PFC watchdog monitors the PFC pause frames received for each port and compares them with a configurable threshold. If the threshold is exceeded, the port is marked as being in a PFC storm.

2. **Mitigation:** When a queue has a PFC storm, PFC watchdog can choose to either drop or forward packets in that queue. If it chooses to drop, this is what it needs to do:

   - Discard all the packets that are already in the output queue.

   - Discard any new packets that are meant for the output queue.

- Discard any new packets that come from the same priority group as this queue, including any pause frames. This limits propagation of the pause frame to the neighbor to signal congestion in this output queue.

Dropping is the most commonly used mitigation technique.

If PFC watchdog chooses to forward the packets, the queue ignores the PFC frames that are received. It forwards all the packets that are meant for the queue as well as the packets that were already in the queue.

Spine1 in Figure 7-15 receives PFC pause frames from LeafC, and as the queue continues to fill up, the pause frames are propagated. When PFC watchdog detects abnormality, Spine1 clears the queue and discards further PFC frames received from LeafC. As a result, the PFC pause frame is not sent to LeafA.

3. **Restoration:** PFC watchdog monitors the port that is impacted by the PFC storm and unpauses the traffic when the received PFC pause frames are below a configurable threshold. This ensures that the device resumes lossless Ethernet functionality.

Data Center Quantized Congestion Notification (DCQCN)

As discussed earlier, both ECN and PFC face challenges with respect to performance. Whereas ECN is lossy, PFC is lossless, but it can result in unfairness. DCQCN combines ECN and PFC over DSCP to achieve better performance.

Figure 7-16 illustrates an example of ECN and PFC thresholds with DCQCN. ECN is normally configured below the PFC XOFF threshold. When the buffer utilization increases beyond the ECN threshold, the switch marks ECN bits in the packets of that flow. The packet continues its path to the destination. The destination acknowledges the ECN marking and generates a CNP toward the sender. The sender reduces the rate of traffic. If the buffer utilization continues to increase and crosses the PFC threshold, a PFC pause frame is triggered. The PFC frame is sent hop-by-hop upstream toward the source.

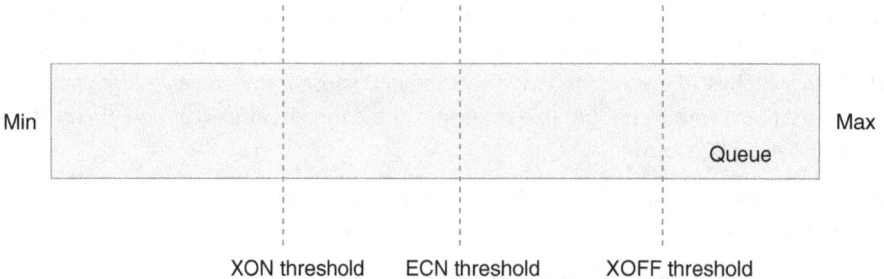

Figure 7-16
ECN and PFC thresholds

Data Center Quantized Congestion Notification (DCQCN)

This is the sequence of steps that occur when the switch receives a PFC pause frame:

1. The PFC frame is received on an egress interface.
2. The switch pauses traffic in the corresponding egress queue.
3. A lossless buffer build-up causes a breach of the PFC XOFF threshold on corresponding ingress ports.
4. An ingress port generates a PFC pause frame toward the upstream node.

This continues hop-by-hop until the PFC reaches the sender, assuming that all transit nodes have PFC configured.

Figure 7-17 illustrates the DCQCN behavior. When the SpineA-to-LeafD queue buffer utilization exceeds the ECN threshold, SpineA marks the ECN bits in the packets and forwards them to the destination server attached to LeafD. As the server receives the ECN 11 bits, it acknowledges them with a CNP to the sender (the source of the write/read) attached to LeafA. Congestion mitigation occurs only when the sender receives the CNP and reduces the rate of traffic. In the meantime, if the buffer utilization crosses the PFC threshold, SpineA sends a PFC frame to LeafA that pauses the traffic on the egress queue. LeafA pauses the flow of traffic for the class of traffic and sends a PFC pause frame to the source.

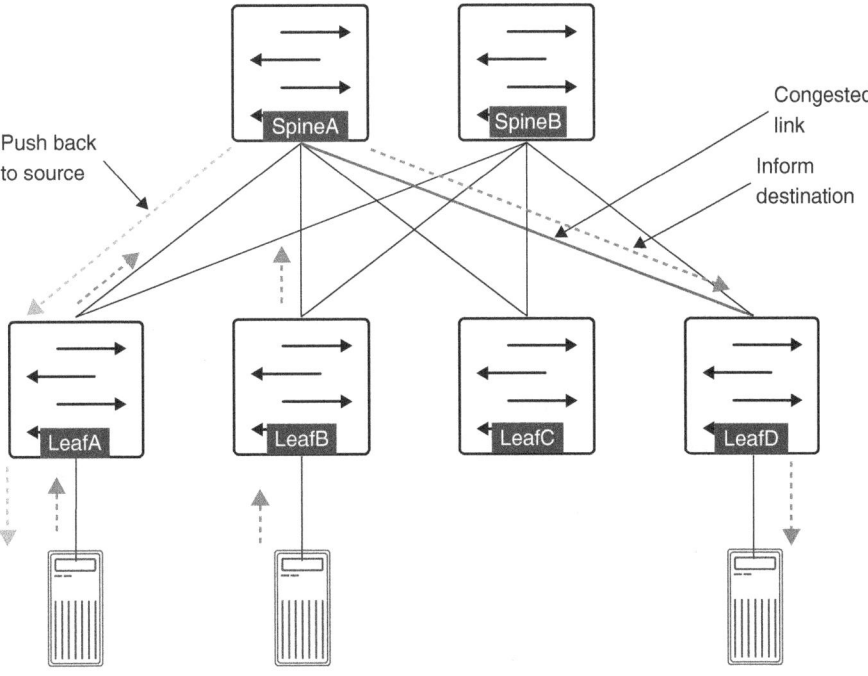

Figure 7-17
DCQCN behavior

In summary, while ECN congestion mitigation is slower than PFC, PFC results in a higher impact on traffic because it pauses the traffic for an entire class and not just the flow. Therefore, the ECN threshold is kept lower than the PFC threshold. If the congestion situation is resolved by ECN, the other flows of the queue remain unaffected. But if the congestion situation worsens quickly, PFC is triggered, and it provides congestion mitigation before any packet loss occurs.

Most setups implement ECN for congestion control. The implementation for PFC varies. In some setups it might not be configured at all, while in others it may be configured only on leaf switches and servers. PFC may be configured on all nodes as well. The implementation depends on the environment and the service-level agreement (SLA) that is in place.

Source Flow Control (SFC)

Source Flow Control (SFC), which is specified in a new IETF standard (802.1qdw), is also referred to as Source PFC. Whereas PFC goes hop-by-hop, SFC directly sends the congestion signal from the congested switch to the source. The congested switch can trim the packet payload and reverse the source and destination in the header. The packet payload is then sent directly to the source. This prevents the congestion mitigation delay that occurs in ECN, where the ECN marked packet is first sent to the destination, which then sends a CNP to the source. Also, because SFC is flow based, it also prevents the class-level impact that occurs with PFC.

Figure 7-18 illustrates the flow of packets for SFC:

1. The server attached to LeafA initiates the packet flow.

2. LeafA forwards the flow toward SpineA.

3. Congestion is detected in the link between SpineA and LeafD, based on the queue usage and the SFC threshold.

4. SpineA sends SFC signals for the flow experiencing congestion. An SFC signal is created with the source and destination IP addresses reversed. This signal is destined to the source of the flow.

5. LeafA receives the SFC signal. It may intercept the signal and take actions such as pausing the traffic in the queue or take another action (for an area under exploration). LeafA can either forward the SFC signal downstream toward the server if the server NIC supports SFC or can translate it to PFC before forwarding.

6. Upon receiving the SFC signal or PFC pause frame, the server pauses the flow for the duration marked by the timer field in the frame.

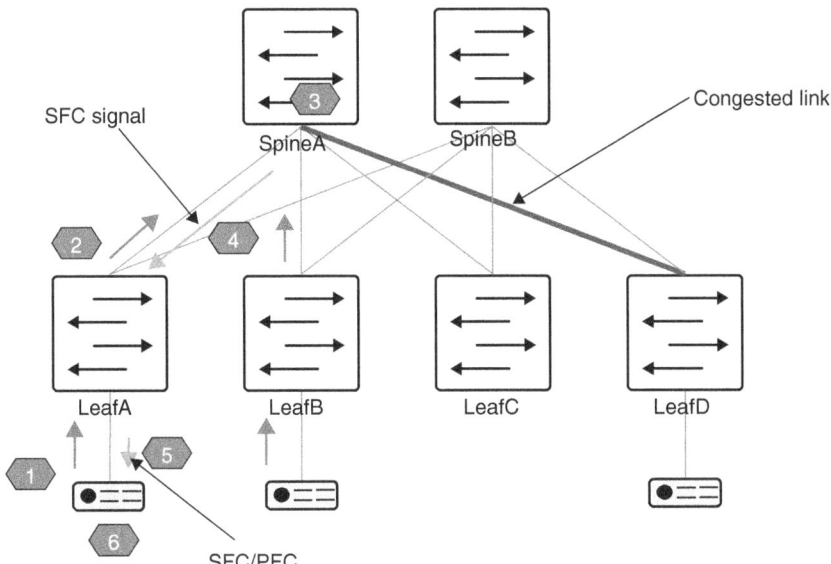

Figure 7-18
Source Flow Control (SFC)

Congestion Signaling

A new draft submitted to the IETF (draft-ravi-ippm-csig-01) talks about Congestion Signaling (CSIG). CSIG provides direct, real-time, in-band signals that network control loops can incorporate for performance and efficiency. It uses in-band network telemetry (INT) features on the switches that incorporate multi-bit signals in live data packets. It provides a simple low-overhead and extensible packet header mechanism to obtain fixed-length summaries from bottleneck devices along a packet path. This summarized information is collected over Layer 2 CSIG tags along the path. Receivers can reflect this information to senders via CSIG reflection headers. CSIG could be the next phase in congestion management that has traditionally been handled via PFC and ECN.

Figure 7-19 illustrates CSIG congestion mitigation. The CSIG signal is generated by the source server, GPU1. On each hop, the CSIG tags get added to the signal. Destination GPU2 receives the signal with CSIG tags from each hop. The destination server sends this signal with all the tags to the source. The source adjusts the traffic based on the information received.

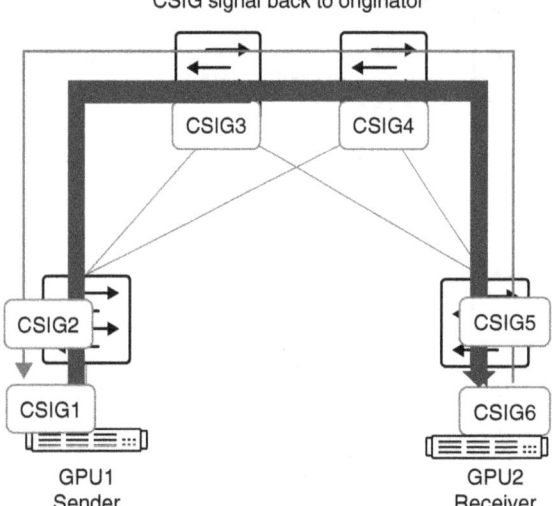

End-to-end congestion control with CSIG updated at each hop

Figure 7-19
Congestion Signaling (CSIG)

These are some of the key points of the CSIG draft:

- A new CSIG tag includes congestion management information.
- CSIG quickly identifies path bottlenecks and suggests better path selection.
- A CSIG tag is between the Layer 2 and Layer 3 headers. Hence, the IEEE needs to allocate a new Ethernet tag.
- Servers are informed end-to-end via the CSIG reflection function.

Figure 7-20 illustrates the frame of a CSIG tag, and Figure 7-21 shows the information contained in the CSIG tag.

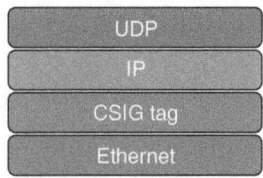

Figure 7-20
CSIG frame

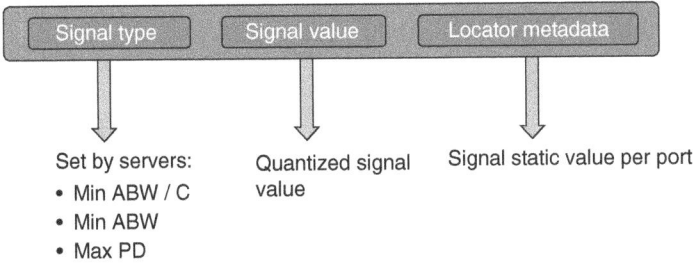

Figure 7-21
CSIG tag information

The locator metadata contains the following information:

- Capacity of the bottlenecks
- Stage of the bottlenecks
- Device ID
- Link identification (uplink or downlink)

Congestion Signaling is new but has good potential and will evolve with time.

Summary

In an AI/ML network, congestion can be mitigated using ECN (Explicit Congestion Notification), PFC (Priority Flow Control), or DCQCN (Data Center Quantized Congestion Notification) mechanisms. All these mechanisms avoid persistent congestion by sending signals to the source, which can then slow the data rate temporarily. The frequent use of the PFC over DSCP techniques may, however, result in a significant reduction in the speed of data exchange.

It is important to enable efficient load-balancing techniques that minimize the risk of congestion. Also, additional mitigation techniques such as the PFC watchdog must be implemented to avoid persistent deterioration of application performance that results from an avalanche of PFC pushbacks. Alternatively, in situations where PFC is likely to be triggered frequently, it is simply better to implement only ECN techniques and focus on efficient fabric load balancing, thereby reducing the probability of congestion.

Test Your Knowledge

Chapter Review

The following questions are designed to test your understanding of the content covered in Chapter 7. Following the questions, answers are provided so you can verify your conclusions.

Questions

1. What is RoCEv2, and how does it enable RDMA over Ethernet in AI/ML clusters?
2. Describe the main congestion points in RoCEv2-based AI data center networks and their impact on performance.
3. How does Explicit Congestion Notification (ECN) function in RoCEv2 fabrics, and what are its operational parameters?
4. Explain Priority Flow Control (PFC) and its limitations in lossless Ethernet fabrics for AI/ML.
5. What is Data Center Quantized Congestion Notification (DCQCN), and how does it combine ECN and PFC for end-to-end congestion control?
6. How does Source Flow Control (SFC) differ from traditional PFC, and what are its advantages in RoCEv2 fabrics?
7. Describe the role and operation of Congestion Signaling (CSIG) and in-band telemetry in RoCEv2-based AI fabrics.
8. Summarize the relationship between ECN, PFC, DCQCN, and the newer SFC in achieving lossless, high-performance RoCEv2 fabrics for AI/ML.

Answers

1. RoCEv2 (RDMA over Converged Ethernet version 2) encapsulates RDMA traffic in UDP/IP packets, enabling RDMA capabilities over standard Ethernet networks. It leverages lossless Ethernet features (for example, PFC, ECN) to provide low-latency, high-throughput, zero-copy data transfers between servers, bypassing the CPU and kernel. RoCEv2 is widely used in AI/ML clusters for distributed training, where rapid synchronization of large data volumes is required.

2. Congestion can occur at multiple points:
   - Local leaf link congestion: Multiple servers sending line-rate traffic to a local storage or compute node
   - Leaf-to-spine and spine-to-leaf congestion: Multiple flows converging on the same uplink/downlink, especially in Clos topologies

- Leaf-to-server congestion: Oversubscription or bursty traffic exceeding NIC or server bandwidth
- Spine-to-super spine congestion: Aggregation points in multi-stage fabrics
- Congestion at any point can cause packet loss, increased latency, and degraded JCT, especially for synchronized AI/ML workloads.

3. ECN enables end-to-end congestion signaling by marking packets when switch buffer utilization exceeds a configurable threshold. Marked packets trigger the receiver to send a congestion notification packet (CNP) to the sender, which then reduces its transmission rate. ECN thresholds must be carefully tuned to balance responsiveness and avoid excessive packet drops. ECN is effective for early congestion detection but may be too slow for microbursts or rapid congestion events.

4. PFC is a link-layer mechanism that pauses traffic for specific classes when buffer thresholds are exceeded, preventing packet loss. It operates on a per-priority basis, using XOFF/XON frames to control flow. Limitations include head-of-line blocking (pausing all flows in a class), risk of PFC storms (cascading pauses), and unfairness (one flow can block others). PFC must be carefully configured to avoid deadlocks and ensure fairness in high-throughput AI/ML environments.

5. DCQCN is a hybrid congestion control protocol for RoCEv2, combining ECN (for early, end-to-end signaling) and PFC (for lossless link-layer flow control). DCQCN uses ECN marks to adjust sender rates via a quantized feedback loop, reducing transmission rates before PFC is triggered. If congestion persists, PFC provides immediate lossless backpressure. DCQCN requires NIC and switch support, and its parameters (for example, ECN/PFC thresholds, rate reduction factors) must be tuned for optimal performance.

6. SFC (Source Flow Control) is a new IETF standard that allows congested switches to send congestion signals directly to the source, bypassing hop-by-hop PFC propagation. SFC can trim packet payloads and reverse source/destination headers, enabling faster, flow-based congestion mitigation. Unlike PFC, which operates at the class level, SFC targets specific flows, reducing head-of-line blocking and improving fairness.

7. CSIG is an emerging mechanism that embeds multi-bit congestion signals in live data packets using in-band network telemetry (INT). Switches add CSIG tags indicating buffer occupancy, congestion stage, and device/link IDs. Receivers reflect this information to senders, enabling real-time, path-aware congestion management. CSIG supports fine-grained, low-overhead congestion detection and can inform adaptive routing and rate control algorithms.

8. ECN provides early, end-to-end congestion signaling, enabling proactive rate reduction. PFC ensures lossless transport at the link layer but can cause head-of-line blocking and PFC storms if overused. DCQCN integrates ECN and PFC, using quantized feedback to adjust sender rates and minimize PFC activation. SFC offers fast, flow-based congestion mitigation, reducing reliance on class-based PFC. Together, these mechanisms provide a layered approach to congestion management, balancing responsiveness, fairness, and lossless operation in high-throughput, synchronized AI/ML workloads.

8

IP Routing for AI/ML Fabrics

The key technologies used in AI data centers today are load-balancing efficiency techniques (such as dynamic load balancing and global load balancing), congestion management Data Center Quantized Congestion Notification (DCQCN) techniques (such as Priority Flow Control DSCP and Explicit Congestion Notification), and RDMA over Converged Ethernet version 2 (RoCEv2). However, the dynamic IP routing protocol is also an essential factor to assess when working on a new network engineering project. Making the IP routing protocol more plug-and-play can have an impact on the convergence, scale, and simplicity of deployments, much as it does in InfiniBand networks. From a topology perspective, most AI data center cluster deployments use IP Clos three-stage/five-stage fabrics; more demanding projects might use newer topologies such as DragonFly+ and full mesh in order to reduce the number of hops for better latency or to optimize the north–south bandwidth usage. In all of these cases, there must be a decision about which dynamic IP routing protocol to use. Sometimes this decision is driven by the type of topology, sometimes by the target scale, and sometimes by the organization's experience with a specific IP routing protocol.

In this chapter, we will evaluate the existing well-known IP Clos dynamic routing approaches used frequently by cloud providers (as described in RFC 7938: Use of BGP for Routing in Large-Scale Data Centers) but in the context of AI data center deployments. We will also consider emerging BGP technologies, such as BGP DPF (BGP Deterministic Path Forwarding) and BGP Link Bandwidth Extended Community, as well as how an IGP-based IP routing using RIFT (Routing in Fat Tree) and IS-IS flood reflections can simplify and optimize the AI data center.

BGP in the context of data center multi-tier fabric has become the most popular deployment option in many cloud providers' data center networks to connect regular compute nodes. In the context of GPU server connectivity, additional requirements have emerged to leverage even more links between nodes and added queue-level awareness besides the link to control and adapt to best-performance conditions. Link- or queue-level awareness is not a native characteristic of the BGP routing protocol. BGP was originally designed for service IP prefix advertisement, so for the data center use case, BGP is fine-tuned to behave like an interior gateway protocol (IGP); for example, it might advertise IP prefixes with a bandwidth community to influence the routing decision process (using route policies) based on link speeds, or it might keep the BGP AS-PATH attribute length the same at each level of the fabric topology.

In this chapter we will also review the key pros and cons of traditional IP routing protocols (such as BGP and IS-IS) and emerging routing protocols (such as RIFT). Before we get there, we will dig into the details of BGP options that may be useful for the concise deployment of backend AI/ML cluster fabric.

Dynamic IP Routing Options

The choice of the dynamic IP routing protocol to use in an AI data center depends on several factors, including scalability, performance, reliability, and security. Some of the commonly used protocols are BGP (including eBGP and iBGP Border Gateway Protocol), IS-IS (Intermediate System to Intermediate System), and OSPFv2/OSPFv3 (Open Shortest Path First).

Each of these protocols has unique advantages and disadvantages, and the optimal solution depends on the network topology, traffic patterns, and management requirements.

OSPF is a link-state protocol that floods the network with information about the links and their states. It uses the Dijkstra algorithm to compute the shortest path to each destination. OSPF is widely adopted in large-scale networks, as it supports hierarchical design, load balancing, fast convergence, and authentication. However, in WAN core IP enterprise networks, BGP took the lead among different routing protocols, particularly in data center fabrics. OSPF has some drawbacks that make it less suitable for data center fabrics, such as high memory requirements and CPU consumption when an intensive flood of routing updates occurs (which is not a problem with today's multi-core CPU switches). In addition, OSPF involves complex configuration and troubleshooting, and it is vulnerable to routing loops, whereas routing loop prevention is built into BGP and RIFT (Routing in Fat Trees).

While it is simple to implement routing protocols for OSPF/IS-IS (by just enabling them on the appropriate links), there are fewer IP routing traffic engineering options. When there's no real need to enable any route policy and no need to enable traffic engineering for each prefix, IGPs such as OSPFv3 or IS-IS may still be relevant to simplify the way IP-routed underlay is put in place; however, this was not sufficient to get better traction in the data center context, and OSPF and IS-IS became less popular compared to BGP implementations in data centers.

IS-IS is another link-state protocol that shares many similarities with OSPF, but it has some notable differences. IS-IS uses a single protocol for both IPv4 and IPv6, whereas OSPF requires separate instances for each address family. IS-IS also uses a simpler metric system, based on link bandwidth, as opposed to the arbitrary cost values that OSPF uses. IS-IS is often preferred in service provider networks, as it is more scalable and stable than OSPF. However, IS-IS is less familiar and supported than OSPF in the data center and enterprise industry, so it may have compatibility issues with some devices and applications in a multi-vendor data center fabric.

BGP is a path-vector protocol that exchanges information about the reachability and attributes of different autonomous systems. It is the standard protocol for interdomain routing, as it allows for policy-based routing, traffic engineering, and multihoming. BGP can also be used for intradomain routing, especially in data center networks, where it offers simplicity, scalability, and flexibility. BGP can support various network topologies, such as Clos, DragonFly+, and full mesh, and it uses various criteria, including latency, bandwidth, and hop count, to select the optimal path. However, BGP also has some limitations, including slow convergence and complex configuration.

In conclusion, there is no definitive answer to which dynamic IP routing protocol is the most suitable to implement in AI data centers. The decision should be based on a careful analysis of the network's requirements, characteristics, and constraints, as well as a comparison of the benefits and drawbacks of each protocol. A possible approach is to use a hybrid solution, where different protocols are deployed in different layers or segments of the network, to achieve the optimal balance between efficiency and flexibility.

eBGP Underlay for Three-Stage/Five-Stage Fabric for an AI Data Center

In an AI data center network, there could be different dynamic IP routing protocols in the backend, where the GPU/NIC servers are connected for AI/ML training purposes, and in the frontend, where the inference is happening with the trained model deployed next to the regular IP storage (either using the RoCEv2 transport and DCQCN control, as in a backend network, or with different transport options for data storage over IP—such as iSCSI, NVMEoTCP, or iWARP). We discuss these options in Chapter 3, "Network Design Considerations."

It is possible to have different scenarios regarding the type of IP routing protocols or different options within the same routing protocol. For example, even if we were using an eBGP three-stage/five-stage deployment in both the backend and frontend AI data center networks, the BGP capabilities and service might be different in those distinct routing domains; the backend might run native IP eBGP without any overlays, whereas the frontend might be enabled with overlays to support multi-tenancy. In this case, the frontend could be enabled with EVPN-VXLAN eBGP on top of the underlay eBGP, and the backend could be enabled with eBGP with global load balancing or BGP Link Bandwidth Extended Community. Similarly, for the IP ECMP setting and load balancing, the backend might use weighted IP ECMP combined with bandwidth community advertisements, whereas the frontend might use regular IP ECMP with the same next-hop BGP weights and limited adaptive routing capabilities.

eBGP Underlay and BGP Unnumbered

One of the popular IP routing approaches in AI data center fabric is to use eBGP combined with the BGP unnumbered implementation specified in RFC 5549 to simplify and automate the way peerings are established between leaf and spine nodes. With this approach, typically, the admin relies significantly on IPv6 link-local addressing, which is unique at each segment/link of the fabric topology because it's derived from the interface MAC address (and is also unique per interface at each node). With this type of BGP implementation, the admin only needs to define the BGP ASNs (Autonomous System Numbers) for different levels of the topology and define in the automation tool the ToR's unique ASNs, either from the 16-bit private range (64512 to 65535) or the 32-bit ASN private range (4200000000 to 4294967294). With this approach, most of the peering establishment tasks are done automatically, and the admin just needs to define which local node server prefixes are to be advertised to the rest of the nodes in the fabric.

Alternatively, the admin can define a simple route policy rule that all the locally connected interfaces advertise into the BGP protocol. This means all GPU NIC server prefixes will get full IP reachability in a much simpler way. The key point to understand here is that instead of using the traditional IPv4 BGP next-hop attribute, the IPv4 server or services prefixes will be advertised by the switches using the IPv6 link-local address as the next hop. This means that between two ToR switches, the eBGP spine device will, by default, perform the BGP next-hop rewrite and change for the given server prefix the IP next hop to the local value and update the AS-PATH attribute, adding the local ASN after the ASN of the switch node that originated the IP prefix.

The rewrite of the next hop would not happen with an iBGP approach with route reflectors at the spines and where all switches in the fabric are using the same ASN. This is not a very popular approach for most cloud providers because, with a unique ToR ASN, the prefixes are easier to identify from the origin perspective. Still, it's easier to eventually enable additional route policing in the event that some server prefixes are removed from operation temporarily for maintenance purposes. It's much simpler to include a route policy that isolates specific switch nodes from the rest of the fabric or that accepts just prefixes coming from a subset of nodes from the same fabric. In the context of data center fabric, this method is mainly interesting for maintenance purposes or from a security perspective. You could easily define the ranges of ASNs and accept the length of AS-PATH that corresponds to the diameter of the AI data center fabric (for example, with up to two ASNs in the AS-PATH attribute).

Figure 8-1 shows the BGP session-establishment process using the "unnumbered approach" of IPv6 link-local addresses. You can see how information is initially exchanged at the link level with the IPv6 neighbor solicitation message and neighbor advertisement, followed by the router advertisement information containing the ICMPv6 info on the link-local address and MAC address of the neighbor. Only after this phase is complete is the BGP TCP session establishment initiated by the routing daemon of spine1 and leaf1.

To better understand the initial phase of the BGP session establishment, let's analyze the Open message content, where the given switch capabilities are advertised—not only those that are BGP unnumbered related but also many other capabilities, such as GR (Graceful Restart). If the peering node cannot work with these switch capabilities, when it's enabled, a less relaxed session establishment approach will typically just tear down the BGP peering by sending the notification BGP messages. In our lab, that didn't happen because the spine1 and leaf1 nodes could support the next-hop extension where the IPv4 destination prefix is advertised with an IPv6 link-local address.

eBGP Underlay for Three-Stage/Five-Stage Fabric for an AI Data Center   **147**

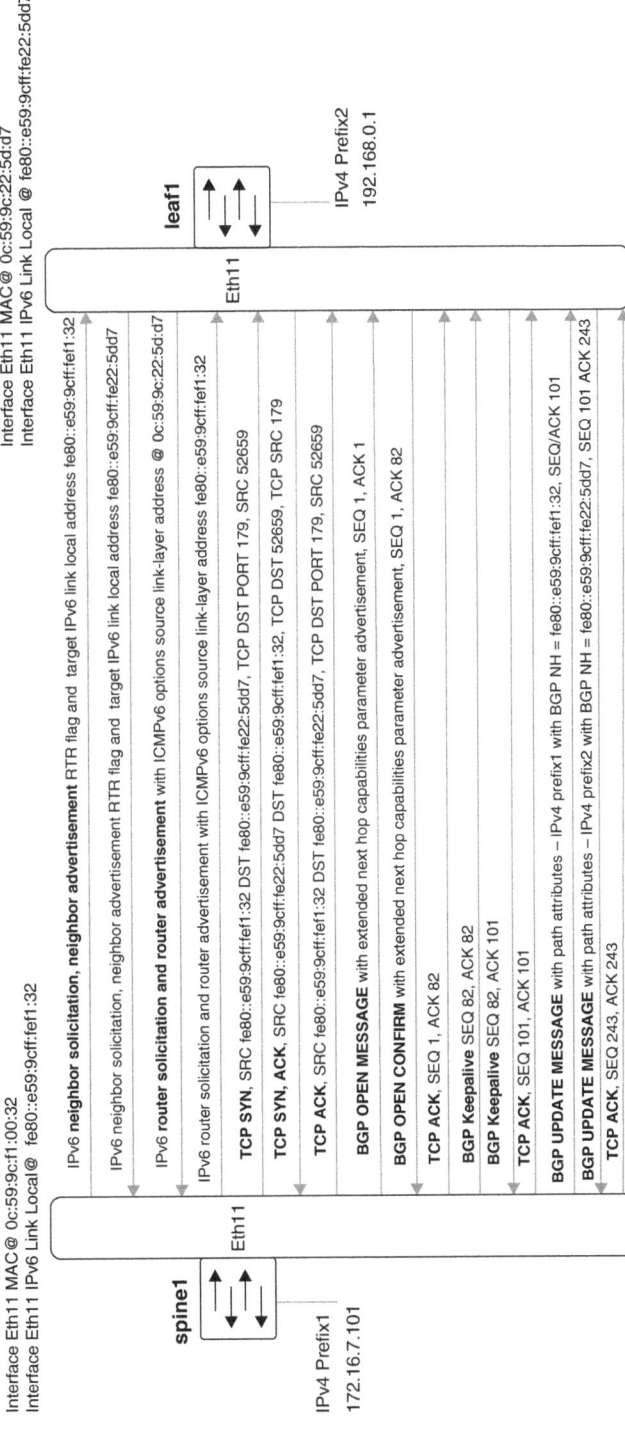

Figure 8-1
eBGP session establishment using BGP unnumbered

Figure 8-2 shows a packet capture from the Open message where the spine1 node advertised many different capabilities and where we highlight the Extended Next Hop Encoding capability, which neighboring BGP switch nodes need to agree on before starting to exchange the IPv4 and IPv6 destination prefixes over the IPv6 peerings in the context of BGP unnumbered.

Figure 8-2 also highlights the optional capability parameters, which indicate that for Extended Next Hop Encoding in particular, the BGP TCP session would come up anyway.

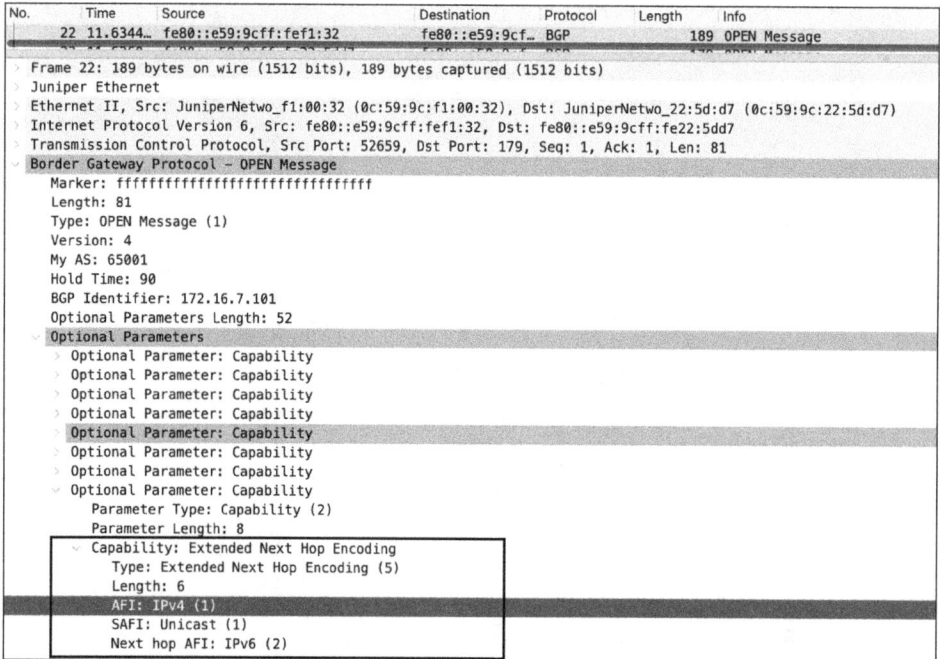

Figure 8-2
BGP Open message with an Extended Next Hop Encoding advertisement

Figure 8-3 shows the next packet view in the context of BGP unnumbered–based routing—the Update message, which is the main message to advertise the server and services prefixes.

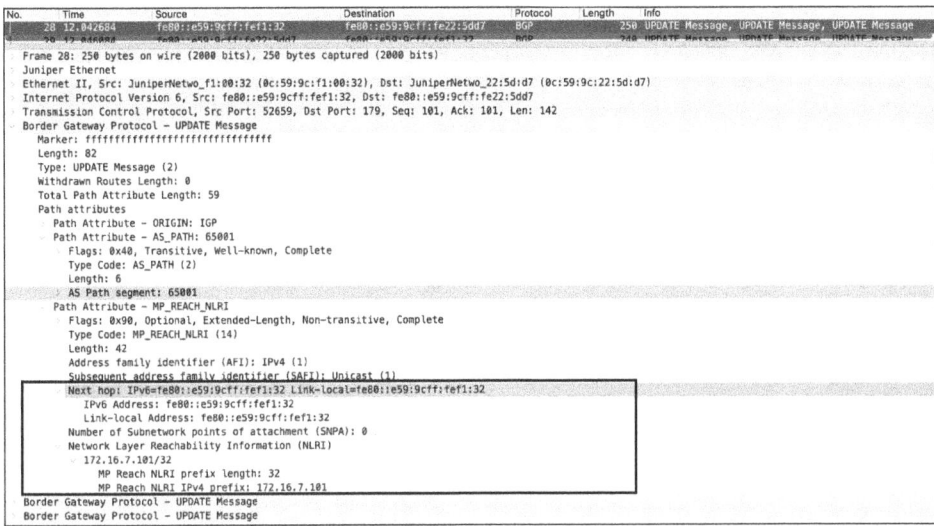

Figure 8-3
BGP Update message with an IPv4 prefix advertisement and IPv6 next-hop information

As you can see, the NLRI IP prefix of the server is an IPv4 address, but the next-hop information is an IPv6 link-local address.

BGP ASN Allocation

BGP unnumbered simplifies the establishment of BGP sessions. For example, there is no longer a need to assign point-to-point IPv4 addresses on each link, thanks to IPv6 link-local addressing, which is used on each link and advertised to neighboring nodes via the ICMPv6 Neighbor and Router Advertisement messages. This can be particularly useful in an AI data center backend Ethernet IP fabric, where many links are typically activated between the leaf and spine to achieve a 1:1 ratio of bandwidth oversubscription. However, some planning is still required to decide which BGP ASN type and which numbers will be used for the ToR leaf switch and spines and super spines within the fabric. The need to specify the neighbor's peer ASN can be eliminated by defining the range of ASNs; although the local ASN must be set, this can be easily automated, and the rest of the BGP configurations can remain intact.

With the eBGP approach shown in Figure 8-4, where each spine uses the same ASN and each rack switch uses a different ASN, you can easily prevent suboptimal forwarding from occurring in the event of a link failure. This is possible thanks to the default BGP loop-prevention mechanism, which won't accept prefixes with an AS-PATH attribute that contains two instances of the same BGP ASN as it considers this a potential routing loop.

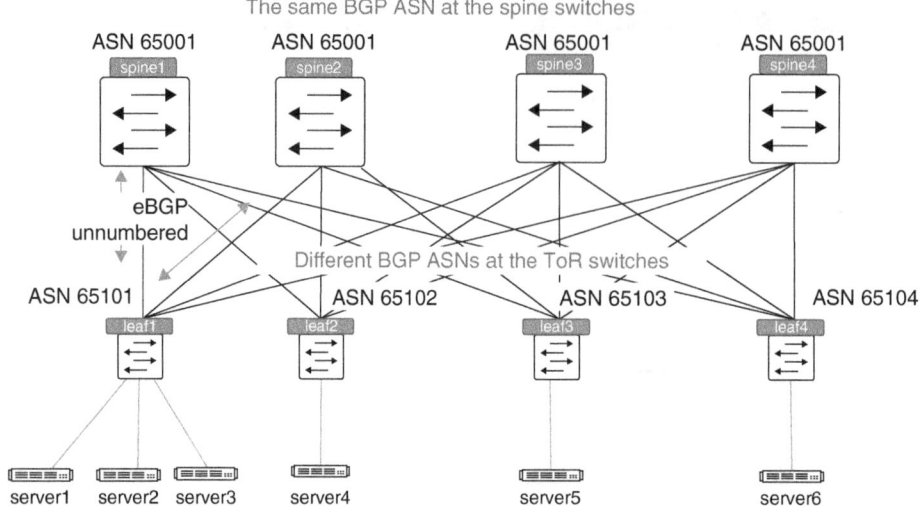

Figure 8-4
BGP ASN allocations in an AI data center with the same BGP ASN at the spines

In some situations, the suboptimal IP routing is accepted, although it is limited to two occurrences of the same ASN. Figure 8-5 illustrates the situation of suboptimal routing inside the data center fabric. In this case, when spines have different ASNs, in the event of failure, the path from server 1 to server 5 would result in suboptimal forwarding.

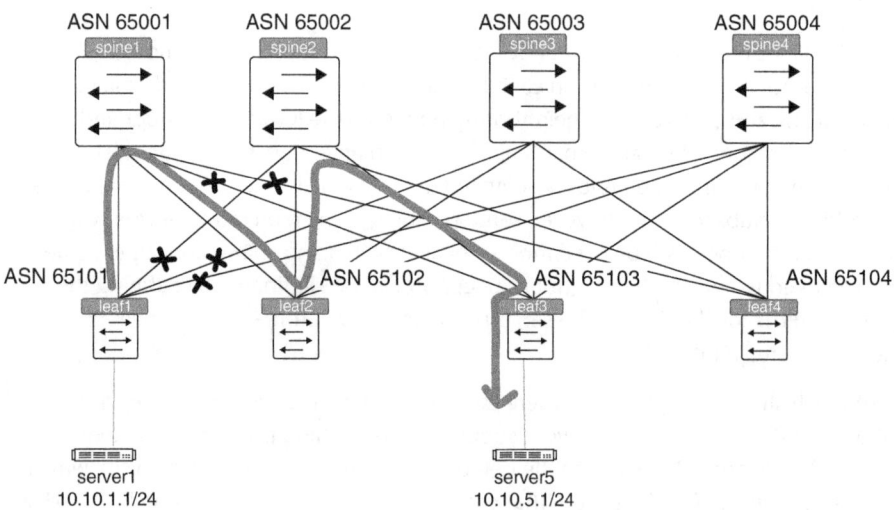

Figure 8-5
BGP ASN allocation and suboptimal forwarding

The situation illustrated in Figure 8-5—with more than two links failing simultaneously—is unlikely to occur in reality, but a well-designed network always accounts for worst-case scenarios. For the IP routing context of an AI data center where many elephant flows are present and consume significant bandwidth on 400 Gbps/800 Gbps Ethernet links, the link failure scenario mentioned previously will easily saturate the leaf2 bandwidth and impact the performance of servers connected to leaf2.

The ASN design shown in Figure 8-4, with the same ASN at the spine level, is preferred as it prevents the suboptimal IP routing situation highlighted with the arrow in Figure 8-5, as it includes the default BGP rule of AS-PATH loop prevention and does not accept any path that crosses the same ASN twice. In this case, if you were using the same ASN at the spine level, the service between server1 and server5 would be declared down, and the switchover to other servers would occur, delivering the same performance. In the event of different ASN BGP numbers at the spines, the communication would still happen between both server 1 and server 5—but with potentially degraded performance (higher latency) due to the suboptimal routing and potentially additional risk of congestion to manage at the spine2 level.

BGP Advanced Capabilities

The baseline peering and IP prefix advertisement BGP feature set may not be sufficient for AI/ML deployments, and one of the more advanced capabilities may be needed. When the scale of the network infrastructure is growing, some of the advanced feature sets will help optimize the fast convergence, even if the number of GPU clusters is continuously increasing at the ToR switches, as well as control the capacity of the network at different levels of the IP Clos architecture.

BGP ADD-PATH

There are several advantages to using BGP ADD-PATH inside a data center, including improved network efficiency, load balancing, and security. BGP ADD-PATH is especially beneficial if the fabric uses the iBGP and route reflector (RR) functions. The RR, instead of just advertising the best path for the prefix, also advertises other paths toward the IP destination prefix.

In addition, BGP ADD-PATH can be used to protect against network failures and implement route diversity. BGP ADD-PATH enables more efficient use of network resources. When there are multiple links toward the same prefix originated from the ToR, instead of having the spine advertising just the best path to other ToR leaf nodes, all paths to a given destination IP prefix will be included. This improves the resiliency of the network; in the event that one path fails, for example, only a portion of the traffic will be affected.

The simplified topology shown in Figure 8-6 can help you understand the ADD-PATH options. First, let's look at how spine2 will advertise the server2 IP prefix 10.10.108.0/24 to leaf2. Typically, it will take one of the BGP updates—either from border-leaf1 or border-leaf2—and send it to leaf2 based on the local best-path selection. If the ADD-PATH send option is enabled for BGP peering on a switch, spine2 will send both path options for the same prefix instead of just one.

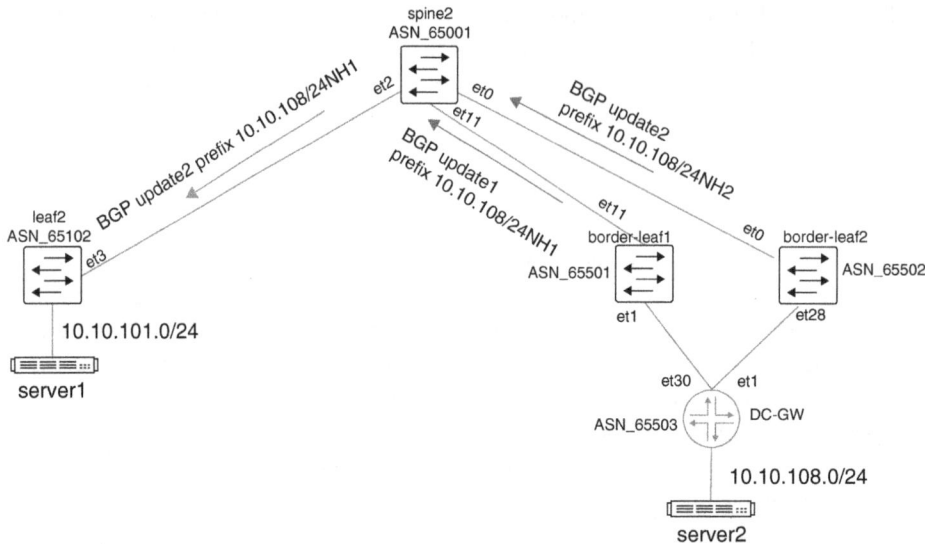

Figure 8-6
BGP ADD-PATH in an eBGP fabric deployment

Figure 8-6 illustrates ADD-PATH in an eBGP scenario. However, in many cases, the iBGP ADD-PATH is the primary supported approach for advertising all possible paths to the same destination IP prefix from the route reflector.

BGP AS-PATH Strip and Replace

In some cases, AI data center BGP IP fabric is deployed with private ASNs, and it may connect to an IP private core network that also uses the private ASN ranges. In the reference topology shown in Figure 8-7, to make the services located behind the core IP network available to the rest of the local fabric, servers may sometimes have to appear from the IP routing perspective of the locally connected GPU servers, in the same way they would appear directly to the fabric. In the figure, server101 is physically located in a different data center location. Normalizing the AS-PATH becomes relevant by stripping private ASNs and replacing them with a predefined list of AS-PATHs at a specific level in the IP fabric topology. In our example, this is enabled at the border–spine level. It's typically done to normalize the unified processing of routes at the border–spine or border–leaf nodes, but it can also be done to avoid any overlapping of ASNs with the numbers deployed inside the fabric via some form of automation, for example.

In Figure 8-7, each of the spines would have the same IP routing policy, dictating the replacement of the server101 prefix AS-PATH BGP attribute with an ASN of the same length. Therefore, from an IP routing perspective, the fabric servers will consider server101 to be accessible equally through all border devices.

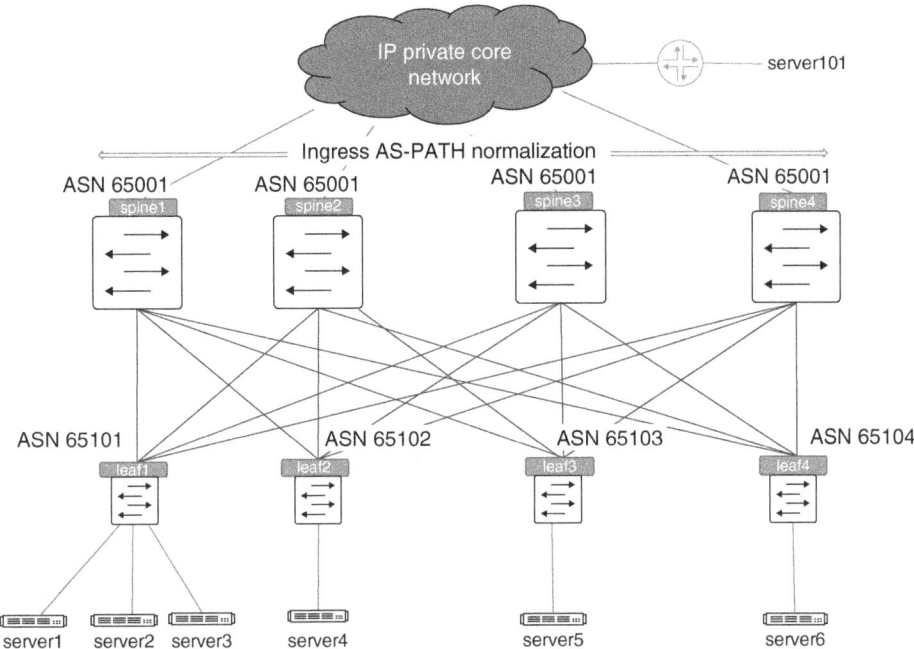

Figure 8-7
Ingress AS-PATH normalization with strip-and-replace function

Another use case where the strip-and-replace ingress routing policy might become relevant is when the servers themselves are running the BGP daemons and inject prefixes into the fabric with various AS-PATH lengths. In such a case, the ToR switches may need to be enabled with a policy that slashes the originally imported one and replaces it with the "operator"-approved list of ASNs. In the AI/ML use case, when server-level multi-tenancy is used, it may become necessary to unify and standardize the BGP ASNs sent to the rest of the topology.

While ingress AS-PATH replacement provides a useful tool for fabric operators to normalize the list of ASNs at each level of the topology for equal processing, when used within the traditional core IP Internet, it can lead to IP routing loops or may be considered a security threat.

BGP Link Bandwidth Extended Community

When dealing with 400 Gbps/800 Gbps Ethernet fabrics for AI/ML, there is sometimes a preference for weighted ECMP (equal-cost multipathing), where the weight for the given next hop depends on the bandwidth community encoding for the given path. For example, when the AI/ML services in the fabric illustrated in Figure 8-8 are extended across the core IP network, the outgoing links of the fabric have different bandwidths. Encoding BGP Link Bandwidth Extended Community based on the link speed is one way to impose weighted ECMP from the forwarding perspective at the leaf nodes.

When all the rest of the BGP attributes are the same, weighted ECMP (proportionally to the value of BGP Link Bandwidth Extended Community) results in a more intelligent way of sending traffic in the south-to-north direction.

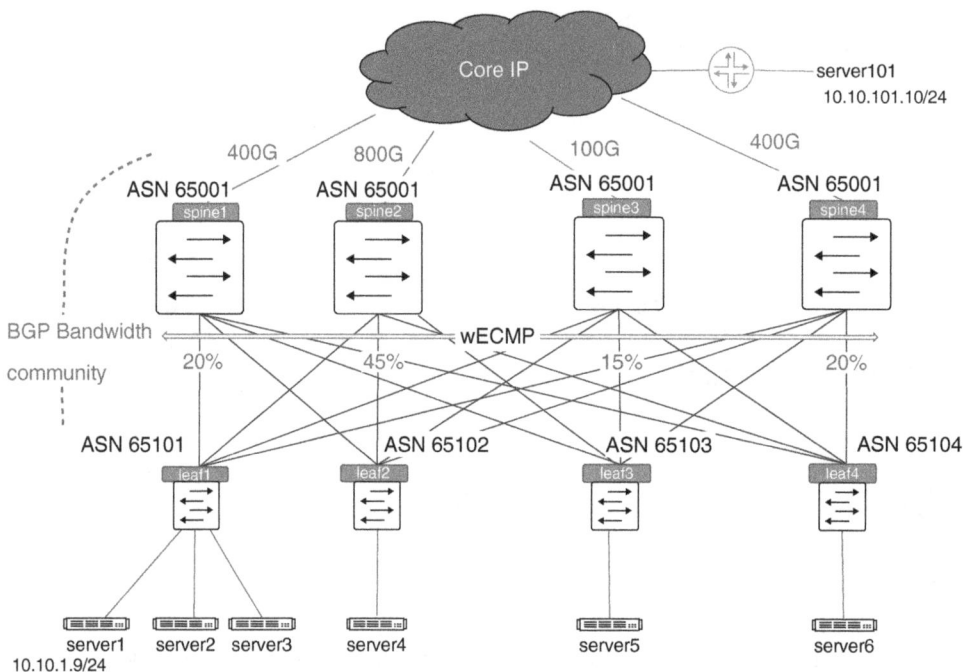

Figure 8-8
Weighted ECMP and BGP Link Bandwidth Extended Community

Sometimes the decision of which BGP path to use for the north–south traffic is evaluated based on the bandwidth of the outgoing link. In Figure 8-8, for example, the servers would send more traffic destined for server101 over spine2.

Addressing ECMP per destination IP prefix within the data center fabric would be more complicated than doing so for prefixes external to the fabric and would result in too many states. Therefore, it should be considered for a select list of prefixes or services that are very bandwidth intensive.

The same bandwidth community information can also be used to influence proportional load balancing at the leaf node level when the IP fabric is a five-stage topology with super spines. In this scenario, the leaf switch sends the traffic and runs adaptive load balancing, also at the ASIC level, based on the IP routing BGP information. When the east–west destination IP prefix is reachable through the IP ECMP group, for the cases where multiple links from leaf to spines are used, the source leaf can adapt the weight of the given spine next hop and send fewer packets over the link to the spine when the aggregated capacity of the given spine connected to the destination leaf node is reduced. This is particularly useful when multiple 400 Gbps or 800 Gbps links are used, such as from leaf to spine or from spine to super spine. The same Link Bandwidth community information can also be used at the ToR switch level to make more intelligent weighted load balancing directly at the ASIC level. If, for example, there are multiple links from the spines to super spines and one of the links goes down, then the leaf node, based on the BGP Bandwidth community, can adapt the weights of the IP ECMP and send proportionally less traffic to the spine that has reduced total forwarding capacity to the destination leaf node. This is something referred to as Weighted Packet Spraying (WPS) in some vendors' implementations.

BGP: Minimum BGP peers per IP Prefix

When using BGP extensively inside data center fabric for backend or frontend IP networks, for specific services, the number of active downlink or uplink BGP peers must be deterministic to guarantee performance and capacity. For example, when the destination service running in 10.10.101.0/24 becomes available through just three paths instead of four-way ECMP, the spine will withdraw the prefix from its advertisement. Therefore, the destination prefix will be reachable via the other three spines, offering full bandwidth capacity. This differs from the situation where only a conditional route advertisement is performed; in this case, the condition is based on the number of BGP peers per IP prefix.

BGP DPF for AI Data Center Path Diversity

In the data center network infrastructure for recent software developments in AI and ML, such as large language models (LLMs), massive amounts of data are exchanged between many GPU servers to deliver the data processing outcomes. It is therefore important for the backend AI/ML fabric to guarantee the following:

- It should efficiently use IP ECMP with multiple fabric 400 Gbps/800 Gbps links between leaf and spine because concurrent massive data chunks are being exchanged east–west between the server's GPU.
- It achieves predictable latency performance for parallel computing. For example, when you are consistently receiving the same low JCT numbers, the given data processing job initiated by the NCCL scheduler must be completed within the provided time window, and the outcome of the job must be synchronized across the entire GPU infrastructure.

In today's implementations of AI/ML servers, RoCEv2 is the primary transport protocol used to synchronize the data chunks between distributed GPU servers. This is the case, for example, with Nvidia H100 and H200 servers. However, the entropy characteristics pose challenges from a networking perspective in the case of RDMA transport over UDP, which can lead to short or persistent traffic congestion within the network. This congestion, in turn, slows down the data synchronization between GPUs, even if the frame loss is mitigated by the RoCEv2 DCQCN mechanisms Priority Flow Control (PFC) and Explicit Congestion Notification (ECN), which help avoid congestion by signaling to the end nodes that congestion occurred and that it needs to slow down the data rate temporarily.

There are different ways to prevent congestion in a data center network. For example, you can use packet spraying by including the RoCEv2 BTH header QPairs in the load-balancing implementation. Dynamic load balancing (DLB) can include the local bandwidth utilization at the node level, and global load balancing (GLB) can include the next-next-hop information on the link quality. These mechanisms, however, may still result in packet reordering at the end-node GPU server level or yield different performance for each job iteration. While this is not a significant issue in most cases, it can be mitigated by incorporating a lightweight IP traffic engineering mechanism for well-selected AI/ML workloads and providing path diversity within the data center fabric.

Today's data center fabrics typically use eBGP for underlay routing in IP Clos three-stage and five-stage architectures. Even though eBGP underlay routing is scalable and straightforward, it only provides a single best-effort SLA for all traffic flows. The data center fabric network represents a shared common pool of resources (as illustrated in Figure 8-9) without any user or application control over the forwarding path.

To provide better SLAs for the drop- and latency-sensitive AI/ML flows, BGP routing needs to be enhanced to deliver IP path diversity inside the data center fabric.

The goal with BGP DPF (Deterministic Path Forwarding), proposed by HPE Juniper Networking and the IETF draft-wang-idr-dpf, is to divide a physical IP Clos fabric (three-stage/five-stage leaf, spine, super spine, or T0/T1/T2 multi-tier fabric) into multiple logical fabrics so that specific flows can be mapped to certain logical fabrics based on the SLA (Service Level Agreement) requirements.

BGP DPF can efficiently identify the flow path, prevent elephant and mice flows from going over the same path, reduce or eliminate packet reordering, and allow a regular compute node and AI/ML GPU traffic on the same path ID. The shared pool of resources shown in Figure 8-9 in the context of backend AI/ML fabric can be divided into multiple logical fabrics to deliver more deterministic path forwarding for the GPU servers (with, for example, the black GPU going through path-id-1 and gray GPUs going through path-id-2). This helps deliver path diversity between different GPUs when their servers are connected to different leaf nodes. Figure 8-10 illustrates the path diversity and fabric logical partitioning achieved using BGP DPF.

BGP DPF can be used in rail-optimized designs as well as rail-unified designs. In a rail-optimized design, if a server has eight GPUs, then a given rail is deployed with eight leaf nodes, and each GPU from the same server goes to a different leaf node. In a rail-unified design, all GPUs from the given server are connected to the given ToR. The advantage with a rail-unified design is that the customer can reduce spending on the cabling infrastructure. However, the resiliency for the whole server GPU is reduced in this case; if the leaf goes down, then four H100 servers go down. With a rail-optimized design, if a given leaf goes down, the compute capacity of the whole rail is impacted.

Figure 8-10 highlights the use case of GPU multi-tenancy where seven tenants are spread across two rails, and tenant black gets a predictable capacity within the fabric by allocating it to the fab-id black. This becomes interesting especially when the black tenant LLM has high priority in terms of execution time and must be offered very low JCT (Job Completion Time): The outcomes of the learnings must be completed as soon as possible. In this case, capacity determinism may become

eBGP Underlay for Three-Stage/Five-Stage Fabric for an AI Data Center

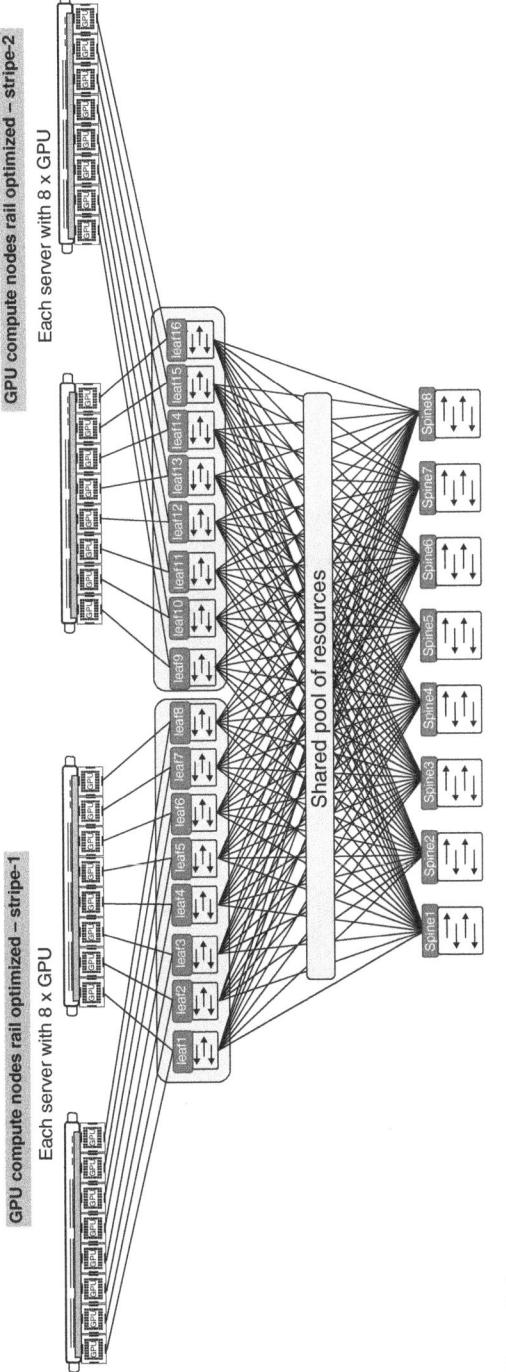

Figure 8-9
IP Clos data center fabric with a shared pool of fabric resources

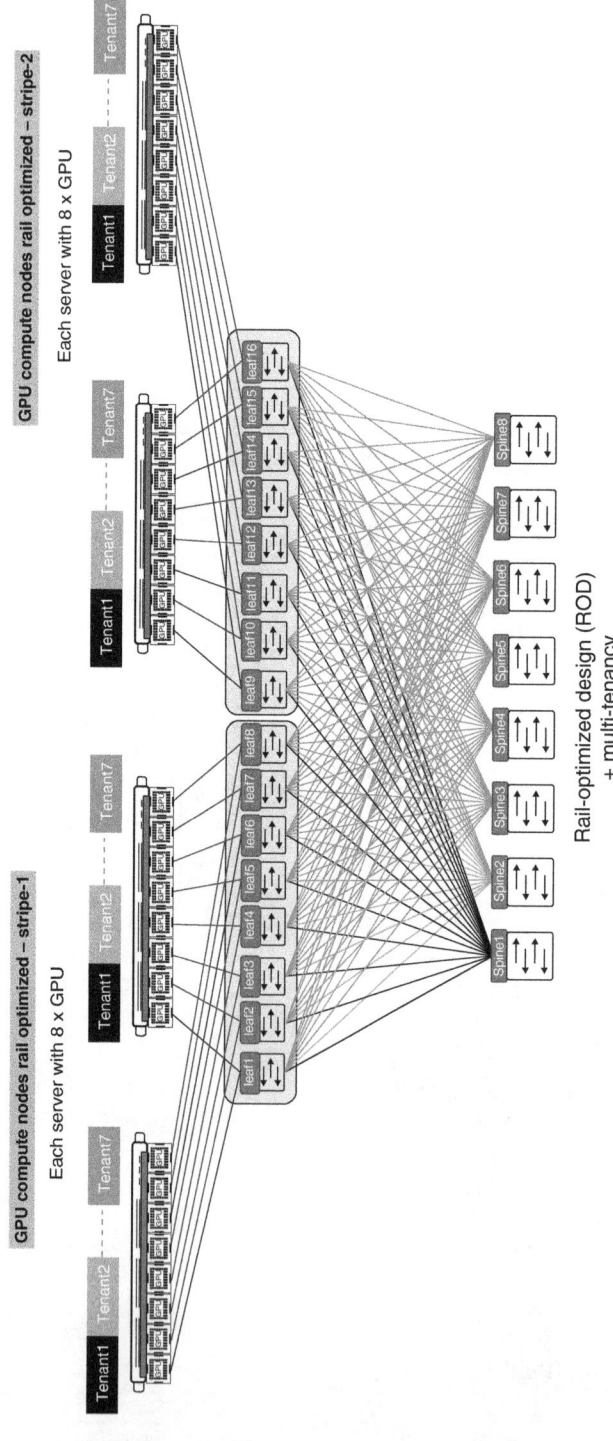

Figure 8-10
BGP DPF path diversity inside the AI data center with rail-optimized design

relevant. In the multi-tenancy scenario, we still have other tenants to be distributed across the fabric when their workloads require synchronization across different rails. In this case, some tenants might simply follow the random packet spraying and use DLB without any specific determinism for path forwarding. Between the black tenant and others, real-time performance measurement will reveal whether any additional fabric load balancing is required for the given tenant and whether light-weight traffic engineering through BGP DPF is needed or whether simple random packet spraying gives better performance results.

When an AI/ML cluster is deployed in such a way that all the GPUs from the given server connect to the same ToR switch, you can use BGP DPF for load balancing with a specific GPU ID by pinning it to a specific logical fabric ID and offering more predictable capacity for communication between the servers. With this scenario, instead of using the full capacity of the given server for every GPU (as described in the case of rail-optimized deployment), you pin the given GPU ID or RoCEv2 QPair value from each of the servers to the given logical fabric and execute the data processing across a large server pool. For example, you might use 128 × GPU-id 0 from 128 servers and allocate to it specific fabric forwarding capacity, such as 1.2 Tbps inside the fabric, with three 400 Gbps links from each leaf node logically allocated to the fabric ID black.

BGP DPF can help the ingress switch automatically discover the paths toward the egress router via different logical fabrics (such as black fabric in Figure 8-11). This can help to map traffic flows with different SLA requirements to different logical fabrics. It's achieved via coloring underlay eBGP sessions and the transport routes.

Another use case for BGP DPF is inside the frontend network, where storage and inference domains are delivered with logical demarcation for both workloads with the same physical infrastructure, offering clear path diversity for each type of workload.

The most important idea of BGP DPF is to color eBGP overlay sessions based on the underlying logic fabric to which they belong. A session can be colored as a single color, as multiple colors, excluding one or more colors, or left uncolored.

Only routes with at least one matching color are advertised over a colored eBGP session. When advertising a route over the colored eBGP session, the unmatched colors of the route are pruned out. This ensures that a colored route can reach the endpoint following the fabric of the route's color(s).

In Figure 8-12, besides coloring specific destination IP prefixes with color community, we use the BGP session coloring option at the establishment phase of the peering so that at the same link, one color or more colored sessions become available. Traditionally, BGP routing is used to advertise the community and other attributes for a specific IP prefix; in this case, we have it enabled at the peering level.

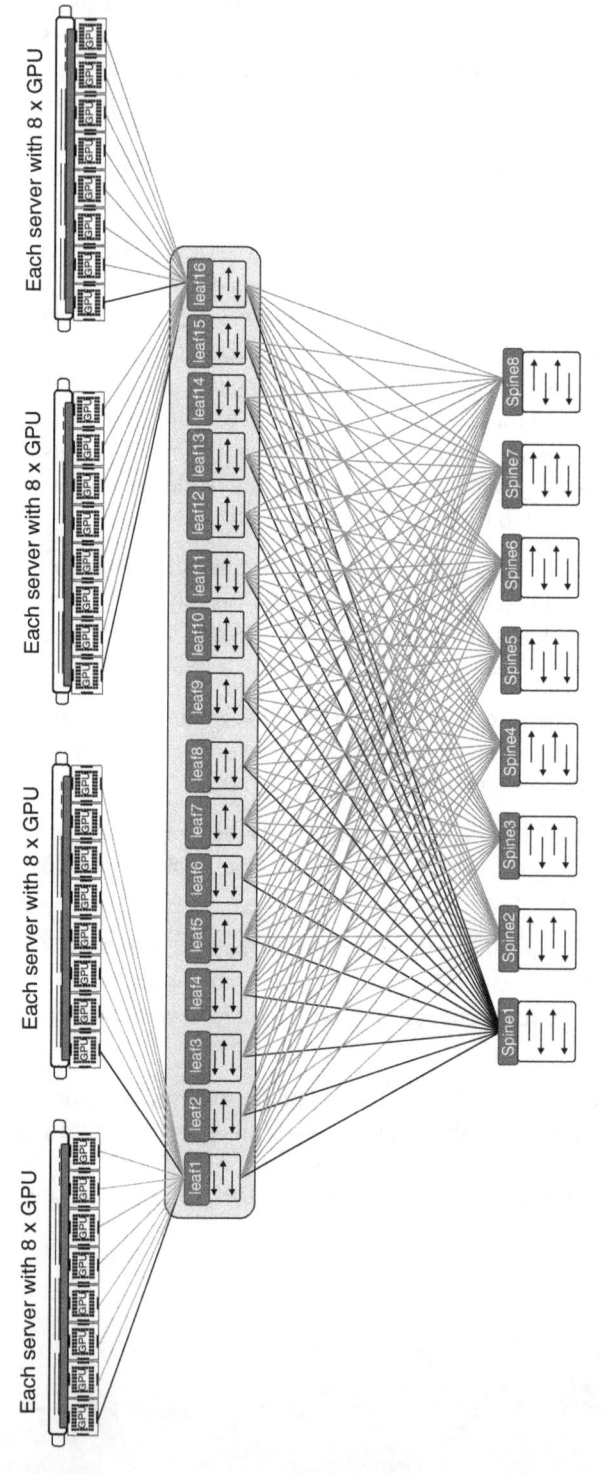

Figure 8-11
BGP DPF path diversity inside an AI/ML cluster with rail-unified design

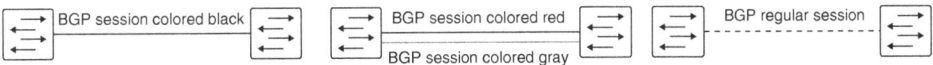

Figure 8-12
BGP DPF session coloring with black and gray colored IP BGP peers

Figure 8-13 shows a scenario with two logical fabrics and two paths, active and backup, where the black fabric is active, and the gray fabric is a backup. When route 10.10.1.4/32 originates from egress router leaf4, it is not colored (which means it matches all colors). When it is advertised toward spine1 over the black BGP session, the color is pruned as black. When spine1 further advertises the black route over the black session toward leaf1, it keeps the black color. Similarly, when the uncolored route is advertised from leaf4 to spine2 over the gray session, the color is pruned as gray. When spine2 further advertises the gray route over the gray session toward leaf1, it keeps the gray color. Now, the ingress router leaf1 has two paths toward 10.10.1.4/32: one black active path and one gray backup path, set as a backup locally at leaf1. If it chooses the black path, it guarantees that traffic is routed over the black fabric. If it's the gray path, it guarantees that traffic is routed over the gray fabric. Spine-level setting of the colors is shown here as optional, and leaf4, where the originating server is connected, can also advertise the given IP prefix with active and backup color settings.

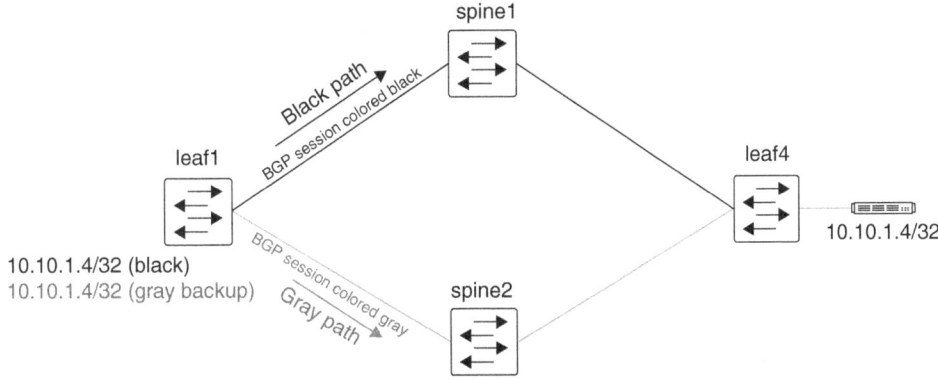

Figure 8-13
BGP DPF server colored prefix advertisement

Traffic-to-Fabric Color Mapping

The given GPU to fabric ID/color ID traffic can be mapped using the following options:

- **Filter-based forwarding (FBF):** With this approach, the admin is globally saying that the following interfaces will be enabled with the given fabric ID or using the firewall filters. The RoCEv2 flows are identified with source UDP (or range or UDP ports) or with the destination QPairs (from the RoCEv2 BTH header) to be mapped to the given fabric ID in order to isolate different flows and perform controlled load balancing across the fabric leaf-to-spine outgoing links.

- **On-box agent:** An on-box agent can use probes to measure the path quality and distribute the new AI/ML workloads to different path IDs to improve the efficiency of the load balancing. RoCEv2 or UEC flow awareness at the ASIC level is required to implement load balancing, using the color ID as an action item.

- **Central controller:** A central controller has a view of the whole fabric topology and understands globally how the fabric resources are used and which parts of the fabric are underused. This is possible with an HPE Juniper Networking implementation by leveraging the existing CPCE (Containerized Path Computation Engine) developments and adding BGP DPF support.

- **EVPN-VXLAN MAC-VRF or RT5 IP EVPN routing instance associated with a specific-colored IP address:** The AI data center admin can introduce EVPN multi-tenancy for AI workloads (sometimes referred to as GPU as a service, or GPUaaS) within the fabric and also control the forwarding correlation between the EVPN-VXLAN overlays and underlay forwarding. This is highlighted in Figure 8-14, where the two different EVPN MAC-VRF instances are mapped to different-colored path IP addresses.

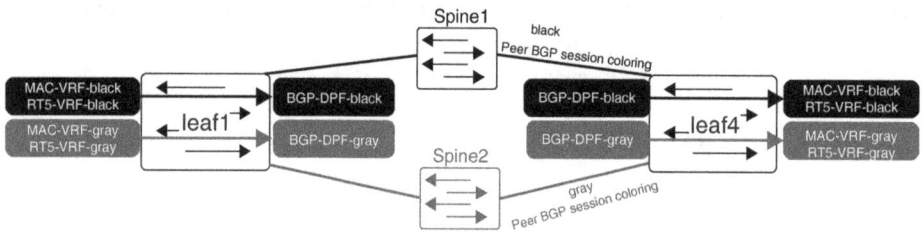

Figure 8-14
BGP DPF and EVPN-VXLAN underlay-to-overlay correlation

With this approach, the AI workloads connected to MAC-VRF-black/RT5-VRF-black instances will follow the black IP path forwarding, and the AI workloads from MAC-VRF-gray/RT5-VRF-gray will be on the gray path, which efficiently isolates both tenants at the control plane and data plane. The rest of the tenants from other MAC-VRF or RT5 instances in this scenario can use both spines' IP ECMP for the forwarding and reachability. Besides the isolation of the tenants, the fabric admin also gets better explicit control of the load balancing per tenant. In the case of multi-tenancy with EVPN-VXLAN, when only RT5 IP VPN instances are used, the same underlay-to-overlay correlation can be applied, and selected IP instances can be mapped to a specific IP-colored path within the AI data center fabric.

Interior Gateway Protocols for AI Data Center Fabric

We saw in the previous section how BGP addresses data center needs within IP Clos three-stage and five-stage fabrics. Many cloud providers have chosen to use this protocol for very large conventional data center topologies, and there are some good reasons for this, including scale, service diversity, multi-vendor interoperability, and advanced routing policy. However, for backend AI networks, some extra requirements have arisen that may not be readily met by the BGP protocol stack:

- Reacting at the microsecond level to changing link/queue utilization
- Leveraging the collective communications information
- Understanding the full topology
- Having link and queue awareness

BGP needs the full power of the CPU processor and more significant compute power to react to changing conditions inside the fabric. Therefore, with AI data center backend networks (where the training is taking place), one of the existing or new IGPs, such as RIFT or IS-IS, may be more suitable for implementation at the lower level of the switching infrastructure.

IGPs have better built-in heartbeat and flood capabilities than BGP, which can make them more suitable for leveraging information related to link and queue quality. With BGP, you might need to rely on some third-party protocol, such as BFD or OAM extensions, to react to changing link conditions. Such solutions may not always scale for larger infrastructures, such as where 16,000 to 32,000 GPUs need to be interconnected using the switching infrastructure—especially when microsecond accuracy is required. IGP routing has a greater chance of combining IP routing information and link-quality advertisements across the entire fabric.

As we previously discussed, BGP can be fine-tuned to behave like an IGP routing protocol. It is possible that some IGPs might start adding features that were initially designed for BGP.

RIFT in an AI Data Center

The Routing in Fat Trees (RIFT) protocol, defined in the IETF RFC 9692, was natively designed for larger-scale data center fabrics with more than 1,000 switch nodes and is another example of an Interior Gateway Protocol (IGP) for AI IP Fabrics, as an alternative to IS-IS or OSPFv2/OSPFv3.

RIFT has the following main characteristics:

- Scales to 1,000 or more switch nodes
- Offers fast convergence
- Balances traffic based on the northbound capacity available
- Supports wide ECMP and unequal-cost multipathing (UCMP)
- Can leverage additional metadata in advertisements, such as the devices' overlay configurations or link/queue information
- Offers Zero-Touch Provisioning (so there is no need to assign any ASNs, for example, to individual switches)

RIFT also offers several specific IP routing features:

- It enables the use of link-state flooding northbound and distance-vector routing southbound.
- The number of routes on the leaf is reduced to a minimum.
- IPv6 ND (Neighbor Discovery) can address links without requiring that IP addresses be set up on them.

The last point is attractive, but we already talked about using BGP unnumbered to automate peering establishment, so we wouldn't consider this as a big differentiator. With RIFT, the adjacency formation is fully based on "hello" UDP messages and not on TCP full state, as is the case with BGP. In addition, with RIFT, the node and link-level information is not tied to any specific prefix. In contrast, with BGP, all the information sent is typically related to a destination IP prefix, for which you may not yet have full information inside the data center; for example, additional server prefixes might be added later. So, with BGP, if any policy is needed, it may have to be updated. This is not necessarily a problem for fully automated data centers, which can adapt their configurations when new servers get deployed.

From an architectural perspective, the three-stage/five-stage IP Clos fabric also supports RIFT, which offers the benefits mentioned previously for data center operation. However, from a topology perspective within the backend network, you may also need to consider a DragonFly type of topology to achieve optimal performance and gain more direct connectivity at various levels of the multi-tier topology. Reducing the number of hops between nodes means less latency for AI/ML workloads. Enabling the DragonFly topology at scale in a backend network with BGP might become very complex, even with an automation tool, and the IGPs RIFT and IS-IS might be very useful. DragonFly topology might also be considered in the case of scale-up fabric management, where more direct links exist inside the data center rack, and the system appears more like a single big GPU server.

Figure 8-15 shows a topology where there are many more connections at each topology level. In the most extreme case, every node would be fully connected to all other nodes to minimize the chance of frame loss and maximize the network's speed while preserving lower latency compared to the traditional IP Clos fabric, where all leaf-to-leaf communication is done through the spines.

While Figure 8-15 shows the connection for just one group of switch nodes in the canonical DragonFly topology, it is easy to extend it to a second group. Figure 8-16 shows group-2 as well as group-1 connected to the other switches.

In this theoretical DragonFly example, we have so far connected two groups of switches. When we have connected all seven groups, as shown in Figure 8-17, we realize that to use such a topology, we would need to ensure that only a subset of the data gets exchanged from one group to another at a given time or that at the software level, the collectives communicate mainly within the group.

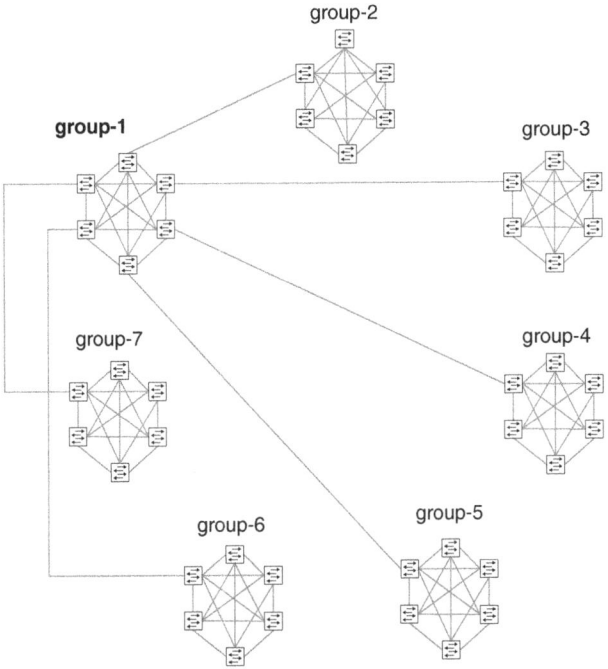

Figure 8-15
DragonFly canonical topology where group-1 connects to all the other groups

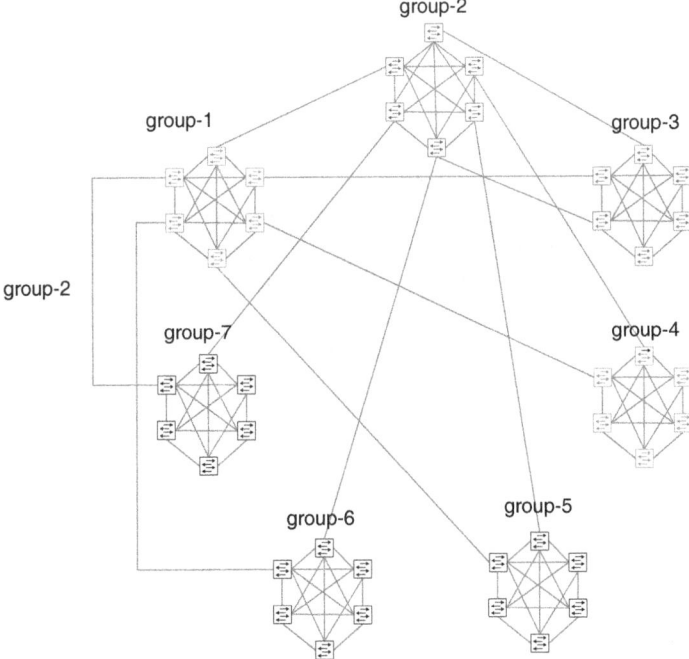

Figure 8-16
DragonFly canonical topology where group-1 and group-2 both connect to all the other groups

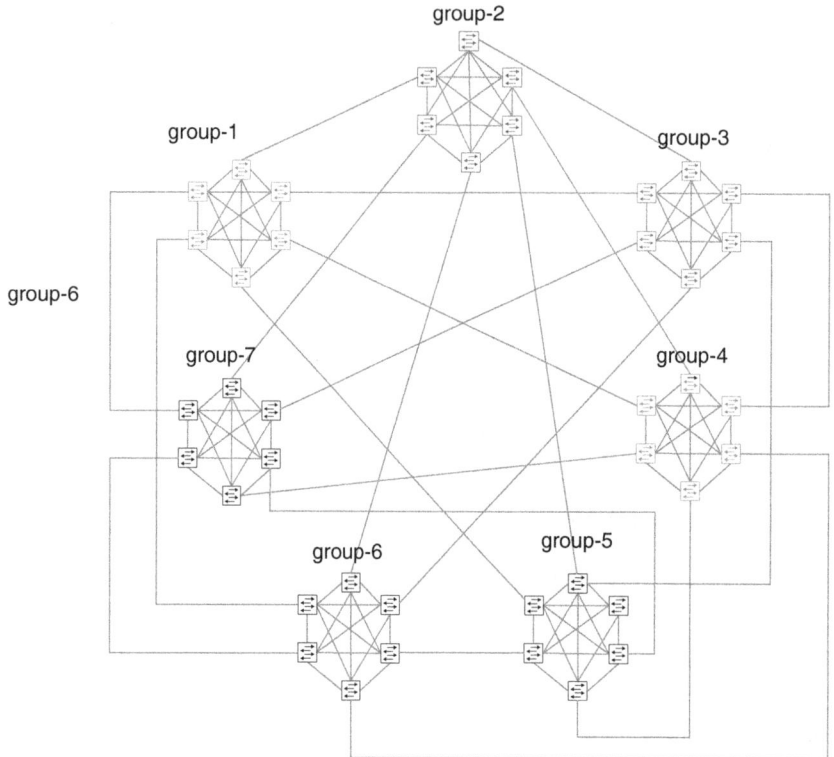

Figure 8-17
DragonFly canonical topology with all the groups connected to each other

The number of links from each group is typically higher than one, and there could be other ways of connecting more than one selected device from a group to other group IDs. The topology shown in Figure 8-17, with each group of switches interconnected to all the other groups via selected switches, is challenging from a cabling perspective; usually, to simplify it, only the higher-density spine switches would be connected in either a full mesh or in a canonical way to the other groups of switches (in pods). This can be addressed by using a DragonFly sparse topology, as shown in Figure 8-18, where the group itself, instead of being a full-mesh or partially meshed topology, is simply a leaf–spine IP Clos fabric, and only from the perspective of the T2 spines is the DragonFly topology delivered.

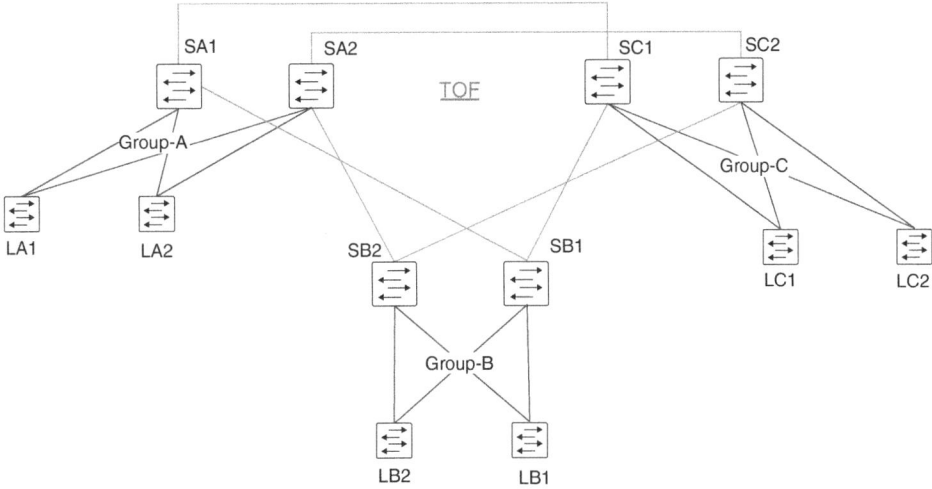

Figure 8-18
RIFT DragonFly Sparse topology

These are the main characteristics of the DragonFly Sparse topology:

- Reduced network diameter/reduced number of long links
- Less latency
- High number of server connections
- Path diversity
- Fabric partitioning
- UCMP and non-shortest-path forwarding
- Identification of inter-group global links
- Topology and link awareness
- Adaptive routing (An IGP such as RIFT in DragonFly topology can react to third-party quality information implemented at a lower level in the ASIC or incorporate link quality information in the K-store values.)

While reducing the network diameter is important in AI and HPC data centers due to the performance aspects (more optimized bandwidth utilization with directly connected elected nodes from each group of switches), the costs of cabling infrastructure and standardization of additional links may be considered too heavy. In such situations, traditional IP Clos fabric, where at each level of the architecture there is no connectivity between the members of the given level, may be more appropriate.

In the topology shown in Figure 8-18, the SA1/SA2 spine devices are the top-of-fabric (ToF) nodes and have a view of the topology of the local group of switches and the other directly connected ToF nodes from the other group of AI data center switches. This type of topology was originally not supported as the ToR-to-ToF link is not typically considered supported and would be withdrawn from routing. Here, the group-to-group connection is part of the added advertisement from the control plane perspective and was encoded in the K-store values as additional information. These advertisements also allow forwarding over the horizontal links, which was not part of the initial definition of the RIFT protocol.

The control plane aspects of the DragonFly topology, such as partitioning of the fabric and split-horizon rule implementations, are covered in more detail in the recent IETF Draft https://datatracker.ietf.org/doc/draft-przygienda-rift-dragonfly/, which was specifically written for the AI data center backend networks.

The RIFT protocol was initially implemented in the open-source community for server-level routing, and some vendors have now also developed it as a separate routing package to be installed on switches.

IS-IS for IP Fabric: Flood Reduction and Flex Algo

From an IGP routing perspective, RIFT is not the only option, and over the past couple years, other legacy protocols have emerged to support additional capabilities in backend data center networks. For example, IS-IS was recently remodeled from its initial definition to become more suitable for data center use cases.

IS-IS Optimal Distributed Flooding for Dense Topologies and Flex Algo topology support for pure IP fabrics are both interesting technologies to consider when designing backend networks. They offer better scalability, fast convergence, and path diversity of the workloads than traditional IP Clos frontend fabrics.

Similarly to RIFT, IS-IS runs at the lower level of the protocols, and it is sometimes considered more secure than other protocols because of the link-local nature of the link-state advertisement. With IS-IS, TCP-level attacks cannot be more easily originated outside the fabric.

For IS-IS in the data center backend use case, we can highlight the following arguments:

- IS-IS enables flood optimization of advertisements to speed up convergence and route learning. From the list of neighbors, just one is elected for update flooding. This improvement minimizes the number of LSP (Link State PDU – Protocol Data Unit) fragments received by individual intermediate systems.
- IS-IS can incorporate additional link/server information inside the TLV (Type–Length–Value) advertisements.
- IS-IS can scale to 2,500 switch nodes.
- IS-IS offers multi-topology and a flexible algorithm (Flex Algo) for different path/fabric plane computations.

Figure 8-19 shows that leaf1 elected spine2 to send the new server IP prefix updates instead of replicating them to both spines. This optimization may not be very important in this basic topology, but when the number of spine nodes in the backend network increases to 32 or 64, it may play a more significant role and help to speed up the convergence of the network.

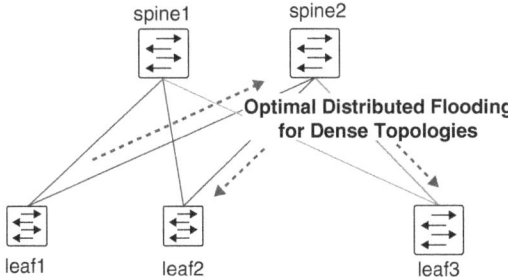

Figure 8-19
IS-IS link/prefix update reduction optimization

This type of modification becomes even more relevant in a dense leaf–spine multilevel topology, such as T1/T2/T3 and sometimes T4, with many switch nodes at each level. Many parallel links are used between each pair of nodes. (This is typically the case when an AI/ML cluster uses a non-oversubscribed fabric.)

The optimization for data center IS-IS is described in the IETF Draft draft-white-lsr-distoptflood, and it has already been implemented in open-source networks and by some vendors.

Another capability of IS-IS that is even more useful in the AI data center backend network context is the support of path diversity through the Flex Algo mechanism. This is standardized as part of IETF RFC 9502 for IP networks, without the original requirement for Segment Routing (SR) or Segment Routing over IPv6 (SRv6) for path computation.

Flex Algo may become one of the options considered for a multi-plane backend topology to help build logical routing planes for different types of AI workloads and different performance requirements. It can be used either to isolate the workload or to make load balancing possible by imposing different constraints, such as lower latency or better congestion management capabilities (for example, lower backpressure statistics). Flex Algo used in pure IP networks without any SR-MPLS or SRv6 encapsulation is something like what we discussed in the case of BGP DPF, where some constraints are known and used to define the plane over which the traffic will be forwarded.

Flex Algo is one of the IGP algorithms for IS-IS that the IETF has defined as part of RFC 9350, where the combination of calculation type, metric type, and constraints is known as a flexible algorithm definition (FAD). When a switch node uses IS-IS Flex Algo, it assigns a Flex Algo value to the combination of calculation type, metric type, and constraints specified with a set of TLVs. An extension of the constraints and additional user-defined constraints were also added as part of the IETF Draft draft-ietf-lsr-flex-algo-bw-con and can be considered in the AI data center use case where specific performance information must be exchanged to offer the best quality for the given learning model. For example, one learning model might require higher bandwidth (via the min-bandwidth setting, where bandwidth thresholds can be defined and advertised as requirements in the TLVs) but may not be sensitive to latency (via the max-link delay setting). Based on these constraints, the metric calculation also takes place for the given Flex Algo identifier. In the topology shown in Figure 8-19, all the switches participating in the same Flex Algo must agree on the FAD information by advertising it at the link level.

Figure 8-20 shows a very basic IS-IS IP fabric topology where all three main types of network domains are combined on the same physical infrastructure and sent with clear path isolation to avoid any disturbances.

Figure 8-20 shows spines participating in distinct Flex Algos, so the negotiation for a unique non-default algorithm number occurs at the link level, from leaf to spine, for the given set of performance constraints (latency, bandwidth, and so on). All the spines and leaf nodes are part of the default algorithm as well and will be used as a fallback in the event that the given constrained deterministic Flex Algo fails.

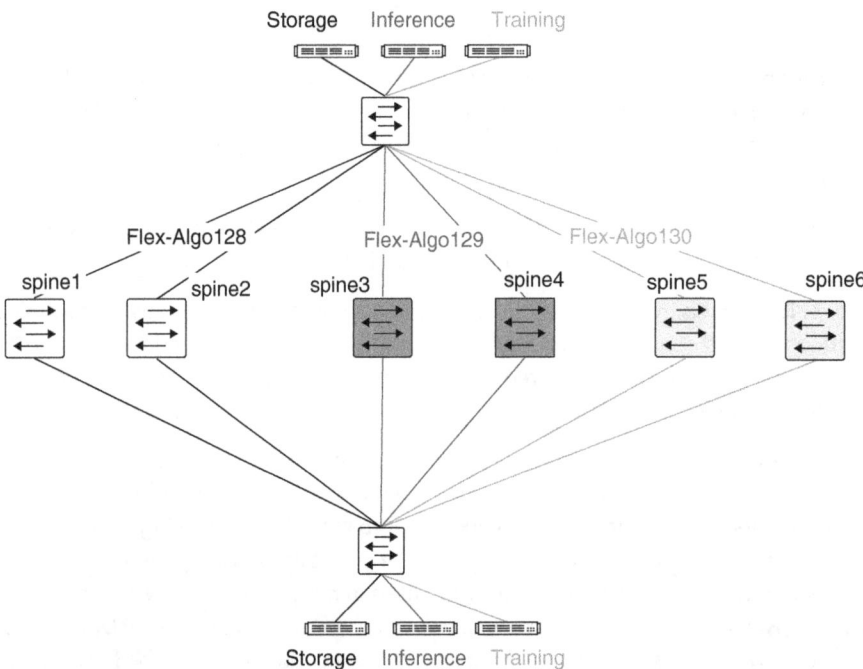

Figure 8-20
IS-IS Flex Algo as a logical separation on the same physical leaf–spine fabric

In the context of the AI backend, Flex Algo and FAD concepts can even be used for load-balancing purposes to simply balance the workloads with different characteristics over different fabric paths. For example, elephant and mice flows can be sent over different Flex Algos at a given time based on the measurement and performance constraints matching. Similarly to what we described in the case of the BGP DPF, tenant isolation is another use case where Flex Algo path diversity can be used to ensure that more critical tenants always get a predefined path with the imposed path bandwidth and latency constraints. The IPv4 Algorithm Prefix Reachability top-level TLV (Type–Length–Value) in the Flex Algo specifies how to announce IPv4 flexible algorithm prefix reachability with IS-IS.

The IS-IS IPv4 Algorithm Prefix Reachability TLV also contains the MTID (multi-topology identifier) to include the specific topology ID. After the MTID, the IPv4 prefix information with the algorithm information is advertised as part of the IS-IS IPv4 Algorithm Prefix Reachability TLV.

In the case of BGP, we've seen that the NLRI and specific IP prefix attributes are propagated. In the case of IS-IS, the TLVs handle many things, including the algorithm information and the associated metrics calculated based on the given algorithm constraints, such as bandwidth or latency expectations.

Multi-tenancy for an AI/ML Cluster Data Center Network

When building larger AI/ML clusters, GPUaaS is often proposed for the training and inference network infrastructures to better monetize and control the new AI data center infrastructure (for example, by offering the GPU as a service in the public cloud or enabling a private cloud in a larger organization). In this case, tenant GPU isolation may be required for the following reasons:

- **Security:** Two different tenants are required to keep their learning phase of the AI/ML cycle completely isolated to prevent any data breach.
- **Performance:** Switch ports and bandwidth are dedicated to specific tenants for the best latency across the network when connecting distributed ToR switches from different AI/ML cluster rails.
- **Capacity planning:** If GPUaaS in the cloud is used, tenant GPU isolation makes it easier to plan the server and network capacity based on the number of logical tenants enabled on the ToR Ethernet switch.

Network-Level Multi-tenancy

Multi-tenancy can be as simple as dedicating switch ports to the tenant. For example, if a tenant purchased a whole GPU server and wants to connect all eight Ethernet ports on different ToR switches, then on each switch from a given rail (which is a group of eight Ethernet ToR switches), one port will be reserved for that tenant. This may happen, for example, when the cloud provider is offering a whole bare metal GPU server as a service (BMSaaS).

In other situations, when a server is enabled with different tenants (for example, four GPUs to one tenant and four other GPUs to another tenant), EVPN-VXLAN segmentation can be used. With VLAN-VNI to MAC-VRF mapping, each tenant can be mapped to a MAC-VRF instance or a combination of MAC-VRF and Type-5 IPVRF instances using a one-to-one mapping approach. Figure 8-21 illustrates this approach within a rail, but it could also be applied to a multi-rail AI data center design.

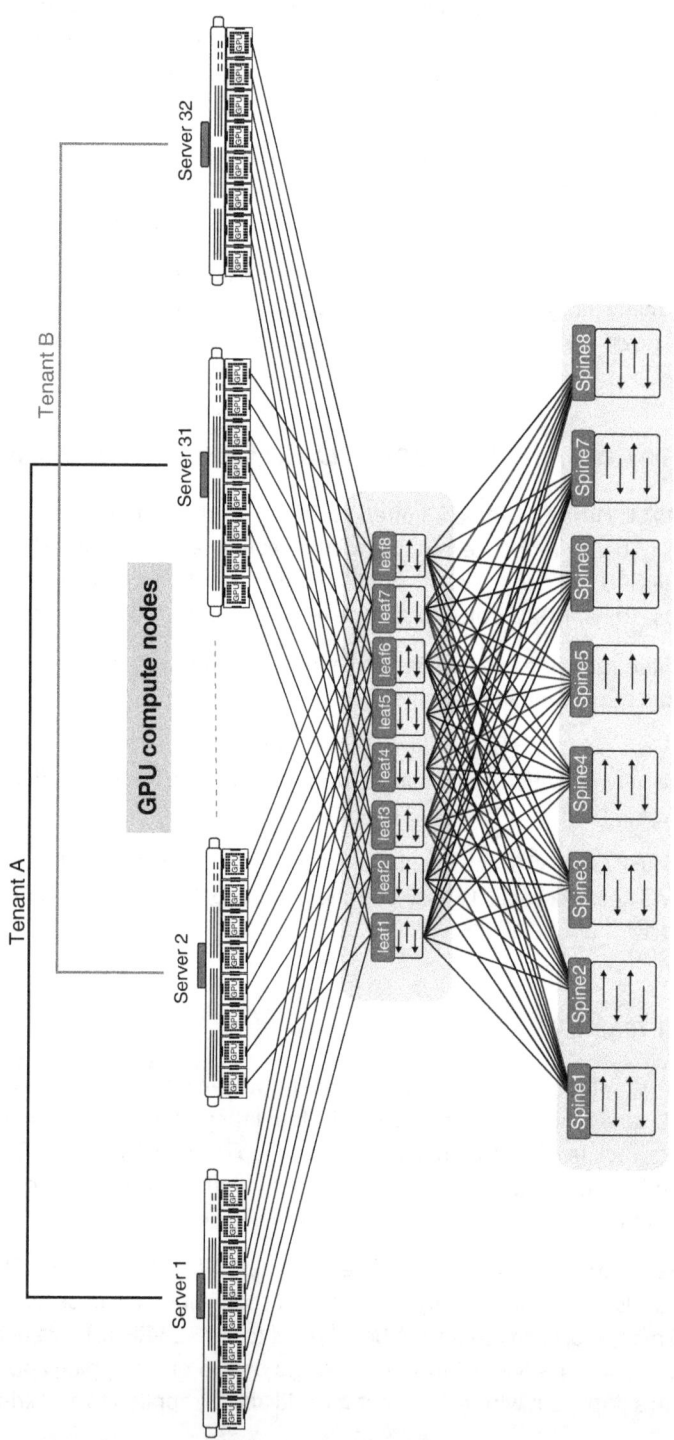

Figure 8-21
Multi-tenancy with dedicated servers for each tenant

When using a simple topology with 8 leaf switches and 8 spine switches and a 1:1 ratio (that is, no oversubscription), it may be possible to obtain, for example, 64 × 800 Gigabit Ethernet switches and servers featuring 8 × GPUs per server. In this scenario, the total number of server ports per ToR is 64 (2 × 400 Gbps breakout × 32), so the total number of GPUs in the rail would be 512, assuming that 32 × 800 Gbps links are enabled to the spine.

When using multi-tenancy with dedicated physical AI servers for each tenant, it is possible to deploy up to four tenants, each with 128 GPUs per tenant ID, within the same rail. Whenever the number of GPUs needs to increase, additional rails can be added, and the number of spines/links will be increased to offer full line-rate capacity to all tenants. Figure 8-22 illustrates such a scenario, where two rails are interconnected through the spine layer, and multi-tenancy is delivered with only RT5 (Route Type-5) EVPN IP instances between two rails. In this case, the spines are playing the role of route server for the tenant routes and transit IP forwarding. All the tenant definition is done at the ToR leaf nodes, so server1-to-server2 communication for tenant-A will happen over the RT5 VXLAN tunnel, signaled by the BGP EVPN session between the leaf and spines and forwarded using the routing VNI. Server4 or server5 will use a different VXLAN tunnel and also a different routing VNI value. In Figure 8-22, each link to the GPU server NIC is allocated a unique IP address subnet. To reuse the same IP subnet across multiple ToR leaf nodes, the combined MAC-VRF and RT5 EVPN needs to be used to allocate just eight subnets per tenant and allocate them across all the fabric rails. The longest prefix match will happen in this case based on the RT5 IP host advertisements or through the MAC-IP RT2 EVPN routes if the symmetric inter-IRB routing is used at the switch for the given tenant IP instance.

Server-Level Multi-tenancy

Some AI server vendors have added multi-tenancy options at the server level. For example, the H100 server from Nvidia introduced a software solution for multi-tenancy called Multi-Instance GPU (MIG), which allows it to be securely partitioned in up to seven separate GPU instances for CUDA applications, offering separate GPU resources for efficient GPU utilization. With MIG, up to seven instances can be defined, and they can be mapped to seven different VLANs, as illustrated in Figure 8-23.

Inside the server, multi-tenancy can be delivered, for example, with the concept of vGPU and scheduled across multiple servers using the NCCL or RCCL collective communication manager.

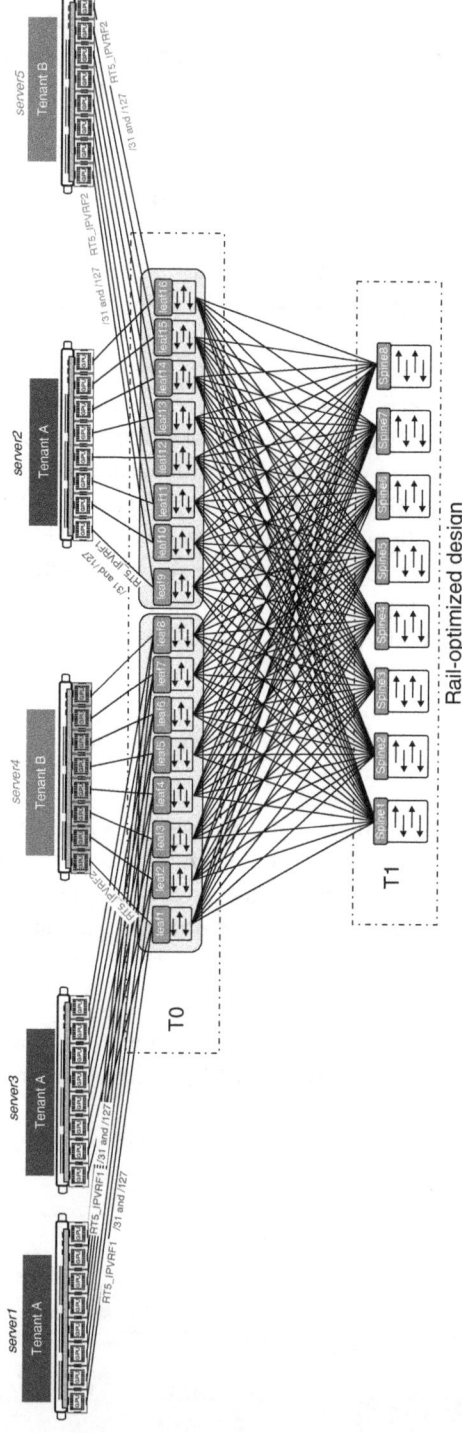

Figure 8-22
Multi-tenant BMS deployment of the GPU servers in two different rails using just RT5 EVPN IP VRF

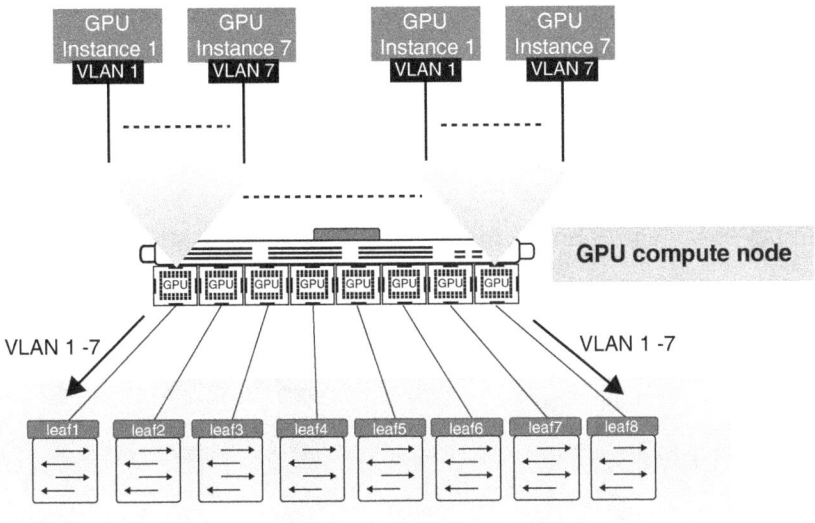

Figure 8-23
Multi-tenancy at the GPU compute node

Combining Server- and Network-Level Multi-tenancy for AI/ML Clusters

When multi-tenancy is enabled at the server level (for example, with Nvidia MIG) as well as at the AI/ML data center fabric level, the given leaf node will enable seven instances at the MAC-VRF level and seven instances of EVPN at the IP level. Each server-connected interface will leverage seven L2 VLAN tags, each allocated to a different tenant.

In the network topology shown in Figure 8-24, seven tenants have been enabled on the AI/ML cluster at the server level as well as inside the network. A given tenant can use all the resources in a particular server, but when communicating between different servers' GPUs, the tenant inter-server traffic is fully isolated; for example, Tenant 1 and Tenant 7 are two different organizations, and the AI/ML data center operator must guarantee, per the contract, that the learning process is fully isolated between the two tenants at the given switch level inside the rail or between rails.

An alternative approach for network level multi-tenancy is to use the dynamic ACLs (Access Lists) enabled at the ToR switch data plane level, based on what the Radius authentication server tenant profile is. The scale of the TCAMs at the switch level may, however, become an obstacle when a very high number of tenants is present at the same time. Having a centralized Radius server-based tenant management is a different approach when compared to a fully distributed EVPN-VXLAN-based multi-tenancy.

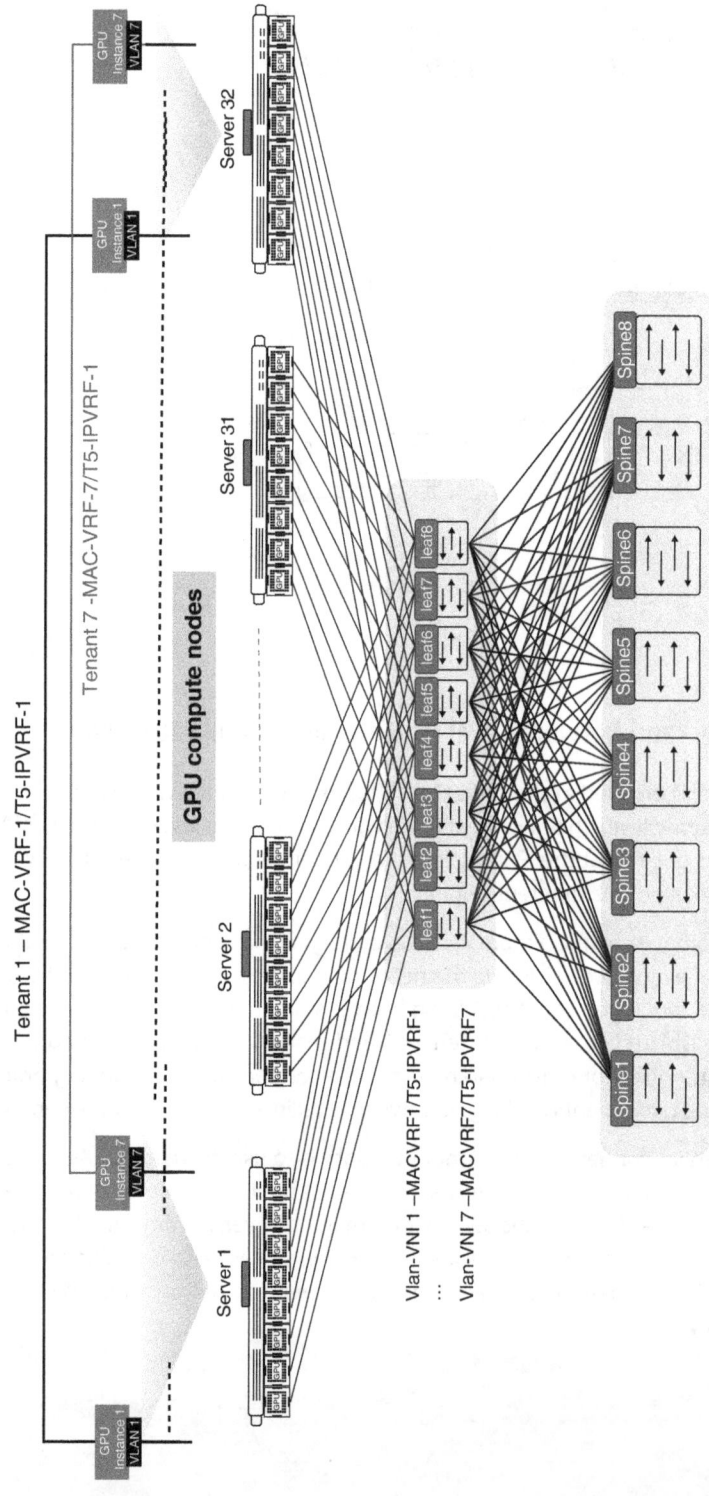

Figure 8-24
AI/ML cluster server multi-tenancy

Microsegmentation and Multi-tenancy for an AI/ML Data Center

If the decision has been made to deliver multi-tenancy inside the backend (learning network domain) and frontend (inference network domain) using the EVPN-VXLAN at the ToR switch level, even within the given VNI/VLAN corresponding to a specific IP subnet, there's a way to add another level of services or tenant segmentation: You can use the VXLAN group-based policy (GBP), where a VXLAN header leverages the VNI ID, and there can be different GLB tag values within the VNI.

For example, if an AI/ML data center operator decided to use the same IP subnet for two tenants but wanted to prevent them from communicating, they could implement GBP by setting the GBP tag ID for a specific tenant ID for ingress.

Extending IP Routing to the Server

In some cases, it can be beneficial to extend the dynamic routing protocol running from the fabric to the GPU server itself. This may be the case, for example, when using a separate routing package for Linux BGP, such as FRR. With this approach, the server can select which of the leaf nodes to forward the traffic to. You can also implement multi-tenancy directly at the server (with IP-VRF for L3 multi-tenancy or MAC-VRF for L2 multi-tenancy). In some cases, you might also implement anycast-type services, where the IP anycast address is advertised through the routing protocol to the fabric from multiple servers. Figure 8-25 illustrates this type of implementation, where each server also gets a BGP ASN.

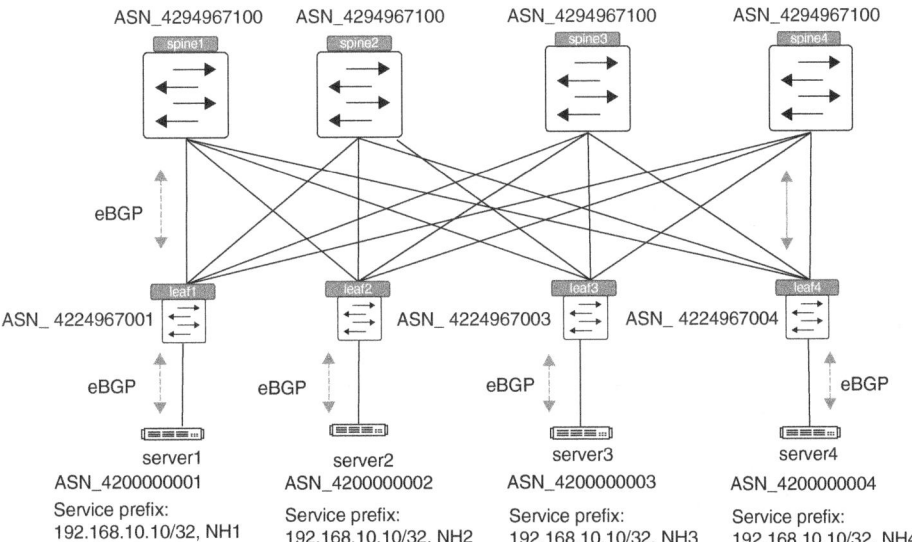

Figure 8-25
eBGP from the server to the ToR switch

You can also optimize a design by enabling a BGP route reflector or even a hierarchical route reflector to which all the servers as well as other nodes peer to optimize the number of peerings or simplify the deployment at scale. In some cases, instead of having the server peer with the ToR switch directly, you can use a virtual appliance BGP route reflector and then let only the selected fabric nodes peer with the virtual applicable BGP server, as illustrated in Figure 8-26.

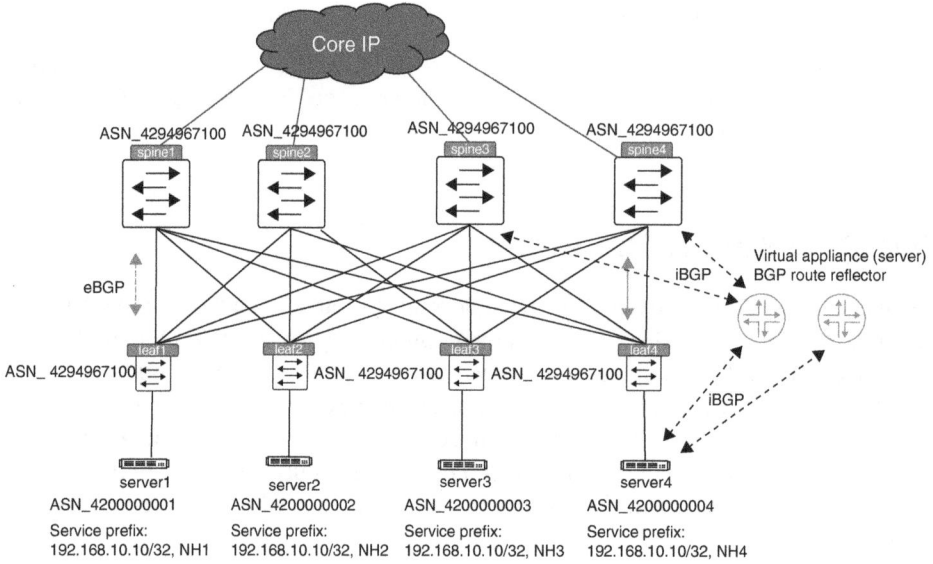

Figure 8-26
Server-level iBGP with a virtual appliance BGP route reflector

With the IP routing design highlighted in Figure 8-26, the service behind the prefix 192.168.10.10 is advertised with a different BGP next hop to the virtual appliance route reflector, which then advertises it to the spines, which are directly connected to the backbone IP network for full IP reachability of the end users to the service inside the data center.

Traffic Engineering in the AI Data Center Fabric

We've mentioned the option of using a central controller, which can influence dynamic IP routing path selection based on the following:

- The telemetry information from all fabric nodes is used to make a decision based on bandwidth and latency utilization.

- The local agent enabled at each node measures the end-to-end performance using active probes and reports it to the central controller.

- DCQCN message telemetry is reported to the central controller, which will decide whether to forward the AI/ML traffic or avoid it (for example, because much of the PFC backpressure was triggered and occurred across many segments of the fabric).

We mentioned that telemetry statistics can be collected and analyzed to make a path decision over the AI data center fabric, but what kind of telemetry data should be considered? Possibilities include queue buffer (shared versus dedicated buffers trends), sFlow, and egress BGP statistics, as well as simple interface statistics at the interfaces for each queue, such as the total cumulative statistics as well as per-second statistics.

The controller connected to the fabric to make any decisions about routing would also need to understand the full fabric topology, so any form of BGP or IGP protocol extension to understand the fabric topology (making sure the connectivity is as designed) would be instrumental as well. It wouldn't make any sense to impose IP routing on incorrectly understood topology; for example, if the leaf nodes were connected incorrectly, it wouldn't make sense to run best performance between the two nodes for specific traffic while letting the rest of the traffic suffer. This is why understanding topology in the context of a controller-based solution for AI data center routing is so important and must be done before triggering any changes for the forwarding of individual AI/ML destination IP prefixes.

The challenge with a traditional controller-based fabric solution is that it can't react to all the performance changes inside the fabric. This is why a controller-driven TE (Traffic Engineering) should be reactive but based on some learnings performed over the fabric, such as over the telemetry data reported over time, to analyze and learn from it. It also needs to preserve stability, so the algorithm used to fine-tune the path forwarding is yet to be defined for each vendor's implementation.

An alternative approach for the AI/ML use case in the context of controller-based dynamic routing would be to make IP routing adaptive for destination hosts while maintaining full synchronization with the GPU job scheduler. For example, if many jobs are scheduled within the fabric for the given path and are ongoing, the new set of GPU jobs will be sent over a different number of paths across the fabric. Consequently, the flows within the given job will use a more deterministic path across the fabric. Figure 8-27 illustrates the building blocks and the controller-driven traffic engineering inside the AI/ML cluster network.

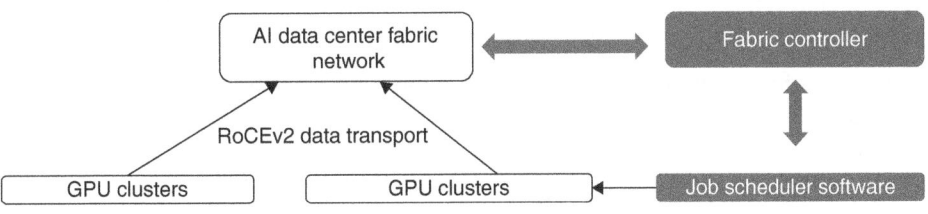

Figure 8-27
Fabric controller connected to the AI data center fabric and job scheduler

Segment Routing and SRv6 for AI/ML Fabrics

As we have discussed in earlier chapters, the major challenge with AI/ML fabrics is to maximize the scale and performance. We have discussed different options to handle load balancing to avoid congestion. Many of the solutions we have talked about have focused on distributed load balancing, where each node decides to balance the traffic. We have also explored global load balancing, where a node knows the link utilization of other nodes in the network so it can make more informed local decisions. Another approach would be to use a centralized controller to make these decisions. The controller would have information about all the nodes, interfaces, and utilization. A controller could have an algorithm to find the optimum paths to enable communication between all the GPUs, and it could push this information to all the nodes to switch the traffic in the required manner.

A centralized controller to make load-balancing decisions would use Multiprotocol Label Switching (MPLS) and Segment Routing (SR). These protocols install additional metadata header information into a network device, and that information is added to the packet at the ingress node in the network. Then all the transit uses this metadata information to make forwarding decisions. The egress node removes the leftover metadata when the packet goes out the network. This approach has the advantage of making much more informed decisions at a central location, resulting in better path utilization across the network.

Segment Routing is a variant of source routing where the decision of the path throughout the network is enforced at the ingress networking node. The node does not store state information; instead, it looks at the segment identified in the packet header and forwards it out the required interface.

The network domain consisting of all networking devices running Segment Routing is referred to as the SR domain. For example, the whole AI/ML cluster can be treated as a single SR domain. Each interface connection between networking devices is referred to as a segment. In the SR domain, each segment is assigned an identifier, called an SR identifier (SID). The path from the ingress node facing the source server to the egress node facing the destination server will include multiple transit nodes and segments. This whole path, from ingress to egress, is referred to as the SR path. Figure 8-28 illustrates the different terms used with Segment Routing.

There are two commonly used SR identifiers: Node SID and Adjacency SID. The Node SID is an identifier attached to a node that is a lot like a loopback address for a node. The Adjacency SID is the identifier attached to each adjacency between the nodes. There are a few other SIDs, including the Anycast SID and the SID for Egress Peer Engineering (EPE).

Figure 8-29 illustrates the operation of Segment Routing. The ingress leaf attaches two SIDs on the Layer 3 header: SID 5 (the node spine) and SID 1 (the egress leaf). Each node removes the SID that is pointing to itself and then forwards traffic based on the underlying SID. This is how a packet is moved from source to destination. Different combinations of SIDs can result in different paths in the fabric. Hence, Segment Routing enables better control of paths in the fabric.

The control plane for Segment Routing mostly resides on the controllers outside the nodes. A controller learns topology information via a routing protocol—either an IGP or Border Gateway Protocol—Links State (BGP-LS). Path Computation Element Protocol is used to install the computed path information on each of the nodes.

The data plane may be either SR-MPLS or SRv6. SR-MPLS uses MPLS labels as the SID. SRv6 adds metadata to the IPv6 header as part of the optional header. This extension header is referred to as the Segment Routing Header (SRH).

Segment Routing and SRv6 for AI/ML Fabrics

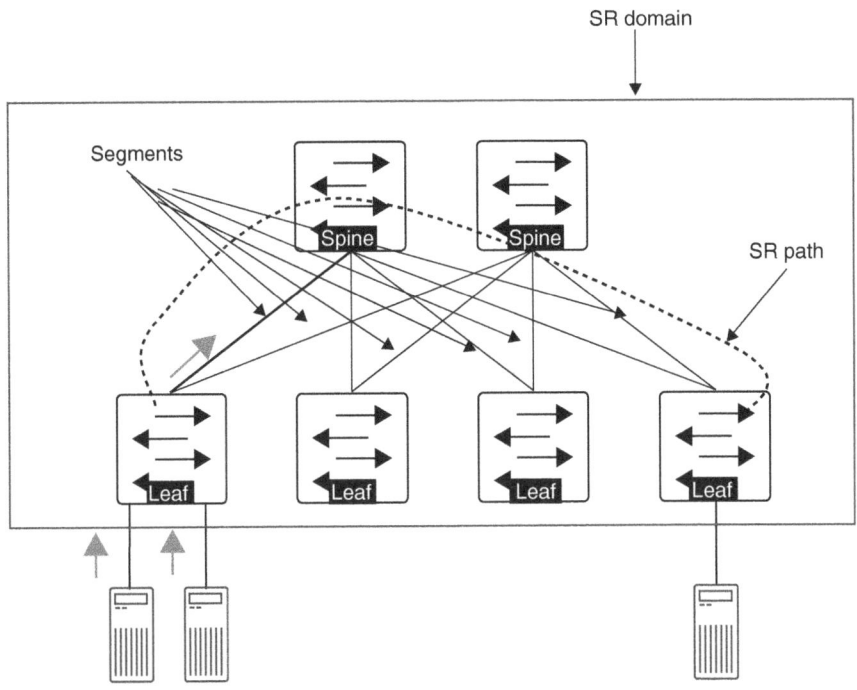

Figure 8-28
Segment Routing terms

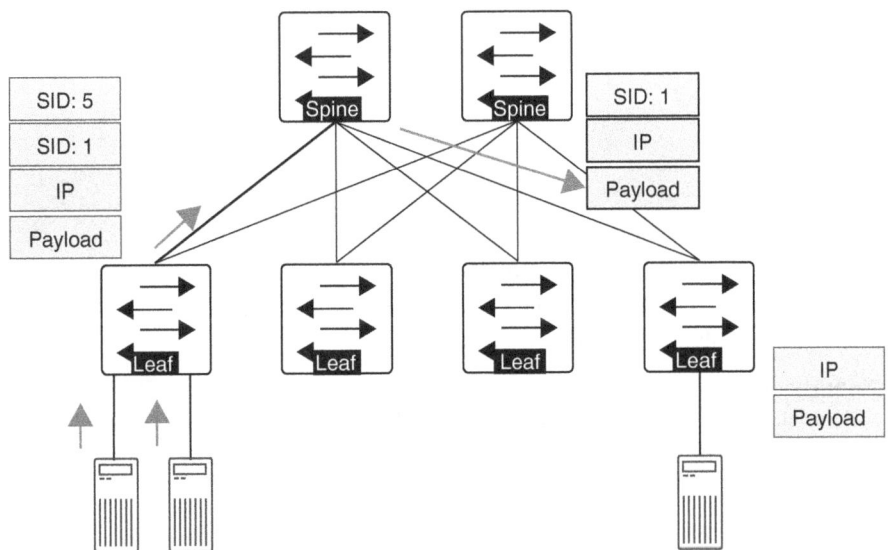

Figure 8-29
Segment Routing in operation

SRv6-Based Traffic Engineering

IPv6 allows 0 to *n* extension headers between IPv6 and the next header. The SRH, illustrated in Figure 8-30, is an extension header that resides between IPv6 and Layer 4 protocols (RDMA in case of AI/ML clusters).

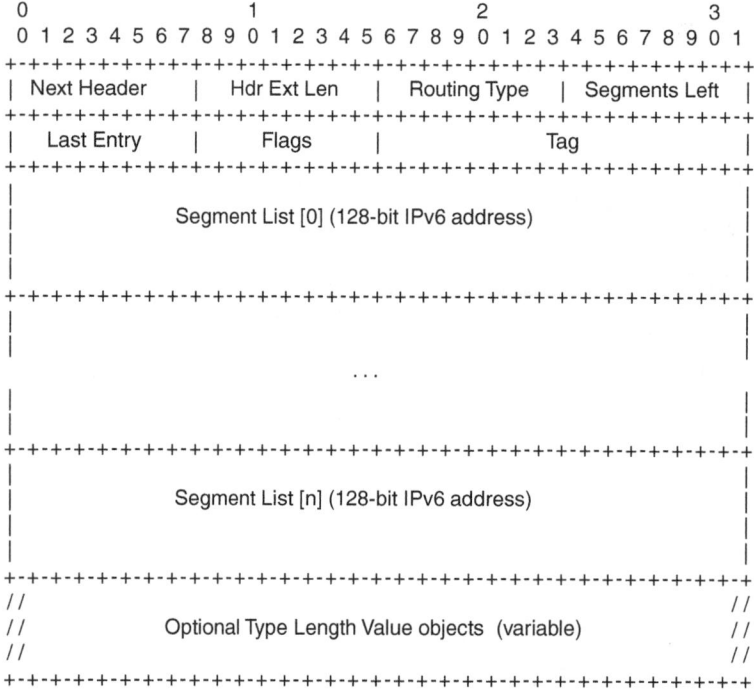

Figure 8-30
SRH frame format

Each SR extension header has three important pieces of information:

- **Locator:** The locator is the first part of a SID, and it consists of the most significant bits representing the address of a particular SRv6 network. The locator is very similar to a network address that provides a route to the parent node.

- **Node function:** The node function typically encodes the node SID function (End SID), an adjacency SID function (End.X SID), or a service function that is the equivalent of a service label in SR-MPLS. Several functions have already been defined in the IETF Draft draft-ietf-spring-srv6-network-programming-07draft.

- **Argument:** The argument function typically encodes a value that identifies the source Ethernet segment for EVPN services that require multihoming. It can be used to carry service or application metadata.

The SR extension header is used to perform network programming. It enables the network to encode a program of individual instructions and insert it into the IPv6 packet headers. The network instruction is the SRv6 SID represented by a 128-bit IPv6 address. Along with the addressing, network instructions define a particular task or function for each SRv6-capable node in the SRv6 network.

An IPv6 header with SRH can be used to encapsulate either IPv4 or IPv6 traffic from the server.

SRv6 Compressed SID

Multiple SRHs may be stacked to provide information about the multiple nodes in a network path. Certain SRv6 applications, such as strict path traffic engineering, may require long segment lists. Compressing the encoding of these long segment lists in the packet header can significantly reduce the header size.

In an SR domain, all SRv6 SIDs instantiated from the same locator block share the same most significant bits. In addition, when the combined length of the SRv6 SID locator, function, and argument is smaller than 128 bits, the least significant bits of the SID are padded with zeros. The compressed segment list encoding seeks to decrease the packet header length by avoiding the repetition of the same locator block and reducing the use of padding bits.

A segment list can be encoded in the packet header using any combination of compressed and uncompressed sequences.

Micro-segment SRv6 (also called SRv6 uSID, or uSID for short) is defined in the IETF Draft draft-filsfils-spring-net-pgm-extension-srv6-usid-16. The micro-SID instruction is an extension of the SRv6 network programming model that does not change the SRv6 control plane and data plane encapsulation. The SID can carry micro-segments. Micro-segment SRv6 provides the same functionality as regular SRv6 but uses 16-bit SIDs (referred to as micro-SIDs), whereas regular SRv6 uses 128-bit SIDs. The benefits of Micro-segment SRv6 are that it reduces packet overhead and helps with scaling in cases of multi-domain deployments.

The SRv6 detailed use-cases for the AI/ML backend training are also covered in the IETF draft draft-filsfils-srv6ops-srv6-ai-backend. It includes the network side and server side SRv6 use-cases for the AI data center.

Segment Routing for AI/ML Clusters

Segment Routing is a major topic, and we don't intend to go deeply into it. However, with basic infrastructure in mind, we can understand the use of SR in AI/ML clusters.

With the help of a controller, paths from each GPU to all the required GPUs can be derived. The algorithm at the controller can help define the paths in such a way that all paths are chosen in the most optimal way to avoid congestion in the network. These path instructions are installed on each node of the network. A node just needs to follow the instructions, and there is no requirement for an advanced load-balancing mechanism; just the per-flow load-balancing mechanism is good enough.

There could be scenarios where interface or node failures occur, and a network needs to be able to handle such failures. The controller must also push the alternate paths or enable OSPF Loop-Free Alternate to handle these scenarios.

In general, Segment Routing technology is gaining momentum in service provider networks to achieve better path utilization. It is also a good contender for exploration from a networking perspective in AI/ML cluster data centers and lossless fabrics as long as the DCQCN and other mechanisms specific to RoCEv2 lossless fabrics can also be leveraged across SRv6 topologies.

Summary

There's no single answer to which IP routing is the best option for all possible AI cluster deployments. While most of the AI data centers will continue to use eBGP-based three-stage and five-stage topology deployments, we recommend analyzing networks in more detail. When topology requirements change to DragonFly or when the number of links to manage between the leaf and spine is increasing over time, some IGP protocols may become better options. Table 8-1 lists some of the most common criteria in this decision-making process, but there are other aspects to incorporate, such as the scale of the FIB and RIB (depending on the product) and how the given routing protocol can coexist with the other functionalities.

Table 8-1 IP Routing for AI Data Centers Summary Table

Characteristic	eBGP	RIFT	IS-IS
IP Clos ECMP topology support	Yes	Yes	Yes
DragonFly topology support	No	Yes	No
Multi-tenancy options for the frontend	Many	Limited	Limited
Convergence speed	Medium	Fast	Fast
Link awareness	Low	High	High
Full topology awareness	Medium	High	Medium
Automatic disaggregation on failure	No	Yes	No
Advertising the fabric configuration data	No	Yes	No
Wide ECMP - Equal Cost Multi Pathing or UCMP – Unequal Cost Multi Pathing	Yes	Yes	No

Test Your Knowledge
Chapter Review

The following questions are designed to test your understanding of the content covered in Chapter 8. Following the questions, answers are provided so you can verify your conclusions.

Questions

1. Why is BGP (Border Gateway Protocol) widely adopted for routing in large-scale AI data center fabrics, and what are its key configuration considerations?
2. How does BGP Deterministic Path Forwarding (BGP-DPF) enhance traffic engineering in AI/ML clusters?
3. What are the advantages and limitations of using RIFT (Routing in Fat Trees) as an IGP in AI data center backbones?
4. How does IS-IS with FlexAlgo support path diversity and workload isolation in AI fabrics?
5. What are the trade-offs between BGP, IS-IS, and RIFT for AI/ML data center routing?
6. How does Segment Routing (SR/SRv6) enable advanced traffic engineering in AI data centers?
7. What is the role of telemetry and real-time monitoring in adaptive routing for AI/ML fabrics?
8. How does multi-tenancy impact routing and segmentation in AI data center networks?

Answers

1. BGP is favored for its scalability, very advanced IP routing policy control, and ability to handle large numbers of prefixes in Clos and non-Clos topologies. In AI fabrics, eBGP is often used with unique ASN assignments per rack or switch, leveraging BGP unnumbered (RFC 5549) for simplified peering via IPv6 link-local addresses. Key considerations include ASN allocation to prevent routing loops, use of BGP add-path for multipath redundancy, and route policies for prefix advertisement and filtering. BGP's path-vector nature and loop prevention via AS_PATH attributes are critical for maintaining stable, deterministic routing in multi-tier, high-bandwidth environments. On the same eBGP session within the fabric, different types of services can be enabled, such as EVPN for multi-tenancy using EVPN RT5 (Route Type 5) for IP prefix isolation and L2 MAC-VRF services for the MAC@ advertisements. Peering from the ToR using BGP to the server is also possible using open-source BGP stack at the server level, which makes an end-to-end IP routing protocol implementation more consistent.

2. BGP-DPF enables logical partitioning of the physical fabric into multiple "colored" paths or logical fabrics. By associating specific flows (for example, based on GPU ID or QPair) with a logical fabric, deterministic path selection is achieved, isolating elephant flows and ensuring predictable latency and bandwidth. This is implemented via BGP community attributes and session coloring, allowing for tenant isolation, SLA enforcement, and optimized resource utilization in multi-tenant or multi-workload environments.

3. RIFT is designed for large-scale, hierarchical fat-tree topologies. It offers fast convergence, automatic disaggregation on failure, and built-in support for wide ECMP and unequal-cost multipathing (UCMP). It uses northbound link-state and southbound distance-vector propagation, reducing FIB size on leaf nodes and supporting zero-touch provisioning. However, RIFT is less flexible for policy-based routing and less mature in multi-vendor environments compared to BGP.

4. IS-IS FlexAlgo allows the definition of multiple logical topologies (algorithms) with distinct constraints (for example, bandwidth, latency). Each FlexAlgo computes its own SPF tree, enabling traffic to be steered over different paths based on workload requirements. This supports isolation of critical AI flows, multi-tenancy, and traffic engineering without requiring MPLS or SRv6 encapsulation, making it suitable for pure IP fabrics.

5. BGP offers policy control, scalability, and multi-vendor support but slower convergence and more complex configuration. IS-IS provides fast convergence and FlexAlgo for path diversity. It is a link-state protocol, but it is less commonly used in data centers. RIFT is optimized for fat-tree topologies and offers fast convergence and automatic disaggregation, but it is newer and less widely supported. The choice depends on scale, required features, and operational familiarity.

6. Segment Routing enables explicit path control by encoding a list of segments (nodes or links) in the packet header. SRv6 uses IPv6 extension headers to carry segment lists, enabling deterministic routing, bandwidth guarantees, and fast rerouting. This is valuable for pinning AI workloads to specific paths, isolating tenants, and optimizing resource usage, but it requires hardware support and careful management of segment lists to avoid MTU issues.

7. Telemetry provides real-time data on link utilization, latency, buffer occupancy, and congestion events. This information can be fed into routing protocols or controllers to dynamically adjust path selection, reroute around congestion, and optimize load balancing. Technologies like in-band network telemetry (INT) and streaming telemetry (gNMI/gRPC) are essential for closed-loop, adaptive routing in high-performance AI fabrics.

8. Multi-tenancy requires strict traffic isolation, often implemented via VRF instances, EVPN-VXLAN overlays, and routing policies. Routing protocols must support per-tenant segmentation, route leaking where appropriate, and scalable handling of overlapping address spaces. BGP-EVPN is commonly used for control-plane signaling, enabling flexible, scalable multi-tenant architectures with fine-grained policy enforcement.

References

Premji, A. Internet Engineering Task Force (IETF) P. Lapukhov Request for Comments: 7938 Facebook Category: Informational Use of BGP for Routing in Large-Scale Data Centers. 2016.

Przygienda, Tony, et al. "RFC 9692: RIFT: Routing in Fat Trees." IETF Datatracker, Apr. 2025, datatracker.ietf.org/doc/html/rfc9692. Accessed 8 Nov. 2025.

Rosen, Eric C., and François Le Faucheur. "RFC 5549: Advertising IPv4 Network Layer Reachability Information with an IPv6 Next Hop." IETF Datatracker, 2025, datatracker.ietf.org/doc/html/rfc5549. Accessed 8 Nov. 2025.

White, Russ, et al. "IS-IS Distributed Flooding Reduction." IETF Datatracker, 2025, datatracker.ietf.org/doc/draft-ietf-lsr-distoptflood/. Accessed 8 Nov. 2025.

Ferguson, Dennis, et al. "OSPF for IPv6." IETF, 1 July 2008, datatracker.ietf.org/doc/html/rfc5340.

Filsfils, Clarence, et al. "SRv6 for Deterministic Path Placement in AI Backends." IETF Datatracker, 2025, datatracker.ietf.org/doc/draft-filsfils-srv6ops-srv6-ai-backend/. Accessed 25 Oct. 2025.

"Juniper Networks." Juniper.net, Juniper Networks, 2025, www.juniper.net/documentation/us/en/software/junos/ai-ml-evo/topics/topic-map/dpf-clos-net.html. Accessed 4 Nov. 2025.

"Juniper Networks." Juniper.net, Juniper Networks, 2025, www.juniper.net/documentation/us/en/software/jvd/jvd-ai-dc-qpp-bgp-dpf/juniper_rdma-aware_load_balancing_lb_and_bgp-dpf_gpu_backend_fabric_implementation.html. Accessed 8 Nov. 2025.

Filsfils, Clarence, et al. "RFC 8754: IPv6 Segment Routing Header (SRH)." IETF Datatracker, Mar. 2020, datatracker.ietf.org/doc/html/rfc8754.

Filsfils, Clarence, et al. "Segment Routing over IPv6 (SRv6) Network Programming." IETF, 1 Feb. 2021, datatracker.ietf.org/doc/html/rfc8986.

Wang, Kevin, et al. "BGP Deterministic Path Forwarding (DPF)." IETF Datatracker, 2025, datatracker.ietf.org/doc/draft-wang-idr-dpf/. Accessed 15 Dec. 2025.

9

Storage Network Design and Technologies

Data storage is a fundamental part of the design of a new AI data center. Storage must be well defined for each phase of the life cycle: data preparation, cleanup, data ingestion, and post-training model storage. Retrieval-augmented generation (RAG) and agentic RAG can utilize storage networks for various types of operations.

The life cycle phases often have different storage requirements in terms of scale, performance, and cost. The target storage media type (such as Flash memory media or a hard drive) sometimes also dictates the type of storage network to be used. Today's storage systems are primarily based on modern solid-state drive (SSD) Flash memory media; some legacy deployments still use high-capacity and low-cost hard disk drives (HDDs). For HDD media, the type of networking storage system will also be reduced to legacy storage networking techniques, such as Fibre Channel (FC) or iSCSI.

The storage networking domain is increasingly essential because, to train LLM models, we need the correct data (curated data), and we need a significant amount of up-to-date data to achieve satisfactory LLM training outcomes. While each GPU-equipped server could, in theory, use the local Peripheral Component Interconnect Express (PCIe) local server interconnect passive component and access the storage that is local to the server, this type of solution is not scalable and is not optimal for larger-scale training. An AI data center needs a dedicated Ethernet/IP, Fibre Channel, or InfiniBand storage network for shared storage memory access to high-capacity servers.

Storage networks are commonly HDDs or SSDs that are not local to the server. They use various logical access methods, such as block, object, or file system access, with a regular NIC or a more advanced specialized NIC with special driver characteristics. Typically, a more advanced NIC is needed for block-level access, while file access and object access are even supported on regular server NICs.

With or without storage networks, a PCIe connection is typically used to interconnect different components within the server with a high-bandwidth bus. In storage networking, a dedicated storage NIC or multiple NICs, once connected directly to the PCIe connection, are used to access remote SSDs rather than the local one. The current generation of PCIe connections (PCIe 5.0/6.0) inside the server can theoretically offer 32 gigatransfers per second (GT/s) per lane. (Gigatransfers are used because the real capacity may change depending on the encoding used.) Even if the networking will always bring small overhead compared to pure native PCIe, the flexibility of adding and removing storage volumes over time is very important, and microsecond or nanosecond latency is still acceptable for most storage deployments with NVME over Fabrics (NVMe-oF). Figure 9-1 shows a CPU and NIC connected to a high-speed server storage PCIe connection. With the generation 5 or higher, such a connection offers 32 GT/s, and so with x16 slots/lanes, it offers approximately 63 Gbps in one direction, with very low latency, which helps to fully exploit the I/O and go line rate of 400 Gbps at the NIC level.

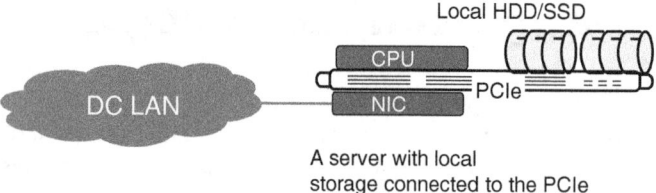

Figure 9-1
PCIe-connected SSD/HDD

Figure 9-2 shows a network-connected SSD/HDD with a storage NIC and a LAN data center NIC.

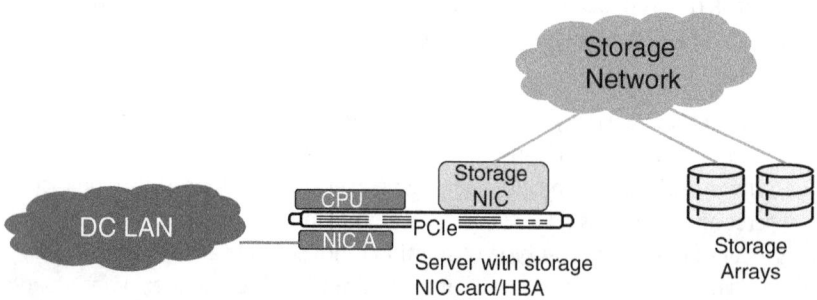

Figure 9-2
Network-connected SSD/HDD storage

In both cases, the servers have CPU and LAN data center NICs as standard parts. This is considered a frontend part for an AI data center. In the case of PCIe-connected HDDs/Flash memory media, access to the file system is facilitated by the high bus speed (that is, lanes). The key advantage of a PCIe-connected SSD is its latency in accessing local storage arrays, which is around 100 nanoseconds for generation 5. In contrast, the Figure 9-2 storage option uses a dedicated NIC for

NVMe-o-TCP/NVMe-o-RDMA, Fibre Channel, or InfiniBand-capable NICs, enabling connection to a dedicated network for accessing remotely connected storage arrays with a latency of around 300 nanoseconds for InfiniBand and 800 nanoseconds for the Ethernet switch. The network-based storage system supports various read and write operations and from the user's perspective—exactly the same as the PCIe option. In the context of AI data center training, both types of storage are sometimes used, with local storage using the file system, backed by one of the NVMe-oF systems. Because parallel accelerated file systems offer shared access by different server nodes and files, additional metadata information is usually helpful during the training phase, as well as when regular snapshots of the training jobs need to be performed.

The LAN data center highlighted in Figure 9-1 can also be used for storage purposes, thereby reducing infrastructure costs. This is not commonly done in AI data centers where dedicated frontend and backend storage systems and storage networks are deployed.

On the topic of the latency advantage of a PCIe connection, when the network is reduced to one to three hops and the port-to-port switch latency is at the nanosecond level, the storage performance in terms of IOPS is very good and comparable with what the PCIe-connected storage is offering. For storage purposes, 700- to 900-nanosecond port-to-port switch latency offers very high bus bandwidth and low latency for write/read operations.

The AI Data Center Life Cycle and Storage Networks

We briefly mentioned the different storage access methods available over a network. We will not detail all of them in this book; our primary focus here is on AI data center–related storage aspects. We will look at how they differ from traditional storage networks and how various storage access technologies can be used to scale and improve performance during the AI training phase. For example, getting up-to-date information in real time in the AI inference may require different storage performance than the AI training phase.

As mentioned earlier, one of the crucial steps in the workflow is data preparation, which involves ingesting data before any training jobs start. The data might be accessed from a storage device that is locally attached to the PCIe connection or, more commonly, it might be accessed from a remote array using some form of dedicated storage network fabric (such as an Ethernet/IP-based parallel high-performance file system or NVMe-oF block storage access, which is the most popular way of integrating a new storage system). The traditional Fibre Channel–based block storage transport (typically deployed in older data center ecosystems) can also be used, but it is typically limited to brownfield data centers, where the AI data center domain is connected to the existing storage domain instead of using a newly built dedicated storage system. The data ingestion step is crucial for transforming existing data stored on various disks to prepare it for the training phase. The data can be organized in both structured and unstructured formats. To optimize it for further training phases, this data is often stored using a modern parallel high-performance file system (such as NFS) or a block access approach with various NVMe-oF options (such as NVMe-o-TCP, NVMe-o-RDMA, or NVMe-o-FC).

After the data preparation phase comes the training and tuning stage. During this phase, it is vital to implement mechanisms for saving and restoring model checkpoints. This practice safeguards the investments made in training and ensures that GPU resources are used effectively for new training jobs. To avoid burdening the GPUs with storage-related tasks, it is important to have a data storage system. An efficient data storage system in the backend network facilitates quicker access and minimizes the time required to save checkpoint data. This, in turn, reduces the frequency and duration of training pauses, which can hinder progress.

The speed of the storage solution in the backend network is critical. Fast-write storage is essential for optimizing the efficiency of the entire training cluster, as it allows continuous training processes to run smoothly, without unnecessary interruptions. Ensuring that this infrastructure is in place is vital for maximizing the overall performance of AI training operations.

Figure 9-3 illustrates the positioning of data storage in the AI training life cycle.

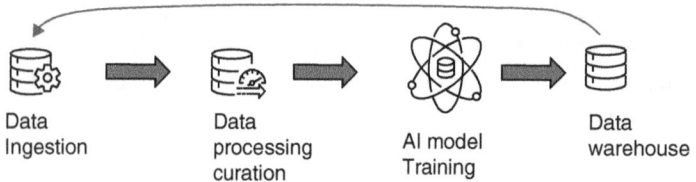

Figure 9-3
Data storage positioning in the AI training life cycle

Figure 9-4 shows how the training server connects to the storage network. Typically, server PCIe-connected local storage flash or disk memory is not sufficient and not scalable for larger-scale deployment of an AI/ML cluster. Therefore, a dedicated storage network is built to offer read/write access using a parallel file system (typically Parallel NFS for higher performance) or one of the NVMe-oF options, such as NVMe-o-TCP or NVMe-o-RDMA, to access larger volumes of flash arrays.

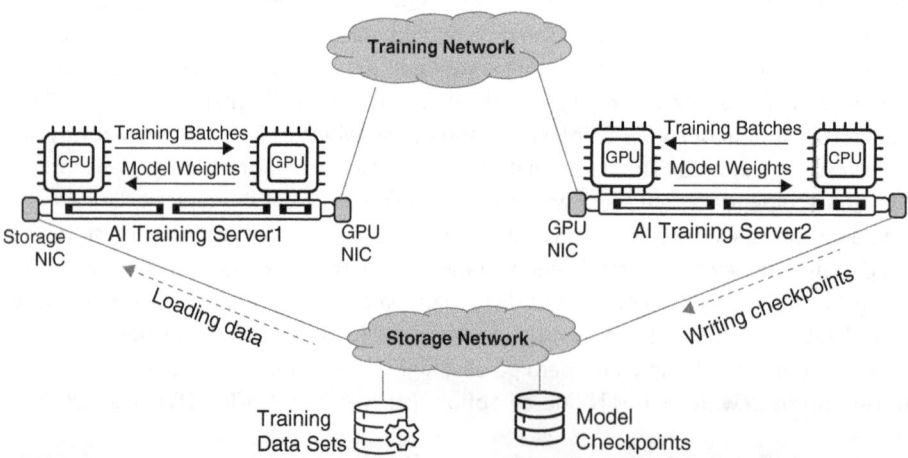

Figure 9-4
AI training server storage network connection

The faster-speed connectivity of the NIC to the storage network is very important here to ensure that the training data sets loaded through the server CPU and delivered in data batches to the GPU have high performance and no bottlenecks; this connectivity is typically achieved by using at least 100 Gbps/200 Gbps NICs. The bandwidth is not the only discriminator. The type of storage system—either the block-level or file-level system—has an impact on the efficiency of the training process.

In the next section, the focus is on the different storage systems that can be considered during the development of a dedicated AI training system. The choice isn't always clear. For example, the storage KPI high continuous I/O might be suitable. However, when integrated with the very frequent training model checkpoint write operations, it may turn out that the whole training system is not as efficient as needed. In an ideal situation, the entire model should fit into the capacity of the GPU local memory. Then, when loading the data, the entire model is loaded, and the data training outcomes are stored progressively within the data warehouse. Suppose the data loading is performed sequentially because of the LLM's larger size and the limited capacity of the GPU memory. In that case, additional time is required to load the data sequentially from the external storage device.

Storage Network Design Types

While considering a storage network's design, the choice of storage technology is sometimes already set, and it affects some aspects of the design. For example, if the design follows NVMe over TCP (NVMe-o-TCP) or NVMe over RDMA (NVMe-o-RDMA), there's more flexibility in terms of design best practices than with the Fibre Channel and NVMe over Fibre Channel (NVMe-o-FC), which are more rigid. This may be related to the fact that standard storage technology has a more rigid definition of redundancy, or the design best practices might have been defined when the density and speed of networks were 10 times slower and virtualization techniques for storage were minimal. While requirements for storage may vary depending on the end goal application (for example, getting a real-time data feed, downloading specific data on demand when needed), there's one common requirement across all the options: the stability of the storage. In fact, the stability of the storage is often even more critical than the performance, which may vary depending on the type of application; for example, storage latency requirements may be different for a financial RAG/agentic RAG system than for a general public RAG system.

When designing the storage infrastructure for an AI data center, two different storage networks are typically built: one for training-related tasks (such as ingesting data) and one for inference (retrieving up-to-date files from various sources). Within the training and inference storage domains, a mix of file and block storage may be used to make the storage both efficient and scalable.

Within each of the storage networks, node- and link-level redundancy is offered, and often there is path diversity between active storage A and backup storage B. Path diversity can be achieved using different methods, depending on the type of storage transport network—Fibre Channel, InfiniBand, or Ethernet/IP—but it offers the same outcomes: full capacity on the backup logical fabric B when fabric A is not available or offers reduced capacity.

From a design perspective, both storage networks must include local site-level redundancy and inter-site replication post-read/write for both storage domains. Inter-site redundancy typically uses a different type of storage transport, such as Fibre Channel over IP (FCoIP), when Fibre Channel storage is used within the data center site, even if object storage is still in use and dedicated site-to-site data center replication gateways are employed.

When the NFS file system is used as a storage technology instead of a SAN, a unified application and storage disaster recovery design can be employed as a single solution for local storage purposes. The inter-site data redundancy tasks can be performed using the same data center interconnect link as the applications.

If the storage is also using RDMA over Converged Ethernet version 2 (RoCEv2) locally within the site, then between the sites, the other inter-site data storage replication technique, RDMA, is typically used. However, inter-site RDMA lossless fabric is rarely used because it's harder to ensure totally lossless fabric with Data Center Quantized Congestion Notification (DCQCN) mechanisms in play over a long-distance link of 40 km or more.

In contrast, data replication over large distances with NVMe-o-TCP can run on a lossy IP core network and won't engage any DCQCN pushback mechanism such as Priority Flow Control (PFC) and adapt to the network conditions using the reliable transport and adaptable and less-restrictive MSS (Maximum Segment Size) requirements compared to the training cluster storage.

The design of a typical storage network should respect the path diversity for redundancy. Data can continue to be read through path B when path A is not available anymore without performance degradation. This means the diverse paths both offer the same capacity in terms of IOPS, bandwidth, and latency. This is sometimes offered using just physical path diversity, where storage A and storage B are two different fabrics, or using logical path diversity with a storage NIC driver capable of switching over from storage A to storage B.

Let's look at the physical level separation, where each storage NIC (independently of the type of transport used) is connected to different physical fabric top-of- rack (ToR) switches, which can be Ethernet/IP, Fibre Channel, or InfiniBand switches. The storage arrays also follow the physical separation. Servers can be set to use the Fab A storage as a primary connection and storage Fab B as a fallback connection, as shown in Figure 9-5.

The design shown in Figure 9-5 is preferred in enterprise environments because there's a complete physical demarcation and precise capacity planning of the resources. The A and B fabrics are identical in terms of capacity: The same number of leaf-to-spine links and the same speed are used, so when one fabric needs to be upgraded or goes offline, the other fabric will offer the same capacity for the data replication. The cost of such infrastructure is high, and that's why, in some cases, logical Fab A/B separation may be desired.

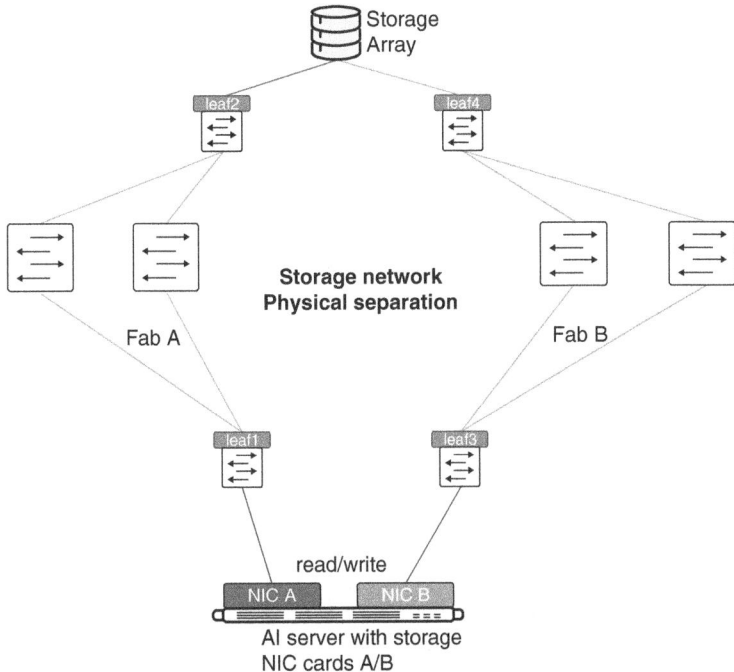

Figure 9-5
Physical Fab A/B separation storage design

With physical separation, the local system must also be set so that, at the nominal level, one path is used. In most critical data replication scenarios, this approach is used. However, for smaller deployments, logical separation is also common. In this case, the same fabric is logically set up with path separation using various path attributes in the case of IP fabrics and using logical zoning in the case of Fibre Channel networks. In the design shown in Figure 9-6, a single link is also used from the leaf to each spine; however, in many cases, at least two links connect each leaf to the spine to ensure that local repairs are triggered at the ASIC level. As with physical separation, storage fabrics are not necessarily 1:1 scheduled, and an oversubscription of 1:3 is very common for both physical and logical fabric separations. When it comes to the logical Fab A/B provisioning for NVMe-o-TCP or NVMe-o-RDMA, as well as for the file systems, pure IP fabrics are used, and the L2 domain isolation is maintained within the given ToR only.

Leaf1 and leaf2 will have dark and light gray fabric connections in the case of logical fabric isolation. In contrast, for physical separation, the given ToR will connect to only NIC A or NIC B. The storage SSD controllers are also provisioned in the same way and with the same approach—either physically or logically separated.

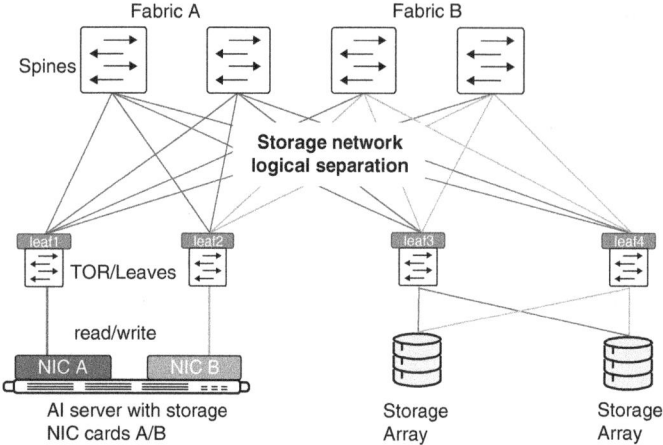

Figure 9-6
Logical Fab A/B separation storage design

With logical separation, overlays using EVPN-VXLAN may be in place, and the Fab A and Fab B control is set to two separate RT5 EVPN instances. Or the same bridging domain may be used for two separate MAC-VRF instances. The point of attachment for these instances (VXLAN tunnel termination) will have a dedicated IP address at each logical instance level, which will be signaled through separate underlay paths—dark gray and light gray underlay paths. The same approach can also be used outside the fabric for storage replication between data center sites: Two separate replication paths, Path A and Path B, can be used, and replication can be done through controlled overlay-to-underlay paths.

While most of the fabrics for storage are moving to IP storage with three-stage IP Clos designs, there's sometimes a need to distribute the data collection in many locations or closer to the end users. This is typically not required in AI training use cases, but when it comes to the inference use case, live data may have to be available closer to the end user. Geographically distributed storage is required for such use cases. This is also where the collapsed storage design shown in Figure 9-7 is useful and where just a pair of two switches will be back-to-back connected, with storage targets and server hosts all connected to the same pair of collapsed spine switches. As we mentioned, this might be more relevant for distributed storage, so some part of the site-to-site storage synchronization may still be required; therefore, a combination of high-performance file storage as well as NVMe-o-TCP block storage may be used. From the Ethernet switching perspective, it may be better to consider deep-buffer switches when the connection to the remote locations is a long distance of 40 km or more to avoid any extensive retransmissions.

The last storage design option we would like to highlight here is the hybrid fabric storage, which involves a combination of on-premises and off-premises storage. In the case of off-premises storage, cloud-based replication ensures that locally stored AI training cluster snapshots are not lost. Therefore, instead of using the site-to-site replication mentioned earlier, a cloud-based AI training outcome is also conducted, typically using two different cloud providers. In most cases, the local site storage and cloud-based storage use a unified approach; therefore, an end-to-end efficient file system or object storage is used both on site and in the cloud. In the context of the AI data center backend fabric, typically the newly efficient file system approach is used to unify the local and remote replication, with the same type of storage technology.

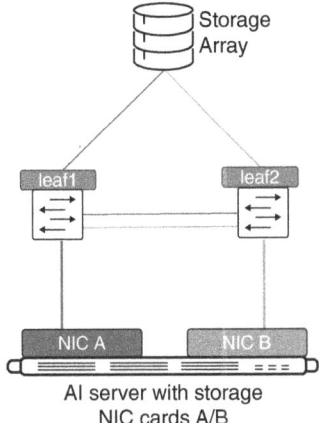

Figure 9-7
Collapsed Fab A/B storage design

The main difference with cloud-based file systems, as shown in Figure 9-8, is that access happens over the firewall cluster. An additional security tunnel layer will be implemented—either IPsec or HTTPS—so for any inference applications, the local file copy is typically used when the storage file system is locally connected and then the backup of the AI training outcomes is just performed to the cloud. When training and inference applications are enabled in the cloud, the natural choice is to also use cloud storage systems for all phases of the AI life cycle.

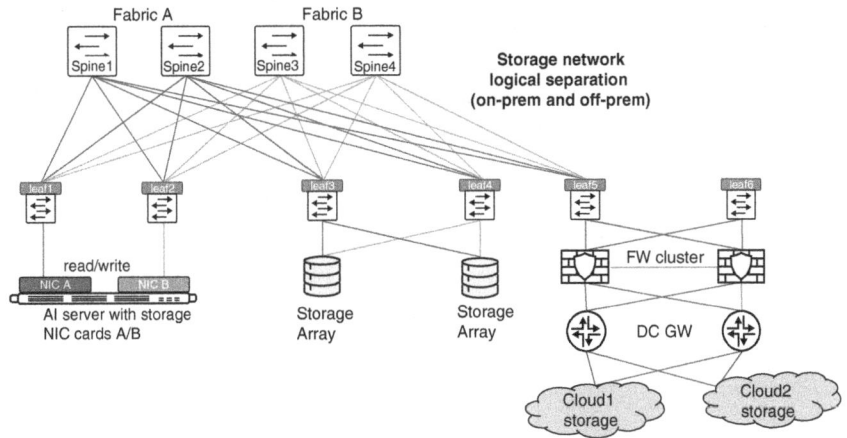

Figure 9-8
Logical Fab A/B design with hybrid cloud redundancy/replication

Block, Object, and File Storage Systems

With AI/ML clusters, the storage system (block, object or file) is typically not directly attached to the network transport type (InfiniBand, Fibre Channel, Ethernet/IP) used by the storage itself, even though some types of storage systems may be limited to a particular kind of network transport or may perform better using a special type of storage network transport. So, while the storage access system can be of the same type (for example, a block storage system), the kind of network storage can be different (for example, IP/Ethernet or Fibre Channel or InfiniBand), and the performance may be different (for example, higher IOPS or better latency).

In the context of AI/ML servers, the high-performance NFS file system may benefit from operating system page caching when multiple model instances are trained on a single server, such as when the training infrastructure is offered as a service.

However, the operating system page cache is not available in the context of block storage, so the local server's CPU cannot access the cached data directly and must retrieve it from the storage array using block-level commands. Table 9-1 compares various types of storage systems with different types of storage networks.

Table 9-1 Comparison of Storage Systems

Feature	Object Storage	Block Storage	File Storage
Data organization	Objects with metadata	Fixed-size blocks	Files and directories
Access method	HTTP-based requests	Block-level access	File-level access
Transport type	TCP/HTTPS, Ethernet/IP	Fibre Channel (FC), FCoIP, Ethernet/IP, InfiniBand (IB)	Ethernet/IP
Scalability	Highly scalable	Less scalable than object storage	Scalable, but less scalable than object storage
Performance	Lower performance than block and file storage	High performance	Moderate performance
Cost-effectiveness	Cost-effective for large-scale storage	More expensive than object storage	Cost-effective for large-scale storage
Use cases	Big data, backups, archives	Databases, virtual machines, high-performance computing, Training/inference, large scale	Training/inference, medium scale, general-purpose file storage, collaboration
AI domain	Post-training data replication in the cloud, RAG/agentic RAG	Post-training local on-premises replication	Training and inference
NVMe-oF	No	Yes	No
SAN	No	Yes	No
NAS	No	No	Yes

NVMe-oF for Block-Level Access

You have just seen the advantage of block-level access, and this type of access is precisely what an NVMe-oF storage network uses. This method of storage networking gained extreme popularity due to its ability to boost storage performance and efficiency in modern data centers with the efficiency of flash media and an open-standard approach. This approach doesn't impose rigid requirements, and it offers a high level of flexibility when it comes to the choice of the storage transport network while still maintaining the common baseline for session establishment and using a boot specification that is common across different types of transport. Figure 9-9 shows that various components remain the same, though the fabric transport part changes, as shown in the section labeled "Transport specifications."

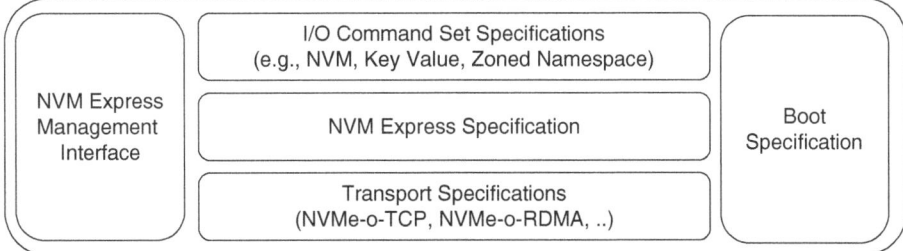

Figure 9-9
NVMe storage specification building blocks

Whereas traditional Fibre Channel involves a limited vendor ecosystem, NVMe storage allows data center administrators to choose different transport options within the same NVMe base storage standard and pick the type of fabric transport based on the application requirements (for example, fast ramp time, lower latency, better scalability). With NVMe-o-TCP, scalability is better than with NVMe-o-FC, but the latency may be higher than with InfiniBand or RDMA.

In the context of the AI fabric, the NVMe flavors may also change according to the AI/ML phase. Either the training or inference phase may use NVMe, but one can run over TCP and the other over RDMA or InfiniBand.

NVMe-oF leverages the high-speed, low-latency characteristics of NVMe, extending its benefits beyond the PCIe bus, which is not scalable for larger AI clusters and for larger-size LLM training. NVMe-oF also makes it possible to enable ingestion and cleanup of the data in parallel and run fast writes of the AI model snapshots. In all cases, NVMe I/O is higher compared to traditional storage protocols like Fibre Channel or iSCSI.

Many criteria can be used to compare the storage types, but scalability, performance, and costs always come first. NVMe-oF enables flexible scaling of storage resources, allowing for both horizontal and vertical scaling. It is therefore ideal for handling increasing data volumes and diverse workloads.

From a performance perspective, there is reduced CPU overhead with NVMe-oF because it offloads many storage tasks from the CPU to the storage controller, freeing up valuable CPU resources for other applications. This is especially optimized in the case of RDMA transport compared to the TCP transport option. NVMe-oF offers significantly lower latency compared to traditional storage protocols, leading to faster response times and improved application performance. NVMe-oF is well suited for software-defined storage (SDS) environments, where its flexibility and programmability enable efficient management and provisioning of storage resources. Finally, from a cost perspective, NVMe-o-TCP is helping to drive down costs, as it involves fewer network prerequisites and lower NIC costs compared to RDMA or Fibre Channel transport options for NVMe-oF.

NVMe over Fibre Channel (NVMe-o-FC) leverages the existing Fibre Channel infrastructure, provides a reliable and high-performance solution for enterprise storage environments, and offers seamless integration with existing Fibre Channel SANs. NVMe-o-FC provides advanced features like lossless data transfer and robust error handling. It also offers all the capabilities of the Fibre Channel transport, such as Credit-Based Flow Control (CBFC) and security of the storage fabric with the zoning system. However, the cost of the infrastructure in greenfield NVMe-o-FC deployments may not be as attractive as the cost of the infrastructure with TCP or RDMA, and the increase in the overall storage fabric bandwidth is not as simple as in the case of RDMA or TCP-based storage fabrics. On the other hand, in brownfield designs where a Fibre Channel network is already in place, NVMe-o-FC may be an attractive alternative. In this case, only the flash system of the storage array can be changed, rather than the entire storage network.

NVMe over RDMA (NVMe-o-RDMA) uses the RoCE protocol over Ethernet networks, enabling high-performance, low-latency storage connectivity. It can also sometimes be considered in AI storage networking because RoCEv2is currently the main option for the AI training phase, so the same transport technology could be used not only in the case of the training network domain but also in the case of the storage network. When the same technology is used in both storage and training networks, it is often a good idea to have the same team operate both of the networks. When RDMA over Ethernet with IP/UDP as the outer encapsulation is also used in the case of NVMe-o-RDMA, the semantics of NVMe are preserved for session establishment and teardown; the SQ (submission queue) and the CQ (completion queue) are both used across all different fabric type options. (We will look at the NVMe-oF state machine in the next sections as well.) From a cost perspective, in most cases, Ethernet/IP-based transports over fabric for TCP and RDMA remain more attractive; however, some additional fine-tuning of the lossless storage fabric is still required for RDMA, mainly related to fine-tuning the queue depth and buffer utilization or adjusting the DCQCN parameters. This means the DCQCN parameters for the RDMA-based NVMe-oF may also differ from the AI training cluster DCQCN setting; the ECN and PFC thresholds may also be different. This type of fine-tuning is not required in the case of NVMe-o-TCP, where even without a lossless network, the storage efficiency in terms of IOPS is good and compatible with most AI training and AI inference requirements.

NVMe over TCP (NVMe-o-TCP) is very popular because it has limited prerequisites on both the NIC side and the network side. The lossy fabric can be used so that a dedicated storage infrastructure can be enabled with a more competitive cost. The TCP transport for NVMe does, however, engage more CPU local to the server, whereas the RDMA and Fibre Channel can place the data directly on the memory space. However, outcome of high IOPS is comparable especially for higher number of threads. Even if latency of the TCP transported read/write operations is higher in case of TCP versus RDMA, among different types of NVMe-oF, the TCP option is the most popular one from the deployment perspective.

NVMe-o-TCP State Machine

We've already discussed the main advantages of NVMe-o-TCP, which will continue to be used for cold file storage in AI/ML data centers. Now let's focus on how session establishment and teardown, as well as the transport data plane, work.

From a higher-level perspective, when the host initiates a read or write operation to the controller target (where the data is stored in a flash array system), communication begins with the establishment of an initial TCP session to the destination TCP port 8009, which is typically used. After that, the NVMe subheader will have the QID setting negotiated between the two nodes. Afterward, NVMe commands will be sent, including the opcode values that describe the type of operation (read/write), with 0x02 for read operations and 0x01 for write operations. The NVMe header information, which is sent before the NVMe command capsule, includes the command ID value, which is either QID or IOQ for the given session. Only then is the NVMe CMD part sent; it contains more detailed information regarding the opcode values and namespace ID (NSID). The NSID is a logical block unit of storage that an NVMe controller (SSD array) presents to a host; the host writes to and reads from the NSID. A single NVMe SSD or a larger NVMe storage array (target) can contain multiple namespaces to enable more precise management of storage capacity allocation and control. For instance, an enterprise storage array could offer multiple namespaces to various hosts or applications, each with distinct performance traits, block sizes, or access permissions.

Figure 9-10 illustrates the communication between the two nodes—a server host (originator) and the target, which, in the context of NVMe-oF, is referred to as a controller. The session establishment commands and the data are sent using IP/TCP encapsulation, which means the fabric over which they are sent is Ethernet based and usually enabled as a pure IP fabric. When multi-tenancy is required, some form of overlay is used with EVPN-VXLAN; however, this is done only when NVMe-oF is offered as a managed service, such as when two parallel LLM trainings are to be conducted at the same time; in this case, the same dedicated storage network domain can be used to deliver backend storage for the two tenants, and the IP fabric shown in Figure 9-10 will also have an overlay with IP VRF instances and VXLAN tunnels signalized with EVPN BGP control plane RT5 (Route Type 5) between the ToR Ethernet/IP switches. The networking design will use the same options as a generic storage design. Hence, here we will focus on the concept of send/receive capsules used in NVMe-o-TCP and the key command structure exchanges over the network.

The communication presented in Figure 9-11 typically occurs in a one-to-one fashion between the originator and the target, so a unique set of command IDs is used to identify the connection. An NVMe/TCP connection is associated with a single admin or I/O SQ and CQ pair, which means a 1:1 mapping for the given TCP connection.

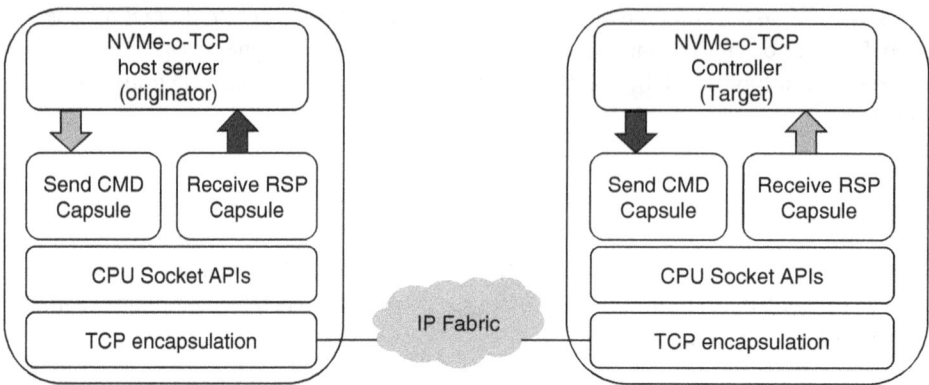

Figure 9-10
NVMe-o-TCP send and receive capsules

Figure 9-11 shows a more detailed view of session establishment, where the initiator presents the IC Req PDU (initialize connection) with the parameters and feature support information and awaits the controller target's response with acceptance of the requested parameters.

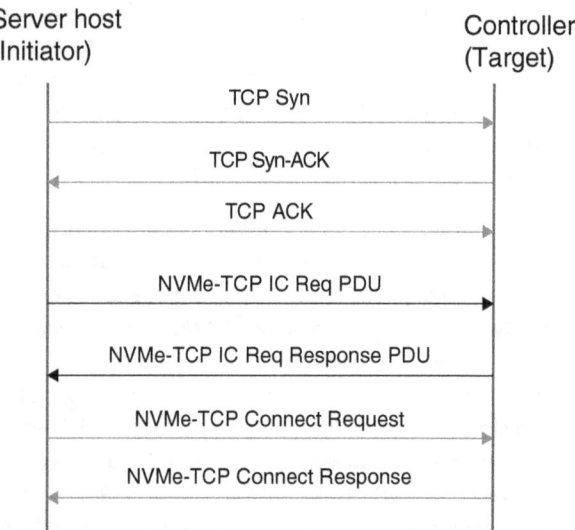

Figure 9-11
NVMe-o-TCP data transfer after the initialization phase

The initial part pf this communication is a classic TCP standard handshake that is completed by the TLS handshake for a secure connection, and the IC Req PDU follows. An originating host and a target controller in an NVM system communicate over TCP by exchanging NVMe/TCP protocol data units (PDUs) (NVMe/TCP PDUs). Different types of PDUs are used during the initialization, transfer, and completion, while the main format of the header stays the same; the PDU format also allows for including PDU type-specific information.

During the initialization part, the type of information included in the IC Req PDU helps to announce the host capabilities (such as the NVMe version used, data integrity info, or the requested data offset and identification unique to the NVMe-oF). In some cases, the server host may also express its preferred controller ID. The last part of the connection establishment in the NVMe-o-TCP connect request and connect response includes the controller's successful binding and the queue sizing. Only after the phase of initialization and connection request/response, the capsule command information is exchanged—CapsuleCmd (controller host) and CapsuleResp (controller to host)—with more detailed information on the namespaces and the opcode with the type of operations requested. After this, data transfers will occur using the H2CData and C2HData PDUs (Protocol Data Units).

Four different types of capsules are used with NVMe-o-TCP communication: the command capsule from the host to the controller, the response capsule, which is from the controller to the host, and the data capsules from the host and the controller, with capsule type IDs 0x03 and 0x04, respectively. So, for example, when the host server wants to run the read operation, the NVMe command capsule includes the capsule type 0x01, a command ID value, an opcode value (which is 0x02 for read), a namespace ID, the data length, in bytes, and the PRP1/PRP2 host memory address (where PRP stands for physical region page). PRP1 and PRP2 are pointers that tell the NVMe device where in host memory to read from or write to. The PRP1 is a 64-bit pointer to the start of the data buffer in host memory, and PRP2 is a 64-bit pointer to either the next contiguous page or a PRP list.

In many cases, instead of using the PRP, the initiator (client) uses the SGL (scatter gather list) to describe multiple discontinuous memory regions. Both the PRP and the SGL, which are the memory block descriptors, will be exchanged at the NVMe command (64B) level just after the NVMe-oF/TCP header, which contains the capsule type and length information. So what's the difference between SGL/PRP and the namespaces, which are all related to the memory block identification? SGL specifies the target's location in host memory for placing (or retrieving) the data payload during I/O operations (such as read and write), indicating where the data buffers reside in the initiator's memory. The namespace information is a logical volume unit exposed by the NVMe target controller. It represents a region of storage, like a virtual disk or a partition ID. Both pieces of information are required for the successful establishment and teardown of a session and are part of the NVMe-o-TCP protocol stack information. With SGL, there is DMA memory mapping, and with a namespace, there is a logical device identification (a more abstract storage device).

For the read operation, we have already mentioned that the namespace ID represents the target logical storage block (i.e., the volume to access), and the SGL descriptors send the information of the originator's memory region address, along with the buffer memory information. When it comes to data transfers, the state machine shown in Figure 9-12 highlights the fact that the acknowledgment sequence numbers are not part of the NVMe headers when TCP is used as a transport because this is handled directly at the TCP level with the SYN/SYN-ACK/ACK standard approach.

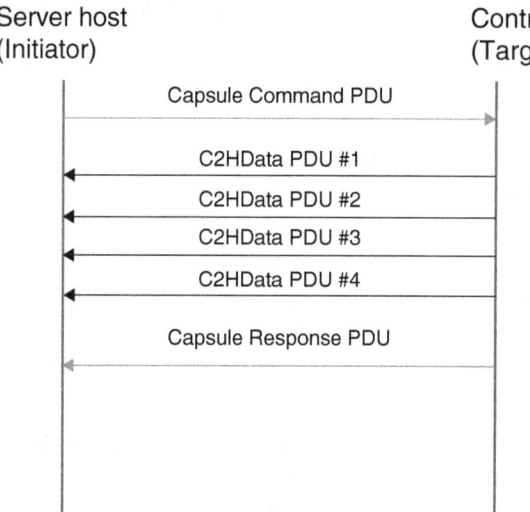

Figure 9-12
NVMe-o-TCP data transfer after the initialization phase

In case of the NVMe-o-TCP, the write operations represented in Figure 9-13 are achieved using in-capsule even if the "off-capsule" transfers are also possible.

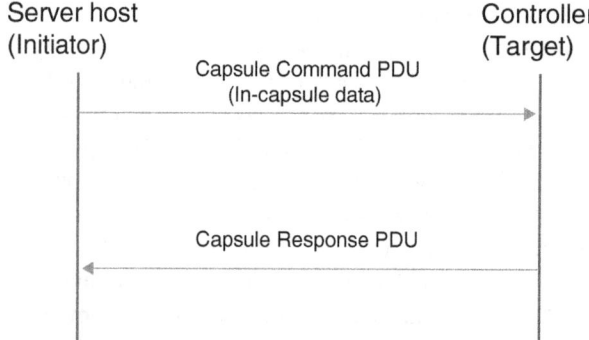

Figure 9-13
In-capsule data write operation

The main difference is that off-capsule transfers may support much faster write operations; this method is used when out-of-order data write operations are preferred. With in-capsule transfers, data write operations are always done in order, and the LAST-PDU flag is used to indicate that the transfer sequence is completed. The size of capsules is variable when in-capsule data is supported and fixed when in-capsule data is not supported.

In the context of native PCIe-attached NVMe SSDs, the NVMe PDU commands are sent to the controller in SQEs (submission queue entries), which are enqueued in the host driver. The controller (target node) enqueues the CQEs (completion queue entries) and sends them to the originating host to notify it about the completion of the given command ID. In the case of NVMe-oF, the concept of the capsule is used; similarly, the command capsule includes the SQE. In contrast, the response capsule includes the CQE, a concept also employed in the native PCIe NVMe use case. With NVMe-oF and also with NVMe-o-TCP, the command capsule becomes the payload of an NVMe-o-TCP CapsuleCmd PDU. For an NVMe completion, the target constructs a CQE and wraps it in an NVMe-oF response capsule, and then this response capsule becomes the payload of an NVMe-o-TCP CapsuleResp PDU.

We mentioned earlier that the capsules concept is used in NVMe-oF and that it's included in the PDUs, where the PDU header contains information about the type of capsule sent in the payload—for example, the common PDU header (PDU Type = CapsuleCmd). Figure 9-13 shows a general view of the PDU format, just before the PDU is encapsulated in the larger TCP payload.

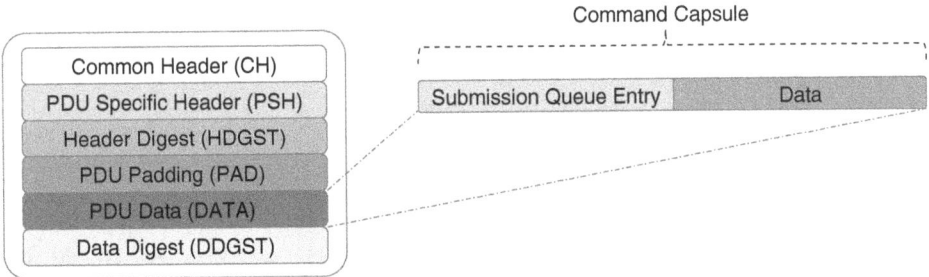

Figure 9-14
NVMe-o-TCP PDU structure with a capsule inside the payload

The PDU standard format inserts the capsules in the data payloads. In the example shown in Figure 9-14, the NVMe command SQE is followed by the in-capsule data, and other PDU is then added either within separate TCP segments or within the same TCP segment. For example, in Figure 9-15, we show a single TCP segment that leverages two NVMe PDUs. Each of these PDUs may include different capsules.

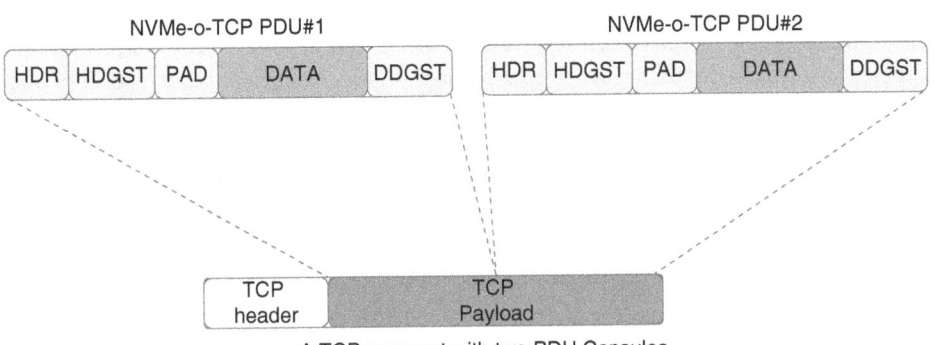

Figure 9-15
A TCP segment encapsulating two NVMe-o-TCP PDUs

Usually, TCP segments are large enough to include multiple segments, so the size of the network interface's MTU is typically set to accommodate jumbo frames and is around 9,000 bytes end to end within the dedicated storage Ethernet/IP fabric, allowing for the delivery of multiple PDUs as part of the same TCP segment.

For session termination, the H2CTermReq (host to controller) and C2HTermReq (controller to host) PDU names are used to gracefully terminate the given NVMe-oF session and subsequently tear down the TCP connection. The PDU CapsuleResp type is used, and the more detailed information is again part of the PDU DATA payload, where the CapsuleResp contains the CQE (command ID, status, and so on) for which the session is terminated. As a result, the given namespace, command identifiers, and SQ/CQ identifiers are also relaxed, and the next session initialization can use them.

With a multi-core CPU system inside a server, each core may have a dedicated session with the target controller and enqueue the messages independently to a dedicated namespace and dedicated memory regions. This is why, outside of the efficient TCP offload at the NICs, the multi-core CPU architecture is typically used in the NVMe-o-TCP environments. This is more optimized in the NVMe-o-RDMA/RoCEv2 systems on which we will focus next.

NVMe-o-RDMA/RoCEv2 State Machine

The RDMA option for NVMe is sometimes considered when the initial ramp-up of storage traffic requires fast performance and when less efficient CPUs are available in the servers. We have already mentioned that for NVMe-o-TCP, each core of the CPU will help handle the session with the given target controller. We have also noted that in case of the NVME-o-TCP storage, the IP fabric network can be a loosely set end-to-end BGP IP or any other IGP IP routing protocol network without any specific QoS settings. This can still be optimized when the servers' CPUs have medium performance and the storage network already offers lossless capabilities. In this case, NVMe-o-RDMA can be considered to offload CPU load and accelerate the initial phases of session establishment. Because the RDMA transport delivery of the NVMe uses UDP connectionless encapsulation instead of TCP, it means there won't be native support for flow control. Flow control will be incorporated at the upper level of the RDMA state machine because the native guarantee of packet delivery is not part of UDP.

From a benchmarking perspective, there are also situations in which write operations with RDMA over RoCEv2 get better latency results (such as 66% lower write latency) but are still dependent on many parameters, such as the number of write jobs initiated, the block sizes, and queue depth. Due to the ramp time and general write latency, better results are achieved with RDMA over RoCEv2 for storage NVMe systems. Some deployments are implemented in this manner, even if additional requirements are necessary on the NIC and in the IP fabric to leverage the lossless approach. The difference for the IP fabric part is that while the transport will be using the RoCEv2, which we have already covered in earlier chapters, the design will typically have 100 Gbps/200 Gbps NICs for storage. The leaf-to-spine dedicated network won't be 1:1 scheduled; that is, it will be oversubscribed (for example, 1:3 scheduled).

The storage longevity of the RoCEv2 workloads will also be shorter compared to AI training, which may involve workflows with very long scheduled times. Therefore, the load-balancing requirements can be slightly relaxed in cases where RDMA is used for IP storage networking. In contrast, the dynamic load balancing (DLB) flowlet mode, described in Chapter 6, "Efficient Load Balancing," will still be applicable in the case of NVMe-o-RDMA.

NVMe/RDMA over RoCEv2 runs NVMe-oF capsules and data over RoCE (InfiniBand over UDP). The reliable connection is controlled at the NIC RDMA driver level instead of at the host-level CPU, as is the case with NVMe-o-TCP.

Figure 9-16 illustrates the key parts of the initial state machine, where just after the UDP initial phase, the RoCEv2 CM (Connection Management) request/reply mechanism will take place over the destination UDP 4420, before any NVMe-specific information is exchanged. That is, without the controller and host negotiated QP ready state, any next phases won't happen properly for the NVMe part of session initialization with the command capsules. During the discovery phase, before any RDMA_CM_REQUEST handshake occurs to negotiate the QPAIRs, the RDMA_PRTYPE (RMDA Provider Type) information is exchanged, which indicates the type of RDMA transport. For example, for ROCEv2, the RDMA_PRTYPE value 04 is used, for InfiniBand, the value 02, and for iWARP, the value 05. The server host sends the Get Log Page – Discovery Log Pages and receives the response from the target server, which gives an indication of the capabilities in terms of transport, and determines which verbs must be used further. This initial phase is a standard NVMe-Fabrics Discovery Controller protocol phase and happens over TCP default destination port 8009, before any RDMA Connection Management (CM) handshake happens using the destination UDP 4420 (in case of the ROCEv2). Only after these two initial phases, the actual data transfer of the ROCEv2 over the destination UDP port 4791 will take place, to carry the NVMe capsules and data.

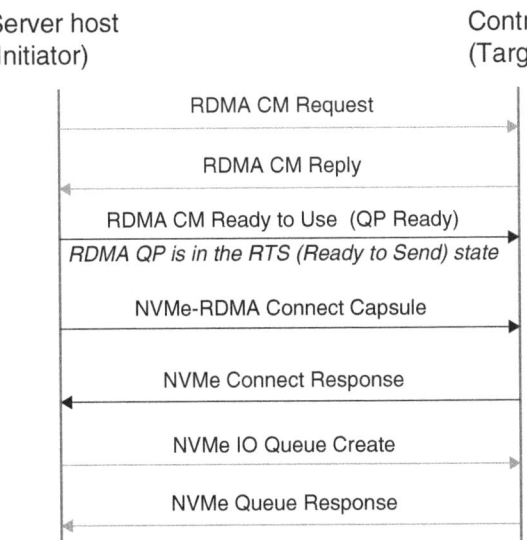

Figure 9-16
NVMe-o-RDMA session initialization summary

From the state machine shown in Figure 9-16, you can see that even if the TCP encapsulation is replaced with the UDP connectionless approach, the initial RDMA handshake is very similar to the TCP handshake.

Once the RoCEv2-driven session establishment is completed, the NVMe-level queue creation happens. The RDMA-based NVMe will place the capsules immediately after the UDP and InfiniBand headers, so the new NVMe information is leveraged with the standardized namespace ID, command ID, and the SGL, which describe the memory buffers on the host where data will be read from or written to.

Figure 9-17 provides a simplified representation of the layered approach of the NVMe-o-RDMA over RoCEv2 data plane.

Figure 9-17
NVMe-o-RDMA over RoCEv2 storage data packet format

The NVM CMD block leverages the namespace ID, command ID, and SGL messages, which are common to the NVMe standard.

The concept of the QPair is specific to RDMA and, in the case of RoCEv2, it is used inside the BTH, so every SQE and CQE will be associated with the specific RoCEv2 QPair value.

At the completion phase, the response capsule is placed into RoCEv2 and sent directly over the network. A single I/O SQ and I/O CQ pair is mapped to a single RDMA QPair in a 1:1 relationship. Multiplexing multiple I/O SQs and I/O CQs onto a single QPair is not supported with NVMe-o-RDMA over RoCEv2. The baseline NVMe queueing operational model is also maintained in the context of NVMe-o-RDMA over RoCEv2. The host server enqueues the SQEs into the SQ. The NVMe controller (target) dequeues the SQEs and enqueues the CQEs into the CQ capsule. The host driver dequeues the CQEs once they are received.

The RDMA transport at the host uses RDMA_SEND to transmit command capsules. An RDMA_SEND contains up to one command or response capsule. All RDMA_READ and RDMA_WRITE operations are initiated by the controller, which is specific to the RDMA transport of the NVMe-oF framework.

From the description, we could think that some of the information from the NVMe block is overlapped with what the native InfiniBand header includes, such as the type of operation or the QPair in the BTH, as well as the RETH (RDMA Extended Transport Header). The DMA length, virtual address, and remote key are sent as well before any of the NVMe memory information is processed for the given namespace ID.

High-Performance File Systems

So far, we have looked at the main protocol stack of the standard storage systems, which are usually used in combination with more modern parallel file systems, such as Lustre, GPFS (General Parallel File System), or BeeGFS (which is open source), or in many cases with more industry-proven end-to-end AI storage systems such as WekaFS and VAST.

In some of these distributed parallel file systems, transport flexibility is still offered with the initial session establishment over RoCEv2 or InfiniBand. However, the namespace shared access part in larger-scale clusters may play a more critical role (as all server nodes can see the same file path, without manual replication or remounting) and help to avoid the limitations of the 1:1 session mappings of the traditional storage systems between the host and the controller, such as with traditional NVMe-oF systems.

Earlier in this chapter, we mentioned that different phases of the AI training life cycle may have specific storage requirements, and a combination of storage technologies can be used to achieve the outcomes such as high I/O, low latency, or high bus bandwidth. This is sometimes a problem because managing the different storage technologies requires different software stacks and different monitoring and provisioning tools. When the design for storage also includes cloud-based storage replication, modern file systems can help unify the integration of on-premises and off-premises storage under the same storage management system. Modern file systems are not exactly the same as traditional NFS systems, and they sometimes use a more efficient transport (such as RDMA). In addition, when a system offers direct integration with the Nvidia GPUDirect Storage software stack, the whole AI data center storage ecosystem becomes much easier to manage and scale.

File metadata information and shared access are often mentioned as advantages of parallel high-performance file systems, but it's important to keep in mind the main characteristics of a file system for storage and the differences with a parallel file system.

A file system typically has the role of organizing and maintaining the file namespace and storing the contents of the files and the attributes of the files using extensive metadata information, such as file size, data owner, and access permissions. A parallel file system is designed to allow multiple clients to access a file system simultaneously, no matter where the file is located. The main difference with a simple shared file system is the level of parallelism. Multiple clients can read and write simultaneously instead of doing so in a sequential way.

For example, the WekaFS storage system, which is particularly designed for AI data center clusters, distributes and parallelizes both data and metadata across the entire cluster in small chunks. This distribution provides low latency and high performance regardless of the I/O size (small, large, or mixed). Because the data and metadata across all nodes are represented in the form of a data lake (a scalable repository that stores structured and unstructured data from various sources), WekaFS maximizes the aggregate bandwidth and IOPS of the system, eliminating the overhead of sequential access to each file and the complexity of supporting various storage state machines. Such a file system can be used on-premises and off-premises as well as in a hybrid mode, where it uses the S3 (Simple Storage Service) implementation to integrate on-premises and off-premises environments. In the case of modern file systems that understand the popular POSIX (Portable Operating System Interface) semantics used in ML software frameworks such as PyTorch and TensorFlow, there's no traditional protocol state machine with a sequential message exchange. POSIX has a set of standardized APIs and behaviors that define how applications interact with the file system and operating system. A POSIX-compliant interface allows AI/ML training applications to run standard Linux file APIs (open, read, write, rename, mkdir, unlink, and so on).

The hot data on on-premises backend servers is connected to a storage IP fabric or InfiniBand fabric, and the cold data is off-premises, in object storage. All of this is accessed by using S3 system calls over the HTTPS API; to be more precise, TLS over HTTP (S3 REST API) is used in the case of hybrid deployments. With an application such as TensorFlow, the POSIX file system interface is used, and the AI parallel file systems will understand the associated semantics, such as open(), read(), write(), stat(), unlink(), and so on, and will, when needed, move the data files from the performance back-end storage domain (local SSD flash system with NVMe-o-PCIe) to the scale-optimized domain using the S3 interface, in the case of the AWS cloud. This stays transparent for the TensorFlow/PyTorch machine learning software frameworks used by the ML developers. These application frameworks use the tensor multidimensional array data structure, which PyTorch or TensorFlow converts to bytes.

When the PyTorch is used, it generates serialized files such as .pt, .npy, .ckpt, .h5, and .bin files, which are written to a disk via POSIX I/O calls. This is why with a storage system capable of understanding the POSIX calls, the files can go into local site and remote cloud storage. For example, with a WekaFS system, the WekaFS over RDMA (RoCEv2 or IB) (Tier 1) is used locally and later S3 object storage (Tier 2) is used into the cloud based storage such as AWS, Google Cloud or Azure Cloud.

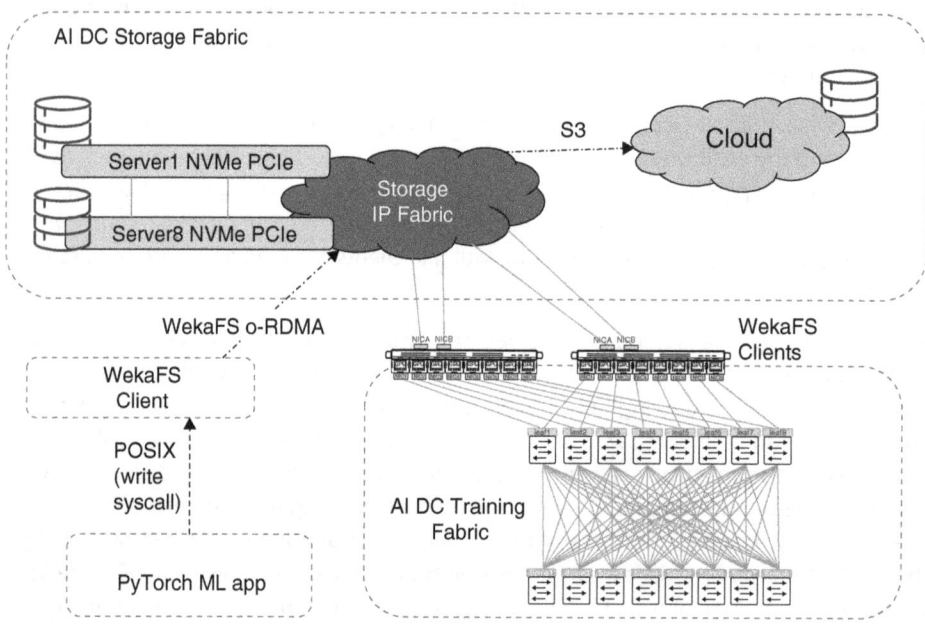

Figure 9-18
High-performance file system in integrated WekaFS storage

In Figure 9-18, the PyTorch app running in the training domain initiates the POSIX write syscall over the storage domain. The WekaFS client running on the GPU-equipped server translates this message to a WekaFS client via a RoCEv2 request when it's an IP fabric. The exact state machine beyond the RoCEv2 transport is not fully published, but the initial RDMA state machine is consistent with what we mentioned in the case of the NVMe-o-RDMA storage. However, this is only used as a transport layer; the rest of the state machine for storage read/write with the accelerated file system remains proprietary to Weka. When the client is not used at the application servers, the traditional NFSv3/v4.1 can also be used; however, it may offer lower IOPS compared to POSIX-driven client deployments. In the figure, on-premises servers 1 to 8 form a local storage cluster, offering redundancy for ongoing training operations. The WekaFS servers have local high-capacity SSD storage arrays where the hot data is stored. There are frequent read/write operations during the training phase.

In the case of on-premises deployments, NVMe-o-RDMA with proprietary file system chunks is used from the protocol stack. Figure 9-18 shows an IP fabric to which the GPU-equipped servers are connected using dedicated storage NICs with 400 Gbps/800 Gbps connections. Each NIC is connected to a different ToR, and the other two storage NICs are connected to the dedicated IP storage network, using 100 Gbps/200 Gbps connections. In addition, when there's a requirement to deploy locally backed storage servers using the traditional NVMe-o-TCP server technology, they can also be accessed over the same storage network for cold file storage usage. The same storage system can also be used in the context of Nvidia AI/ML GPU servers to run the GPUDirect Storage system, where the GPU places the partial outcomes of the training jobs directly into the SSD storage, using the RoCEv2 as transport, but still with the modified file system on top of it. No raw block storage is used when such a file system is employed for hot data storage during the training phase of an LLM model. In this case, the POSIX semantics are also used as part of the state machine. RoCEv2, which is used in this case, is primarily designed to deliver low latency and facilitate fast session establishment, while the accelerated file systems provide improved I/O and simplicity of deployments.

VAST storage systems employ a similar concept of running NFS over RDMA and using existing IP storage networks to accelerate IOPS and bus bandwidth and demonstrate better read/write latency. These systems are also compatible with Nvidia's GPUDirect Storage.

GPUDirect Storage

GPUDirect Storage from Nvidia enables direct memory access between GPU memory and storage devices, such as NVMe SSDs or network-attached storage (NAS), without the need for intermediate data copies through the CPU or system memory. It typically offers less jitter, much better bus bandwidth, significantly lower CPU load, and a reduced number of competing connections.

With GPUDirect Storage, RDMA access is the only form of storage where the GPU to remote SSD is directly placed over the InfiniBand network or over IP/Ethernet using the RoCEv2.

GPUDirect Storage systems provide a direct path between GPU memory and local or remote storage devices, such as NVMe or NVMe-oF, for efficient data transfer. Bypassing traditional data paths and the CPU to move data reduces latency and CPU overhead in data-intensive applications. GPUDirect Storage solutions include DMA (Direct Memory Access) capabilities. They may have different product names depending on the partner storage system. Still, all the solutions share a common goal: to provide direct communication between GPU memory and storage devices, thereby eliminating data copies that pass through local system memory and the CPU, which results in improved performance for training- or inference-intensive applications.

Figure 9-19 provides a high-level look at GPUDirect Storage, where GPUs directly place the outputs of computations onto storage arrays over RoCEv2 NICs, without interrupting the CPU core and thereby relaxing system memory utilization. The GPU can, after the direct placement, take care of the next job task execution, and the given AI/ML server is not required to support high-end CPU multi-core systems as well as expensive local memory for each server. This may not be terribly important with smaller cluster deployments, but when it comes to 100,000-cluster or bigger AI/ML deployments, GPUDirect Storage can have a significant cost impact.

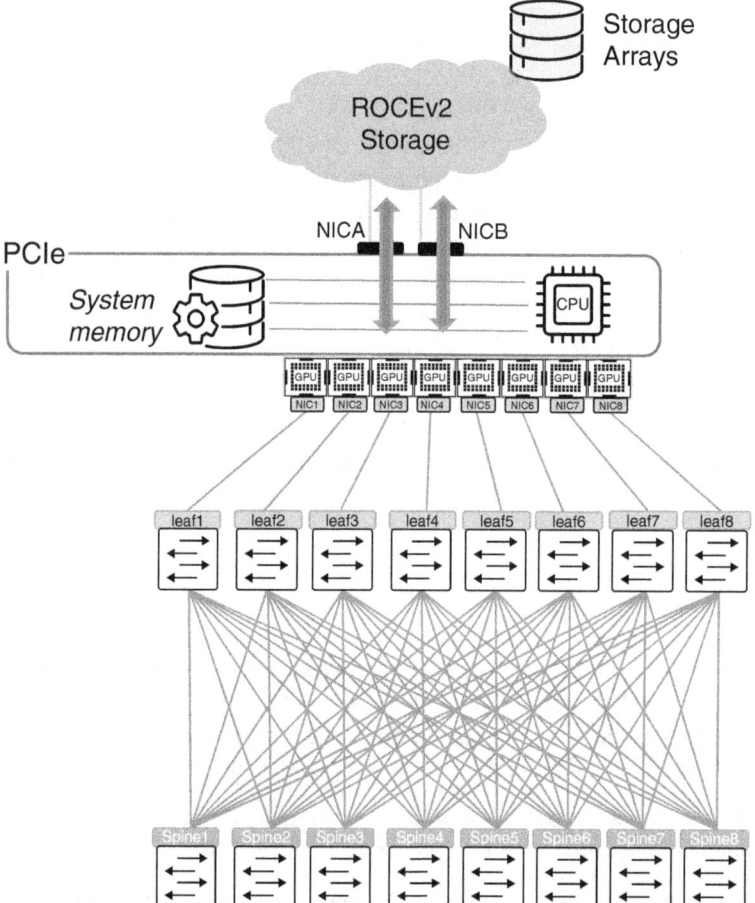

Figure 9-19
GPUDirect Storage logical view

GPUDirect Storage is also used because it's supported directly at the CUDA API level. Compute Unified Device Architecture (CUDA) is a parallel computing platform and application programming interface (API) developed by Nvidia. In the context of GPUDirect Storage, the CUA API serves as an orchestrator or an execution environment, with a memory management interface that enables zero-copy I/O between storage and GPU memory.

Figure 9-20 highlights the CUDA orchestrator positioning in the context of GPUDirect Storage, specifically in allocating memory and pinning it (that is, locking the physical address mapping) to a specific DMA/RDMA. When this occurs, the interaction with the NIC driver also takes place directly from the CUDA orchestrator, preparing the InfiniBand or RoCEv2 communication without engaging any CPU core and without using any other system memory.

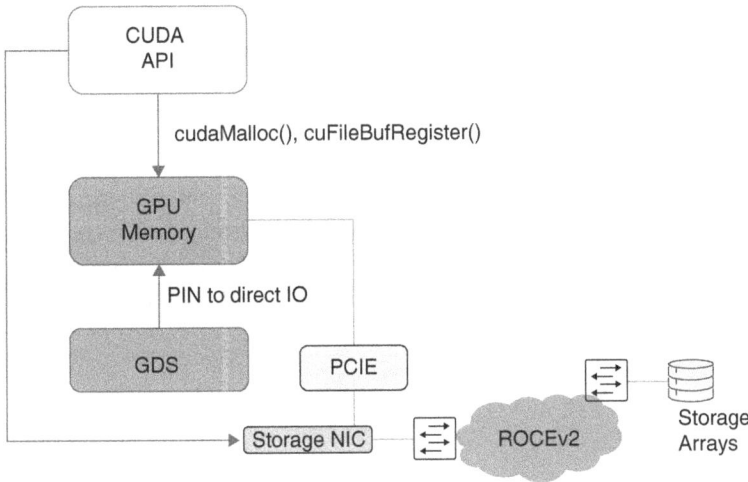

Figure 9-20
CUDA orchestrator interaction with GPUDirect Storage from Nvidia

The CUDA development framework provides native support for GPU memory pinning to storage. However, other development frameworks in machine learning, such as PyTorch v2.7.0 and later, also directly support API calls for GPUDirect Storage.

InfiniBand for Storage

The InfiniBand Trade Association (IBTA) was established at the end of the 1990s, and InfiniBand (IB) became the preferred transport method for deploying HPC for some organizations. InfiniBand was also used as a transport for storage in the case of NVMe-o-RDMA, where native InfiniBand is the underlying storage network. The same protocol stack has achieved even greater success more recently, with AI/ML training implementations in Nvidia GPU-based servers.

With InfiniBand-type storage for AI training, GPUDirect Storage is considered in the Nvidia environment. InfiniBand features ultra-low-latency capabilities, thanks to its simplified packet-processing pipeline within the switches and lightweight encapsulation, the plug-and-play approach for address allocation (local identifier [LID]) from the InfiniBand Subnet Manager, as well as the built-in congestion control mechanism with the support of credit-to-credit between the NICs and at the link level of the InfiniBand switches. Nvidia primarily proposes InfiniBand switches, which are not used only for storage networking but also for newer AI/ML training use cases. These IB switches will eventually be replaced with Ethernet 400 Gbps/800 Gbps, which currently still matches the performance of InfiniBand.

In the storage context, the InfiniBand frame format and semantics are the same as in the case of AI/ML fabrics, but they can also be completed with the NVMe capsules described earlier in this chapter. Therefore, some details of the InfiniBand network for storage transport are also fully applicable for training use cases, where InfiniBand still has a strong presence, especially when Nvidia GPU servers are deployed.

In the context of InfiniBand networking, transport encapsulation is considered lightweight and differs from Ethernet/IP; an InfiniBand switch, rather than an Ethernet switch, is used for deploying a native InfiniBand network for storage. Even if the transport part requires dedicated InfiniBand switches, the RDMA session establishment and state machine are preserved, as explained in Chapter 7, "RoCEv2 Transport and Congestion Management." This is because the InfiniBand data payloads and BTH portions are used in both cases—in RoCEv2, which uses Ethernet/IP transport, and with native InfiniBand. In the case of the Ethernet/IP transport for RoCEv2, the outer encapsulation transport and the quality-of-service part differ mainly from those of native InfiniBand networking.

Typical InfiniBand Designs

From a design perspective, InfiniBand topologies primarily follow a leaf–spine design. In smaller deployments, they use the collapsed-switch designs we covered at the beginning of this chapter as generic storage designs. The flexibility of InfiniBand designs may be limited compared to Ethernet/IP RoCEv2 or Ethernet/IP UET designs, primarily due to the limited number of vendors supporting InfiniBand switches and network adapters with native InfiniBand capabilities. The scale of LID addressing for mega-cluster design and the multi-stage bandwidth capacity control are sometimes considered limitations of the InfiniBand design. The logical isolation may also be more difficult to achieve for storage; therefore, the easiest InfiniBand storage design would be to consider physical isolation, which we also covered earlier in this chapter.

Network virtualization and multi-tenancy are also more limited with InfiniBand than with standard Ethernet/IP. The distances mentioned in the IBTA specification are for optics of up to 10 km, but when writing the book, we couldn't find any references to InfiniBand being used over such a long distance.

Finally, some customers using InfiniBand consider it a black box, where troubleshooting options are limited compared to Ethernet/IP or the telemetry for real-time observability.

The 2D/3D torus type of design or mesh designs are mentioned in some literature, but they are not very popular compared to fat tree leaf–spine topologies. However, it's worth knowing at least the format of the InfiniBand frame as well as the addressing schemas when dealing with storage networking or when InfiniBand is used for AI/ML.

LID: InfiniBand Addressing and Frame Formats

The addressing within an InfiniBand network uses centralized address allocation, and the InfiniBand Subnet Manager (SM) is incorporated into one of the selected switches from the given InfiniBand topology, but each switch runs a subnet manager agent (SMA).

With InfiniBand, the local identifier (LID) is part of the LRH. The S-LID (source LID) and D-LID (destination LID) are used for forwarding purposes at the InfiniBand switch, as well as the outgoing interfaces associated with the D-LID.

A LID is a 16-bit address assigned by the Subnet Manager. InfiniBand allows for up to 48,000 end nodes within a single subnet. When a subnet is reconfigured, new LIDs are assigned to the various endpoints within the subnet. Figure 9-21 shows the base data frame format used by InfiniBand, where the LID is part of the outer LRH, unique across the fabric, and the Global Routing Header (GRH) is used with routing between the subnets. The GRH part of the header is used to route packets between different InfiniBand subnets, but in many cases, the packet may not have it when it's part of the same subnet.

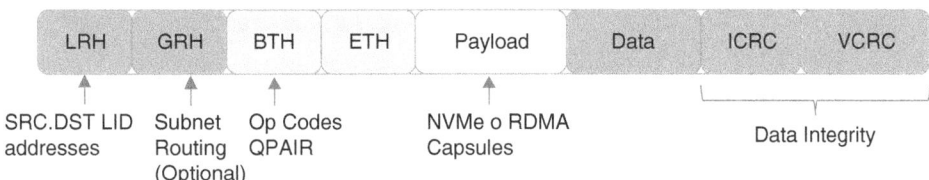

Figure 9-21
InfiniBand data frame format

The LRH part of the packet frame is dedicated to addressing, and the GRH part is ignored when the incoming packet is part of the same subnet as the destination LID. The LRH part of the InfiniBand packet is comparable to Ethernet, and the GRH part is comparable to the IP layer.

In Figure 9-21, before the data payload is a BTH part of the frame that is used for the destination QPair and opcode information and an ETH (Extended Transport Header) part that contains source QPair information. Here, as in the case of the RoCEv2, the destination QPair is used on the receiving end to place the data into the specified data buffer in its memory.

InfiniBand session establishment uses the CM connect request and CM connect reply, as well as CM ready, where QPair values are advertised and partition key information is shared to facilitate a direct storage write operation.

In the context of storage with InfiniBand, when the NVMe base specification is used, the NVMe headers, including command capsules/response capsules, the NVMe common header, and SGL description information, will also be leveraged inside the InfiniBand payload, similarly to what we described for NVMe-o-RDMA over RoCEv2. This part of the encapsulation is specific to storage purposes and is not used, for example, in the case of training, where the raw InfiniBand data format may be used for even faster job completion time and better tail latency. The QPair values from the BTH in the native InfiniBand are also mapped to the NVMe SQEs and CQEs, which is similar to what we've observed already with the RoCEv2 option of NVMe-oF.

InfiniBand QoS Support

InfiniBand supports QoS through virtual lanes (VLs), which are separate logical communication links that share a single physical link. Typically the VL number is higher (up to 16) and each of 8 to 12 queues can become a queue for a storage or AI workload. Besides the VLs, InfiniBand uses additional QoS mechanisms, which are often cited as a key advantage of InfiniBand, such as CBFC, where a credit attribution mechanism is used at each segment level. Each sender tracks the number of receive buffer credits available on the next-hop port. A credit typically represents the ability to send 64 bytes of data. The credits are exchanged at the LLH (Link Layer Header). At each segment, buffer space credits are handled at the per-VL level. This way, the sender gets a guarantee that the next-hop switch node has enough reserved resources in the buffer memory to handle the given packet. Figure 9-22 illustrates CBFC from IB switch 1 to IB switch 2, as well as at the NIC-to-InfiniBand access switch level.

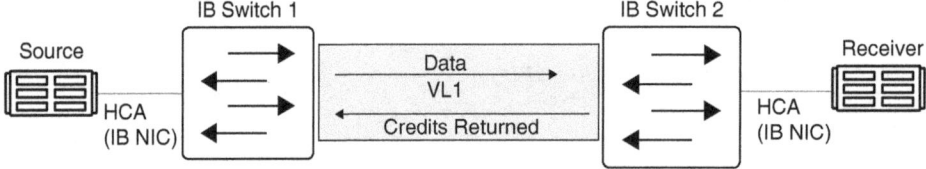

Figure 9-22
InfiniBand Credit-Based Flow Control

In Figure 9-22, IB Switch 2 sends credits to IB Switch 1 based on its buffer status. IB Switch 1 will send the packets to IB Switch 2 at the VL1 level only if sufficient credits are received. So, for a total of 16 VLs, this mechanism can be handled individually at each VL.

In a larger topology, when many switches concurrently request the same resource, there may be no buffer space available. Consequently, the originating switch might keep the packet in the buffer, increasing latency when the receiver does not grant credits. This doesn't mean, however, that the InfiniBand switches are a deep buffer.

The InfiniBand CBFC mechanism was also incorporated in the UEC (Ultra Ethernet Consortium) protocol link layer, as discussed in Chapter 12, "Ultra Ethernet Consortium (UEC)."

Summary

In this chapter, we have covered some generic storage design aspects and introduced the protocol state machines for the most popular NVMe-oF storage networks, as well as the newer network file systems with parallelism, which help speed up access to the storage in an AI data center. In many cases, RDMA is used to achieve lower latency and faster session establishment for storage workloads.

It is crucial to consider the various transport and forwarding options covered in this chapter. RoCEv2 is covered extensively in Chapter 1, "Wonders in the Workload," for the training network use case. In this chapter we have seen how the basic semantics and network encapsulation formats are proposed when the NVMe baseline protocol stack is used on top of RoCEv2 for storage networking with SSDs.

There are also, of course, legacy storage technologies and systems, such as iSCSI, FCoIP, Fibre Channel, and Fibre Channel over Ethernet. However, we have intentionally limited the scope of this discussion to storage options that can be used in the context of AI/ML data centers.

Table 9-2 provides a summary of the various storage network options for an AI data center.

Table 9-2 Comparison of Storage Network Options

Characteristic	(P)NFS	NVMe-o-TCP	NVMe-o-RDMA	InfiniBand
Inference optimized	Yes	Yes	Yes	No
Training optimized	Yes	No	Yes	Yes
Fast access to the same files in parallel	Yes	Yes	No	No
Ultra-low latency	No	No	Yes	Yes
IOPS performance	High	Medium	High	High
Block-level access	No	Yes	Yes	Yes
File-level access	Yes	No	No	Yes
Easy to extend and scale	Yes	Yes	Yes	No
Cost competitive	Yes	Yes	Yes	No
Server local cache can be used	Yes	No	No	No
Can use Ethernet/IP	Yes	Yes	Yes	No
Built-in security and partitioning	No	No	No	No
High port scalability	Yes	Yes	Yes	No
Requires lossless fabric	No	No	Yes	Yes
Built-in reliability	No	Yes	No	Yes
400 Gbps, 800 Gbps, and 1.6 Tbps support	Yes	Yes	Yes	Yes
Network architecture flexibility	Yes	Yes	Yes	No
Multi-vendor support	Yes	Yes	Yes	No

Test Your Knowledge

Chapter Review

The following questions are designed to test your understanding of the content covered in Chapter 9. Following the questions, answers are provided so you can verify your conclusions.

Questions

1. What are the primary storage network architectures used in AI data centers, and how do they differ in performance and scalability?
2. How does NVMe over Fabrics (NVMe-oF) work, and what are its protocol options?
3. What is GPUDirect Storage, and how does it accelerate AI/ML workloads?
4. Compare InfiniBand and Ethernet (RoCEv2) as storage network transports for AI clusters.
5. How do parallel file systems support large-scale distributed AI training?
6. What are the key design considerations for redundancy and path diversity in storage networks?
7. How does storage network design differ between training and inference phases in AI pipelines?
8. What are the challenges and solutions for integrating on-premises and cloud storage in hybrid AI data centers?

Answers

1. AI data centers use block storage (NVMe-oF), file storage (parallel file systems like Lustre, GPFS, and WekaFS), and object storage (S3-compatible storage). NVMe-oF provides low-latency, high-throughput block access over Ethernet (TCP or RDMA) or InfiniBand. Parallel file systems enable simultaneous, high-speed access to shared data sets by multiple nodes, which is essential for distributed training. Object storage is used for scalable, cost-effective archival and RAG workloads. Each architecture has trade-offs in latency, throughput, scalability, and management complexity.
2. NVMe-oF extends the NVMe protocol over network fabrics, allowing remote SSDs to be accessed as if they were local. Protocol options include NVMe-o-TCP (which runs over standard Ethernet and provides easier deployment and higher latency), NVMe-o-RDMA (which uses RoCEv2 or InfiniBand for ultra-low latency), and NVMe-o-FC (Fibre Channel). NVMe-oF uses submission and completion queues, with capsules and PDUs for command and data transfer, supporting high IOPS and parallelism.
3. GPUDirect Storage enables direct data transfers between GPU memory and NVMe storage, bypassing the CPU and system memory. This reduces data movement overhead, lowers latency, and increases throughput for training and inference workloads.

GPUDirect Storage leverages RDMA and DMA engines, and it is supported by Nvidia's CUDA and compatible storage systems.

4. InfiniBand offers ultra-low latency (around 300 nanoseconds), lossless transport, and credit-based flow control, making it ideal for high-performance storage fabrics. Ethernet with RoCEv2 offers similar RDMA capabilities over standard Ethernet, enabling greater scalability and vendor diversity; however, it requires careful tuning of PFC, ECN, and DCQCN for lossless operation. InfiniBand is often used in HPC and legacy AI clusters, while RoCEv2 is preferred for large-scale, cost-sensitive deployments.

5. Parallel file systems distribute both data and metadata across multiple storage nodes, enabling concurrent access by thousands of compute nodes. They support POSIX semantics, high aggregate bandwidth, and redundancy. Examples include Lustre, GPFS, BeeGFS, and WekaFS. These systems are optimized for large, sequential reads/writes and can integrate with object storage for tiered data management.

6. Redundancy is achieved through dual fabrics (A/B), multipath I/O, and RAID or erasure coding at the storage layer. Path diversity ensures that failure of a switch, link, or storage node does not disrupt access. Storage networks must be designed with non-blocking topologies, sufficient buffer space, and failover mechanisms to maintain high availability and performance.

7. Training requires high-throughput, low-latency access to large data sets, favoring NVMe-oF and parallel file systems. Inference often involves smaller, random-access workloads, where object storage or distributed file systems may be more appropriate. Storage architectures must be optimized for the specific I/O patterns and concurrency levels of each phase.

8. Hybrid architectures require seamless data movement between on-premises NVMe/parallel file systems and cloud object storage. Solutions include S3 gateways, data movers, and unified namespace file systems (for example, WekaFS with S3 tiering). Challenges include maintaining consistency, minimizing data transfer latency, and managing security and access control across domains.

References

Alan Adamson, "NVMe over TCP," Oracle Linux Blog, September 9, 2020, blogs.oracle.com/linux/post/nvme-over-tcp.

NVMe Network Storage Protocol: NVMeTM/TCP vs. RDMA with RoCEV2. 2025.

Nvidia, "GPUDirect Storage Design Guide v1.14," docs.nvidia.com/gpudirect-storage/design-guide/index.html.

Nvidia, "CUDA C++ Programming Guide v13.0," docs.nvidia.com/cuda/cuda-c-programming-guide/index.html.

InfiniBand Trade Association, "IBTA Releases New InfiniBand Architecture Specification," November 14, 2012, www.infinibandta.org/ibta-releases-new-infiniband-architecture-specification/.

10

AI Network Performance KPIs

Significance of Performance Benchmarking

Key performance indicators (KPIs) are very helpful for evaluating and moving technology in the right direction. To understand the importance of KPIs, let's consider an example of the evolution of wheels. Wheels have evolved over time to meet the demand for transporting people and goods over long distances. Initially, humans walked and carried goods themselves. Then they began to use animals for traveling and carrying goods farther, but the amount and weight that could be transported were limited. The desire to transport more faster led to the invention of wheels, which were first made of stones. Pulling carts that had stone wheels required a lot of effort, and the speed was still speed. The desire for greater speed led to further evolution into wooden wheels, which were lighter, required less effort to pull, and could travel greater distance. But wooden wheels had a short lifespan and provided a rough ride, which led to the introduction of an outer band to absorb the shock and make the ride smoother. The band initially was made of leather, then metal, and then rubber. The outer band reduced the force needed to move, increased the distance that could be covered, and improved the overall ride quality. Since then, there have been many enhancements in the rubber as well as the rims, which have changed from wooden to metallic to alloys. Wheels continue to evolve.

When evolution happens, benchmarking can be helpful to measure the progress with each iteration. AI/ML workloads have become popular in recent years and have accelerated the growth. It is important to monitor the evolution of these workloads with metrics. Benchmarking provides a way to compare systems based on standardized metrics. These metrics should cover different aspects, and the results should be consistent across runs. As evolution occurs, benchmarking helps to find the right system among various options being explored and designed.

The main metric for measuring the performance of AI data centers today is job completion time (JCT). In this chapter, we'll explore some different ideas and methods. With AI/ML data centers, it's not enough to just keep track of server availability and energy usage; there are a few additional important KPIs that reflect the specific challenges these systems face. For example, AI data centers are facilities that house high-performance computing (HPC) systems and applications for AI and ML. These data centers need a lot of power, cooling, and network bandwidth to run the sophisticated and demanding workloads of AI and ML. Therefore, it is important to track and enhance the performance, efficiency, and scalability of AI data centers using suitable KPIs.

As we have discussed in previous chapters, an AI/ML data center consists of two main components—the model and the data—and there are KPIs tied to both of these components.

Performance Benchmarking for AI Data Centers

- **Model:** These are a few of the indicators of model performance:
    - **Accuracy:** How well does the model perform its intended task? Common metrics include mean squared error (MSE) for regression tasks and classification accuracy for prediction tasks.
    - **Precision and recall:** These metrics measure a model's ability to correctly identify true positives and avoid false positives and negatives. Precision is expressed in terms of the number of bytes, for example, as 8-byte, 16-byte, or 32-byte floating-point numbers or integers.
    - **Latency:** How long does it take for the model to generate a prediction or complete a task?
- **Data:** These are a few of the indicators of data performance:
    - **Data efficiency:** What is the quality of the data used for learning? Data should have little redundancy and should cover as many scenarios as possible. Variety helps improve the model and make it robust.
    - **Training time:** This is the most important aspect of AI/ML training fabrics. Because data sets can be petabytes in size, processing can take a lot of time, and the goal is always to reduce that time. Thanks to new generations of GPUs and parallel processing, training time is being reduced.

For training workloads, time to train is the most important metric as it encapsulates how quickly it is possible to get to a trained model. High-precision training can result in achieving a solution faster. With lower precision, it may take multiple iterations to reach the right trained model, whereas with high precision, it might be possible to get there in one longer iteration. For inference, the metric could vary based on use case. OpenAI reportedly used 1,023 A100 GPUs to train ChatGPT, with a training time of around 34 days.

AI data center KPIs are metrics that quantify the performance, efficiency, and scalability of AI data center systems and applications. These are some of the common KPIs for AI data centers:

- **Throughput:** This KPI measures the number of operations or tasks completed per unit of time by an AI data center system or application. Throughput can be measured at different levels, such as node, rack, cluster, or data center. Throughput can also be expressed in terms of operations per second (OPS), floating-point operations per second (FLOPS), or queries per second (QPS).
    - **Latency:** This KPI measures the time elapsed between the start and the end of an operation or a task for an AI data center system or application. Latency can be measured at different levels, such as node, rack, cluster, or data center. Latency can also be expressed in terms of milliseconds (ms), microseconds (µs), or nanoseconds (ns).
- **Accuracy:** This KPI measures the degree of correctness or quality of the output or the result of an AI data center system or application. Accuracy can be measured using different metrics, such as precision, recall, F1-score, or mean average precision (MAP).
- **Power:** This KPI measures the amount of electrical energy consumed by an AI data center system or application. Power can be measured at different levels, such as node, rack, cluster, or data center. Power can also be expressed in terms of watts (W), kilowatts (kW), or megawatts (MW).
- **Efficiency:** This KPI measures the ratio of the output or the result of an AI data center system or application to the input or the resource consumed. Efficiency can be measured using different metrics, such as throughput per watt (TPW), FLOPS per watt (FPW), or QPS per watt (QPW).
- **Scalability:** This KPI measures the ability of an AI data center system or application to maintain or improve its performance, efficiency, and accuracy as the input or the resource increases. Scalability can be measured using different metrics, such as speedup, efficiency, or strong scaling and weak scaling.

MLCommons for AI Data Centers

One of the difficulties of AI data center KPIs is the absence of standardization and comparability among different platforms, architectures, and applications. To overcome this difficulty, a group of industry leaders and researchers have established MLCommons, a nonprofit organization that aims to develop common and fair benchmarks for AI data center systems and software. MLCommons provides a set of tools and best practices for assessing and improving the performance of AI data centers.

MLCommons was established in 2020 by a group of experts and researchers in the field of AI and ML. The goal of MLCommons is to speed up the progress and deployment of AI and ML workloads by developing standard and equitable benchmarks, data sets, and best practices for AI data center systems and software.

MLCommons Initiatives

MLCommons has the following objectives:

- Allow fair comparison of different systems while still promoting ML innovation.
- Advance ML progress through fair and helpful measurement.
- Ensure reproducibility to guarantee reliable results.
- Benefit both the commercial and research communities.
- Keep benchmarking costs low so everyone can join.

MLCommons has three main initiatives:

- **MLPerf:** This is a suite of benchmarks that measures the performance of AI data center systems and software across different domains, such as computer vision, natural language processing, recommendation systems, reinforcement learning, and HPC. MLPerf provides standardized and rigorous methodologies, metrics, and data sets for measuring and comparing the throughput, latency, accuracy, power, and scalability of AI data center systems and software.
- **MLCube:** This is a set of tools and best practices that enables the portability and reproducibility of AI data center systems and software across different platforms, architectures, and environments. MLCube provides a common interface and a container-based framework for packaging, deploying, and running AI data center systems and software on any hardware and software configuration.
- **People + AI Research (PAIR):** This program supports the research and education of AI and ML by providing access to data, compute, and expertise for academic and nonprofit organizations. PAIR also fosters collaboration and communication in the AI and ML community by organizing events, workshops, and publications.

MLCommons Benchmarking Suites

MLCommons benchmarking suites aim to provide fair assessments of training and inference performance for hardware, software, and services. They all follow certain rules. To keep up with industry changes, MLPerf is updated regularly, new tests are periodically run, and new workloads are added to reflect the latest in AI.

MLCommons offers the following suites for benchmarking:

- **MLPerf Training:** This benchmarking suite evaluates how quickly systems in training models reach a desired quality metric. Different suites are created for AI/ML workloads and for HPC workloads.
- **MLPerf Inference:** This benchmarking suite evaluates how quickly systems can take inputs and generate outputs using a trained model. Different suites are created for data center, edge, mobile, and tiny workloads.

- **MLPerf Storage:** This benchmarking suite tests how quickly storage systems provide training data when a model is being trained.

A working group community of experts defines each benchmarking suite, and they set the fair benchmarks for AI systems. The working group specifies the AI model to use, the data set to run it on, the rules for modifying the model, and the metrics for measuring how fast the hardware runs the model. By using this AI model tripod, MLCommons AI systems benchmarks assess the speed of hardware and also the quality of training data and of the metrics of an AI model.

Benchmarking a Data Center for Machine Learning

Evaluating a data center's performance for machine learning involves using the MLPerf benchmarks and a standard set of tests from MLCommons that follow a structured multistep procedure. The objective is to provide a fair, open, and repeatable assessment of a system's capabilities on real-world AI workloads. The specific methodology varies between tasks like model training and model inference, but the general process is as follows.

1. **Benchmark selection and division:** The initial step involves choosing the appropriate benchmarking suite. For a data center, this will be either the MLPerf Training or MLPerf Inference data center suite. Within these suites, one of these divisions must also be chosen:
   - **Closed division:** This division is designed for direct comparisons of hardware and software. Participants are required to use the same model, data set, and official reference implementation. This is the standard path for vendors seeking to compare their systems directly.
   - **Open division:** This division is intended to showcase new research or algorithmic advancements. It allows participants to use different models or training methods, as long as the system achieves the same predefined quality metric.

2. **System and software setup:** The hardware and software stack for the benchmark must be carefully configured. This includes:
   - **Hardware:** The hardware is the physical components of the system, such as servers, GPUs, CPUs, and the network interconnect.
   - **Software:** Software includes the operating system, device drivers, chosen machine learning frameworks (e.g., PyTorch, TensorFlow), and any proprietary optimization libraries.
   - **Reference code:** The official MLPerf benchmark source code for the specific workload must be acquired. This code, typically found on platforms like GitHub, includes the model architecture, data loading scripts, and a load generator utility for performance measurement.

3. **Benchmark execution:** The actual benchmark runs are automated by MLPerf tools.
   These tools are used for inference benchmarking:
   - **Load generation:** A utility known as LoadGen is used to dispatch inference requests to the system under test (SUT) in a controlled manner.

- **Scenarios:** Data center inference is evaluated across two primary scenarios. The first scenario is offline, where all queries are delivered to the SUT at once to measure the maximum throughput (queries per second). The second scenario is server, where queries are streamed to the SUT following a Poisson distribution to evaluate latency and throughput under a stringent latency constraint.
- **Metrics:** The key performance metric is throughput, measured in samples per second or queries per second. For the result to be valid, the SUT must also achieve a specified accuracy target. Both a speed test and a separate accuracy test must be conducted.

These tools are used for training benchmarking:

- **Time to train:** The core metric is the time required to train a model to a predefined target quality metric (e.g., a specific accuracy level).
- **End-to-end process:** Timing begins with the data loading process and concludes when the model reaches the accuracy target. This comprehensive approach is used to evaluate the entire system, including the data pipeline, storage, compute power, and communication efficiency.
- **Distributed training:** Data center training benchmarks often involve the use of multiple servers and accelerators to train models at scale and assess the system's ability to scale efficiently.

4. **Results and code submission:** Once the benchmark runs are completed and validated, the results, along with the detailed system configuration and all the source code used, are submitted to MLCommons. The submitted code must be made available to the public.
5. **Peer review and publication:** The final, critical step for ensuring fairness is the review and auditing of the submissions by MLCommons and its member organizations. The goals of this peer-review process are to verify that the rules were followed, the accuracy targets were met, and the results are reproducible. Verified results are then published in a publicly accessible, interactive table on the MLCommons website, https://mlcommons.org.

Summary

AI data centers are crucial for the development and innovation of AI and ML. However, they also present significant challenges and opportunities for assessing and improving their performance, efficiency, and scalability. AI data center KPIs and MLCommons are two key elements that can help tackle these challenges and opportunities by offering common and fair measures, data sets, tools, and best practices for AI data center systems and software. By using AI data center KPIs and MLCommons, AI data center operators and users can enhance their knowledge, testing, and comparison of AI data center systems and software and, ultimately, improve their AI and ML abilities and results.

Test Your Knowledge

The following questions are designed to test your understanding of the content covered in Chapter 10. Following the questions, answers are provided so you can verify your conclusions.

Questions

1. What are the most critical KPIs for evaluating AI data center performance, and how are they measured?
2. How does MLCommons' MLPerf benchmark suite standardize AI performance evaluation?
3. Why is job completion time (JCT) a key metric for AI/ML clusters, and what factors influence it?
4. How do throughput and latency metrics differ in their significance for training versus inference workloads?
5. What is the role of power- and energy-efficiency metrics (for example, FLOPS/Watt) in AI data center benchmarking?
6. How does scalability (strong and weak scaling) affect AI data center design and KPI interpretation?
7. Why is reproducibility essential in AI benchmarking, and how is it enforced in MLPerf?
8. How can benchmarking results inform architectural and operational improvements in AI data centers?

Answers

1. Key KPIs include job completion time (JCT), throughput (FLOPS, IOPS), latency (per operation and tail), accuracy (model quality), power consumption (Watts, PUE), and scalability (speedup, efficiency). These are measured using standardized benchmarks (for example, MLPerf), telemetry data, and application-level metrics. Accurate measurement requires synchronized clocks, representative workloads, and consistent test environments.
2. MLPerf provides closed-division (fixed model/data set) and open-division (innovation allowed) benchmarks for training, inference, and storage. It specifies reference models, data sets, accuracy targets, and test harnesses, enabling fair, reproducible comparisons across hardware, software, and cloud services. Results are peer reviewed and published for transparency.

3. JCT measures the total time to train a model to a target accuracy. It is influenced by compute performance, network bandwidth and latency, storage throughput, parallelism efficiency, and tail latency. Reducing JCT accelerates model iteration and deployment, directly impacting business agility and research productivity.

4. Throughput (samples/sec, FLOPS) is critical for training, where large batches are processed in parallel. Latency (response time) is more important for inference, especially in real-time applications. Both metrics must be balanced to optimize resource utilization and user experience.

5. Power efficiency determines operational cost and sustainability. Metrics like FLOPS/Watt and PUE (power usage effectiveness) quantify how effectively hardware converts electrical power into useful computation. Energy-efficient designs reduce cooling requirements and environmental impact.

6. Strong scaling measures how performance improves as more resources are added for a fixed problem size; weak scaling measures performance as both resources and problem size increase proportionally. Poor scaling indicates bottlenecks in network, storage, or software, guiding optimization efforts.

7. Reproducibility ensures that results are reliable and comparable across systems and over time. MLPerf enforces this by requiring open-source code, fixed data sets, accuracy validation, and peer review. This builds trust in published results and drives industry progress.

8. Benchmarking identifies bottlenecks (for example, network congestion, storage latency), validates design choices, and guides investment in hardware/software upgrades. Continuous benchmarking enables data-driven decision-making for scaling, tuning, and evolving AI infrastructure.

References

Chuan Li, "OpenAI's GPT-3 Language Model: A Technical Overview," June 3, 2020, https://lambda.ai/blog/demystifying-gpt-3.

Nvidia, "MLPerf Benchmarks," https://www.nvidia.com/en-us/data-center/resources/mlperf-benchmarks/.

MLCommons, "Benchmarks" https://mlcommons.org/working-groups/

11

Monitoring and Telemetry

Exploring Monitoring Options

Monitoring a data center's health is critical and is not just limited to the network infrastructure. Power, temperature, and humidity monitoring is crucial for the efficient operation of the data center infrastructure and involves many data points taken from sensors and other hardware devices. In this chapter, we focus on IP networking infrastructure monitoring and telemetry, which may sometimes include power consumption statistics but is mainly limited to networking infrastructure monitoring that is specific to an AI data center.

Different types of monitoring are commonly used in AI data center networks. The networking equipment supports Syslog, SNMP, and telemetry for exporting the data from the devices. The same mechanisms are being used for the AI data centers. The data export mechanisms remain the same and are evolving more toward telemetry. The advent of AI data centers presents a challenge of exporting data faster so that decisions are taken and applied to the devices at the correct time. Exporting the data at the interval of seconds or milliseconds is not good enough, it has to go to micro and nano seconds intervals. Even the SNMP trap generation could be faster to handle the scenario of microbursts.

Let's look at some of the most common AI data center monitoring tools, which are sometimes used in parallel on networking devices such as switches, routers, and firewalls in the backend AI data center as well as in the frontend network.

- **SNMP polling:** With SNMP polling, SNMPv2c or the more secure SNMPv3 is used to look every couple of seconds or minutes at a specific MIB. SNMP polling can focus on interface stats, queue stats to get the total current counter or the current rate per second, the total buffer utilization at the switch of the shared or dedicated buffers, per-interface buffers, and queue buffers. It can also focus on node capacity information for the FIB, RIB, or MAC table; TCAM utilization; or standard performance of the node at the CPU level, the memory used globally at the node, or the CPU and memory of the individual line card and ASIC of the switch.

- **SNMP traps:** SNMP traps are generated based on the threshold set for specific parameters on the device. For example, an SNMP trap may be sent to the collecting node when the CPU of the device reaches a certain level of utilization. Or, in lossless fabric, an SNMP trap may be generated by a device automatically when the rate of the Priority Flow Control (PFC) pushbacks received on the interface on the specific queue is reached.

- **Syslog monitoring:** Syslog monitoring may be carried out for specific Syslog messages that are reporting critical or fatal errors for global device parameters or for specific interface-level problems.

- **Telemetry streaming interface:** Instead of just using the legacy SNMP-based polling approach, a device might send information on specific statistics to a telemetry collector—either periodically or when a change occurs. Telemetry uses a push mechanism instead of a pull method (SNMP). Telemetry data can be pushed by the forwarding engine directly via the revenue ports. Periodic exports require continuous monitoring of the devices from the collectors and data has to be sent from the device continuously. Change-based telemetry is a method where the networking device exports information only when there is a change from the previous state or value. For example, if there's no change in a statistic, why would the telemetry interface continue to send the same information to the collecting device? In some cases, on-change telemetry is more suitable. Telemetry streaming may provide global node-level information, or it may operate per interface or per queue. Global telemetry streaming may export information related to buffering, shared versus dedicated monitoring, monitoring of the CPU, node memory, the Forwarding Information Base (FIB), the Routing Information Base (RIB), or TCAM utilization (which is related to the use of access lists to protect the IP network from various attacks). Interface-level telemetry provides details on buffer utilization (with accuracy at the per-queue level), the rate of packets per interface, and cumulative statistics for IPv4 and IPv6. The telemetry interface uses the gRPC or gNMI approach, allowing for the simultaneous establishment of multiple concurrent sessions from a given device to different collectors.

- **In-band flow analyzer (IFA):** An in-band flow analyzer can be used with on-data plane metadata information or data plane cloning probes to measure latency and congestion in the data center fabric.

- **RPC query:** Like SNMP polling, an RPC query can help automate information gathering at the command-line interface with XML, JSON, or similar structure.

- **Agent-based network monitoring:** A dedicated agent runs TWAMP probes to measure RFC 2455 benchmarking of the network. Various probes can be used, including UDP- or TCP-specific probes, and latency and loss can be measured.
- **sFlow and IPFIX:** These tools are used to monitor traffic characteristics and analyze applications used over the network.

Both historical and real-time monitoring are used to analyze data center networks.

With historical network monitoring, the statistics data trend is identified, and corrective actions are taken on the network isolated node or specific interface. The collected historical data helps predict the situation. For example, it might be possible to see that bandwidth utilization grew 10% over the course of a couple weeks, and we might believe there's a good chance it will continue to grow in the next couple weeks, assuming that applications continue to be deployed in the new data center or more customers use the infrastructure.

The large language model (LLM) is used to analyze the historical data, and the generative AI takes corrective actions even before the problem appears; the AI agent suggests taking corrective action based on the monitored data.

Real-time network monitoring is typically streaming telemetry based instead of polling based. Data is collected from the data center Ethernet/IP switches, routers, or firewalls to get a better situational awareness. Real-time network monitoring uses real-time data statistics for flow tail latency; these statistics include packet drops per queue, fat flow information, and entropy scores for the flow. Real-time network monitoring seamlessly moves part of the server traffic to other nodes of the Ethernet fabric.

Real-time network monitoring involves analyzing real-time data for a given network node; the data might include memory utilization of the ASIC, CPU of the switch/router/firewall nodes, or remaining storage space. Corrective action might involve reducing the load on a node by blocking specific sources if the origin of the churn was related to a security breach. Currently, exporting most amount of data from network equipments is very important. The data received on the collectors needs to be stored. The data stored is being used to analyze the patterns that help corelate the events with the data collected. As the AI models evolve, the corelation detection will become better. This corelation will help in predicting the upcoming events in networks and flag alarms, potetically suggest mitigation steps and in future, remediate the issues as well.

Network Monitoring in an AI/ML Data Center Network

InfiniBand technology has been the most used technology when it comes to lossless fabric. Ethernet has undergone significant improvements in telemetry and monitoring over recent years and is even more advanced in Ethernet AI data center scenarios compared to the traditional InfiniBand networks. In an AI data center, RDMA is considered as a technology that can be enhanced to achieve similar performance with Ethernet. The monitoring and telemetry allow you to determine if lossless Ethernet fabric delivers on its promises after deployment and provides the similar performance experience as InfiniBand with Ethernet fabric.

The collector software that is involved in network monitoring is necessary to handle real-time data from switches in telemetry streaming mode. In the AI/ML data center context, however, it's more helpful to have a switch produce telemetry data as well as the server telemetry, to allow greater correlation of the server and switch telemetry data to identify the performance consistency or the changes and trends across the entire system.

Advanced software that examines and connects different indicators is crucial to the success of AI data center monitoring. With many data collection tools, having a large amount of data is beneficial. However, the primary goal is to ensure that we understand how to utilize the information collected from various network nodes and correlate the data across different points within the network at different points in time. For example, within data center fabric, frame loss or latency differs at the aggregation point compared to nonaggregation point, such as a spine, compared to a leaf, which connects only a subset of servers.

With telemetry data, it is possible to collect vastly more data than is possible with the traditional SNMP polling mechanism. In addition, use of telemetry data requires more ability to store information on servers, and servers need to be able to analyze real-time data. Also, more resources are required on the server side, including CPU memory to process data in real time and create visualizations such as graphs, also in real time. The metadata in the telemetry data received by the collector server is also typically more significant and more accessible for comparison between nodes.

In the context of AI data centers, monitoring of network utilization focuses on the following aspects:

- **Utilization of egress buffers:** Monitoring the utilization of egress shared buffers or dedicated egress buffers is essential even if applications are not yet experiencing related issues. This monitoring can enable you to take corrective action such as adding more bandwidth between leaf and spine or moving part of the server traffic to other links (assuming that you can run some form of traffic engineering inside the fabric).

- **Latency changes:** In-band telemetry (with probes and timestamps) makes it possible to observe latency changes between different leaf nodes in the network and ensure consistency in latency across all leaves in the fabric.

- **Bandwidth utilization:** By monitoring bandwidth utilization trends from leaf to spine and spine to leaf, you are equipped to determine whether any spine is getting overutilized. Overutilization can be a symptom of load-balancing issues related to an increasing number of elephant flows in the network with lower flow entropy.

- **Application flows:** It is possible to analyze application flows by using sFlow information.

- **Mirroring on demand:** Mirroring packets on demand allows you to analyze user content and examine dropped packets.

- **Mirroring on the drop:** Mirroring on the drop is also helpful to make sure you know what kind of packets are getting dropped or were dropped. You can collect dropped packets at the collecting station and use them to determine if drops were related to application malformations or the security rules in place. The packet drops in a network are not all bad; sometimes they occur because the network is defending itself against an attack or because the control plane or data plane load on the network is too high, and the network starts to protect itself. Perhaps DDoS is triggered at the switch ASIC because too many ARP requests are observed per second. In response, the switch may begin dropping packets randomly, or egress queue loss may occur on lower-priority queues.

Even with numerous monitoring options available, it may still be impossible to react to a performance degradation trend quickly. For example, when network congestion happens at the microsecond level, a monitoring station may not have a sufficient level of accuracy to capture and report it correctly.

On the other hand, even if the occurrence and reporting of some negative symptoms can't be fixed immediately (with automated corrective actions), at least the origin and size of the problem will be known, allowing the network administrator to make an informed decision. Is the network constantly dropping packets? Is it happening on a single interface or on many interfaces? Is the problem isolated to one switch node, or is it occurring on multiple switches simultaneously?

It is important to know whether you need to be able to react immediately with corrective actions or whether the server application is robust enough to handle drops. In the context of an AI data center, for example, monitoring might report the following types of real-time statistics:

- **Frame loss:** You might get reports about the egress per queue frame loss reported via telemetry or SNMP.
- **PFC stats**: You might monitor the PFC XOFF backpressure augmented rate across all the queues and on many interfaces of the spines or leaf nodes.
- **Latency:** The latency of the sample traffic may be higher than usual.
- **ECN stats**: Explicit Congestion Notification (ECN) stats may be increasing on all queues, and many GPU servers may be slowing down their learning process and reporting higher JCT numbers than usual.

Depending on the magnitude of a problem reported in real time, the following worst-case situation decisions may need to be made:

- You may need to shut down the server at the origin of the congestion (in which case it's helpful to have switch software that is capable of identifying the origin).
- You may need to restart the learning process at the scheduler level.
- You may need to evacuate the entire data center to a location that has better network capacity and restart the jobs in that new location.

Monitoring the network and taking minor corrective actions won't help if overall network capacity planning was not done correctly—for example, if the oversubscription ratios were incorrectly designed, the wrong packet load-balancing method was implemented on the switches, or the quality of the optics was not suitable for the 800 GbE or 400 GbE interface connection. You need to ensure that monitoring is done on an AI data center network that was correctly designed and included the proper capacity planning analysis to support the target GPU connection and the target number of concurrent jobs in the backend network.

In-Band Flow Analyzer (IFA)

Earlier we mentioned monitoring GPU workloads and the types of corrective actions that can be taken. What if you could add extra metadata to a data packet to gain better visibility into performance, or what if you could add specific probes to the network to measure it with greater accuracy? This is precisely where IFA-based telemetry comes into play.

Besides doing traditional real-time monitoring, you can include more information in the original data packets or add specific probe packets (which are copies of the original packet) to the data plane network to better measure its performance (such as its latency). If you use IFA and set the measurement metadata on the original packet or a copy of the original packet as a probe, you have a good chance of getting a more accurate latency measurement than if you used an artificial agent, which has a different packet payload content compared to the original user flow. With IFA, the original data plane packet is tagged with info, or a packet clone is used for probing purposes.

So, IFA enables you to tag packets in a flow with metadata, and then the server can analyze this information to detect any network faults and bottlenecks. The IFA header on a packet is set to tag the packet accordingly at each hop along a network. The initiator, transit, and termination nodes are well identified with IFA. A data center fabric typically uses a three-stage IFA model or a five-stage IFA model (for rail-to-rail communication).

IFA consists of the following nodes:

- **Initiator:** The initiator IFA node samples the traffic of interest and converts it to an IFA-capable flow with specific header information. Sometimes, depending on the implementation, specific traffic may be cloned and set with IFA metadata dedicated to the measurements in real time; for example, the initiator node might add timestamps and node information to every cloned packet traversing the fabric for the given flow. The node also adds the initiator tag so that the collecting server correlates all the information received in the metadata, from the number of hops to the timing information.

- **Transit:** The transit IFA node, which may be a spine or a super spine in the data center fabric, appends metadata with local information. It adds local updates to the metadata stack information.

- **Termination:** The termination IFA node is typically an egress leaf node or a border-leaf node. When the IFA metadata is not set on cloned traffic, the metadata information is removed; when it is set on cloned probe traffic, the metadata stack of information is sent to the collecting IFA server application (for example, in the IPFIX format), but the cloned data packet is typically dropped at the egress switch in the IFA telemetry system.

Figure 11-1 illustrates the IFA process.

In-Band Flow Analyzer (IFA)   235

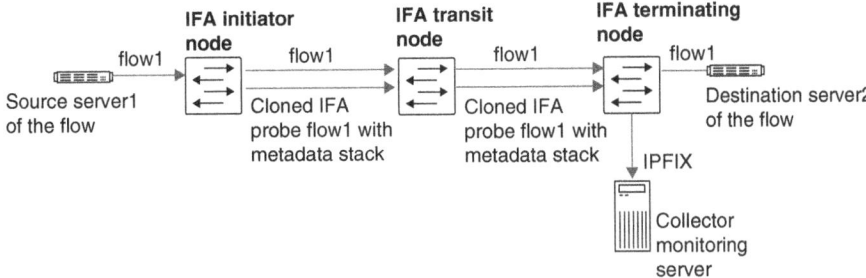

Figure 11-1
IFA for in-band telemetry monitoring

IFA collects data such as the following:

- Residence time (how long a packet spends within a single hop)
- Per-hop latency (cumulative latency for a packet to travel between two adjacent network devices, which includes residence time plus the time on wire)
- Per-hop ingress port number
- Per-hop egress port number
- Received packet timestamp value
- Queue ID
- Congestion notification
- Egress port speed

Figure 11-2 illustrates the L3 data packet format with the IFA metadata to highlight that new portions are stacked before the original payload appears inside the packet.

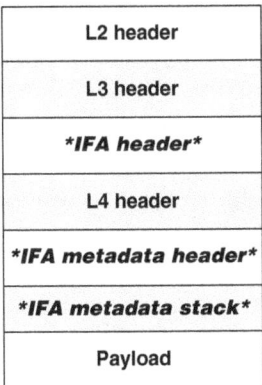

Figure 11-2
IFA packet format with metadata information

As you can see in Figure 11-2, the IFA header is the first header after the IP header. The MTU of the interfaces in the fabric must be large enough to support additional headers of IFA. This is typically not a big problem, and most switches in a data center have the MTU size set to 9000 bytes or more.

The IFA header identifies the packet. Figure 11-3 shows the contents of the IFA header.

IFA version (4 bits)	Global name space (4 bits)	Protocol type (8 bits)	Flags (8 bits)	Max length (8 bits)

Figure 11-3
IFA header format

Just after the IFA header is the original L4 transport header, but then comes the IFA metadata header. This header is pushed by the initialization node. Metadata header contains information on the action to be performed on the given IFA packet: either by transit or termination egress node. It also includes the hop limit, in case the initiator would like to reduce the scope of the IFA packet at the initiator itself. Then the most important part of the IFA packet is the IFA metadata stack, which contains relevant information.

Figure 11-4 shows the contents of the metadata stack.

Local name space (4 bits)	Device ID (20 bits)		IP TTL (8 bits)	
Egress port speed (4 bits)	**Congestion (2 bits)**	Queue ID (6 bits)	Rx timestamp seconds (20 bits)	
Egress port number (16 bits)			Ingress port number (16 bits)	
RX timestamp nanoseconds (32 bits)				
Residence time nanoseconds (32 bits)				
Opaque data 1 (Reserved) (32 bits)				
Opaque data 2 high (Reserved) (16 bits)			Opaque data 2 low (Reserved) (16 bits)	
Opaque data 3 (Reserved) (32 bits)				

Figure 11-4
IFA metadata stack contents

For a complete description of each field, you can see the IETF document https://www.ietf.org/archive/id/draft-kumar-ippm-ifa-08.txt. For now we will focus on fields related to receipt timestamps, nanoseconds, congestion, and residency time.

For an AI data center, it is important to know whether a packet experienced congestion; in order to know this, though, ECN must be enabled on the egress port. The residence time, in nanoseconds per hop, is a latency value that depends on a given switch node's capacity to calculate it; therefore, it is sometimes best to keep nodes with the same computational capacity at the given architecture level in order to make the latency stamp accurate. Latency is usually calculated based on the metadata received, by subtracting the receipt time from the transmit time.

The IFA stack also contains other information, such as device ID, port speeds, and port numbers. However, depending on the implementation, they may not be used, and only the latency and congestion information may be relevant.

To summarize our discussion about IFA in the context of an AI data center, these are the main benefits:

- IFA probe packets traverse the same network path as the original flow, helping you monitor the network for faults and performance issues.
- IFA monitors live traffic and thus helps to perform packet-level latency analysis and queue-congestion monitoring to optimize network performance.

As with all other technologies, there are limitations with IFA that will get addressed as the feature matures. For example, for general networking purposes, the way multicast traffic metadata information is handled will need to be addressed though this is less relevant for the AI data center use case, where multicasting is less commonly used in the backend network. However, IFA offers significant improvements in network monitoring, such as tracking congestion points inside the fabric by using unique metadata and monitoring latency to the microsecond level of accuracy based on the copy of the original data packet.

Corrective Actions

We have covered different monitoring options available that can be used in the AI data center fabrics. As we get feed of data from the networking devices through any of the available mediums, the data can be stored on the servers. It is also important to understand how the data can be used:

- The data stored over a period of time can be used to derive the patterns.
- The patterns can be tagged with the corrective measures taken.
- Over a period of time, there may be different measures taken to address similar issues.
- The data can also be used to measure the effectiveness of the measures taken.

Currently, in most cases, humans are involved when any action needs to be taken. As the pattern identification and actions correlation matures, the monitoring platforms can be enabled to take the corrective action when patterns are identified. This will enable us toward more autonomous networks or self-driving networks. The use of artificial intelligence models has the potential to enable us to move toward it.

With AI data centers, the congestion occurs in milli, micro, and, in some cases, nano seconds. There are features being explored where the system takes decisions to handle these scenarios.

- It could be an individual hop taking the decisions.
- It could be the source of the stream taking the decisions by learning about congestion anywhere in the network.
- It could also be a monitoring platform, which is able to predict the recurrence of a known issue by looking at the pattern and taking corrective measures.

It is also important to note that each node may be doing its best to deliver the best network performance but as a system, the performance may not be good enough. Hence, end-to-end monitoring between the applications is being explored to achieve better results.

Some of the explorations are underway in UEC and covered in Chapter 12, "Ultra Ethernet Consortium (UEC)." Also, there is exploration by the vendors as well as the large-scale network deployment companies.

Summary

This chapter highlights key features of network monitoring. As you have seen, telemetry in-band and out-of-band capabilities have become the de facto standard in the AI/ML context. When dealing with much broader performance statistics, such as when using active probes to clone traffic or when using measurements of buffer occupation to analyze latency trends, it is important to use an analyzer server. For analysis of telemetry data, open-source systems are still relatively limited, and typically a specific vendor fabric manager is used to read the centrally collected data; the manager has a better chance of success at giving real-time analysis if the server also integrates an AI engine that is capable of gathering logic from different sources of data and presenting it to the end user in a simplified way. AI engine–based corrective actions are typically not yet integrated even in professional fabric managers and monitoring tools; human-based decisions are still currently involved to mitigate any issues that are reported by various monitoring tools, such as SNMP or telemetry.

Reference

Inband Flow Analyser (IFA): https://www.ietf.org/archive/id/draft-kumar-ippm-ifa-08.txt

12

Ultra Ethernet Consortium (UEC)

The recent Ultra Ethernet Specification v1.0 represents a significant advancement in network technology, developed to satisfy the growing requirements of HPC, AI, cloud infrastructure, and data-intensive enterprise environments. By addressing the inherent limitations of traditional Ethernet, Ultra Ethernet introduces advanced capabilities that deliver GPU cluster scalability and improved reliability. Released on June 11, 2025 by the Ultra Ethernet Consortium (UEC) under the Linux Foundation, this specification presents a comprehensive Ethernet-based architecture explicitly optimized for AI and HPC workloads. Key features include modern RDMA over Ethernet/IP, support for multi-vendor interoperability, and scalability to millions of endpoints. The updated specification incorporates new transport and congestion management protocols, as well as enhancements at the physical and link layers, facilitating seamless integration across NICs, switches, optics, and cables. Emphasizing performance, scalability, interoperability, and adherence to open standards, Ultra Ethernet establishes a robust foundation for meeting the rigorous demands of contemporary AI and HPC applications.

The recent success of Ethernet/IP fabrics in AI data center clusters has been confirmed through production-level deployments, which have reached 100,000-GPU server clusters and thousands of 400 Gbps/800 Gbps ports deployed to interconnect these servers. Traditionally deployed with InfiniBand, Ethernet 800 Gbps, which was tuned to support lossless fabrics, offered a more cost-competitive solution than InfiniBand, with the same performance, better scalability, and an open-standard approach, with a larger number of vendors supporting both the switch and NIC server card sides.

The fine-tuned Ethernet with RDMA over Converged Ethernet version 2 (RoCEv2) and Data Center Quantized Congestion Notification (DCQCN) still had some minor drawbacks, such as the operational requirement to change the tuning over time when AI workload characteristics were changing. For example, there might be changes in the way end-to-end reordering capability was announced between the server NICs and how the network settings were made to align to what the NICs at the source and target servers were capable of really doing, or there might be changes in the handling of reordered packets or how many sessions could be handled in parallel (based on the server buffer size). There's still a need for the network to understand the end-host capabilities within the AI clusters and seamlessly adapt to them (such as by dynamically setting buffers or enabling a specific load-balancing mechanism for that workload and maintaining consistency over the job execution time).

As AI models grow in terms of parameters and tokens, data center networks will need ports of 400 Gbps or more to support larger networks and synchronize GPU servers. Therefore, for a network training domain, the IP Fabric should be ready to achieve over a million GPU nodes. To handle such giant clusters, more network optimizations are needed. This is one of the reasons the UEC wants to standardize optimizations at the industry level and make Ethernet more scalable for scale-out, while maintaining increased performance, such as faster ramp time, delivery mode detection, link-level, and end-to-end congestion control. To make this possible, the standardizations at the industry level—not only for the network switch level, but also at the end host NIC drivers level—are required. This is to form a full-stack solution in which the switch understands the end host's requirements, and the end host understands the real-time network conditions. As an example, in the case of UEC the NIC card can automatically adapt to the congestions, by changing the source UDP port.

The UEC decided to define a new transport, link, and software stack that will not only increase performance but also offer an easier way to deploy the AI data center fabric infrastructure (in a plug-and-play fashion).

Table 12-1 summarizes the UEC's main motivations in redesigning the whole protocol stack, with a big focus on end-host NIC optimization.

Table 12-1 Key Motivations of the UEC in Redesigning AI/ML Fabrics

Lossless fabric fine-tuning	If zero-touch DCQCN is missing, the UEC will offer a plug-and-play approach for lossless Ethernet.
Ultra-large scale and performance	AI data center infrastructures are increasing. Today they have 100,000+ GPUs. The UEC wants to create fabric and communication libraries that can support more than a million nodes. Faster workloads mean shorter session negotiation.
Full-stack AI fabric	Current fabrics are not connected to the upper-layer collective communication managers. With the In-Network Collectives (INC) defined under the UEC Software working group, collective communication will be included in the specification. Transport and upper software layers will be synchronized.

We have already mentioned that optimizations are being made for LLMs in the training domain. To make these optimizations fully efficient, it's essential to also optimize other building blocks, such as storage networks, management, benchmarking standards, and KPIs; all these aspects motivated the UEC. From a services perspective, besides training, the HPC use case is also included as part of the target improvements for the protocol stack.

The UEC formed different working groups to focus on defining the requirements at the use case level, even if some of the technologies eventually become applicable across multiple use cases. The UEC defined three main use cases to focus on: the AI Base, AI Full, and HPC profiles. It maps features as must or optional, depending on the type of service profile. For example, the AI Base profile may need to support only one packet delivery mode—out of four possible by the UEC standard—RUD, ROD, RUDI, and UUD. The AI Full profile will have to cover the first three packet delivery modes and keep the last UUD packet delivery as optional. The information about profile feature support is exchanged during connection setup and is managed at the Libfabric software level. Libfabric provides a standard user-space API for RDMA. Within UEC, Libfabric is expected to be the primary application-facing interface that abstracts the complexity of the UET (UEC Transport) stack and allows high-level frameworks (like MPI, NCCL, SHMEM, etc.) to run over UEC fabric. Libfabric defines the requirements and translates them into semantics for end-to-end session establishment. For example, if both servers confirm the type of UEC profile to use, the specific software features will be enabled accordingly at the NIC driver level. Of the three profiles, the most advanced one is the HPC service profile, where, in addition to the feature set requirements, performance and latency requirements are also very strict.

To sum up the UEC's motivation, we can highlight the following:

- **Performance:** Traditional Ethernet protocols may result in unpredictable delays caused by packet collisions and a lack of deterministic routing. Ultra Ethernet includes features designed to guarantee bounded latency for critical workloads.
- **Scalability:** Modern AI training clusters and supercomputers can comprise tens of thousands of nodes. At this scale, legacy protocols often struggle to maintain optimal performance.
- **Reliability and congestion control:** Effectively managing network congestion is vital when multiple high-bandwidth applications operate simultaneously.

UEC Developments and Working Groups

With an ambitious plan to expand the scale of AI cluster networks and enhance their performance, a group of more than 70 vendors and institutions established various working groups focused on specific areas of improvement. For the UEC specification v1.0, the work of these different groups was consolidated into a single document and released in June 2025 as a standard reference.

It isn't necessarily important to know the key working groups and their roles in order to understand different technologies. However, it's useful to know which groups are out there so you can see what features and capabilities might be included in the next version of the UEC standard. In this chapter, we'll mainly focus on the Transport and Link Layer working groups (WGs) and how they connect to the Software working group.

Link Layer Working Group

The Link Layer WG is focusing on everything related to improvements that can be made at a connection between the two end nodes, such as between the two UEC switches or between a UEC switch and a server. The group has looked at how congestion or reliable transport can be improved at the per-link level to ensure that key AI workload performance yields better outcomes, such as faster job completion times or reduced tail latency. These are some of the functions the WG has explored:

- **Link Layer Reliability (LLR):** The Link Layer WG proposed the LLR tool, aiming to mitigate the latency impact of packet loss by minimizing the need for end-to-end retries. Instead of engaging with the end host for retransmissions, control is performed at the link level. (We will revisit the LLR when we delve into more details of its various features.)

- **Packet Rate Improvement (PRI):** The Link Layer WG also proposed PRI at the link level, with the goal of increasing frame rate by reducing per-frame overhead and using only the header components relevant for the AI workload transmissions.

- **Credit-Based Flow Control (CBFC):** The Link Layer working group also proposed CBFC, with the goal of replacing the current RoCEv2 PFC with a more efficient credit-based system at the link level. We mentioned CBFC in Chapter 9, "Storage Network Design and Technologies," when discussing InfiniBand transport for storage networking. The same approach is taken in the Ethernet context of the UEC, where credit-based communication is conducted. We will dig into the details of this functionality later this chapter.

Transport Working Group

The Transport WG is developing Ultra Ethernet Transport (UET), which is one of the most important developments from an end-to-end integration perspective. We believe many future developments will be attributed to the work conducted in this working group. UET is a new data packet format that uses an entirely new set of headers after the UDP frame instead of using RoCEv2 with BTH and InfiniBand payloads encapsulated in the UDP frame.

Let's look at how UET packet forwarding differs in the next-generation AI/ML data center compared to current implementations with RoCEv2 and DCQCN for reactive congestion control. Congestion management is not done only at the link level with credit-based CBFC but also in the context of end-to-end congestion control. The Transport working group is proposing packet trimming, as well as Receiver Credit Congestion Control (RCCC) and Network Signal Congestion Control (NSCC), which influence the entropy of multipathing.

The entire UEC protocol stack employs a two-level approach for congestion control and other signaling: One level is handled end-to-end between the servers, and the other level is accessible via the link, where some functionalities remain optional. The UET transport, which we will explain later in this chapter, incorporates authentication, encryption, and a new UET security header as part of the UET packet format—instead of going through the separate MAC-SEC functions currently used in the context of RoCEv2 encrypted transport. The last part of the communication between the servers supporting UET, which is probably the key one for the end-to-end orchestration, is the Semantic Sublayer (SES). The goal here is to be in sync and let the software layer (that is, the Libfabric, which is a key software layer component in the UEC context) of the intended transaction track the transaction's state.

The Transport WG is also defining fundamental packet delivery modes and how the two end hosts agree on how they will communicate with each other and handle the reliable transport (in order versus out of order) of packets.

Software Working Group

The Software WG is defining In-Network Collectives (INC) and how the collective communication libraries (CCLs) are used to organize and efficiently use data center fabric resources. This working group is proposing the INC manager and INC switch agent application as new components for AI/ML data centers; similar components are currently used in InfiniBand deployments. The UEC is indeed taking inspiration for the components from the InfiniBand mechanism. UET is using the best capabilities of InfiniBand (credit mechanisms, the CCL/INC, and the plug-and-play behavior) as well as the best capabilities of Ethernet, which is a more distributed model where various entries are not dependent on the centralized state (for example, the massive scale of IPv6). The plug-and-play address assignment with SLAAC technology, defined natively in IPv6, will also be considered for the newer UET-based fabrics.

An important focus for the Software WG is the API part. The WG is looking at the well-known open-source Libfabric, which allows applications to express workload-specific requirements for message and packet ordering and directs UET's choice of appropriate transport services. It involves the definition of specific UEC profiles: the AI Base, AI Advanced, and the HPC profiles.

Other Working Groups

The UEC's working groups helped deliver the first version of the Ultra Ethernet Specification in June 2025, combining functionalities from the link and transport layers and finishing at the software level. We mention the working groups in this chapter to highlight the key building blocks of the new AI data center standard, which will help organize our understanding of the layered approach and glue all the pieces together.

In addition to the three working groups we will be focusing on in this chapter, there are other WGs that are also very important for the entire data center ecosystem. For example, the Compliance WG is defining testing frameworks, and companies such as Spirent and Keysight are helping to define how the performance measurements will be done and how to measure the KPIs (which the Performance and Debug WG is defining). The Management working group is involved in making the new UET standard deployable in production networks. The Physical Layer WG is probably the most disruptive as it is defining optimizations at a very low level of the protocol stack, where the existing Ethernet infrastructures will not be fully compatible. This group will probably take the longest to have its ideas adopted in scale-out solutions. The Storage working group is, in some sense, distinct from the rest of the groups and will become relevant only when the first implementations of the Transport and Link Layer groups become a reality at the switch, particularly at the NIC/network adapter level.

To summarize, these are the UEC working groups that were involved in Ultra Ethernet Specification v1.0:

- **Physical Layer working group:** This working group aims to create specifications that enhance the performance, latency, and management of the Ethernet physical layer, including the medium below and the clients on the physical layer (link layer).

- **Link Layer working group:** This working group focuses on creating specifications that improve the performance, latency, and management of the Ethernet link layer.

- **Transport Layer working group:** This working group is responsible for creating specifications for an AI/HPC transport with better throughput, latency, scalability, and management for Ethernet networks.

- **Software working group:** This working group aims to create specifications and an open-source software API for various AI/HPC use cases and applications.

- **Storage working group:** For AI and HPC workloads, storage services are an important part of the infrastructure. The Storage working group is focusing on compatibility of storage service with industry-standard physical connections, link-level capabilities, and different packet-encoding mechanisms. It is also focusing on the integration of transport services, enhanced security, and RDMA API compatibility through collaboration with the Software working group.

- **Compliance working group:** This group's focus is to ensure that devices and services are compliant with UEC standards. This group is responsible for defining the specifications and tests to validate the implementation.

- **Management working group:** This group is focusing on fabric manageability. It is investigating topology discovery, monitoring, and interoperability across different vendors.

- **Performance and Debug working group:** This group is focusing on defining performance benchmarks and the addition of debugging capabilities.

UEC Key Terminology

If you read the Ultra Ethernet Specification v1.0, you might notice that it includes a number of new acronyms and terms, and it may take some time to understand the relationships between some of them. In this section, we review some of the important acronyms and terms and relate them to existing concepts in order to help you understand the relationships and terms used in the following sections.

We believe it is best to start from the server with any AI data center requirement, so this is the order we have used to discuss key terms here. A fabric endpoint (FEP) is a node inside the fabric, which can be a server NIC or a switch port on which the fabric address (FA) is set. The FA is typically an IPv6 or IPv4 address. A FEP can be considered both an initiator and a target node.

Now let's talk about session establishment and teardown, starting with packet delivery context (PDC) creation. All negotiations between two FEPs (two end nodes connected across the fabric or a switch and a server directly connected) are part of a given PDC, which can be thought of as a logical communication channel. A PDC represents one logical connection or session. Two servers communicating with each other may have multiple PDCs enabled, and they are managed by the Packet Delivery Sublayer (PDS), which implements the logic for delivery mechanisms. The PDS is, in fact, part of the UET packet field linked to the Semantic Sublayer (SES) fields, which manage the high-level communication semantics, including message types, memory operations (such as RMA or atomics), and API compatibility. This means the AI application will communicate through the Libfabric software layer, which will then translate the requirements and include them in the negotiation between the two servers at the SES.

During session negotiation, the type of packet delivery mode is negotiated between the two FEPs (two servers equipped with GPU/NICs). Packet delivery modes include the following:

- Reliable unordered delivery (RUD)
- Reliable ordered delivery (ROD)
- Reliable unordered delivery idempotent (RUDI)
- Unreliable unordered delivery (UUD)

RUD, ROD, and RUDI, which are specific to UET, are all reliable transports; above the L4 UDP transport, there's a mechanism of sequence numbers that guarantees packet delivery and retransmission in the event of packet loss. Only UUD is an unreliable packet delivery method; it provides best-effort delivery of packets without handling any positive or negative acknowledgments, as is the case with the RUD, ROD, and RUDI methods of packet delivery.

As part of the GPU operation on the servers, the UEC has introduced the concepts JobID, PIDonFEP, and Resource Index:

- The JobID uniquely identifies a job in a cluster, and it has a field in the data packet within the SES that can be used to process packets accordingly. Multiple JobIDs can be scheduled in parallel on a particular GPU. Consequently, a single network interface connected to the fabric will send multiple JobIDs for various logical communication contexts.
- According to the specification, the PIDonFEP identifies a service available on a specific FEP.
- The Resource Index identifies a resource within a service.

A combination of JobID, PIDonFEP, and Resource Index values is leveraged at the UET frame level and can be used for more advanced network forwarding decisions, such as selecting the end-to-end path or running more efficient packet spraying inside the AI data center fabric.

There are many other acronyms in use, and they are all well documented in the UEC specifications. However, for the purposes of this chapter, we believe these are the most important ones to highlight. We will delve into some of them further when reviewing the packet delivery modes and examining various packet encapsulation formats. It's going to be much easier to understand them when you look at the Wireshark first packet captures we present later in the chapter.

The UEC and Network Architectures

Before we focus on the details of the new protocol stack for transport and the session setup details, we need to look at how UET impacts the architectures. Fortunately, network design changes are not required, and the existing IP Clos three-stage/five-stage design principles will continue to dominate, even in the case of UEC-based AI/ML scale-out clusters. As with other protocol specifications, such as InfiniBand and RoCEv2, the network design aspect is left open with UET and will depend on the target scale and expected performance of the applications. For example, when the target scale is ~100,000 or 1 million GPUs, a five-stage or seven-stage architecture is required, along with various other protocols and load-balancing mechanisms enabled at the Ethernet/IP switches, to ensure that the new UET protocol stack functions properly.

From an architecture perspective, the lossless fabric remains optional for the UEC, and the NIC-level reliable packet delivery modes and end-to-end congestion control mechanism are supposed to deliver high performance even if the fabric itself is not set at each segment of the network topology as a lossless fabric. This is why the first version of the UEC specification keeps the link layer optimization optional, even if it may significantly contribute to increasing the scale and performance of the AI/ML clusters.

When the UEC's new protocol stack is used for a latency-sensitive inference use case, the five-stage topology may not be used, and a collapsed spine-type design or a three-stage IP fabric topology will be used instead.

Some of the UEC networks will implement INC/CCL features on top of the leaf-spine type of topologies to optimize the bandwidth and latency. This will require more advanced spine devices and higher-end management platforms. In this case, the fabric three-stage/five-stage architecture may need an additional controller component, such as an INC manager (IM), and the spines or super spine will have a further role to play in this context as well, besides a typical transit and BGP route server function. (We will come back to the INC/CCL and how the new components of the design are placed in the UEC architecture.)

Most of the UEC IP Fabric designs will continue to have high port radix from leaf to spine and, therefore, will also have to be capable of balancing traffic based on the semantics negotiated at the SES layer.

UEC and the Existing Ethernet

Some feared at the beginning of the UEC work that the Ethernet header would be modified to optimize the segment latency with some form of compression or removal of the unnecessary fields. This remains an option; however, it is clearly mentioned as optional, just like all the link layer optimizations, such as CBFC and LLR. This means even the existing 400 Gbps/800 Gbps switches with the proper density of Ethernet/IP ports will be able to be used for the UEC for at least the AI Base profile. Because over time many UEC physical and link layer options became optional, the UEC-ready switches will be mainly Ethernet switches that were designed for the correct packet depth processing to include some of the UEC fields as part of the load-balancing mechanism. With the new data plane packet fields—either the JobID or Resource Index—the source UDP will have to be included in the load-balancing hash computation to perform the correct load balancing. The current QPair-based load balancing from ROCEv2 can't be used here anymore, because the BTH header is no longer there in the UET packet format. This proves that it's the advanced software feature-set at the Ethernet switch that will have to be updated and not the design itself. In most cases networks will continue to use the leaf–spine–super spine type of design and have a higher density of 800 Gbps/1.6 Tbps/3.2 Tbps ports to support larger numbers of GPUs inside the same cluster (more than a million, according to the UEC). At the time of writing this book, we expect most of the architectural changes to move from the traditional leaf–spine architecture to DragonFly or DragonFly+ and Torus, but we expect to see scale-up systems, rather than scale-out.

When thinking about the network design in the first implementations of the UEC, the same fabric will likely have to handle the existing RoCEv2 traffic coming from the existing servers, so the network design will have to in some way support two concurrent types of workloads on the same ToR the UEC-ready servers as well as RoCEv2 GPU servers. The RoCEv2 servers will continue to use the lossless approach, while the UEC-ready servers may simply use the best-effort approach and rely solely on end-to-end congestion management via RCCC or NSCC (discussed later in this chapter). Enabling the lossless fabric mechanisms from legacy networks at the link level, such as PFC-DSCP for RoCEv2 and the new LLR and CBFC, will require more attention, and either one or the other mechanism will have to be considered. In most cases, RCCC or NSCC will be used at the NIC level. Whenever the design requires handling two types of traffic, the lossless queue will still use RoCEv2. The rest of the congestion management will be controlled at the extremity of the architecture—at the server NIC level. For native UEC fabric deployments, a combination of link-layer congestion control and reliable transport, as well as end-to-end congestion control, will make much more sense. In certain cases, logical path isolation may be considered for the two types of AI/ML workloads. Whenever needed, the multi-tenancy options described in Chapter 8, "IP Routing for AI/ML Fabrics," can help introduce new UEC workloads as a separate overlay network, isolated from the existing AI/ML workloads.

A New Protocol Stack

During the initial phase of UEC communications, most industry experts believed that the Ethernet and physical layers would not be compatible with the existing Ethernet IEEE standards. If this were the case, it would significantly slow down the future adoption of the UEC specification, as well as other fundamental features from the transport layer, such as SES/PDS and the new end-to-end congestion management optimization. This is why the key focus for the initial adoption of the UEC specification will be on preserving the existing standard Ethernet and using the new UET packet format, optimizing only the post-UDP protocol layer and end-to-end semantics. Figure 12-1 provides a high-level view of the new UEC protocol stack.

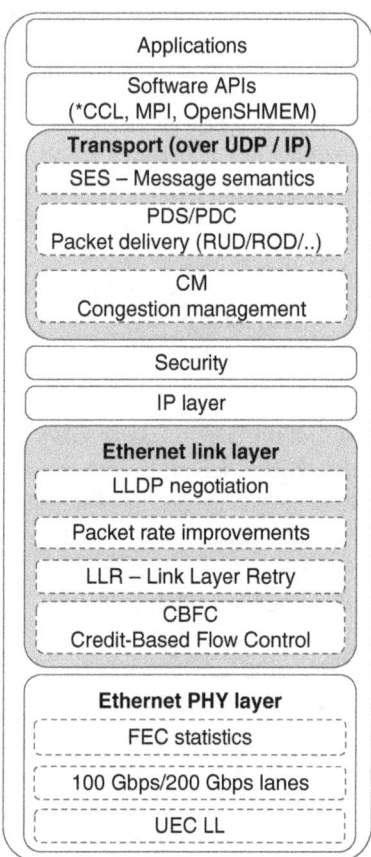

Figure 12-1
UEC protocol stack

The UEC Ethernet physical layer (PHY) is considered a longer-term option from the new technology adoption perspective, and the main things it takes care of are FEC (Forward Error Correction) statistics for the prediction of link quality, link fault signaling, and modified 64B/66B PCS encoding to run out-of-band signaling within the physical layer instead of the upper layers. The physical layer also defines the optional control ordered set (CtlOS) message mechanism used by the UEC link layer in conjunction with credit-based flow control (CBFC) and Link Layer Reliability (LLR) for each segment.

The relationship between the protocol stacks of the two servers is shown in Figure 12-2, where the initiator and target servers form a 1:1 relationship initiated from the top at the API and Libfabric levels. That relationship is translated to the relevant network and target memory parameters that are leveraged in the SES and PDS.

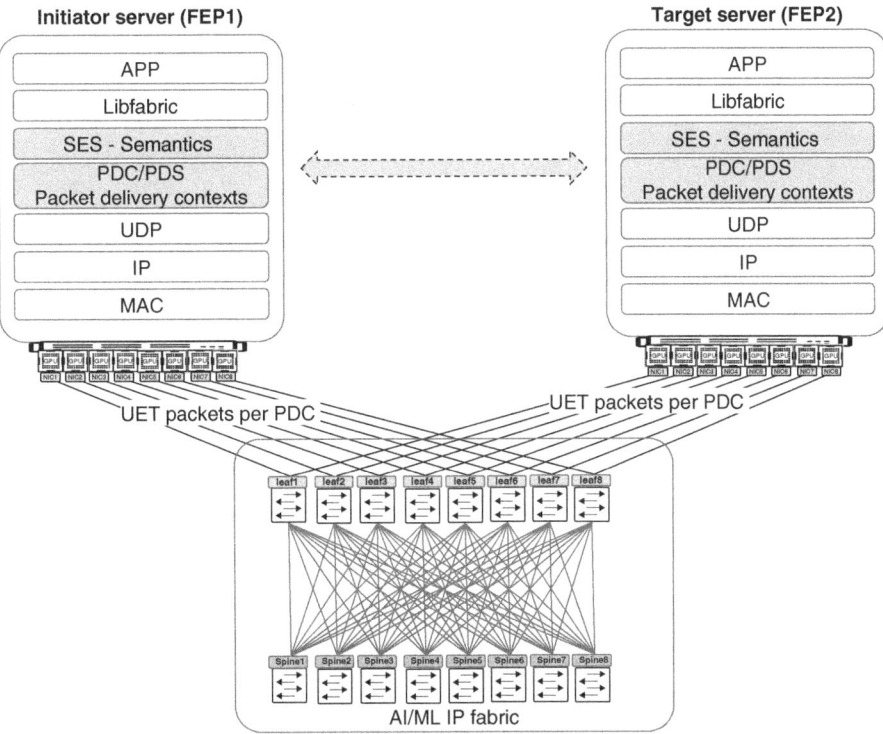

Figure 12-2
Initiator-to-target server session establishment over the Ethernet/IP fabric

When it comes to session establishment, the first phase is endpoint discovery with address assignment, where each FEP (initiator/target server) has a fabric address (FA)—typically an IPv4 or IPv6 address—and relative addressing based on the JobID and PIDonFEP values for the given PDC.

The second phase of session establishment involves the exchange of supported profiles (for example, AI Base, AI Full). The transport capabilities (for example, supported packet delivery negotiation modes, RUD/ROD/RUDI/UUD) and the reordering support information are exchanged. During the session establishment, the congestion management method supported between the initiator and target is negotiated for the given PDC (Packet Delivery Context). If two servers per GPU NIC establish more than one PDC, all packets from a single message use the same PDC. When the packet delivery mode is set to ROD, all messages between {JobID, source PIDonFEP, destination PIDonFEP, RI, TC} always use a single PDC. Only after this phase does the protocol state machine reach an established state on both sides, and the data transfer can begin.

Control messages (ACK, NACK, SACK, and so on) maintain session state and reliability. Before any data transfer begins, the type of acknowledgement to use is negotiated and set. Congestion CCC_ID (Congestion Control Context) is assigned when the PDC is created. For cases where the PDS Request control packet is received at the target server and there is insufficient packet buffer to accept the packet, the packet is dropped, and a NACK packet is transmitted to the initiator.

After the data transfer is completed, sessions can be gracefully closed by issuing teardown messages or implicitly timed out due to inactivity or errors.

Figure 12-3 shows two FEPs (servers) establishing a connection as part of the given packet delivery context.

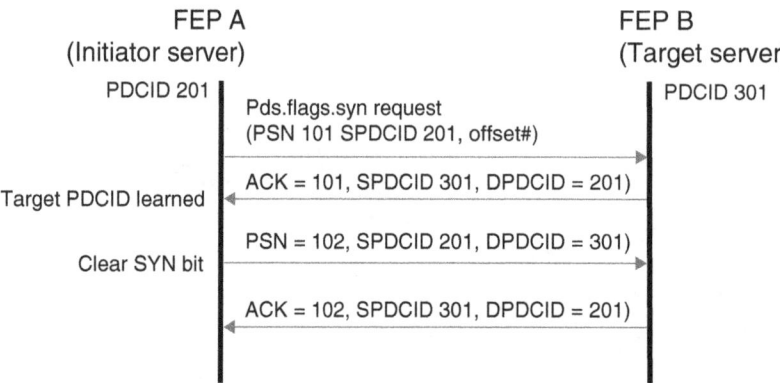

Figure 12-3
UEC session establishment within the PDC between two servers

From the simplified session establishment state machine, we can see that once the target PDC info is received, the SYN state is cleared at the initiator side. The offset information advertised by the initiator FEP is used to calculate the starting PSN for data transfer. The PDC ID remains constant on both sides throughout the session, and the PSNs change based on the acknowledgement status and offset values.

To give you an idea of what the PDS (Packet Delivery Sublayer) field looks like at the protocol level when decoded by Wireshark, we captured a sample PDS packet. We then decoded it using the Spirent implementation of the UEC emulator and read the packet in Wireshark packet decoder software. In Figure 12-4, you can see that the PDC ID Source and Destination, as well as the PSN (Packet Sequence Number) information, are leveraged in the acknowledgement message in the theoretical session state machine. When examining the decoded initial PSN packet, we can see that the delivery mode is advertised. Here, the ROD Request was sent in the PDS and encoded as required by the Libfabric settings at the software level and encoded as part of the capability advertisement for the given PDC. Setting the packet delivery mode at the Libfabric software level was done indirectly in this case.

There is also something specific to notice outside the PDS/SES part of the session information. In Figure 12-4, you can see that the captured UEC packet used raw IP encapsulation and a new Entropy field instead of UDP. (We detail the two specific encapsulation formats later in this chapter.) At the session information level, the SES part with the JobID, PIDonFEP, and Resource Index is leveraged in the SES part of the UET message header and is decoded, as shown in Figure 12-5. The same is true for the UDP and raw IP formats of UET encapsulations.

```
> Ethernet II, Src: d6:3a:fa:94:57:0b (d6:3a:fa:94:57:0b), Dst: 76:51:ee:c7:c2:fb (76:51:ee:c7:c2:fb)
> Internet Protocol Version 4, Src: 10.89.0.45, Dst: 10.89.0.44
v UltraEthernet Transport
  v PDS
      Entropy: 0
      0001 1... .... .... = Type: ROD_REQ - ROD Request (0x03)
      .... .001 1... .... = Next Header: REQUEST_STD (0x3)
      .... .... .101 1100 = Flags: 0x5c
      .... .... .1.. .... = CRC: Yes
      .... .... ..0. .... = RSV: False
      .... .... ...1 .... = RETX (is retransmit): Yes
      .... .... .... 1... = AR (ACK Request): Yes
      .... .... .... .1.. = SYN: Yes
      .... .... .... ..0. = CC state present: No
      .... .... .... ...0 = RSV2: False
      Clear PSN offset: -1
      Packet Sequence Number: 13
      Source PDC ID: 0
      Destination PDC ID: 0
      [ACK in: 3253]
  > SES request
    Payload [...]: 000102030405060708090a0b0c0d0e0f101112131415161718191a1b1c1d1e1f202122232425262728292a2b2c2
    CRC: fcfdfeff
```

Figure 12-4
Ultra Ethernet Transport PDS frame format with the SYN flag set

```
> Frame 3249: 1124 bytes on wire (8992 bits), 1124 bytes captured (8992 bits)
> Ethernet II, Src: d6:3a:fa:94:57:0b (d6:3a:fa:94:57:0b), Dst: 76:51:ee:c7:c2:fb (76:51:ee:c7:c2:fb)
> Internet Protocol Version 4, Src: 10.89.0.45, Dst: 10.89.0.44
v UltraEthernet Transport
  > PDS
  v SES request
      00.. .... = Reserved: 0x0
      ..00 1001 = Opcode: TAGGED_SEND - A tagged send operation using match bits for buffer selection. (0x09)
      00.. .... = Version: 0x0
      ..0. .... = Delivery Complete (DC): No
      ...0 .... = Initiator Error (IE): No
      .... 1... = Relative: Yes
      .... .0.. = Header Data (HD): No
      .... ..0. = End of Message (EOM): No
      .... ...1 = Start of Message (SOM): Yes
      Message ID: 0
      Resource Index generation: 0
      Job ID: 1
      0000 .... .... .... = Reserved: 0x0
      .... 0000 0000 0000 = PID on FEP: 0
      0000 .... .... .... = Reserved: 0x0
      .... 0000 0000 1111 = Index: 15
      Buffer offset: 0 (0x0000000000000000)
      Initiator: 0x00000010
      Match bits: 0x0000000000000001
      Header data: 0x0000000000000000
      Request length: 4096 (0x00001000)
    Payload [...]: 000102030405060708090a0b0c0d0e0f101112131415161718191a1b1c1d1e1f202122232425262728292a2b2c2d2e2f303132
    CRC: fcfdfeff
```

Figure 12-5
SES request packet with JobID and Resource Index information

At the API level, the given JobID is also linked to the registered memory region when authorized at the application/system level. The memory key (RKEY) is validated and used to locate the exact registered memory region, ensuring that access rights (read, write, atomic, and so on) are correct. The Libfabric's various API groups, which are defined as part of the UEC standard, regulate the association of the UET transport protocol semantics with memory buffer regions. For example, the fi_mr API is dedicated to managing the association of memory regions. At the target server, the JobID and

PIDonFEP combination will be used to locate the appropriate operating system process context, and Resource Index will be mapped to a receive queue, which serves as a completion queue.

Data Plan: Packet Forwarding Options

We've already highlighted the fact that there are two main different encapsulation options in the UEC standards: UDP-based encapsulation and the IP-only encapsulation. These two forms of encapsulation are proposed to offer full compatibility with existing networks and to provide a lightweight version of the PDS/SES encapsulation without traditional UDP L4 transport by leveraging only the key UET development information, including entropy options.

In both forms of encapsulation, the SES leverages the same type of information as the PDS, in addition to entropy information that is specific to the native IP version (also known as the raw IP version) of UET encapsulations. With both types of UET encapsulation, the BTH is no longer used with the QPair, as is the case with RoCEv2 encapsulations; it is replaced with the JobID and Resource Index information to find the memory queue pair info mapping, based on the upper-layer Libfabric definition.

UDP-Based Encapsulation for UET

In the case of UDP packet encapsulation, any entropy requirement for packet spraying will use the source UDP port, which in RoCEv2 implementations often stays the same throughout the duration of a session. In case of UET, the intent is that whenever congestion is encountered, the originating host will be informed, and, subsequently, the source UDP port will be changed to influence the hashing at the switch level. UET PDS will include the PSN, which will be acknowledged or negatively acknowledged. If UET uses NSCC for congestion management, the NACK will contain entropy information to allow the originator to adapt its entropy accordingly.

The destination UDP port selected by UEC is 49150, and it will be common for many JobIDs, so naturally the IP fabric switches will—as with RoCEv2—have to adapt the hashing or the load balancing by using a more intelligent approach. It might be as simple as using the source UDP port, which changes during a same session based on the feedback from the NSCC target, or it might be a more advanced option, where the Ethernet switch is capable of inspecting the JobID, the Resource Index, or other fields from the SES and PDS.

From an encapsulation perspective, the UDP-based option covered in this section will be the most acceptable for initial deployments because, in many cases, it will simply just work over the existing Ethernet/IP networks, as long as the switches are capable of efficiently handling load balancing and as long as the NICs inside the servers support at least one of the congestion mechanisms proposed by the UEC. (We cover NSCC in more detail later in this chapter.)

Figure 12-6 provides a horizontal view of UDP-based encapsulation.

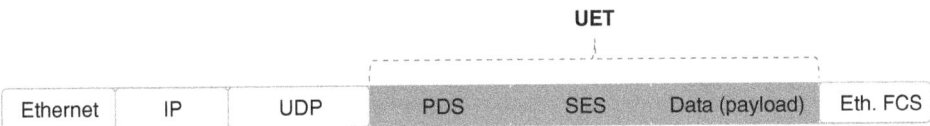

Figure 12-6
UET data packet with UDP encapsulation (horizontal view)

Figure 12-7 shows a more detailed vertical view of packet encapsulation. The first three parts of the UET packet from the top—Ethernet, IP, and UDP—will be processed as in any other IP packet by the switches. The PDS/SES recognition will mainly have to happen at the NIC driver level, which will have to be capable of enqueueing the given PIDonFEP and Resource Index to the correct memory queue.

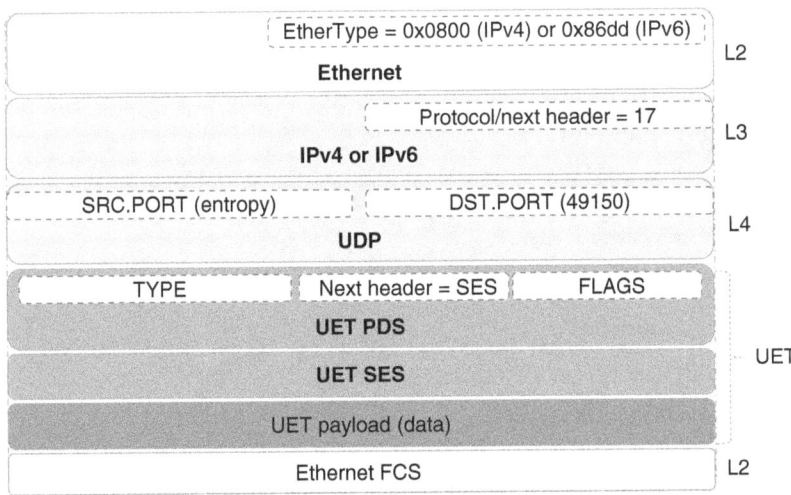

Figure 12-7
UET data packet with UDP-based encapsulation

Figure 12-7 shows the Ethernet Frame Check Sequence at the bottom and Ethernet at the top of the layered stack. It shows that, from the switch perspective, the UET packet will mainly be considered an Ethernet packet with IP inside, based on the EtherType value being set to IPv4 or IPv6. The proposed outer FCS is also just one option to make the encapsulation compatible with the existing switches, but the UET standard also proposes the option of using the UET CRC (check resource) just after the UET payload.

Cyclic redundancy checking is applied at the UET layer to ensure data integrity over the transport path and can be used at the NIC adapters. The use of the CRC is optional and may become an advantage for lossy transport environments where data corruption may still happen outside the

FCS-based hop-by-hop protections. The CRC usage in this case depends on the type of packet delivery mode set for the given PDC; typically for ROD, it can still be considered to check the end-to-end integrity when packets are arriving at the destination server in order.

The additional UET CRC fields are one option for UDP-based encapsulation. There's also an option to include the TSS (Transport Security Sublayer), which is a security encryption layer header, just after the UDP and to include the ICV (Integrity Check Value) output of AES-GCM just after the UET payload. Figure 12-8 shows the TSS.

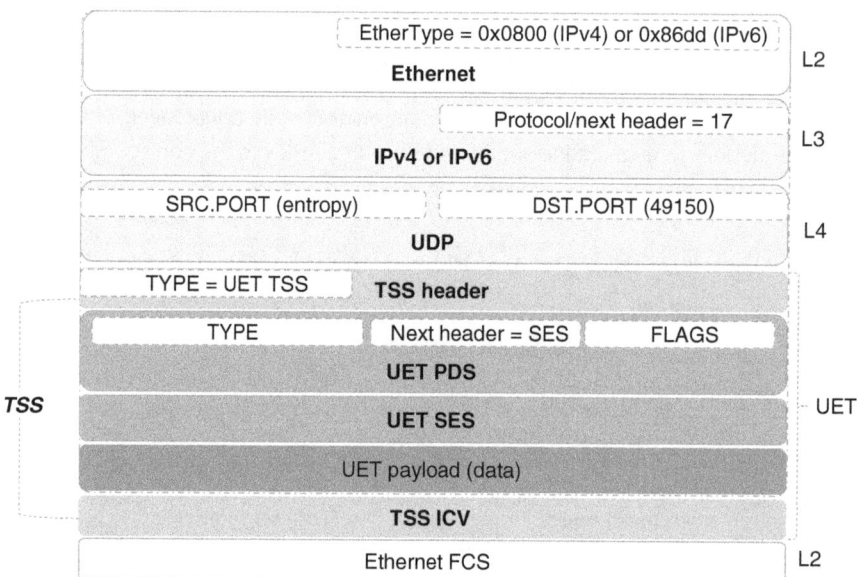

Figure 12-8
UET encapsulation using UDP with the TSS encryption layer

If this method of security is used, the outcomes of end-to-end confidentiality are integrity and anti-replay protection of the UET AI workloads. Because of the encryption used at the load-balancing level, the packet spraying or UDP source port-based LB will have to be used, because the other SES/PDS field (for example, Resource Index, JobID) will be only understood by the originating and target server NICs only when the TSS security enabled.

We may also need to understand the UDP-based encapsulation extended view. We at least need to understand that in the PDS and SES, many important end host–relevant parameters are leveraged. SES-level opcode information on the type of write or send operation conducted is traditionally leveraged as part of the BTH in RoCEv2. To match the memory, the Resource Index, JobID, PID on FEP, and the buffer offset specify where in the target memory buffer the data associated with the SES message should be placed. Figure 12-9 shows a packet capture in which these parameters are included within the SES request message.

As mentioned earlier, the PDC Source and Destination and packet delivery mode information inside the PDS remain intact during the transfer, and only the PSN packets/ACK are updated. The message

ID information from the SES remains constant for a given set of write or send operations and is used for tracking, matching, and completing communication operations, especially in the context of reliability and ordering, where packet reassembly at the target server is also required.

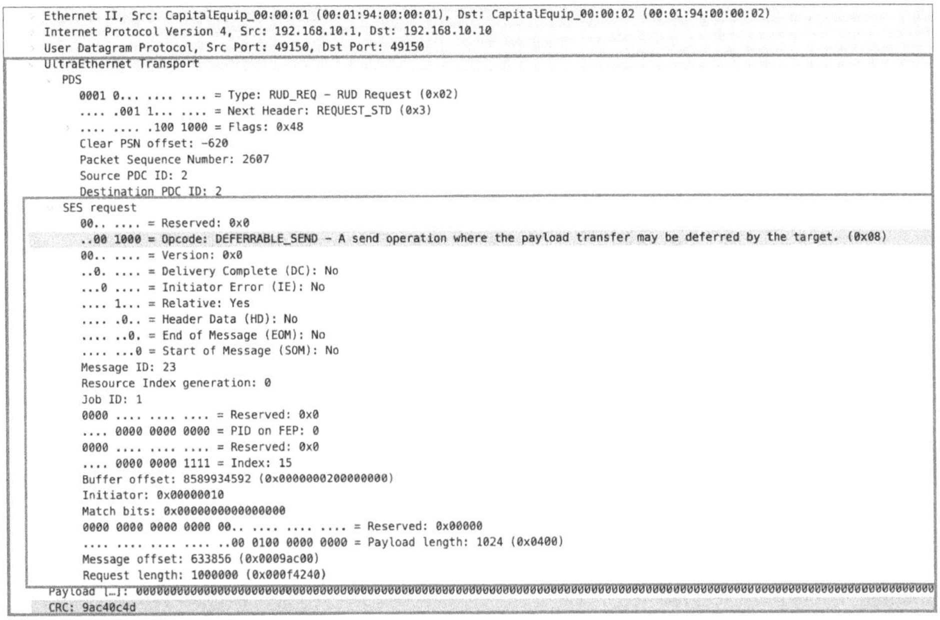

```
Ethernet II, Src: CapitalEquip_00:00:01 (00:01:94:00:00:01), Dst: CapitalEquip_00:00:02 (00:01:94:00:00:02)
Internet Protocol Version 4, Src: 192.168.10.1, Dst: 192.168.10.10
User Datagram Protocol, Src Port: 49150, Dst Port: 49150
UltraEthernet Transport
  PDS
    0001 0... .... .... = Type: RUD_REQ - RUD Request (0x02)
    .... .001 1... .... = Next Header: REQUEST_STD (0x3)
    .... .... .100 1000 = Flags: 0x48
    Clear PSN offset: -620
    Packet Sequence Number: 2607
    Source PDC ID: 2
    Destination PDC ID: 2
  SES request
    00.. .... = Reserved: 0x0
    ..00 1000 = Opcode: DEFERRABLE_SEND - A send operation where the payload transfer may be deferred by the target. (0x08)
    00.. .... = Version: 0x0
    ..0. .... = Delivery Complete (DC): No
    ...0 .... = Initiator Error (IE): No
    .... 1... = Relative: Yes
    .... .0.. = Header Data (HD): No
    .... ..0. = End of Message (EOM): No
    .... ...0 = Start of Message (SOM): No
    Message ID: 23
    Resource Index generation: 0
    Job ID: 1
    0000 .... .... .... = Reserved: 0x0
    .... 0000 0000 0000 = PID on FEP: 0
    0000 .... .... .... = Reserved: 0x0
    .... 0000 0000 1111 = Index: 15
    Buffer offset: 8589934592 (0x0000000200000000)
    Initiator: 0x00000010
    Match bits: 0x0000000000000000
    0000 0000 0000 0000 00.. .... .... .... = Reserved: 0x00000
    .... .... .... .... ..00 0100 0000 0000 = Payload length: 1024 (0x0400)
    Message offset: 633856 (0x0009ac00)
    Request length: 1000000 (0x000f4240)
  Payload [...]: 0000000000000000000000000000000000000000000000000000000000000000000000000000000000000000000000000000
CRC: 9ac40c4d
```

Figure 12-9
UET encapsulation format: UDP-based detailed Wireshark view

When the ACK message is sent for a given RUD request, the SES part of the ACK message is usually shorter and simply refers to the message ID and job ID for the originator to which the acknowledgement is sent.

UET over IP: The New Entropy Field

For the lightweight version of UET data encapsulation, raw IP encapsulation is also proposed for the transport and highlighted as a new UET data packet format (see Figure 12-10). The main difference is that there's no more UDP layer, and entropy is managed directly at the PDS level with a new field called Entropy. UEC-capable Ethernet switches will have to consider that field to handle the load balancing or include it as an additional parameter for the hash calculation or for the path pinning option of the load balancing. In addition, newer UEC-ready switches will be able to process even further inside the SES because the L4 information processing is simply not there anymore. For an ethernet switch packet parsing is typically limited to 128 bytes, which helps to include upper transport and session (SES) layer information. For example, inside the UET this information is positioned at the end of the SES message. For an existing Ethernet switch, the new IP Protocol value 253 (see Figure 12-10) might not work if the Ethernet switch implementation restricts the type of IP Protocol values accepted for port-to-port forwarding. The rest of the SES remains consistent with what the UDP-based encapsulation is running. This means, however, that the two servers must be set to use the same type of encapsulation before any SES data is processed. Both endpoints must be preconfigured and orchestrated to agree on the format before the session is established. There's no encapsulation negotiation process involved, and the preset encapsulation must happen before any session negotiation starts at the PDC level.

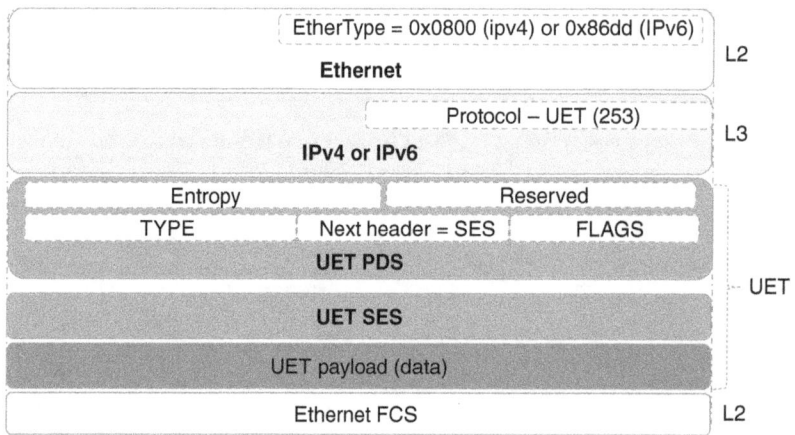

Figure 12-10
UET encapsulation format using IP only

In the case of IP-only UET encapsulation, there's also an option to add the CRC (Cyclic Redundancy Check) for the packet integrity check, to avoid the corrupted data. In addition, an optional TSS security is built into UET, and it is set immediately after the Entropy field. According to the specification, when the CRC is used, TSS security should not be employed, so typically either the UET CRC or the UET TSS security is used.

Similarly to UDP-based encapsulation, the UET PDS includes the PSN and the ACK or NACK to ensure reliable packet delivery. If UET uses NSCC for end-to-end congestion management, the NACK contains the entropy information to let the originator adapt its entropy accordingly. This means that instead of changing the UDP source port with UET over IP, the new Entropy field must be used at the originating server. To better imagine the second option of encapsulation proposed as part of the UEC Specification v1.0, Figure 12-11 shows a Spirent-based data plane and UET control-plane packet emulation and decoding.

We can observe that the PDS now includes the Entropy value and that the UDP layer is no longer set. On the other hand, the remaining SES fields, such as PIDonFEP, JobID, and the Resource Index, are still present and will be used to connect to the GPU memory-specific region, as defined by the Libfabric software application mappings.

```
Frame 46: 1124 bytes on wire (8992 bits), 1124 bytes captured (8992 bits)
Ethernet II, Src: ae:27:7a:03:dc:e3 (ae:27:7a:03:dc:e3), Dst: e2:84:7b:d9:62:e8 (e2:84:7b:d9:62:e8)
Internet Protocol Version 4, Src: 10.89.0.42, Dst: 10.89.0.43
UltraEthernet Transport
    PDS
        Entropy: 0
        0001 1... .... .... = Type: ROD_REQ - ROD Request (0x03)
        .... .001 1... .... = Next Header: REQUEST_STD (0x3)
        .... .... .100 1000 = Flags: 0x48
            .... .... .1.. .... = CRC: Yes
            .... .... ..0. .... = RSV: False
            .... .... ...0 .... = RETX (is retransmit): No
            .... .... .... 1... = AR (ACK Request): Yes
            .... .... .... .0.. = SYN: No
            .... .... .... ..0. = CC state present: No
            .... .... .... ...0 = RSV2: False
        Clear PSN offset: -4
        Packet Sequence Number: 17
        Source PDC ID: 1
        Destination PDC ID: 1
        [ACK in: 50]
    SES request
        00.. .... = Reserved: 0x0
        ..00 0001 = Opcode: WRITE - RMA Write (0x01)
        00.. .... = Version: 0x0
        ..0. .... = Delivery Complete (DC): No
        ...0 .... = Initiator Error (IE): No
        .... 1... = Relative: Yes
        .... .0.. = Header Data (HD): No
        .... ..1. = End of Message (EOM): Yes
        .... ...0 = Start of Message (SOM): No
        Message ID: 1
        Resource Index generation: 0
        Job ID: 1
        0000 .... .... .... = Reserved: 0x0
        .... 0000 0000 0000 = PID on FEP: 0
        0000 .... .... .... = Reserved: 0x0
        .... 0000 0000 1111 = Index: 15
        Buffer offset: 0 (0x0000000000000000)
        Initiator: 0x00000010
        Match bits: 0x0000000000000000
        0000 0000 0000 0000 00.. .... .... .... = Reserved: 0x00000
        .... .... .... .... ..00 0100 0000 0000 = Payload length: 1024 (0x0400)
        Message offset: 3072 (0x00000c00)
        Request length: 4096 (0x00001000)
    Payload [...]: 000102030405060708090a0b0c0d0e0f101112131415161718191a1b1c1d1e1f202122232425262728292a2b2c2
    CRC: fcfdfeff
```

Figure 12-11
UET data packet with IP-only encapsulation: Write operation with ROD

Packet Delivery Modes

We've already mentioned the packet delivery modes proposed by the UEC on multiple occasions, and this section provides more detail about each of the proposed options. Why would the definition of the packet delivery mode matter in the context of AI workloads? The UEC Transport working group has made proposals based on experiences from the existing RoCEv2 networks, where there are many limitations and disconnects in terms of which RoCEv2 packet delivery traffic can run in an ordered way and which can run in an unordered way. Typically, the packet delivery mode is based on the capability of the NIC vendor and the type of data operation performed: writing into the same memory space versus into different memory spaces, writing it once versus writing it multiple times to the same memory sector.

The UEC decided to classify the requirements and allow an AI/ML application developer to define them at the Libfabric level, based on specific API calls. Libfabric connected to an AI/ML application, such as PyTorch, which has an interface to Open MPI (Message Passing Interface), can set some of the settings directly from the API, which will then be translated to the PDS/SES settings and encapsulated as part of the UET transport. The same goes for the settings of the packet delivery modes. Figure 12-12 illustrates the relationship between the AI/ML API, Open MPI, and the Libfabric.

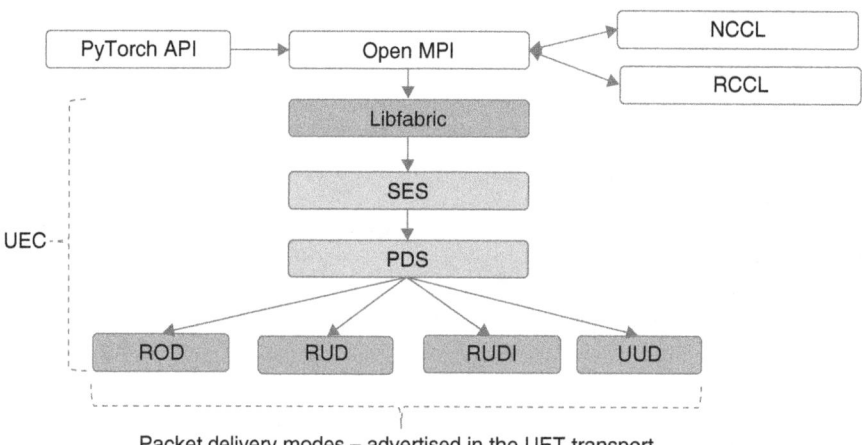

Figure 12-12
Libfabric/Open MPI and SES/PDS relationship for packet delivery modes

Message Passing Interface (MPI) is a widely adopted API standard for communication in parallel computing. MPI was originally used in HPC, and it is beginning to play a critical role as a high-level interface for UEC—where it connects to Libfabric as well as to original AI/ML applications such as PyTorch. OpenMPI, when connected to Libfabric, also provides an interface to NCCL or RCCL for collective communication. These libraries and management software are currently the most popular options for accelerating GPU-based operations, offering faster, topology-aware communication between GPUs. Meanwhile, OpenMPI handles process coordination and CPU-side messaging. The NCCL/RCCL interface connections at the software level won't be required when MPI native collective support is used or when Libfabric managed collective communication is enabled; for example, the MPICH (an MPI alternative to OpenMPI) supports MPI_Allreduce and MPI_Alltoall, and is documented as a supported collective communication type.

We have explicitly mentioned the software/API relationship with the Libfabric, which has an interface to the SES layer of UET. That's where the first initialization is happening, and it is little by little translated to lower-level requirements—including the way packets are delivered across the AI/ML data center fabric (either in a reliable or unreliable way and an ordered or unordered way of delivering packets). In most cases, reliable packet delivery will be used because even if the ACK mechanism has some penalty on the speed of packet delivery, it's preferred to ensure that all the packets from the originator to the target server are confirmed with an explicit acknowledgement. A negative acknowledgement (NACK) can be used as an alternative, when there are still lower packet sequence numbers (PSNs) missing packets, for the given higher sequence number well received packets.

RUD, ROD, and RUDI all use reliable packet delivery methods, and only the ordered versus unordered delivery option changes between these options. On the other hand, UUD offers an unreliable and unordered delivery option. Each UEC profile (AI Base, AI Full, or HPC) has a corresponding packet delivery mode selected for a given type of operation (read/write or send). All profiles support RUD/ROD, and only HPC supports RUDI.

Reliable Ordered Delivery (ROD)

The ROD reordering buffer is engaged at the receiver server when packet spraying is used at the originator. Only if the NIC card does not support the buffer memory to reorder packets, then the network flow-based dynamic load balancing must be set accordingly.

A specific packet delivery mode does not imply that the switch has to be explicitly set for ordered or unordered packet delivery. At the destination server in case of ROD packet delivery, the reordering buffer can be used and the IP Fabric can still perform the packet spraying or the NIC card itself can use the packet spraying. As long as the destination server can reorder it, the ROD can be used at the application level. The top-of-rack switch load-balancing setting may differ between UEC and ROCEv2 when both server types are connected to the same node.

Reliable Unordered Delivery (RUD)

RUD is a reliable mode of packet delivery, in which PSNs are acknowledged, selectively acknowledged, or negatively acknowledged. However, the target server supports unordered delivery for the placement of data in the GPU memory buffer. This mode assumes selective retransmission capabilities and enables semantic processing and out-of-order direct data placement. *Direct data placement* refers to writing data arriving at the Ethernet network port directly into system memory, without CPU intervention and without imposing a higher memory buffer for reordering, which was the case of the ROD. The latency is therefore lower with unordered delivery. On the fabric side, the packet spraying can be used, and there's no need for any additional settings unless the ROCEv2 servers are connected to the same node with limited support for unordered delivery.

Reliable Unordered Delivery Idempotent (RUDI)

In the RUDI (reliable unordered delivery idempotent) packet delivery mode, the word *idempotent* refers to operations that can be safely retried multiple times without changing the result. RUDI does not guarantee ordering, so duplicate or late packets might arrive. With this packet delivery mode set, it's safe to retry packets multiple times—for example, to write the same packet multiple times, which will avoid too many NACKs in the event that one of the write operations isn't successful. At the application level, multiple retries can be conducted without necessarily asking for retransmission. In addition, in the case of RUDI, multiple sources can write to the same destination, and this may be necessary in the context of AI gradient updates.

Unreliable Unordered Delivery (UUD)

UUD is different from ROD and RUD in that the UUD request packet does not have the PSNs (PSN offsets) included, whereas ROD and RUD always have PSNs for the given packet delivery context. With UUD, the two initiator and target servers avoid retransmissions, acknowledgements, or ordering logic, which results in a better JCT value. With UUD, packets can occasionally be lost, so communication is generally a best-effort type of delivery with no acknowledgements; no ACK, SACK, or NACK is used with UUD. On the other hand, when the network is well designed from a capacity and load-balancing perspective, UUD may have performance advantages compared to ROD, RUD, and RUDI as it offers faster session ramp times compared to the other three modes of delivery.

UEC Delivery Modes Comparison

The new UEC packet delivery modes incorporate mechanisms that are improvements over go-back-to-N, such as selective acknowledgments (SACK-like behavior), where instead of discarding all packets after a loss, UEC receivers may buffer out-of-order packets and request only missing packets for retransmission. RUD, RUDI, and UUD can, for example, handle the out-of-order packets inside the buffer. With the improved go-back-to-N in UET, there's no need to flush the entire window of packets. This means that the UEC source server needs to retransmit only the lost packet and not all subsequent ones. If subsequent packets were well received, only the missing one is requested to be retransmitted with RUD or RUDI. In UEC's transport (RUD/RUDI), the sequence space continues forward, and it doesn't have to roll back entirely because it's just scheduled as a retry for the specific missing packet. This saves fabric bandwidth, avoids redundant work, and reduces latency.

Table 12-2 presents a comparison of the different modes of delivery.

Table 12-2   UEC Packet Delivery Modes

Mode	Pros	Cons	Use Cases
ROD (reliable ordered delivery)	Guarantees in-order delivery of packets	Higher latency due to ordering constraints	HPC, MPI, serialized control flow
RUD (reliable unordered delivery)	Lower latency, no order guarantees. Good for many parallel streams	Application must handle reordering	AI model parallelism Bulk data ops
RUDI (reliable unordered delivery idempotent)	Like RUD but ensures safe retry of idempotent operations Supports write multiple times	Requires apps to be capable of retrying the same write operation	RMA writes AI gradients

Mode	Pros	Cons	Use Cases
UUD (unreliable unordered delivery)	Lowest latency	No retransmissions	Telemetry
	No reliability (that is, no PSNs and no ACKs)	No integrity checking	Inference logs
	Can be useful for fire-and-forget AI workloads	Not compatible with UET-driven security	

Congestion Management (CM) in the UEC Specification

With all the flexible UEC packet delivery modes, a congestion management mechanism must still be put in place in order to ensure that the initiator and target servers are reacting to congestion in an efficient way, to reduce the number of retransmissions. It is important to ensure that the CM (Congestion Management) mechanism doesn't slow down the AI workloads for too long and doesn't slow down the workloads that are not at the origin of the congestion. This was one of the drawbacks of the legacy ROCEv2-based AI Workloads, where PFC backpressures used for congestion control were also impacting the servers that were not at the origin of the congestion.

In the standard that the UEC has developed and described, there are two main types of congestion management:

- End-to-end congestion management with one of the following:
    - Network Signal Congestion Control (NSCC), which is managed at the originator
    - Receiver Credit Congestion Control (RCCC), which is managed at the target
- Segment/link-level congestion control with Credit-Based Flow Control (CBFC)

For a given PDC (Packet Delivery Context) between the originator and target, a CCC (congestion control context) is created and preserved for the duration of that PDC. The three UEC profiles are required to support NSCC when a lossy network is used. As of mid-2025, RCCC is optional for lossy IP fabric networks.

Network Signal Congestion Control (NSCC)

NSCC maintains an explicit congestion window. The sender (server1 in Figure 12-13) uses window-based congestion control to estimate packets in flight—that is, packets that have not yet been acknowledged by the target. The sender can send when the congestion window is larger than the number of in-flight bytes in packets that have not yet been acknowledged, negatively acknowledged, or timed out. The sender PDS considers packets to have left the network when they are acknowledged by the receiver with an ACK or SACK. NACK messages may contain the ECN flag.

The sender adjusts the window size based on congestion feedback from the receiver and RTT. Whenever NSCC is used for congestion control, the ACK/SACK used in ROD/RUD packet delivery must be used, and it must contain the congestion control flags.

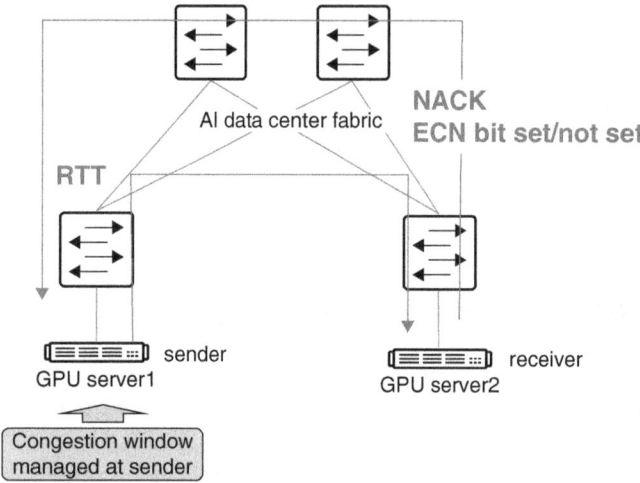

Figure 12-13
Network Signal Congestion Control

When NSCC is used, the ACK_CC (an acknowledgement with congestion control info) includes the congestion control information sent back by the target, with the number of received bytes, the service time, and the out-of-order packet count.

NSCC reuses the ECN part to calculate the congestion window, so for IP fabrics that already support ECN, the adoption of NSCC may become more seamless from the perspective of an Ethernet switch because the state machine of the NSCC is mainly managed at the server NICs.

Receiver Credit Congestion Control (RCCC)

An alternative to NSCC is RCCC, which manages things at the receiver and uses the concept of credit attribution rather than the congestion window calculations used by the NSCC. The sender sends requests for more credit to the receiver via the Credit Target field in data packets. The sender can transmit whenever there is available credit in its local credit pool at the receiver (server3 in Figure 12-14). The originator receives credit back from the receiver through credit control packets. The receiver shares the credit information with the source servers so that, collectively, their rate does not cause congestion at the receiver.

The advantage of this approach is that the target server knows exactly how many of the credits are left based on all the active sessions that are locally controlled—so if there are no more credits left, the credits are not distributed. For the RCCC congestion management credit, the PDS req_cc_state information sent by the source server will include target information that indicates the amount data to be sent. From the destination/target server, the 24-bit ACK congestion control will include the credits allocated in units of 256 bytes.

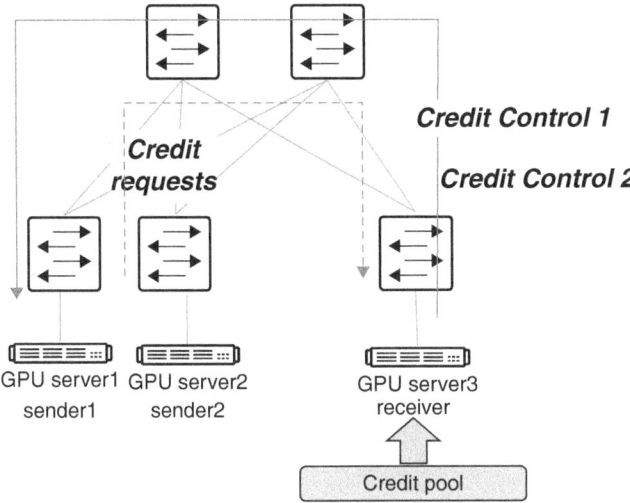

Figure 12-14
Receiver Credit Congestion Control

Credit-Based Flow Control (CBFC)

CBFC is an optional feature that operates as a link-layer function, enabling lossless packet delivery on a priority basis over an Ethernet full-duplex link. Similarly to the end-to-end credit allocation explained for RCCC, the link-level CBFC mechanism also uses credits to manage the available buffer space at the receiver and prevent buffer congestion—but just at the given segment (for example, between two switches from the same IP fabric). InfiniBand's CBFC inspired the UEC version of the CBFC, but with the UEC version here, the number of virtual channels (VCs) is increased from 16 to 32 per port. Some of the VCs are lossless, and others may be best effort (in which case the credits are not exchanged).

CBFC has several advantages over the standard Priority-Based Flow Control (PFC), including the ability to support more lossless classes, better scheduling and load balancing, and less sensitivity to cable length and frame size. The receiver generates the token based on the available buffer and sends the credit to the sender. The scheduler at the sender sends traffic only when there are enough tokens available. Both the sender and the receiver keep track of the credits consumed. The receiver informs the sender of the credits freed when the traffic is out of its input buffer.

In theory, the UEC standard allows PFC and CBFC to be used on two different VCs on the same link. However, the challenges of the PFC running independently to manage the thresholds of the buffers for two entirely different mechanisms may eventually make it very complicated. CBFC mechanism is proposed as a more effective approach compared to the existing PFC/DSCP-driven congestion control in lossless fabrics.

Figure 12-15 shows CBFC between two UEC switches. It works similarly to what we explained about the InfiniBand CBFC in Chapter 9. Here, destination Switch2 will respond with credits based on its port-level buffer state; it's up to the implementation to decide whether these credit allocations will be based on dedicated buffers or a combination of dedicated interface buffers and shared buffer pool.

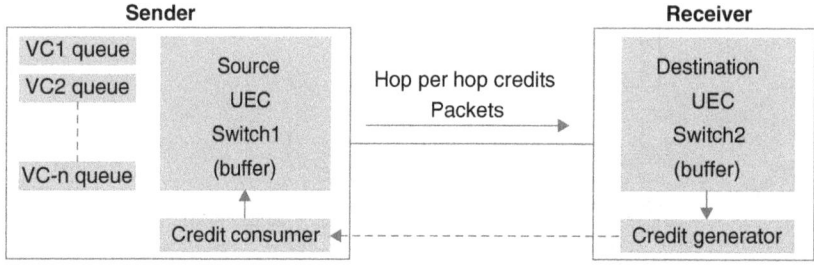

Figure 12-15
UEC Credit-Based Flow Control

CBFC manages the credit mechanism, tracking the consumed and freed credits; the CC and CF counters are mentioned in the UEC specification as counters to monitor at the segment level. Compared to end-to-end congestion management, CBFC requires minor modifications to the link layer to support the CtlOS messages out of band of the link. This ensures that the link layer offers line rate and very fast credit update information. It is also important to note that the explicit credit request information is not sent by switch1 but rather uses the CP_Update message as part of the CtlOS message from the PCS physical sublayer to inform the receiver (switch2) about the consumed credit count.

Before any credit information is exchanged, Link Layer Discovery Protocol (LLDP) is used at the segment that handles the CBFC credit information to recognize the switch-to-switch capability.

Packet Trimming and Fast Retransmissions

While we're on the topic of congestion control, it's worth mentioning the optional packet trimming mechanism, which can be enabled to speed up retransmissions across all three packet delivery modes. With packet trimming, in the event of overutilization of all the buffers, the intermediate switches inside the IP fabric start trimming the packets (that is, cutting them in smaller pieces) and continue to send the traffic over a higher-priority queue to the destination server. The switches expect the destination server to react slightly differently from ECN, which simply sends back the congestion information to the originating host but does not specify which packets must be retransmitted.

With UEC packet trimming, the destination understands that the given packet delivery context is experiencing extreme congestion, which results in packet drop, and it also knows which packets must be retransmitted immediately. The outcome of such a procedure is that the JCT is better than with regular PSN-driven retransmission. UEC packet trimming can also help to identify the exact AI workload that's experiencing severe congestion.

With UEC packet trimming, DSCP-specific values are used to identify whether the packets are trimmable. Only packets from a specific class of service arriving on the port may be trimmed and set with additional information. This means, however, that the packets that were trimmed will not send the ECN information to the destination server at the same time; in addition, the trimming only preserves the original ECN information, such as the ECN-capable flag, which can still be leveraged. When the trimmed packets are received at the destination host, the trimmed packet information is, however, not placed in the memory buffer of the GPU but is instead used for fast retransmission request and telemetry purposes. The trimming implementation engages the support of the NICs and also the support of the Ethernet switches to implement the trimming formats defined by the UEC.

Link Layer Reliability (LLR) Mechanism

At the upper layer, the PSN-based sequence numbers already regulate reliable transport, and packet delivery is guaranteed. The problem is that in the case of any drops in larger fabric, the unacknowledged packets may have to be retransmitted by the originating server, and this will create a delay for the scheduled AI workload job.

This is where LLR comes into play, as it assists communication at each segment by managing retransmissions between end hosts rather than managing them directly. The capability of the LLR is advertised between the two switches (Switch1 and Switch2 in Figure 12-16) or between the host NIC and the switch, so the rest of the state machine is triggered only if there's such an agreement between the two nodes. If only one node supports it, then the LLR is ignored, and a regular end-to-end PSN and ACK/NACK/SACK-based reliable transport is used. When LLR-based acknowledgments are proposed, the other end-to-end semantics are still used, which means there's double-level control for the reliable transport. The result should be a better JCT for the given job, especially where there is a higher risk of congestion. The LLR must be implemented at the ASIC level to ensure that the segment-level mechanism does not slow down the end-to-end communication. If the MAC client does not want LLR for the frame or if the frame is otherwise classified as LLR ineligible, it is sent as a standard Ethernet frame. If the frame is LLR eligible, it is assigned a sequence number and stored in a replay buffer in case the link partner does not receive it.

The sequence number for each LLR-eligible frame passed from the LLR to the MAC (Media Access Control) is placed into the preamble prepended by the MAC.

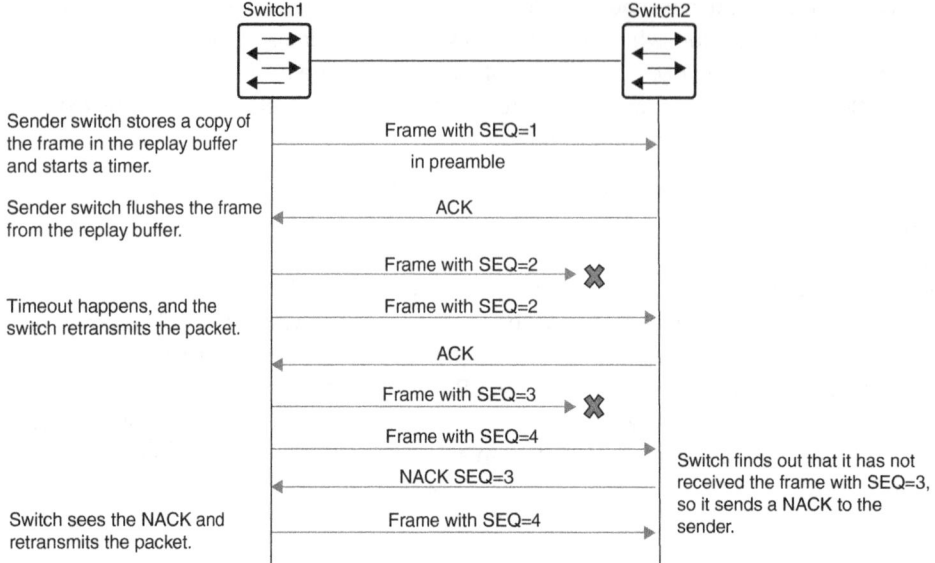

Figure 12-16
Link Layer Retry

The LLR state machine mentioned earlier is still optional. It can complement what end-to-end reliable packet delivery is doing (RUD/ROD/RUDI) with PSN-based retransmissions. Here, the retransmission occurs at the link level instead of at the server level, so for the given PDC, the LLR part can be transparent. LLR is more applicable in the context of latency-sensitive AI applications, such as inference networks that use GPU servers. Segment-level connection-oriented control may yield a positive outcome for such workloads.

In-Network Collectives (INC) and xCCL

The Ultra Ethernet Specification v1.0 does not yet include the INC and xCCL. However, the Software working group is discussing the use of collective communication (for example, Broadcast, AllReduce, AllGather) to offer parallel computing. Collective communication helps accelerate computing at the servers by offloading part of the tasks into the network or by optimizing network forwarding based on the type of collective (such as AllReduce, AllGather, or Broadcast).

MPI (including OpenMPI) is starting to implement collective communication native definitions similarly to the way the NCCL and RCCL versions from Nvidia and AMD do. Adoption of the UEC INC components will happen only when it will interop with these two vendor-specific xCCLs frameworks. Libfabric used by the UEC already supports the API group fi_collective, which will be used for collective operations management. The details of the supported collective operations are available on GitHub and from the Open Fabric Interface Working Group (OFIWG). CCL (Collective

Communication Library) focuses on data movement patterns at the server level and is tightly integrated with training frameworks such as PyTorch and TensorFlow.

INC refers to compute optimizations performed within the network, such as aggregation for AllReduce (originally introduced as part of the SHARP framework from Nvidia). INC will assist a given xCCL type and perform network-level optimizations, such as data transformation, filtering, or in-network routing decisions designed to a specific type of collective characteristics. The outcomes of the INC optimizations (grouping flows of the given collective into the group with specific switches and servers) are that the server GPU and latency are more optimized. From a network perspective, the INC optimizes the communications using the hierarchical aggregations at one of the switch nodes inside the IP fabric supporting the INC (for example, at the spines). decreasing data copies and reducing data movement.

The main differences and similarities between the INC and xCCLs are highlighted in Table 12-3.

Table 12-3 Comparison of INC and xCCL

Feature	INC	xCCLs
Layer	Fabric level (hardware)	Software library (user space)
Primary execution	Inside network switches (sFEPs)	On host CPUs using standard protocols
Integration	Needs Libfabric and INC switches	Integrates with MPI or AI frameworks, and the switch is transparent
Offload capabilities	Yes (to the switches)	When paired with INC
Performance	Lower latency, higher throughput, and optimized GPU utilization	Optimized GPU utilization
Scalability	Very high in supported fabrics, depending on the type of collective set	Limited by server library software optimization
Required infrastructure	INC-capable switches, INC manager, and Libfabric	Standard NICs and the MPI/CCL stack
Implementation	UEC fabrics with INC switches and an INC manager	PyTorch DDP, TensorFlow, and MPI collectives

In network architectures, INC typically supports the following key components:

- INC-capable switches with the switch FEPs (sFEPs) and agents (UEC-capable Ethernet/IP switches)
- INC manager (IM) for control and coordination
- Libfabric software integration

Figure 12-17 shows a topology in which switches as well as pure software components are orchestrated not only at the server level but also at the network level. The sFEP—an Ethernet switch capable of running UEC and INC features—has the INC engine at a basic level or has it enabled in the microkernel of the silicon.

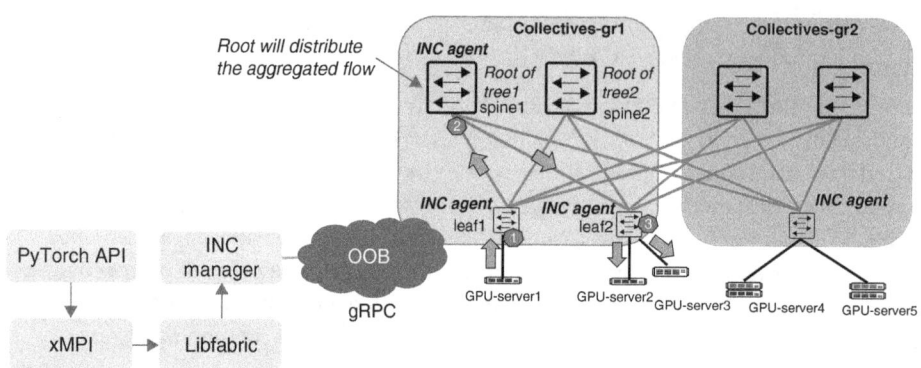

Figure 12-17
INC-optimized AI/ML data center topology

In Figure 12-17, two collective communication groups are enabled at the Libfabric level, based on the requirements set in the PyTorch API, and transferred to Libfabric using the MPI framework: Collectives-gr1 and Collectives-gr2. They are highlighted inside the fabric defined by the INC manager (IM), which is connected through the out-of-band network to each switch INC agent and sends the information about the optimizations needed (for example, when to aggregate the flows to the given destination). In Figure 12-17, GPU-server1 wants to synchronize the exact outcome of the local computation to GPU-server2 and GPU-server3, so instead of sending the duplicate copy twice, it will send it to the top of the fabric spine elected as a root of the INC tree, which then will distribute it to the rest of the switches that are part of the given collective group. A similar type of optimization was observed a long time ago, when multicast replication was optimized by electing a centralized replicator. In the present case, bandwidth is saved from the leaf to the spine, and latency is unified across all servers.

Management and Orchestration

UET is engineered for streamlined implementation and automated functionality at an extensive scale. The network telemetry and analytics system provides fine-grained telemetry, enabling operators to monitor per-flow latency, jitter, and packet drops and also use AI-based analytics for anomaly detection and performance optimization. The Libfabric connection to any open-source MPI, as well as the NCCL/RCCL, is also an example of the orchestration that UEC software vendors will need to include beyond the networking mechanisms detailed in this chapter. In addition, INC must be in sync with the collectives defined at the application level. The orchestration of specific congestion management will also be necessary to ensure that the type of congestion—whether at the link level or end to end—for the given packet delivery format is fully aligned.

Interoperability and Backward Compatibility

Ultra Ethernet Specification v1.0 is designed to maintain compatibility with existing Ethernet devices when possible. It includes dual-mode operation, which enables devices to communicate through either standard Ethernet or Ultra Ethernet protocols, depending on the negotiation during link initialization. With end-to-end congestion management, such as RCCC or NSCC, as well as reliable transport (RUD, ROD, and RUDI), standard Ethernet will be used by the first implementations; at the same IP fabric for AI/ML, lossless RoCEv2 and new UET fabric traffic may have to coexist. When the ECN is used for the lossless RoCEv2 fabric and the PFC at the same time, some of the newer congestion management mechanisms may not work correctly. For example, at the same link, CBFC and LLR won't be easy to manage at the same time with PFC pushbacks, which means the link-level UET congestion management we covered in this chapter will likely go to greenfield deployments, while the end-to-end congestion management with RCCC or NSCC may work in brownfield scenarios as well.

Compliance and Certification

Compliance requirements include the implementation of observability APIs, formalized testing methodologies, and procedures for validating interoperability. Before the Ultra Ethernet Specification becomes a new production-level standard, all related software tooling must be developed, including telemetry for UEC-specific features, such as telemetry for CBFC credits or telemetry for the RCCC credits.

UEC compliance requirements cover observability, testing, and interoperability. The Ultra Ethernet Specification delineates the profiles AI Base, AI Full, and HPC to enable adaptable deployment strategies tailored to various scales and use cases.

The Ultra Ethernet Specification outlines a comprehensive compliance suite that consists of the following:

- Interoperability testing spanning multiple vendors and device types
- Line-rate performance benchmarks to assess latency, jitter, and throughput
- Security validation, including encryption and authentication methods

UEC Challenges and Future Directions

Although the Ultra Ethernet Specification v1.0 introduces new advancements, some challenges persist:

- The cost and complexity associated with upgrading existing infrastructure to accommodate new hardware and protocols
- The need to ensure interoperability across a wide range of existing Ethernet equipment

- Ongoing developments in AI and cloud workloads, which may necessitate higher performance requirements in the future

The UEC is establishing dedicated working groups focused on storage, management, performance, and compliance, and is publishing educational resources to facilitate adoption. Subsequent versions are expected to offer higher data rates, enhanced automation, and increased integration with emerging edge computing models.

The number of optional UEC features from the specification version 1 is relatively high. This may pose some challenges, especially when it tries to address the same problem. For example, the number of congestion control options proposed by UEC is quite extensive. As a result, only a subset of features will be implemented by different switch or server NIC vendors. Finally, in the early phase of implementing the new UEC specification, the diversity of server NIC cards supporting the full UEC software stack may be limited, making interoperability across different server vendors more challenging.

Comparing UEC to InfiniBand and RoCEv2

The Ultra Ethernet Specification v1.0 establishes a new standard for data center and high-performance networking in scale-out architectures. It provides features such as flexible reordering, high scalability, high bandwidth, deterministic communication, enhanced security, and simplified management, and it aims to address the requirements of growing data needs and real-time applications. As it is increasingly adopted, Ultra Ethernet may play a significant role in future AI data center infrastructure. However, it is important to consider some factors related to the cost and complexity of upgrading existing infrastructure to support new hardware and protocols, as well as the need to maintain interoperability with a wide range of current Ethernet equipment.

In this section, we compare some traditional Ethernet features with RoCEv2/DCQCN and the newly proposed Ultra Ethernet Specification standard for AI/ML data centers.

From a performance perspective, Ultra Ethernet is designed for lower latency, increased throughput, and enhanced scalability relative to previous technologies. Determinism for time-sensitive flows is managed through specified delivery intervals (a feature not present in standard Ethernet). Open standards–based programmability is offered via Libfabric, enabling the use of open APIs and programmable hardware to customize network behavior in real time. Finally, Ultra Ethernet has additional security options. It has built-in cryptography and integrity controls that provide security beyond what traditional Ethernet offers.

Table 12-4 compares InfiniBand, RoCEv2, and UET.

Table 12-4 Comparison of InfiniBand, RoCEv2, and UET

Requirement	InfiniBand	RoCEv2	UET
Scale	<100,000	>100,000	~1 million target
Performances (JCT, BUS BW)	High	High; comparable to InfiniBand	High; same as or better than InfiniBand
Multipathing	Yes	Yes	Yes

Requirement	InfiniBand	RoCEv2	UET
Congestion control	Yes; credit/credit	DCQCN (ECN, PFC-DSCP), controller-based auto-tuning	NSCC (RTT/ECN), RCCC, packet trimming, CSIG, CBFC, auto-tunning built-in protocol
Delivery modes	Reliable connect (RC); in-order, unreliable connect	RC; in-order, unreliable connect	Flexible delivery; RUD/RUDI/UUD
Security	N/A	External security stack (for example, MAC-Sec)	Built-in the UEC protocol stack – using the TSS
Encapsulation options	InfiniBand	UDP/BTH in IPv4 or IPv6	UDP/SES and PDS in IPv4/IPv6 or IP and SES/PDS without UDP
Network deployment readiness	Deployed in production networks	Deployed in production networks	Expected first pilot deployments in late 2026
NIC diversity	Low	High	Low
UET-compatible fabric transport	No	Yes	Yes
Interoperability	Bad	Good	Good
Transport	InfiniBand	Ethernet/IP/UDP	Ethernet/IP/UDP
INC/CCL	Yes (optional)	No	Yes (optional)

Summary

Ultra Ethernet sets a new standard for data center and high-performance networking in scale-out architectures. It provides features such as flexible reordering, high scalability, high bandwidth, deterministic communication, enhanced security, and simplified management, and it is designed to meet the growing demands for data and the needs of real-time applications. As the adoption of new 400 Gbps/800 Gbps NICs increases, with UEC software stack support, UET will play a crucial role in future AI data center infrastructures, particularly as UEC tooling expands for scale-out fabrics, driving down even further the TCO (total cost of ownership) for AI infrastructures.

UEC software features will not all have to be enabled at the same time to offer performance outcomes that surpass the limitations of RoCEv2, such as go-back-to-N packet loss recovery, which forces the retransmission of up to N packets even if one packet is lost, which results in an underutilized network fabric and increased job completion time for the AI workload.

With newer UEC packet delivery modes such as RUD, ROD, RUDI, and packet trimming, the originator knows more quickly which selective packets need to be retransmitted. From an Ethernet switch fabric perspective, some mechanisms of the UEC, such as CBFC, will help introduce capabilities known so far only in InfiniBand networks, where guaranteed packet delivery is offered at each segment level. RCCC is an end-to-end mechanism for congestion control that also provides an option to enable fabric-guaranteed delivery with a credit-to-credit mechanism. This mechanism is handled purely at the AI GPU NIC servers, leaving the Ethernet UEC switch-level mechanism as an optional link-level implementation for more demanding AI network accelerator requirements.

Test Your Knowledge

Chapter Review

The following questions are designed to test your understanding of the content covered in Chapter 12. Following the questions, answers are provided so you can verify your conclusions.

Questions

1. What is Ultra Ethernet Consortium (UEC), and what are its primary objectives for AI data center and HPC networking?
2. How does the UEC protocol stack differ from traditional Ethernet and RoCEv2?
3. What are the new packet delivery modes defined by UEC, and how do they benefit AI workloads?
4. How does Credit-Based Flow Control (CBFC) in UEC improve upon Priority Flow Control (PFC)?
5. What is the role of In-Network Collectives (INC) and collective communication libraries (CCLs) in UEC?
6. How does UEC delivered UET (Ultra Ethernet Transport) ensure interoperability and backward compatibility with existing Ethernet networks?
7. What are the key congestion management mechanisms in UEC, and how do they interact?
8. How does UEC delivered UET (Ultra Ethernet Transport) address the scaling and performance challenges of next-generation AI clusters?

Answers

1. UEC is an industry group developing open standards for Ethernet optimized for AI, HPC, and cloud workloads. Its goals include ultra-high scalability (1 million or more endpoints), deterministic low latency, lossless transport, multi-vendor interoperability, and integration of advanced congestion management and collective communication features.
2. UEC introduces new transport and link-layer protocols (UET, CBFC, LLR), supports both UDP-based and raw IP encapsulation, and adds semantic and packet delivery sublayers (SES, PDS) for advanced flow control. It enables flexible packet delivery modes (ROD, RUD, RUDI, UUD), built-in security, and in-network collective operations, while maintaining backward compatibility with standard Ethernet.
3. ROD (reliable ordered delivery) ensures in-order, reliable delivery; RUD (reliable unordered delivery) allows out-of-order delivery with reliability; RUDI (reliable unordered delivery idempotent) supports idempotent operations for collective updates; and UUD (unreliable unordered delivery) is best-effort delivery. These modes enable fine-grained control over performance, reliability, and resource usage for diverse AI workloads.

4. CBFC provides per-priority, per-virtual-channel lossless transport, supporting more classes and better scheduling than PFC. It uses explicit credit exchange between sender and receiver, reducing head-of-line blocking and PFC storms, and enabling more granular congestion management.

5. INC enables switches to participate in collective operations (for example, AllReduce, Broadcast), offloading aggregation and synchronization from servers to the network. CCLs provide software APIs for collective operations, tightly integrated with AI frameworks. Together, they reduce latency, improve bandwidth utilization, and accelerate distributed training.

6. UEC supports dual-mode operation, allowing devices to communicate using either standard Ethernet or UEC protocols, based on negotiation. It maintains standard Ethernet framing, supports UDP/IP encapsulation, and provides compliance and certification frameworks for multi-vendor interoperability.

7. UEC uses end-to-end mechanisms (NSCC, RCCC) for congestion control, segment-level CBFC for lossless transport, and packet trimming for fast retransmission. NSCC uses window-based control with ECN feedback; RCCC uses receiver-managed credits. These mechanisms work together to minimize packet loss, reduce JCT, and maintain high throughput under heavy load.

8. UEC's protocol stack, collective communication features, and congestion management enable scaling to millions of endpoints, deterministic low latency, and more efficient resource utilization; for example, using packet trimming, the originator will re-send well-identified packets if any packet loss is observed. Its open, programmable architecture supports rapid innovation, multi-vendor ecosystems, and future-proofing for evolving AI/HPC workloads. The AI data center admin will be able to cover the backend and frontend as well as storage with the unified administration tooling.

References

Ultra Ethernet Consortium, "Ultra Ethernet Specification v1.0," June 11, 2025, https://ultraethernet.org/wp-content/uploads/sites/20/2025/06/UE-Specification-6.11.25.pdf.

Light Reading, "Spirent and Juniper Combine for Ultra Ethernet Transport Test," June 30, 2025, www.lightreading.com/optical-networking/spirent-and-juniper-combine-for-ultra-ethernet-transport-test.

Mpich.org, " MPI_Allreduce, " 2025, www.mpich.org/static/docs/v3.1/www3/MPI_Allreduce.html.

Github.io, " Libfabric Programmer's Manual: fi_collective(3)." 2025, ofiwg.github.io/libfabric/v1.20.1/man/fi_collective.3.html.

13

Scale-Up Systems

With all the technologies and diverse design options for backend training networks and storage networking for the domains covered so far in this book, you might think that AI/ML data center networking is already well defined with scale-out systems, and most problems can be solved using the current RoCEv2 or the emerging Ultra Ethernet Specification from the Ultra Ethernet Consortium (UEC). Today, however, computing power of xPU accelerators (such as GPUs or TPUs) sometimes increases faster than the capacity of Ethernet and InfiniBand, so newer, higher-capacity XPU-scale-up systems are being developed. In these systems, the xPU is closely connected to a purpose-built interconnect point, which helps memory schematics communicate faster and with even lower latency (typically, below 1 microsecond end-to-end and often within the range of 200 nanoseconds at the scale-up switch device level).

To this point, switches for multiple GPUs have typically used PCIe (Peripheral Component Interconnect Express). However, PCIe legacy systems use point-to-point data links between two devices, which may introduce higher latency due to their shared-bus architecture or reliance on CPU involvement for GPU communication. The transfer rate and network latency of PCIe is not capable of meeting the increasing bandwidth and latency demands of connecting multiple GPUs within the server for AI and HPC. For example, PCIe 6.0 offers 8 Gbps per lane (~128 Gbps bidirectional for x16 lanes), whereas NVLink 5.0 offers 1.8 Tbps bidirectional. Modern scale-up systems also offer lower latency than PCIe for GPU-to-GPU communication. Typical NVLink latency ranges from 100 to 300 nanoseconds (ns), whereas PCIe 5.0 latency generally ranges from 500 ns up to 1 microsecond (µs). The PCIe alternative, CXL 3.0 (Compute Express Link), can reduce latency to 100 ns and provide cache-coherent shared memory and semantics. However, it still offers the same performance as PCIe 6.0, with a transfer rate of 32 GT/s (gigatransfers per second).

The limitations of PCIe and CXL led to the emergence of alternative GPU interconnect solutions, such as NVLink from Nvidia, Infinity Fabric from AMD, as well as newer industry standards such as UALink (from the Ultra Accelerator Link Consortium) and SUE-T (Scale-Up Ethernet Transport), proposed in the ESUN (Ethernet Scale-Up Network) framework from OCP (Open Compute Project).

You might wonder whether these newer scale-up rack systems are intended to replace the scale-out systems discussed earlier in this book. Scale-up and scale-out can coexist in an AI/ML data center, enabling enhanced performance and scalability. The high-level motivation for AI data center scale-up is to create a virtual super-accelerator—a pod of hundreds of GPUs treated as a single computational entity. This is essential for training state-of-the-art models that exceed the memory and compute capacity of any single GPU or a server with just eight GPUs.

Scale-up fabric interconnect points, such as UALink and SUE-T, are also being developed to break vendor lock-in and enable open, multi-vendor ecosystems for super-accelerators. These developments have occurred in response to the success of Nvidia's proprietary NVLink implementations, which offer better performance and scale than legacy PCIe switch-based systems.

While scale-up delivers superior performance for tightly coupled workloads, it is limited by physical constraints: up to four racks/pods with up to 1,000 GPUs. Scale-out can complement scale-up by allowing data centers to expand capacity horizontally, connecting multiple pods or servers for massive, distributed training clusters and using the collective communications to group the participating systems.

Proposed scale-up rack systems have a higher number of accelerators (xPU) per system compared to scale-out systems. (Scale-up offers more than 8 xPUs per server system and up to 1,000 xPUs with multiple scale-up racks interconnected.) Unlike scale-out systems, proposed scale-up rack systems use unified hardware or software memory coherence (a single global memory namespace with PGAS in the case of UALink or coherent memory in the case of Nvidia NVLink switches).

Across all high-density accelerator scale-up systems, the higher-level goal is to offer more straightforward and faster direct memory load semantics for the entire large language model, with a simplified software stack and a more coherent multi-xPU high-bandwidth memory (HBM) view. This can be achieved in the case of the scale-up with less administrative burden (that is, less fabric interconnect setup needed) and with reduced overhead when moving the memory from one xPU to another xPU (no more IP/UDP in case of the scale-up and less multi-stage networking), using just an optimized/compressed version of the Ethernet interconnect switch system with one-hop networking systems.

The scale-up server also helps expose the larger number of xPUs as a single giant AI compute system, ready to train the specific model, rather than thousands of servers, as in the case of horizontally scaled-out compute systems. From a networking perspective, ultra-low-latency systems are typically only built within the rack (sometimes called a point of distribution) and extended in some cases to four racks while still using a single-hop type of topology; an xPU accelerator is directly linked with multiple links to the interconnect point scale-up switches without using a dedicated NIC for each xPU. (One NIC to one GPU is typically used in the case of scale-out systems.) This means that from a topology perspective, for a design with 1,000 accelerators, there will still be a requirement to use a collapsed type of network architecture with a higher density of 800 Gbps/1.6 Tbps/3.2 Tbps ports/

lanes to the same xPU. This also means there is typically no spine layer in the given scale-up rack, and when required, all the xPUs are connected via multiple scale-up switches with many interconnect points from the same accelerator. The speed per xPU is also targeting a higher 1.6 Tbps/3.2 Tbps speed in the case of scale-up systems because the individual xPU compute capacity is also significantly higher than that of the scale-out systems. This is why existing or emerging scale-up systems will mostly use 200 Gbps SerDes (serializer/deserializer) systems to reach higher speeds of packet delivery with lower power consumption goals.

High-density accelerator (xPU) scale-up systems are highly rack-driven designs. It means that the rack total power and space in the rack for compute, number of interconnect switches, or the pre-installed cabling will have a vendor specification. This is different from scale-out systems, where a server with eight GPUs has 8x 400 Gbps/800 Gbps connections to a rail-optimized design (Ethernet or InfiniBand) with switches from different racks. With scale-up systems, most components are already configured and ready to use. The goal is to deliver simplicity and a highly scalable number of xPU accelerators per rack/pod and better interoperability between the interconnect points from one vendor and the xPUs from another vendor. If the standardization process offers comparable, identical, or better performance compared to the vendor-specific options, it will become appealing to end users and provide longer-term advantages. For short-term scale-up projects, a vendor's specific rack systems will be used with proprietary solutions, offering superior scale and performance, which are the goals of most scale-up use cases.

Let's quickly review the applicability and use cases of scale-up systems, focusing on the value proposition:

- **Foundational large language models training use case:** This use case features huge multi-hundred-billion-parameter models (for example, GPT, Claude, Gemini), where each training phase requires faster synchronization of gradients and parameters across xPUs over the dedicated line rate Tbps aggregate bandwidth for gradients. It offers comparable or even better bandwidth compared to PCIe 5.0 systems, using different types of encoding and error correction to increase the transfer performance. In the case of PCIe, each lane can transfer 3.94 GB and reach 64 Gbps of effective data load using a 16-lane system. With PCIe systems, the scale of 1,000 xPUs is challenging to achieve, and this is where the emerging scale-up systems will come into play.

- **Multimodal models training for text to video (Sora-like), audio, and 3D generative models:** These models, known as diffusion models, are extremely bandwidth-hungry tensor exchanges and must synchronize intermediately with frequent inter-GPU tensor exchanges. Communication repeats thousands of times per batch, and a group of input samples (such as images) is processed together before one update is registered; for example, 1024 images are spread across 512 xPUs, and each xPU processes two images (micro-batch) and synchronizes the gradients across the interconnect point for one step. This is synchronized across the entire shared memory so that the given model thinks it is trained on a single xPU.

- **AI inference with mixture-of-experts (MoE) architectures and AI reasoning:** In this use case, each token activates a small subset of experts, requiring all-to-all collective routing of activations between GPUs in sub-microseconds. AI inference with multi-step reasoning requires multiple forward and backward passes across GPUs, involving frequent communication with small messages and shared tensor memory across GPUs. In scale-out systems, the latency for some multi-step reasoning can become too high, and the lack of shared coherent memory can cause performance bottlenecks in traditional distributed AI backend systems.

- **Inference real-time simulation and digital-twin physics:** This is where the workload's data for fluid dynamics and robotics is used and where time-stepped simulation with frequent nanosecond synchronization is required between many xPU—this is not something a scale-out system can achieve—which often operate at the end-to-end micro-econd latency.

- **Graph neural network (GNN)/sparse tensor computation use case:** In this use case, data is structured as a graph (for example, molecular graph, protein graph). This involves frequently gathering feature vectors from neighboring nodes (with irregular memory reads) and updating node embeddings (with irregular writes). This use case enables scale-up interconnect systems offering around 300-nanosecond latency to become more efficient (for example, for new drug discovery and bioinformatics).

- **Financial modeling with nanosecond precision for comprehensive risk analysis use case:** This use case enables traders and analysts to rapidly assess market volatility and potential exposure. Real-time market modeling involves continuously updating financial data with high-frequency algorithms to predict market trends, optimize trading strategies, and manage risk effectively in rapidly changing economic environments.

- **Edge AI and federated learning use case:** This use case features distributed learning, closer to the end user, where rapid sharing and synchronization of model updates between many accelerators are critical. For example, in each service provider point of presence location, an operator can offer proximity inference services.

Key Building Blocks of Scale-Up Systems

Vendors build scale-up systems with different types of hardware components prebuilt into the rack with limited optional characteristics. Such a system is a ready-to-go, high-capacity compute system without physical integration complexities such as intra-chassis cabling, optics, and integration of individual components, management switches, and storage units. All these elements are prebuilt in a scale-up chassis, so when connecting to the system, the end user gets a unified management interface with the xPU, compute, and storage all integrated under one management instance.

Different vendors' scale-up systems differ, and so scale-up-to-scale-up chassis interoperability is not typically addressed. Usually, one to four pods come from the same scale-up vendor and are integrated with the existing scale-out systems. Figure 13-1 illustrates a four-pod scale-up design that features a unified rack-to-rack interconnection using scale-out or scale-up extenders. The number of scale-up racks can be higher if, instead of using a scale-up interconnect between the racks, a three-tier IP Clos scale-out fabric is used.

Key Building Blocks of Scale-Up Systems

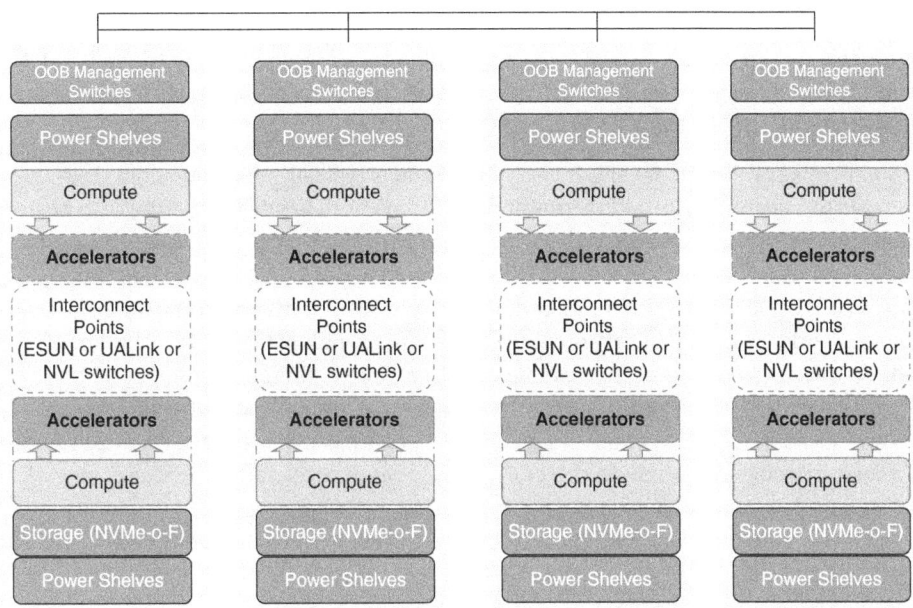

Figure 13-1
Physical building blocks of a scale-up system with a four-pod scale-up design

From a hardware perspective, a large number of accelerators is used—from 72 up to hundreds of xPUs (GPUs, TPUs, etc.) in a four-pod/rack scale-up system. Each accelerator (xPU) has HBM localized physically but exposed as part of the coherent shared memory to the rest of the xPUs—on the order of hundreds of gigabytes of local memory for each HBM module. From a high-level perspective, the HBM module of the xPU is connected directly to the accelerator, and it's managed by the dedicated memory semantic software, typically at the compute level and connected via PCIe (see Figure 13-2), much like a multi-core CPU/ARM. This PCIe connection is not engaged for AI training purposes, when scale-up dedicated interconnect switches (SUE or UALink) are used.

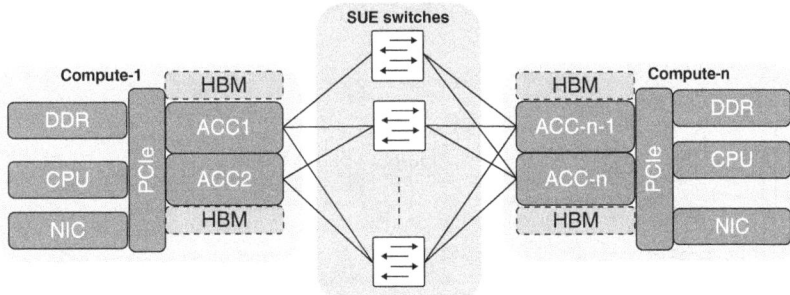

Figure 13-2
Accelerator HBM modules inside a compute node

The number of GPUs/DPUs per compute host will change over time. For example, in the case of the Nvidia B300, four GPUs with a total of 1.152 GB of aggregated HBM3 memory are used. However, for the NVL72 and the NVLink5 generation, the total per GPU is 1,800 Gbps. In this system, 18 NVLink switches are used, resulting in 18 NVLink 5 links per GPU.

Aggregated multi-Tbps bandwidth per xPU is also offered and is typically much higher in scale-up systems compared to scale-out systems in terms of per-GPU memory bandwidth. In the case of a scale-up system, each xPU also connects to the scale-up switch—a purpose-built scale-up switch that uses multiple serialized lanes, typically with 200 Gbps per lane. This means the xPU is not linked through a classic 800 Gbps NIC but rather has an on-die direct networking software stack (UALink, SUE) and sends the encapsulated inter-xPU frames using multiple lanes. The number of lanes depends on the scale-up system; for example, a UALink system has four lanes of 200 Gbps per station (a group of four UALink lanes), and each xPU may have multiple stations connected to it. The UALink specification mentions about eight stations per xPU; this makes 32 lanes of 200 Gbps for each, for a total aggregated bus bandwidth of 6.4 Tbps for each accelerator. The idea is to work within the SUE-T-based scale-up accelerators, where 100 Gbps per lane serialization or 200 Gbps serialization can be offered, using, for example, 12 SUE-T lanes, each connected from xPU to SUE via an interconnect point to the SUE-T Ethernet ultra-low-latency switch.

In Figure 13-3, each accelerator (ACC1 to ACC64) has a number of connections equal to the number of ESUN/SUE Ethernet switches. Here, 12 scale-up switches were enabled within the rack system, allowing each accelerator to connect via 12 lanes or AXI (Advanced Extensible Interface) at the accelerator-to-scale-up Ethernet connection level. As the figure shows, there's always a one-hop connection between accelerators (ACCs), offering ultra-low latency for AI workloads. The physical Ethernet connection remains unchanged, and each SUE-T lane uses a 100 Gbps or 200 Gbps link connection to the SUE-T switch. Each xPU/accelerator is designed to be directly connected to the SUE-T ultra-low-latency switch. In the case of SUE-T, the new AFH transport is used, and optimized Ethernet header encapsulation is employed for remote memory access from ACC1 to ACC64. However, in the case of the scale-up systems, the RoCEv2 or UET frame format is no longer used, in favor of reduced overhead. The advanced entropy requirements are less relevant due to the single-hop design approach, so the RoCEv2 and BTH types of information are no longer needed. The memory access semantics are also simplified in the case of scale-up systems to reduce the time required to write the accelerator outcome into the remote accelerator HBM module.

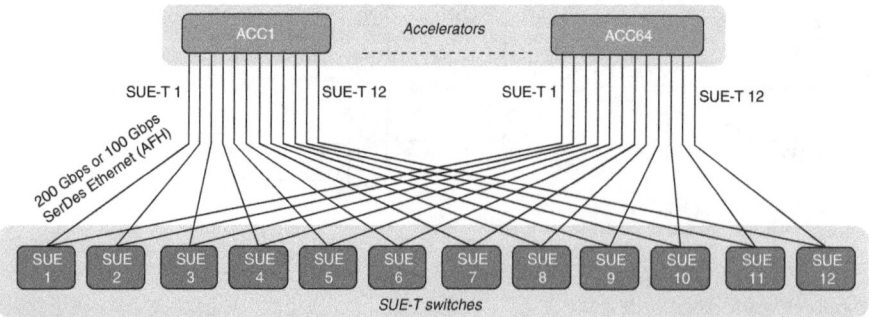

Figure 13-3
Scale-up system with SUE-T switches: Single-hop design

Within the rack, things start to become clearer, but then how does the scale-up rack system shown in Figure 13-1 connect to the rest of the AI data center racks? Each compute system will be using a dedicated scale-out NIC to connect between the scale-up racks. Figure 13-4 shows a multi-planner type of connectivity design, where just two planes are used; in a production deployment, more planners are typically used to offer even better availability of the compute network.

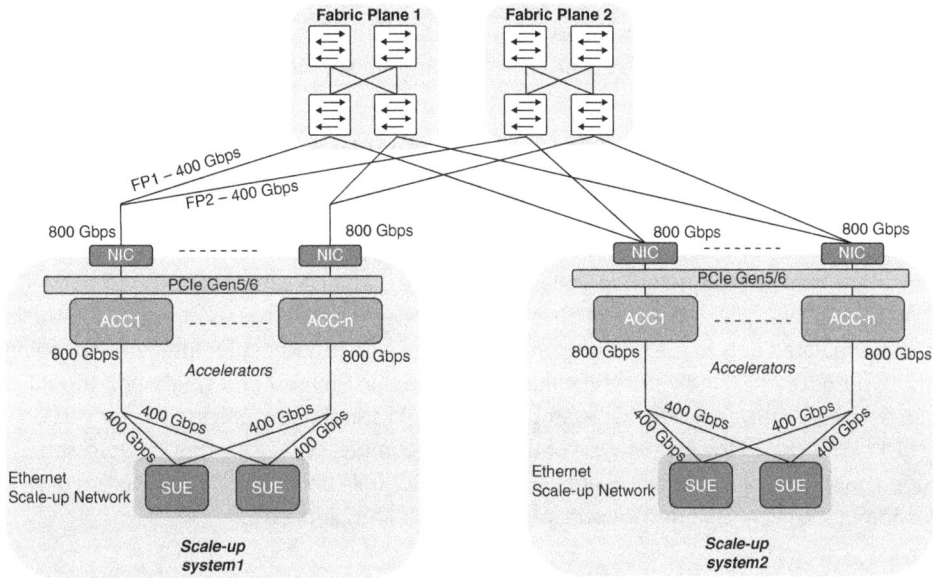

Figure 13-4
Scale-up interconnect design using a multi-planner Fabric Plane1|2

This type of design offers faster convergence and controlled minimal compute capacity across multiple scale-up compute systems. For example, if one planner goes offline, the capacity of the inter-scale-up systems will still be equal to one plane plus the compute capacity of each scale-up system. The number of 800 Gbps NIC ports per compute node inside a scale-up system may vary between two and four if the 800 Gbps NIC card is used and four to eight with 400 Gbps NIC cards connected to the ToR Ethernet switches from different fabric planes. In Figure 13-4, the scale-up systems use PCIe 5/6 generations between the accelerators and the compute scale-out network fabric planes. A single-plane fabric with inter-pod connections is also possible and can be used to enable the logical path diversity options described in Chapter 8, "IP Routing for AI/ML Fabrics."

Scale-Up Ethernet Transport (SUE-T)

The OCP-driven scale-up framework called SUE-T that was announced in October 2025 focuses on addressing open-standard Ethernet-based transport for loading and storage and memory transactions between many xPUs with ultra-low-latency, low-overhead communication. It gives end users the impression of working on a single super-accelerator system with tens or hundreds of xPUs interconnected under rack system(s), using special scale-up Ethernet switches called interconnect points. While baseline Ethernet is preserved with SUE-T, from a transport perspective, SUE-T defines a new frame format called AI Fabric Header (AFH), which is a shim layer that makes the 256-byte frame a scale-up Ethernet flit that is sent over the regular Ethernet PHY, which can be packed with up to a 4,096-byte SUE PDU (protocol data unit) sent over the given virtual channel (VC).

AFH Generation 2 provides an option to use a compressed version, where the destination and source xPUs are encoded as part of the destination MAC and source MAC addresses of the Ethernet frame.

AFH Generation 2, illustrated in Figure 13-5, is an optimized header that includes the xPU source and destination target encoding and is compliant with Ethernet standards while still offering negligible overhead for xPU-to-xPU transactions. As part of the SUE-T transport, two options for the AFH are defined. Compressed (6-byte) and non-compressed (12-byte) headers are used. The compressed header is mainly applicable to single-hop scale-up topologies, while the non-compressed header may be used for two-hop scale-up architectures. IEEE-compliant encoding is used, and the xPU identifiers are populated only in the destination address and source address for interconnect point L2 forwarding purposes. AFH individual bit values mostly remain irrelevant for single-hop topologies but are defined for future usage. For example, the M field stands for multicast, V is for version (currently 0), W is related to the format type of the header (compressed versus non-compressed, with the hop count field), X is a locally assigned value but not fully defined (as it is for future use), and Z is an administratively assigned identifier (AAI) for local MAC addresses.

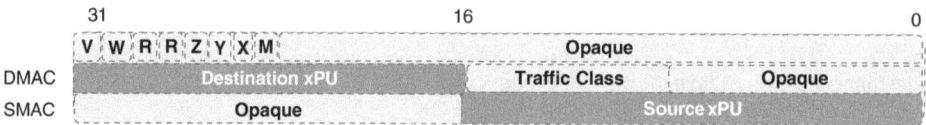

Figure 13-5
Compressed AFH (Generation 2) with the destination and source xPU IDs

The AFH helps route the SUE-T packets between the xPUs. To ensure efficiency and reliability, the Reliability Header (RH) encodes additional XPU information, memory partitioning, and tenant isolation information, following the Ethernet type. We highlight this in Figure 13-6, where the RH field is included just before the payload data plane. It contains the xPU ID, ten 10-bit unique identifiers in the scale-up SUE-T system, and the VC information, which includes four or more virtual channels that can be identified by queue delivery. The NSPN is a 16-bit packet sequence number, and the ASPN is a 16-bit acknowledgment information sequence number. The CRC is also included for data integrity verification before the standard Ethernet frame check sequence (FCS).

With RoCEv2 delivery, reliability is handled at the upper layers. In contrast, for scale-up systems based on SUE-T, reliability is fully managed at the link level with the RH (Reliability Header) shim layer and the Link Layer Retry (LLR). Chapter 12, "Ultra Ethernet Consortium (UEC)," covers this mechanism, where the switch-to-switch link uses link-layer sequence numbers and a local temporary buffer to re-send the L2 packet in the case of negative acknowledgments. However, with SUE-T, instead of re-sending the L2 packet from the originating xPU, the interconnect point switch will re-send it to the target xPU if it was not explicitly acknowledged. The UEC Specification 1.0 originally covered the LLR, and the SUE-T adopts it to ensure hop-by-hop reliability for the SUE-T packets.

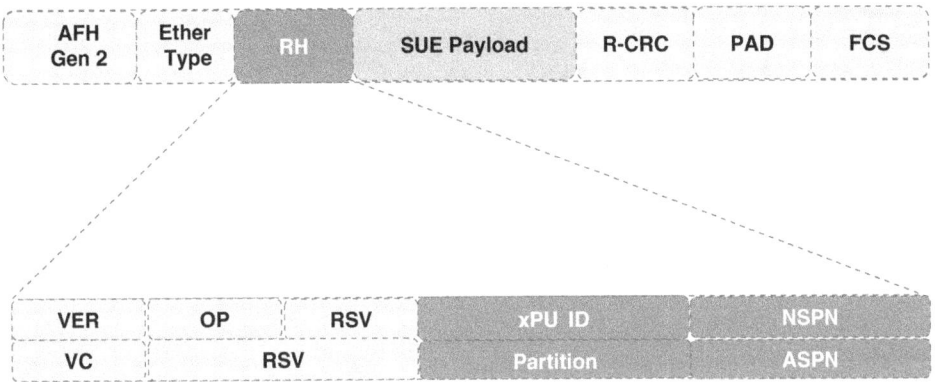

Figure 13-6
Reliability Header (RH) in SUE-T

Meanwhile, the RH header shown in Figure 13-6 provides end-to-end L2 reliability with sequence numbers per source/destination xPU. If the scale-up systems using SUE-T are reliable at the L2 end-to-end level with the RU shim layer as well as with the LLR per segment xPU to IP and IP to xPU, do we still need any congestion management mechanism to make sure the interconnect fabrics are truly lossless? In the case of a single-hop topology, we might still have many xPUs attempting to perform memory write operations at one xPU. In case of the scale-up SUE-T, the Credit-Based Flow Control (CBFC) system will handle the credit mechanism at the link level instead of PFC (Priority Flow Control) unless the xPU used inside the rack is not CBFC capable. The regular pushback of the PFC at the L2 level will reduce the rate based on the quanta value sent from the interconnect point switch. The sender knows the credit usage of each VC, and so if both endpoints xPU and IP are CBFC capable, then the packets are sent, as long as sufficient credits are available. The SUE-T framework uses LLR and CBFC, which are covered in Chapter 12, to provide better local link-level reliability. The SUE-T framework specification also mentions that traffic load balancing can be based on credit usage. The given xPU can load balance traffic across multiple SUE processing channels (lanes), and this load balancing can be software or hardware driven. This part is mentioned only briefly in the SUE-T framework document, so it will likely be implementation dependent for each xPU vendor.

Figure 13-7 shows an end-to-end SUE protocol stack with a single-hop switch used in the middle, capable of handling the SUE AFH data plane header and using the LLR and CBFC per segment to each accelerator. The reconciliation layer shown refers to the process and logic that align (reconciles) the Media Access Control (MAC) layer with the Physical Coding Sublayer (PCS), which handles serialized symbols on the wire.

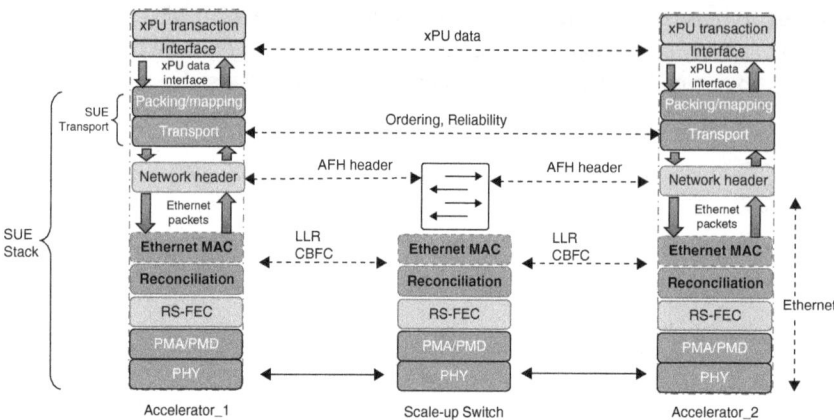

Figure 13-7
SUE-T end-to-end protocol stack

SUE-T uses the shared memory model. In this model, the xPU uses one-sided memory semantics, where data sent to the target node is acknowledged not based on memory placement but on the SUE sequence number. The load/store commands (for example, put, get, atomic) are proposed to the SUE transport, but the type of command is transparent for the transport itself. The RH field shown in Figure 13-6 can also be used to map memory access control from the memory semantic to the network, offering multi-tenancy capabilities within the scale-up system. When the scale-up system boots up, multiple SUE connections are established across different interface types. This is highlighted in Figure 13-8, where an xPU accelerator is connected to multiple SUE instances, which are then linked to the ESUN/SUE-T Ethernet switches, corresponding to the number of SUE interfaces at the accelerator (ACC1/ACC2 in Figure 13-8).

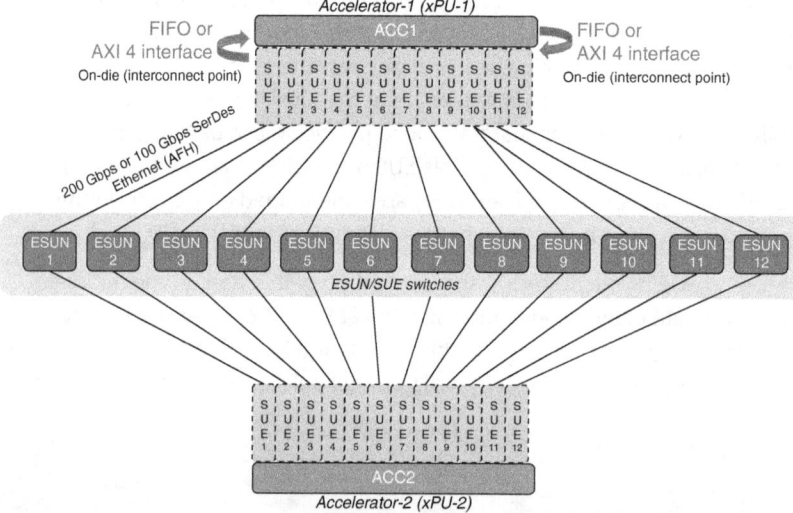

Figure 13-8
SUE-to-xPU interfaces: FIFO and AXI 4

The FIFO xPU-to-SUE interface allows the xPU to write a command or command and data directly to the SUE, which then generates flow control for each destination using a 10-bit xPU and 2-bit VC identifiers. The transmission credit information is updated accordingly. In the case of FIFO interfaces, a streaming approach of raw PDUs is used, without any memory-level transaction state management (no semantics); that is, only packet-level delivery state is handled.

The second SUE-T interface option between the xPU and SUE is the AXI 4.0 from ARM, which was designed for high-performance, high-frequency systems and where independent transaction channels are set for read address, read data, write address, write data, and write response operations over five independent channels, instead of the FIFO raw data stream approach.

At the given accelerator level, an on-die relationship is created (see Figure 13-9) with a primary and a secondary node. The primary is the accelerator xPU AXI interface, on top of which the cache/HBM controller sits, and the secondary AXI interface connects to the SUE instance, which handles AFH encapsulation and reliability flow control logic (credit-based mechanism) when connecting over the SUE-T/SUE switch. On-die integration means components are physically integrated into a single silicon chip, such as a GPU accelerator. The SUE-T transport block is built into the accelerators without the need for an external NIC card.

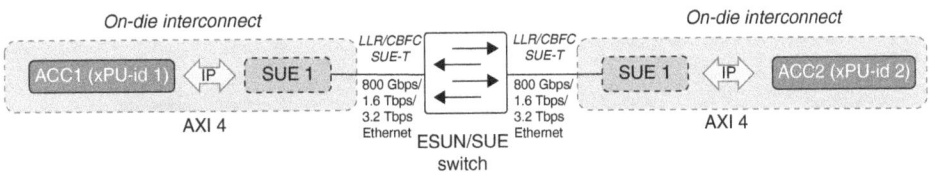

Figure 13-9
On-die interconnect interface using the AXI 4 memory framework

While both on-die interface types (FIFO and AXI) push the transactions on the wire using AFH across the interconnect SUE-T/SUE, the AXI memory semantics offer better inter-xPU memory synchronization, where all transactions are based on AXI requests (AR, AW, and W transactions), which are mapped to VC0, and responses (B and R transactions), which are mapped to VC1. The interconnect point also sets the buffers at the interface for each AXI channel. Each xPU kernel sets a command to SUE over the xPU command interface. The on-die SUE module accepts the operation and packs the control and data to the destination transmit buffer.

The on-die memory and transport functions determine when a queue should be serviced, based on the flow control state. When CBFC (Credit Based Flow Control) is used, it indicates to the AXI scheduler (for example, the CBFC input) when a queue is ready to transmit (based on the credit information status).

Ultra Accelerator Link (UALink)

Scale-up systems have also been defined as part of the Ultra Accelerator Link consortium, which differs from the ESUN (SUE-T) framework and has a much more comprehensive technical specification. Existing fabrics (including NVLink and Infinity Fabric) are considered proprietary or may include components that depend on a single vendor, and UALink is trying to solve the vendor lock-in problem, in addition to the unified super-accelerator option for continuously growing AI models. The PCIe/CXL interconnects are also less scalable in terms of the number of accelerators they can connect and the total bus bandwidth and may have higher latency for GPU–GPU data paths compared to the simplified packet processing on newer UALink switches.

Figure 13-10 illustrates the way UAlink xPU accelerators connect within the same rack system. Each station member connects to a different ULS (UALink switch).

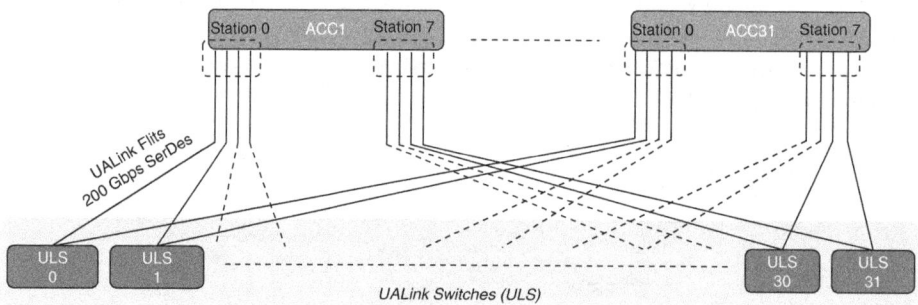

Figure 13-10
UALink scale-up systems within the rack with UALink switches

In addition to ULS switch-based connections between the accelerators (up to 1,000) for UALink, the specification proposes a direct connection between accelerators for smaller-scale xPU systems using a full-mesh topology. We highlight this in Figure 13-11, where instead of using a dedicated ULS, a direct link connects the two or more accelerators.

Figure 13-11
Direct accelerator-to-accelerator connection using UALink interface

UALink addresses similar use cases to SUE-T and NVLink from Nvidia and Infinity Fabric from AMD. It offers a highly scalable xPU interconnect solution with ultra-low latency but a more comprehensive coherent memory view across tens or hundreds of accelerators, with load/store, atomics, and read/write operations with a unified ordering model across local and remote accelerator memory. UALink uses the flit packet format with fixed transmission units of 680 bytes between the communicating xPUs. The shared memory semantics are also defined as part of the UALink specification and do not rely on any third-party semantics proposed by AXI for SUE-T. UALink keeps a uniform memory ordering across local and remote accelerators. It's also proposed as a more open, cost-competitive, and simplified scale-up standard for the continuously growing LLMs, measured by parameters and tokens per second. UALink reuses the IEEE 802.3 Layer 1 physical layer, with modest changes for low latency and alignment to 640-byte flit boundaries. It also targets sub-1 μs round-trip time (RTT) for requests and responses, supporting 200 GT/s per lane and short (< 4 m) cable runs inside racks. This is also different from scale-out systems, where cable lengths are much longer in the rail-optimized design, introducing additional delay per meter. The 200 Gbps SerDes is the main target of UALink and is offered as multiple lanes—more than 12—compared to SUE, and a group of 4 x 200 Gbps lanes is defined as a station inside the accelerator. Eight stations per xPU accelerator can be supported, providing higher bus bandwidth and lower latency than a single 400 Gbps/800 Gbps connection per GPU, used in traditional scale-out servers.

UALink also includes a built-in protection mechanism that provides confidentiality and optional integrity (replay protection) for data exchanged between accelerators. Once the atomic write operation is initiated, it first goes through the transaction layer (TL), where 64-byte flits (packets) are packed into 640-byte data link (DL) flits and sent over the Ethernet PHY. The Ethernet PCS (Physical Coding Sublayer) synchronizes 640-byte DL flits to PCS codewords, which are fixed-size unit of encoded transmission symbols. One DL flit fits exactly into one PCS codeword of 544/514 symbols (each of 10-bit), enabling the alignments for flits to lane transmission, without fragmentations. According to UALink Specification 1.0, PCS overwrites the first several 257-bit blocks of the start flit code sequence with the alignment markers specified in the 802.3. The RS (Reconciliation Sublayer) bridges data-link flits with PCS codewords and adds logic to keep DL flit boundaries aligned to codeword starts. With the PMA (Physical Medium Attachment), a codeword interleave is reduced, and PCS synchronizes 640-byte DL flits to PCS codewords. Because of that, a regular Ethernet switch may not be totally transparent, so purpose-built ULS Ultra switches will have to be used as part of the new scale-up system. On the other hand, minor changes to the Ethernet PCS level are proposed to improve latency for scale-up workloads.

At the Physical Layer (PL), the protocol stack serializes DL flits into 64-byte/66-byte blocks with optional FEC codewords, adds new codeword alignment markers, and includes a reconciliation layer header. It also uses a one-way (no interleaving; sending a single codeword on the wire at a time) and a one-way codeword interleave (mixing two codewords) at the physical level to achieve better latency. This means that instead of the traditional four-way standard Ethernet approach, the receiver must wait for all four codeword pieces to start decoding. In contrast, in a two-way decoding, just two codewords are expected to decode the message at the target node. Again, this is mainly done in UALink to reduce per-hop latency but still preserve some level of error correction.

From a data link perspective, in addition to 640-byte flit packing, the retry is proposed to maintain reliable transmission at each segment of the scale-up single-hop fabric. The retry mechanism is conceptually the same as the one we discussed for SUE-T/SUE. A more detailed explanation of LLR can be found in Chapter 12, even though the retry formatting for UALink is different. UALink includes fewer optional features than the UEC Specification 1.0 for scale-out systems, which includes many optional features, including LLR and CBFC at the link level.

Figure 13-12 illustrates a layered UALink approach, where the initial signals originate at the top application/software level, with direct memory semantics across the protocol layers and the network TL (transaction layer) and DL (data link layer) layers, before reaching the optimized PHY Ethernet transmission.

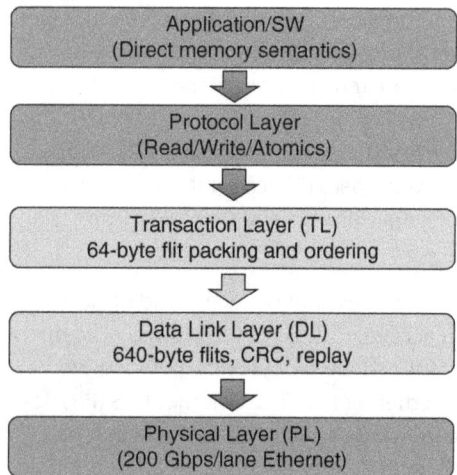

Figure 13-12
UALink high-level protocol stack

The application will initiate the read/write or atomic commands and encode them into the TL transaction 64-byte flits (packets), which are organized into 16 4-byte units, called *sectors*; 16 multiplied by 4 bytes yields a total of 64 bytes per TL. The flit format of the TL is divided into the upper and lower 32-byte parts. The control half flit includes the request, read response, write response, and call control information, while the data payload (write data, read data) can use the 32-byte half or the full upper and lower parts of the flit. Figure 13-13 illustrates the key concept behind the TL when an uncompressed request message is included in the lower flit part.

Upper TL Half-Flit	Lower TL Half-Flit			
Req0.Data.0	Req3	Req2	Req1	Req0
Req0.Data.2	Req0.Data.1			
Req0.Data.4	Req0.Data.3			

Figure 13-13
UALink TL flits frame format with data write request encapsulation

The UALink-based scale-up packs requests/responses from multiple sources/destinations into a single DL flit of 640 bytes, plus an additional 40 bytes for FEC (Forward Error Correction), offering much higher transmit efficiency from the individual xPU perspective and predictable performance compared to the UDP-encapsulated RoCEv2 packet of scale-out systems.

From a multi-tenancy perspective, the UALink specification also introduces the concept of virtual pod partitioning, where a group of one or more accelerators in the pod may communicate among themselves but not with any other accelerator in the other pods. (This is also offered with the partition field we discussed for SUE-T scale-up systems.) The UALink-connected accelerators in a pod have a unique accelerator ID, regardless of the virtual pod partitioning, so they don't need to change when the administrator redefines the virtual pod partitioning.

The UALink specification at the protocol state machine introduces the concept of UPLI (UALink Protocol Level Interface), which is an interface at the higher level (above the TL) that provides channelized request–response links between an originator (requester) and a completer (responder). The originator UPLI initiates requests (read/write/atomic), and the completer UPLI requests and returns responses, as highlighted in the UALink stack's protocol section with four channels. This semantic interface protocol uses the request, write request data (OrigData), read response with data, and write response. The originator sends the request (Req) command to the other accelerators and receives the responses. The TL/DL can include in the same flit the req/resp and send it over the Physical Layer (PL) in a serialized way over the number of lanes equal to the number of UALink switches using the 200 Gbps SerDes.

When packets are moving from the top layer of the originator to the completer, different addressing schema translations are used from the remote memory access (RMA) perspective in the request write command. The destination accelerator identifier is enabled using a 57-bit identifier (ReqAddr), and as part of the request, the request credit number is indicated at the virtual channel of the originator to indicate the number of credits being returned and the number of credits being released. ReqSrcPhysAccID 10-bit physical accelerator addresses are also included in the request message coming from the top of the layered UALink communication.

The ReqCmd (request command) field indicates the command for this request (write, for example, using the data channel called OrigData) and obtains the credits from the request channel with at least one credit or more. The UALink switches shown in Figure 13-14 follow the same semantics at the interface/port level as the accelerator's protocol stack, with UPLI interfaces at the top and traversing the TL, DL, and PL levels before serializing on the outgoing interface, where the completer accelerator is enabled.

UALink and addressing formats for the accelerators have different structures. The standard defines the SPA (System Physical Address), the NPA (Network Physical Address), and the GVA (Guest Virtual Address). Accelerators may use a System Physical Address (SPA) to access memory within a system domain and may use a Network Physical Address (NPA) to access memory in a different system domain (for example, on a different accelerator). The source accelerator uses the memory management unit (MMU) block to translate a GVA to an NPA, which is used at the UALink switch level, and at the destination node, a link MMU is used to translate NPA to a local SPA.

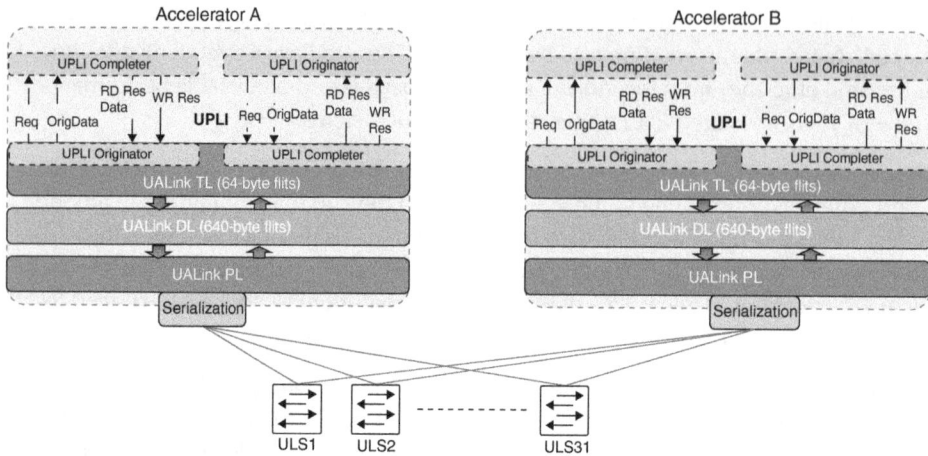

Figure 13-14
UALink Protocol Level Interface (UPLI) completer

The address handle in UALink ties together the logical address space we just discussed (SPA to NPA) with the hardware context and access control needed to perform remote memory access (RMA) across accelerators.

The address handle is a reference object that encapsulates all information needed to access a remote memory region via UALink. For remote access to the accelerator, the originator uses the handle ID when forming UPLI requests to write the data at the remote accelerator. The UALink hardware replaces that handle ID with the corresponding NPA plus key bits for on-wire transmission.

The software layer registers memory regions on each accelerator, defines local SPA ranges, and exports them as an address handle table, where the handle value is then encoded at the UPLI interface level in the request message with the target accelerator identifier. The UALink switch (interconnect Ethernet switch) uses the 10-bit accelerator ID and associates it with the outgoing interface to communicate and route requests/responses encapsulated in serialized DL flits. We can clearly see that MAC address-based switching is no longer used here, while the PHY Ethernet is still present; the switch above the PHY uses a different addressing structure that is directly mapped to the memory addressing scheme. A page table entry (PTE) in the accelerator's memory management unit (MMU) includes the address handle and the accelerator identifier association. At the accelerator level, the request field initiated at the UPLI transaction level (which is later packed into the TL and DL) includes the 10-bit DSTACCID field, which is mapped into the NPA address. The SRCACCID field is also included and later used by the responder to build the NPA destination address as feedback. At the destination accelerator, the TL flit decoder will take the delivered flit from the UPLI and MMU, place it in the queue, and then create the appropriate Rx memory cache entry at the accelerator level.

Figure 13-15 illustrates the end-to-end addressing relationship, including the NPA, SPA, and accelerator ID. The GVA from the source is translated to the NPA, and then the MMU block translates the NPA to the local SPA address.

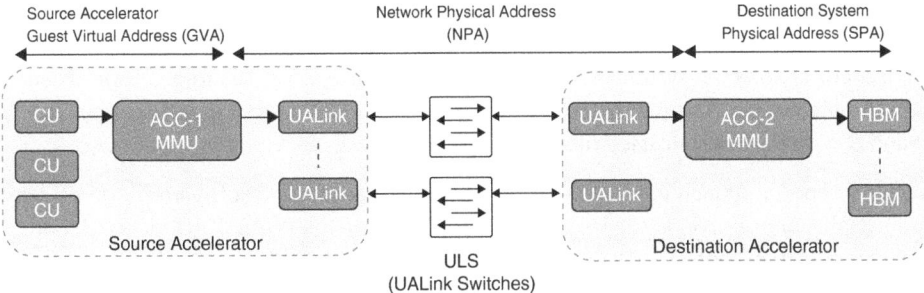

Figure 13-15
UALink scale-up system addresses from the source to the destination accelerator

Memory Coherence in Scale-Up Systems

Memory coherence in multi-accelerator systems means that when multiple accelerators access the same memory space, they must ensure that all devices see the same data at the same address. The synchronization of memory state is called *cache coherence*. One xPU writes to its local memory cache, and then any other xPU can read that from its own cache.

Hardware coherence means the fabric itself enforces cache consistency between devices—entirely in silicon, without software involvement. Hardware-based scale-up coherence is difficult to extend beyond tens of nodes, unlike software-based coherence. With hardware coherence used in the Infinity Fabric, a snoop message is sent to invalidate or update other caches, and the interconnect system of these accelerators ensures that all participating xPUs have a single "truth" for each memory line; that is, the scale-up system ensures that all others see a consistent view. The memory controller tracks which caches hold copies of each memory line (owner, sharers, state). In this context, the memory cache snoop messages are short protocol packets that query or notify other caches about the state of the memory line.

The device that initiates a memory access is called a requestor, and the responder is a peer xPU cache that holds a copy of each memory line. The interconnect point, also known as the interconnect fabric, transports snoop messages across the NVLink (Nvidia) or Infinity Fabric (AMD) or via the CXL/PCIe switch system, guaranteeing that all caches have a consistent view of memory. This is done entirely in hardware, without software or driver involvement. In such systems, directory-based coherence is used, where *home* agents send snoop messages based on the directory state responsible for the directory entries. So, when a GPU wants to write to memory address X, the memory home agent sends invalidate snoop messages to all the other XPUs, which acknowledge them to make the new GPU memory line the most up to date. The ownership is also then granted to the new xPU. Thanks to this process, the other xPUs don't have any memory line stale entries, and the most recent version of the cache line is used. The NVSwitch acts as a coherence router, so when one GPU writes, the NVLink switch sends invalidations to other GPUs that are caching that memory line.

Software coherence means the hardware does not maintain memory consistency automatically. Instead, software layers (drivers, runtimes, communication libraries) coordinate updates and synchronization. Each accelerator (xPU) has its own cache hierarchy, and when data needs to be shared, the software component, such as NCCL, SHMEM, the CUDA runtime, or the ROCm driver, explicitly flushes/invalidates caches. For example, UALink Specification 1.0 focuses on software coherence to scale to hundreds of xPUs per system. Software-based coherence scales to more xPUs and can choose when to synchronize (for example, only after each training iteration rather than every memory access) and can make the fabric itself more vendor agnostic.

The software coherence approach uses transport-level control packets and software-triggered synchronization signals. For example, in the UALink specification case, the PGAS (Partitioned Global Address Space) model maps onto the TL flit transaction layer. The PGAS abstraction layer sits above the TL layer of the UALink protocol stack. PGAS defines what memory operations mean, and TL flits define how they're encoded and delivered between the xPUs of the scale-up system. PGAS in the UALink specification defines global logical memory address and access semantics, and the TL translates them into Network Physical Addresses (NPAs). An NPA is a globally unique physical address within the UALink fabric namespace used by the Transaction Layer to identify a memory location owned by an endpoint; the System Physical Address (SPA) is a local xPU node addressing schema. The memory management unit (MMU) local to the xPU translates the NPA to the SPAs. Each xPU exposes a set of NPA ranges that corresponds to its local memory regions.

In the case of UALink, RMA is used, and the TL flits, which are the atomic transactions of 64-byte packet units, leverage the semantic meaning of an operation (for example, read, write, atomic, fence, notify), which is then packed and encapsulated inside data link flits. Once packets are sent over the DL using a fixed size of 640 bytes (for example, 10 TL flits per DL flit plus 8 bytes for CRC), they can be sent over the UALink scale-up fabric. The DL flits have an atomic replay/flow-control unit, so the reliable transport of the UALink scale-up fabric is delivered. The DL offer also provides reliable flit delivery using the initialization/training control at link bring-up and negotiates the interleave mode/FEC. Once link training is done, the DL handles the CRD (credit update), which periodically informs the sender of available receive buffers. The replay request (RREQ) is sent when the CRC check fails and the request is retransmitted for a specific flit sequence. ACK and NACK handle positive/negative acknowledgment of flits.

Inside the TL, higher-level *control verbs* are included, such as RMA_SYNC, NOTIFY, and RMA_FENCE, which are used to set memory completion of prior atomic operations. The RMA_COMPLETION verb signals to the target GPU that a write or atomic operation was completed. An ATOMIC_ACK message in the transaction flit confirms the success of the atomic RMA operation.

Scale-Up Systems: Key Differences and Similarities

We've just highlighted the key SUE-T/SUE and UALink capabilities of scale-up open fabric systems. To better understand the two open scale-up fabric systems and compare them with the leading Nvidia NVLink-based switch scale-up systems, it is helpful to define a few common capabilities and highlight the differences among the three main scale-up system approaches.

When comparing the NVLink/NVL72 systems, we primarily used the public documentation, which lacked detailed specifications. The SUE-T/SUE capabilities were announced as a framework and may evolve over time. The UALink approach is the best-defined source; besides the transport of

TL and DL well-defined flits over the Ethernet PHY, the request, request data memory semantics, and address translations are very well defined. However, due to the TL/DL changes, implementing UALink may take longer than implementing SUE-T/SUE, which continues to use standard DMAC/SMAC-based addressing.

For the scale-up systems, there are some similarities, such as the type of topology used. SUE-T and UALink take the same single-hop approach, and along the way, the systems can be interconnected using the scale-out leaf-spine IP Clos topology when the given scale-up system must be connected to the rest of the backend data center network infrastructure. Regarding UEC features, the retry link-level mechanism is mentioned for both SUE-T and UALink, but CBFC is only included in the SUE-T/SUN framework documentation. INC (In-Network Collectives) capabilities are not yet included in scale-up systems; they are only part of the scale-out UEC and InfiniBand topologies.

From an architectural scale perspective, the size of the target scale-up fabric domain targeted by UALink, with up to 1,000 accelerators, is already encoded in the 10-bit ACC-ID information; however, higher-density systems with 1.6 Tbps or higher speed and 200 Gbps SerDes will have to be built. When comparing the scale-up systems to the scale-out topologies with rail-optimized or non-rail-optimized design, the flexibility of deploying a full-blown scale-up chassis is lower when it comes to power, cooling, and cabling requirements.

Table 13-1 proposes including various comparison criteria for the three selected scale-up systems. We didn't include the AMD scale-up Infinity Fabric systems because limited documentation was available at the time of writing the book, even though the main differentiator is that it continues to use IP-level tunnel encapsulations, whereas SUE-T, UALink, and NVLink decided to stay at the Ethernet level with newer encapsulation formats.

Table 13-1   Scale-Up Systems Comparison

Capability	SUE-T/SUE	UALink 1.0	NVLink
Wire/PHY	Standard Ethernet PHY (200 Gbps–800 Gbps PAM-4)	Custom PHY aligned to 802.3dj class rates (200 Gbps–800 Gbps PAM-4), non-IP	Nvidia proprietary high-speed links
On-wire unit	Ethernet frame + AFH/SUE-T header (FlowID, PSN, credits, ECN bits)	TL flits (64 bytes) packed into DL flits (640 bytes + CRC)	NVLink flits over NVSwitch crossbar
Memory model	One-sided, PGAS-style (put/get/atomic) over Ethernet; destination is passive	PGAS (load/store/atomic, fence/notify) via NPA-to-SPA translation	Hardware-coherent shared memory within the NVLink/NVSwitch domain
Coherence	Software-managed (fences/barriers in runtime)	Software-managed (fence/notify TL ops; no snoops)	Hardware coherence (cache/directory managed via NVSwitch)
Ordering	Per-flow; strict or unordered per virtual channel; single-hop focus	Per-stream in-order TL delivery	In-order per flow; global fabric ordering via switches
Reliability	Credit-based, PSN/ACK at the link layer; Link-Layer Retry (LLR); CBFC	Credit + CRC + replay (DL level)	Reliable fabric; hardware retry inside NVSwitch fabric
Congestion control	In-band credits (AFH) and endpoint rate control	Credit/credit based	Fabric-internal; scheduler/backpressure in NVSwitch

Capability	SUE-T/SUE	UALink 1.0	NVLink
Topology scope	One-hop Ethernet scale-up (within a pod); multi-plane supported	In-rack pod (tens to 1,000 GPUs), switch-centric	NVSwitch-based systems (for example, NVL72): fully connected 72-GPU domains; multiple chassis via bridges
Latency (1 hop)	Sub-µs (typically 1 µs end-to-end and 250 ns port-to-port switch)	Few 100 ns TL-to-TL per hop and up to 300 ns port-to-port at the switch	Tens of nanoseconds switch hop; system-level, few 100 ns
Per-GPU fabric BW	0.8–3.2 Tbps typical with multiple 200 Gbps/400 Gbps/800 Gbps ports	0.8–3.2 Tbps class (configuration dependent)	Around 1.8 to over 2.0 Tbps per GPU (generation dependent)
Programming model	AXI or FIFO into SUE-T; one-sided verbs; libraries map collectives to SUE-T	PGAS API (load/store/atomic/fence), collectives over TL	CUDA/NCCL/NVSHMEM with coherent pointers; HW collectives
Openness/ecosystem	Open (OCP), leverages Ethernet optics/switches	Open consortium spec (new switches/ASICs)	Proprietary Nvidia stack and hardware
Cost	Medium	Medium	High

Summary

Scale-up systems are the most recent emerging domain of AI data centers, and the standardization progress of some initiatives, such as SUE-T OCP (Open Compute Project) will continue, as the first implementations of the UALink standard will come, provided that the accelerator-level semantics also follow developments. Typically, on the market, more switch vendor switches may exist with Ethernet PHY implementing the UALink or the SUE-T/SUE, but the whole scale-up system will work only if the xPU interconnect point development is done at the same time in order to offer a ready-to-use rack solution.

It's important to note that the new OCP framework includes more dependencies on other standards or frameworks, while UALink is an end-to-end, detailed standard specification that includes many fewer dependencies on other frameworks or standards. From business drivers' perspective, scale-up systems, even when implemented with more standardized protocols, may be more complex to adapt in some environments, especially where their power and cooling requirements are even more challenging than for scale-out systems with just eight xPUs per server. If the training of the model requires hundreds of thousands of xPUs, which scale horizontally, then adding the scale-up rack systems may simplify the deployments. However, it's yet to be proven from a software integrations perspective where a scale-up and scale-out deployment must represent a unified system capable of understanding which xPUs are part of the same scale-up rack system. When precisely the other scale-up racks must be used for communication (that is, the scale-up system from vendor A and vendor B) will need a common top-level orchestration at the software level. This means that the management and orchestration level of the scale-up systems must also provide interoperability with the existing and proven scale-out systems in order to be fully successful in production AI data center networks.

Test Your Knowledge

Chapter Review

The following questions are designed to test your understanding of the content covered in Chapter 13. Following the questions, answers are provided so you can verify your conclusions.

Questions

1. What is the fundamental motivation for scale-up systems in AI/ML data centers, and how do these systems address the limitations of scale-out architectures?

2. How do scale-up systems differ from scale-out systems in terms of hardware topology, memory coherence, and deployment philosophy?

3. What are the main interconnect technologies used in scale-up systems, and how do they compare to PCIe and CXL in terms of bandwidth and latency?

4. What is the role of interconnect points in scale-up rack systems, and how do they impact network topology and performance?

5. How does the SUE-T framework optimize Ethernet for scale-up AI workloads, and what are its key protocol components?

6. What are the memory coherence models used in scale-up systems, and why is coherence critical for AI workloads?

7. What reliability and congestion control mechanisms are implemented in scale-up fabrics, and how do they ensure lossless, efficient communication?

8. How do open standards like UALink and SUE-T address vendor lock-in and ecosystem interoperability, and what are the implications for AI data center design?

Answers

1. Scale-up systems are designed to overcome the limitations of scale-out architectures, which connect multiple servers horizontally but struggle with the ever-increasing computational and memory demands of state-of-the-art AI models. The motivation is to create a virtual super-accelerator—a tightly coupled pod of hundreds or even thousands of GPUs (or xPUs) that can be treated as a single computational entity. By integrating accelerators within a rack or a few racks using specialized interconnects, scale-up systems deliver performance and scalability that scale-out systems cannot match for tightly coupled AI training tasks.

2. Scale-up systems feature vertical integration of a large number of accelerators (often more than 8 xPUs per server, up to 1,000 xPUs across interconnected racks) within a unified hardware or software memory-coherence domain. They use purpose-built new scale-up switches to connect xPUs directly, often with multi-lane, high-speed links, and provide a global software memory coherence (for example, PGAS) or

hardware-coherent memory. The topologies are single hop, and the cabling and optics are all prebuilt in case of scale-up systems; scale-out systems allow many more customization options in terms of network design. There's no three-stage type of scale-up topology, and the accelerators get much higher bus bandwidth compared to the scale-out accelerators typically deployed with 400 Gbps or 800 Gbps link over the network interface adapter. In the case of scale-up systems, there's typically no NIC integration, and the interconnect point of the accelerator offers a direct path to the scale-up single-hop switches.

3. Scale-up systems leverage advanced interconnect technologies such as Nvidia NVLink, AMD Infinity Fabric, UALink (Ultra Accelerator Link), and SUE-T (Ethernet Scale-Up Networking).

   UALink provides up to 6.4 Tbps aggregated bandwidth per accelerator using multiple 200 Gbps lanes, with submicrosecond round-trip latency. It uses a flit-based packet format (640 bytes) and supports up to 1,000 accelerators per domain. SUE-T uses standard Ethernet PHY with optimized headers (AFH), supporting 100 Gbps to 200 Gbps per lane and ultra-low latency (typically <1 μs end-to-end and 200–300 ns port-to-port). PCIe and CXL, while widely used, cannot match the bandwidth and latency of these specialized interconnects, especially for large-scale, tightly coupled AI workloads. CXL 3.0 improves latency (down to 100 ns) and offers cache-coherent shared memory, but its bandwidth remains similar to that of PCIe 6.0.

4. Interconnect points are specialized points of connection at the accelerator level, where the upper-level memory commands are linked directly to the networking instances. An example of an interconnect point is the SUE-T/SUE scale-up system, where the interconnect point streams data write requests over the SUE interface at the accelerator and encodes them using standard Ethernet with an additional shim layer (AFH).

   Interconnect points also facilitate vendor interoperability, as open standards like UALink and SUE-T allow different vendors' accelerators and switches to work together, breaking proprietary lock-in.

5. SUE-T (Ethernet Scale-Up Networking/Scale-Up Ethernet Transport) is an open framework that adapts standard Ethernet for ultra-low latency, high-bandwidth AI workloads. AI Fabric Header (AFH) is used as a shim layer that enables efficient, low-overhead memory transactions between xPUs. AFH supports compressed and non-compressed headers, encoding source/destination xPU IDs in MAC addresses for single-hop topologies. Reliability Header (RH) in SUE-T/SUE adds sequence numbers, virtual channel information, and tenant isolation, enabling end-to-end link-layer reliability and multi-tenancy. Link Layer Retry (LLR), on the other hand, ensures reliable transmission by allowing switches to re-send packets in the case of negative acknowledgments; this is managed at the link level rather than by the originating xPU. Credit-Based Flow Control (CBFC) manages congestion and flow control at the link level, replacing traditional Priority Flow Control (PFC) for more efficient traffic management. The shared memory model supports one-sided memory semantics (put/get/atomic) with PGAS-style addressing, enabling direct memory access and synchronization across xPUs.

6. Scale-up systems employ two main memory coherence models:

    - **Hardware coherence:** With this model, which is used in NVLink/NVSwitch and Infinity Fabric, the interconnect fabric enforces cache consistency automatically via snoop messages and directory-based protocols. This ensures that all accelerators see the same data at the same address, with updates propagated instantly across caches. Hardware coherence is fast but difficult to scale beyond tens of nodes.

    - **Software coherence:** This model is used in UALink and SUE-T, where runtime libraries, drivers, or communication frameworks (for example, NCCL, SHMEM, CUDA, ROCm) explicitly manage cache synchronization. Software coherence scales to hundreds of xPUs and allows selective synchronization (for example, after each training iteration), making the system more vendor agnostic and flexible.

7. Scale-up fabrics implement reliability and congestion control at the link and data link layers. With SUE-T/SUE, Link Layer Retry (LLR) provides hop-by-hop reliability by allowing switches to re-send packets if acknowledgments are not received, ensuring lossless delivery without burdening the originating xPU. Otherwise, the sequence numbers and acknowledgments in L2 packets enable precise tracking and retransmission of lost or corrupted packets.

8. By enabling interoperability, these standards allow data centers to mix and match hardware from multiple vendors, reducing costs, increasing flexibility, and accelerating innovation. Proprietary solutions like Nvidia NVLink offer superior performance but limit ecosystem diversity and long-term scalability. Open standards empower organizations to build scalable, cost-effective AI infrastructure that can evolve with technological advances. UALink and SUE-T are intended to be open standards developed by industry-leading vendors within a consortium or standardization framework to break vendor lock-in and foster multi-vendor ecosystems for super-accelerators. They define interoperable protocols, hardware interfaces, and memory models, allowing accelerators and switches from different vendors to work together seamlessly.

References

Arm.com, "AMBA AXI and ACE Protocol Specification," 2025, developer.arm.com/documentation/ihi0022/e.

"Scale-Up Ethernet Framework Specification," 2025, docs.broadcom.com/doc/scale-up-ethernet-framework.

Open Compute Project, "Introducing ESUN: Advancing Ethernet for Scale-Up AI Infrastructure at OCP" https://www.opencompute.org/blog/introducing-esun-advancing-ethernet-for-scale-up-ai-infrastructure-at-ocp.

Ultra Accelerator Link. "UALink 200G 1.0 Specification Overview and Applications," 2025, www.youtube.com/watch?v=YHkpS_qyl-8.

Nvidia, "Nvidia GB200 NVL72," www.nvidia.com/en-us/data-center/gb200-nvl72/.

Nathan Kalyanasundharam, "Introducing UALink 200G 1.0 Specification," 2025, https://ualinkconsortium.org/wp-content/uploads/2025/04/UALink-1.0-White_Paper_FINAL.pdf.

14

Conclusion

DC Network Role for AI

This book covers fundamental concepts of AI data center network design for scale-out and scale-up infrastructures. It also discusses associated technologies, such as load balancing and congestion management in backend Ethernet networks, where the large language model (LLM) training phase is conducted, as well as multi-tenancy options in the frontend DC network, where LLMs are deployed in the post-training phase. The focus on networking is instrumental when deploying larger-scale AI clusters. Without high-scale, high-performance networks, popular generative AI applications wouldn't exist. Due to the massive number of parameters that describe the patterns and relationships the model learns, as well as the tokens that represent the actual content being processed, a large number of GPU-enabled servers are needed. To achieve the training outcomes, all these servers must be synchronized across the AI DC network. More parameters mean the AI model consumes more memory and requires more FLOPS (floating-point operations per second) per token processed. We have explained how these networking and GPU server components interact and influence each other and how they affect the performance, efficiency, scalability, and reliability of an AI data center ecosystem.

Throughout this book, you have seen the operational advantages of various architectures and technologies. We also purposely kept Chapter 3, "Network Design Considerations," generic to help you tackle the initial phases of creating AI network architecture. We have illustrated how AI data center design can be applied to different use cases: frontend versus backend versus traditional data center deployments. We have demonstrated how AI data center design can support various AI applications and domains, including healthcare, education, finance, manufacturing, entertainment, and social media. We have also looked at some emerging trends and innovations in AI data center design, such as the Ultra Ethernet Consortium (UEC) suite of protocols.

In this book we have discussed the possibilities and challenges of new AI data center technologies, as well as how they can complement and integrate with existing AI data center solutions. The gateway mode of migration, or a transition from traditional Ethernet to UEC, will likely occur. Any newer approach for the backend network developed by UEC will still have to be proven at the NIC driver level, so it will probably require a slower transition from the existing 400 Gbps/800 Gbps Ethernet format. Or perhaps we will see interoperability between the header-optimized UEC and current Ethernet for new 1.6 Tbps backend data center network architectures.

This book provides a comprehensive and practical overview of AI data center design, enabling and supporting your new AI data center projects. The focus on RDMA over Converged Ethernet version 2 (RoCEv2) and UEC, rather than InfiniBand, is justified by the fact that in recent times, many organizations that have decided to deploy large-scale greenfield AI data center backend clusters have preferred Ethernet/IP-based open and distributed architectures with unified tooling, better troubleshooting options, and equal or better performance.

Caveats and Challenges

The implementation of the solutions discussed in various chapters of this book comes with several caveats and nuanced considerations, which can be highly specific to the particular vendor of the AI data center solution being utilized. Even in scenarios where Ethernet and IP protocols are employed, an organization may adopt a proprietary, or vendor-specific, solution to address technical challenges (such as load balancing or congestion control) rather than rely solely on open standards such as those defined by the IETF or IEEE. The development cycles for new protocols and solutions within standardization bodies tend to be lengthy and may not align well with the fast-paced deployment windows characteristic of AI data center infrastructure projects. For instance, the concept of global load balancing (GLB), as described in Chapter 6, "Efficient Load Balancing," remains in an early conceptual stage at the IETF level and has not yet been addressed comprehensively by the UEC, which focuses on ultra-high-speed Ethernet standards. Such incomplete standardization can lead to interoperability challenges when integrating AI/ML data centers from different vendors, complicating seamless communication and data exchange. Typically, deployment scenarios favor using equipment from a single vendor for core network components, such as leaf and spine switches, to ensure compatibility.

Another challenge is that the architecture of AI/ML data centers is continually evolving, particularly as server hardware and processing capabilities continue to advance. For example, current designs such as the rail-optimized design (ROD) for IP Clos fabrics at the T0 level assume that servers support eight GPUs and eight NIC modules. However, these assumptions may change over time as newer, more powerful GPUs with higher computational densities become available and higher-rate NICs are introduced. Eventually, the number of NICs may be reduced, and the overall network architecture might evolve from the ROD approach to a more unified design, such as the rail-unified design (RUD), to better accommodate increased performance requirements and newer hardware configurations. The ongoing evolution of both server architecture and network topology requires flexible, adaptable network designs that can scale and evolve in tandem with technological advancements to ensure optimal performance and interoperability in AI data center environments.

The coexistence of different AI/ML workloads will also become more popular, and the same enterprise infrastructure may integrate both RoCEv2 and UEC-compliant traffic and include a shared storage network for both types of remote direct memory access (RDMA) transport. Such a design should offer sufficient flexibility and scalability to accommodate future modern AI workloads in addition to current RoCEv2 workloads. Some switch silicon may also have limitations in terms of adopting the link-layer functions for the newer AI/ML transport from UEC, which means only a subset of the advantages from the newer protocol stack will be supported in RoCEv2-designed data centers. The adoption of the UEC protocol stack will also depend heavily on the NIC diversity with the new protocol stack support and on the efficiency and the quality of the implementation of the latest features, such as network signal-based congestion control (NSCC) or receiver credit-based congestion control (RCCC) for congestion control, or the possibility of supporting both RoCEv2 and UEC transport from the same NIC to simplify the migration process.

From a design perspective, the leaf–spine–super spine architectures for scaling out will persist, and only in rare cases will the DragonFly design become relevant—primarily due to the simplicity and widespread adoption of the IP Clos fabric, also known as fat tree fabric. The challenge in such designs, particularly with AI/ML, is that the number of fibers and optics required from leaf to spine is very high. Also, a single server has to connect in the ROD design to multiple top-of-rack switches, which is not easy to implement and requires more expensive optical infrastructures.

AI/ML fabric extensions across data center locations is also a challenge. Because of the volume of east–west traffic, the traditional long-reach extensions may not be possible for the same job. However, they may become relevant if different jobs for the same training are executed in different locations; in that case, latency and higher WAN bandwidth will still be required. Hybrid on-premises/off-premises (cloud) AI training has yet to be defined as a unified solution; currently, it's either on-premises or off-premises in most of the cases.

The design of AI/ML data centers faces fundamental challenges beyond just networking and protocol requirements. The primary concern remains power consumption, which is typically much higher in AI data centers than in traditional data centers. As bandwidth increases, fabric network requirements also grow—from 800 Gbps to 1.6 Tbps—leading to a 20% to 30% increase in power use in a common scenario. GPUs with higher compute capacity inside servers will continue to consume more power while providing improved computation and I/O. In addition, cooling capacity must be considered when selecting locations for AI data centers, as insufficient cooling or power supply could hinder compliance with sovereignty requirements for LLM model training. If the power and cooling infrastructures are not available at a chosen site, strict adherence to the country's sovereignty laws cannot be maintained. This could slow the adoption of AI for mission-critical applications such as military systems, banking, or air traffic control.

The costs of AI/ML infrastructure for many organizations are very high, even when excluding the costs of power and cooling systems. GPU server infrastructure costs are significantly higher than the costs associated with traditional CPU-based servers, mainly due to the limited diversity in the AI infrastructure market. Therefore, the speed of AI adoption will in part depend on the evolution of the number of vendors delivering GPU compute and support for the associated development software stacks. Another challenge is that a given vendor may offer alternative GPU systems, but the full stack capabilities may be limited compared to other vendors, or a new GPU vendor's capabilities may not offer the same performance. For example, one GPU vendor's job completion time (JCT) may be better than another's, and the tail latency may also differ between the GPU vendors; it may therefore be challenging to integrate servers from different vendors in the same AI/ML data center infrastructure.

Finally, different software stack versions also offer different levels of performance. For example, a single GPU vendor may provide better performance in one version of the xCCL collective communication library, such as improved consistency in bus bandwidth. After an upgrade, this performance might look entirely different. Telemetry and recording of the AI workload performance becomes critical for the success of a future deployment.

Future Developments

The speed of the recent hardware and software developments for AI infrastructures has been exceptional and will continue at the same pace or even more quickly. Predicting exactly how things will evolve may be difficult, but for sure, scale optimization will become instrumental in the context of the compute software. For some LLMs, training requires much less infrastructure than is needed for some of the mainstream LLMs, so while the infrastructure may still continue to grow, the time spent on training continues to be reduced. For example, the GPT model went from requiring 9 months for training to 3 months, and the size of the training network was just one of the scale improvements; the software related to the training was more optimized than the network itself. For example, mixed precision began to be used with FP16/BF16 for compute and FP32 master weights, which has directly affected throughput (TFLOPs) and memory capacity. The size of LLMs will grow as the precision increases. For example, the 175B parameters result in a 350 GB model size for weights in FP16 precision and 700 GB in FP32 precision. To give a precise real-world example, the GPT-3 (175B) model had 175 billion parameters. In an LLM context, a parameter is basically a number the model learns to help it make better predictions. During training, the computer tweaks these numbers over and over until the model gets really good at predicting the next word. So, when we mention a "175B parameter model," we're simply saying that the model has 175 billion of these small numbers inside that were fine-tuned during training. In the early days of AI/ML training, the number of parameters was continuously increasing, driving up memory and compute requirements; however, sharing or recycling training will save on memory requirements while still maintaining high performance.

Another example of model optimization is the way models store parameters in fewer bits, which means lower memory requirements and faster computation. Another area of future development for models, which will also optimize the way network and compute infrastructures are used in the

AI/ML context, is related to the activation memory—the GPU memory used to store all the intermediate results until training finishes (that is, the temporary results produced when data flows through the model). Even if a model's parameters and weights fit in GPU memory, the activation memory may consume more resources, so future developments will continue to optimize it.

From the model optimization perspective, the dense models mentioned here will also evolve into sparse models, specifically Mixture of Experts (MoE) models, where only a fraction of the parameters are used per input; only the parameters that are most relevant for the given input are used, making model training more innovative and efficient. We mention this because it has a direct impact on the way the network infrastructure will evolve; for example, how quickly the connection to the server GPU NIC will become a 1.6 Tbps connection will depend on whether the compute requirements continue to grow as quickly as they did in the early phase of the LLM developments. With further research on optimizing the models, the 800 Gbps connection to the server GPU NIC card is likely to remain stable for a longer time and require evolutions of 1.6 Tbps and 3.2 Tbps between the leaf and spines to reduce the number of optical links within the fabric. This is why, from the perspective of AI fabric infrastructure evolution, the key future developments will be related to the following:

- **Scale-up systems:** Evolution in fabrics such as NVLink and NVSwitch from Nvidia and UALink standard-based scale-up systems will continue to standardize the interconnections within systems, and the number of GPUs per single system will continue to increase, along with the number of scale-up systems interconnections within the data center site and between the data center sites.

- **Scale-out fabrics:** UEC leaf/spine/super spine fabrics will be used instead of RoCEv2 and InfiniBand or will coexist with RoCEv2 with higher speed of 800 Gbps to the server NIC and 1.6 Tbps or 3.2 Tbps between leaf and spine. Networks will potentially include AI agents on switches to analyze telemetry data and make smarter adaptive routing decisions.

- **Storage optimization:** Optimizations such as NVMe over Fabrics and parallel file systems will be implemented for faster storage networks.

- **Cooling innovations:** We will see significant network infrastructure evolution in liquid cooling for 1.6 Tbps or 3.2 Tbps Ethernet per port and over 100 Tbps per switch node. Many more innovations and standardizations will be coming in the future.

When speaking with customers, we often hear questions about the impact of quantum computing on AI/ML infrastructures and the use of quantum processing units (QPUs) alongside GPUs and CPUs. You might be wondering what quantum computing is and why we haven't mentioned it before this point in this book. We have not included quantum-related topics and technologies because their use with AI training and inference is still highly research oriented and limited to specific model-training use cases, such as quantum physics, chemistry, new drug development, cryptography, and climate-related applications. While the currently deployed LLMs are designed for linear algebra, matrix multiplication, and deep learning, quantum systems can tackle high-dimensional data (such as molecules, proteins, and financial models). Some initial implementations will be hybrid AI models, where part of the network operates using quantum computing.

Let's look briefly at the basics of quantum computing. It's a new type of computing that uses the various rules of quantum physics. Instead of using regular bits that are either 0 or 1, quantum computers use special bits called qubits, which can be both 0 and 1 at the same time. Quantum computers can explore multiple solutions simultaneously, and they can be significantly faster than conventional computers at solving certain problems. Quantum-unique algorithms (like quantum annealing or variational quantum optimization) could, in theory, do a better and faster job setting parameters than the gradients used in the current LLMs. In the context of AI/ML, quantum machine learning (QML) has been referenced in numerous academic papers; it involves the application of quantum computing techniques to enhance or develop machine learning algorithms. Quantum algorithms (such as quantum linear algebra solvers) can accelerate gradient calculations, reducing training time from weeks to days. Data is encoded into quantum states and utilizes quantum properties, such as entanglement, where two things are so deeply connected that you can't describe one without the other. This enables the processing of multiple possibilities simultaneously, potentially reducing training time and memory requirements.

Nvidia, a leader in GPU system development, is integrating quantum-based solutions into its software, such as the CUDA-Q software suite for developers. IBM has announced the Qiskit SDK development framework, which is key to future developments, alongside broader hardware availability.

The quantum server systems that natively support qubit-based computation are highly different from the GPU servers' architecture; they can't just be deployed in traditional data center premises with air or liquid cooling. The first quantum systems required near-zero temperatures, cryogenic cooling, isolation from noise, and vacuum chambers. These unique needs are one of the reasons hybrid systems with QPU, GPU, and CPU on the same server board will become more popular in the coming years rather than native AI data center quantum servers. From a network perspective, such systems will be able to continue to utilize the 800 Gbps/1.6 Tbps AI Ethernet infrastructure and won't immediately require any newer quantum switch infrastructure.

Inside a data center, optical interconnect systems are sometimes considered as a next-generation solution, where instead of the Ethernet spine layer, optical interconnects are used; in some cases, optical interconnects (instead of copper interconnects) are planned for use between all the GPUs, similarly to the current scale-up systems, to interconnect the accelerators. Optical interconnects can provide non-blocking, high-radix topologies (such as Clos and DragonFly) but without the power penalty of electrical switches. They avoid electrical-to-optical conversions at every hop in the infrastructure and also offer ultra-low end-to-end latency. Optical interconnects may become the next extension of co-packaged optics products (silicon photonics integrated directly with Ethernet or InfiniBand ASICs), which are already available on the market.

Final Remarks

AI/ML networking and server systems are an exciting domain, and we hope that this book has inspired you to delve deeper into the dynamic and ever-evolving design and technologies. This multidisciplinary area presents significant technical challenges and exciting opportunities for innovation, creativity, and collaboration among engineers, researchers, developers, managers, and industry leaders who aim to leverage AI to make a positive and transformative impact.

To maximize your understanding, we recommend revisiting certain chapters after completing the entire book, as this approach can help you get new insights and perspectives on complex topics. For instance, you might start by exploring the principles of data center design and then examine the relevant technologies involved, such as routing; to do so, you could review Chapter 3 and then Chapter 8, "IP Routing for AI/ML Fabrics." Such sequential review enhances comprehension by connecting foundational concepts with advanced applications. The next stage would be to apply the knowledge you've gained through hands-on work with specific vendors and their solutions.

We have intentionally kept this book vendor neutral, avoiding configuration templates and show commands from a switch or router, to keep the content broadly applicable without being biased by a particular network or server vendor. Practical application becomes most effective once you have a solid grasp of the baseline concepts discussed throughout the initial phases.

We value your insights and invite you to share feedback and suggestions on how to improve this resource to make it more comprehensive, insightful, and relevant to your needs. Thank you for engaging with this book and becoming part of the community focused on AI data center design and technology.

References

Nvidia, "NVIDIA DGX Quantum," https://www.nvidia.com/en-us/data-center/dgx-quantum/.

Rick Merritt, "What Is a QPU?," https://blogs.nvidia.com/blog/what-is-a-qpu/, Nvidia blog, July 29, 2022.

Pradnya Khalate, Thien Nguyen, and Efrat Shabtai, "NVIDIA CUDA-Q 0.12 Expands Toolset for Developing Hardware-Performant Quantum Applications," https://developer.nvidia.com/blog/nvidia-cuda-q-0-12-expands-toolset-for-developing-hardware-performant-quantum-applications/, Nvidia Developer blog, August 4, 2025.

Bernard Marr, "Quantum Computing Faces 3 Major Barriers Before Going Mainstream," https://www.forbes.com/sites/bernardmarr/2025/07/23/quantum-computing-faces-3-major-barriers-before-going-mainstream/, Forbes, July 23, 2025.

IBM, "Quantum Technology," https://www.ibm.com/quantum/technology.

Henning Soller, "Bringing Quantum Computing to Data Centers," https://www.mckinsey.com/capabilities/mckinsey-digital/our-insights/tech-forward/bringing-quantum-computing-to-data-centers, McKinsey & Company, December 20, 2023.

PhotonDelta, "The Path to Future AI Data Centers Is Paved with Optical Interconnect," https://www.photondelta.com/news/path-to-ai-data-centres-is-paved-with-with-optical-interconnect/, March 17, 2025.

Broadcom, "Broadcom Announces Third-Generation Co-Packaged Optics (CPO) Technology with 200G/lane Capability," https://investors.broadcom.com/news-releases/news-release-details/broadcom-announces-third-generation-co-packaged-optics-cpo, May 15, 2025.

Ashkan Seyedi, "How Industry Collaboration Fosters NVIDIA Co-Packaged Optics," https://developer.nvidia.com/blog/how-industry-collaboration-fosters-nvidia-co-packaged-optics/, Nvidia Developer blog, August 26, 2025.

APPENDIX A

Questions and Answers

Chapter 1: Wonders in the Workload

The following questions are designed to test your understanding of the content covered in Chapter 1. Following the questions, answers are provided so you can verify your conclusions.

Questions

1. How does the data lifecycle influence AI model performance in data centers?
2. Explain the iterative process of training an AI model, including the roles of forward and backward propagation.
3. What are the main types of parallelism in AI training, and how do they address scalability challenges?
4. Define job completion time (JCT) and discuss its significance in AI/ML clusters.
5. How does tail latency affect distributed AI training, and what architectural features help mitigate it?
6. Describe the function and benefits of RDMA in AI/ML data center networks.
7. Compare InfiniBand, RoCEv2, and iWARP as RDMA transport protocols for AI/ML workloads.
8. What are the key requirements for AI data center fabrics to support efficient AI/ML workloads?

Answers

1. The data lifecycle—spanning collection, cleaning, labeling, and tokenization—directly impacts model accuracy and robustness. High-quality, relevant, and well-labeled data enables models to learn meaningful patterns, while poor data can introduce bias or reduce generalization. The robustness of a model is proportional to the diversity and volume of the training data, which is why petabyte-scale data sets are often used in modern AI/ML workloads.

2. Training involves feeding input data through the model (forward propagation) to generate predictions, comparing these predictions to expected outputs, and then adjusting model parameters using gradients (backward propagation). This process is repeated over many iterations (epochs) and across large batches of data, gradually improving model accuracy.

3. Data parallelism involves splitting data across multiple GPUs, each running the same model; model parallelism involves splitting the model itself across GPUs; pipeline parallelism involves dividing model layers into stages that are processed in sequence; and tensor parallelism involves splitting tensor operations. These approaches enable simultaneous computation, reducing training time and overcoming the limitations of single-processor systems.

4. JCT is the elapsed time from the start of a training job to the end of the job. It is a critical KPI because AI/ML workloads are often split into many parallel tasks, and the slowest task (due to tail latency or congestion) determines the overall JCT. Optimizing JCT is essential for efficient resource utilization and faster model iteration.

5. Tail latency refers to the slowest responses among many parallel tasks. In distributed AI training, high tail latency can delay job completion, as all tasks must finish before the job can proceed. Architectural features such as use of high-radix switches, dynamic load balancing, and lossless fabrics (for example, RoCEv2) help reduce tail latency by minimizing congestion and ensuring even traffic distribution.

6. RDMA (remote direct memory access) enables direct memory access between servers, bypassing the CPU and kernel, which reduces latency, increases throughput, and lowers CPU utilization. It is especially beneficial for AI/ML workloads that require frequent, high-volume data transfers between GPUs across nodes.

7. InfiniBand offers low latency and lossless transport but is less scalable and more expensive. RoCEv2 runs RDMA over Ethernet using UDP/IP, providing scalability and compatibility with existing Ethernet infrastructure, but it requires careful congestion management. iWARP is less popular, offering RDMA over TCP/IP, but with higher latency and less adoption in AI/ML clusters.

8. AI data center fabrics must be lossless, support high throughput and low latency, provide dynamic load balancing, and be capable of handling large-scale parallelism. Features like high-radix 400 Gbps/800 Gbps Ethernet switches, RoCEv2 support, and advanced congestion management—such as DCQCN, including PFC and ECN—are essential for optimally maximizing performance in the AI data center. The design should allow for the integration of

a higher number of servers with GPUs; it should help to move, for example, from a three-stage topology to a five-stage topology when the number of AI workloads is increasing over time.

Chapter 2: "The Common-Man View" of AI Data Center Fabrics

The following questions are designed to test your understanding of the content covered in Chapter 2. Following the questions, answers are provided so you can verify your conclusions.

Questions

1. How do the requirements of AI training data centers differ from those of inference data centers?
2. What are the technical trade-offs between InfiniBand and Ethernet for AI training cluster deployments?
3. Explain the concept of low entropy in AI/ML network traffic and its impact on load balancing.
4. What are elephant flows, and why do they pose a challenge in AI/ML fabrics?
5. Describe the proactive and reactive congestion management techniques used in AI/ML fabrics.
6. How does RoCEv2 address the need for lossless transport in Ethernet-based AI data centers?
7. What are the main load-balancing techniques used for AI/ML fabrics, and how do they differ?
8. Why is oversubscription ratio a critical design parameter in AI/ML data center fabrics?

Answers

1. Training data centers require high-performance computing, massive memory bandwidth, and fast interconnects to process large data sets over long periods. Inference data centers prioritize low-latency, real-time responses and typically use smaller, more effective multi-tenant systems.
2. InfiniBand offers sub-microsecond latency, native RDMA, and high reliability but at higher cost and with vendor lock-in. Ethernet is more cost-effective, widely compatible, and easier to manage, but it requires enhancements (such as RoCEv2 and advanced load balancing) to match InfiniBand's performance for AI workloads.
3. Low entropy means that many packet headers are similar, making it difficult for switches to distinguish flows and distribute them evenly. This can lead to inefficient load balancing, congestion, and underutilization of network resources, especially in one-to-one or small-group GPU communications.

4. Elephant flows are large, sustained data transfers and are typical in AI/ML clusters. They can monopolize bandwidth, cause congestion, and require specialized load-balancing and congestion management techniques to prevent performance degradation.

5. Proactive techniques include dynamic and global load balancing to prevent congestion before it occurs. Reactive techniques, such as ECN (Explicit Congestion Notification) and PFC (Priority Flow Control), respond to congestion events by signaling endpoints to slow down or pause traffic.

6. RoCEv2 uses UDP/IP encapsulation and relies on lossless Ethernet features (such as PFC and ECN) to provide RDMA capabilities over standard Ethernet, enabling the high-throughput, low-latency data transfers required for AI/ML workloads.

7. Static load balancing (SLB) uses fixed rules, dynamic load balancing (DLB) adapts to real-time link and buffer utilization, global load balancing (GLB) incorporates remote link quality, and per-packet spraying distributes packets across all paths. Each technique offers different trade-offs in complexity and efficiency.

8. The oversubscription ratio determines how much aggregate server bandwidth exceeds the available network bandwidth. High oversubscription can cause congestion and increase JCT, so AI/ML fabrics aim for low or no oversubscription to ensure predictable, high-performance communication. In rare cases, an undersubscription type of design is used (with more links to the spines and fewer to the servers) to include better packet spraying from leaf to spine and also get more dedicated egress buffers in a shallow buffer switch deployment.

Chapter 3: Network Design Considerations

The following questions are designed to test your understanding of the content covered in Chapter 3. Following the questions, answers are provided so you can verify your conclusions.

Questions

1. What are the main architectural stages in AI/ML workload processing, and how do they influence network design?

2. How do rail-optimized design (ROD) and rail-unified design (RUD) differ in terms of GPU-to-leaf connectivity, and what are the implications for scalability and fault tolerance?

3. What are the key considerations and trade-offs in rack design (top of rack, middle of row, end of row) for AI/ML data centers?

4. How does the Clos (fat-tree) topology enable scalable, non-blocking AI/ML fabrics, and what are the challenges at extreme scale (for example, 32,000+ GPUs)?

5. What are the benefits and limitations of alternative topologies like Dragonfly and Torus for AI/ML clusters?

6. How do scheduled fabric architectures (for example, cell-based switching, VOQ) improve congestion management and link utilization in AI/ML data centers?

7. What are the power and cooling implications of high-density AI/ML racks, and how do they influence network and facility design?

8. How do deterministic path forwarding and traffic engineering support performance and reliability in large-scale AI/ML fabrics?

Answers

1. AI/ML workload processing typically follows three main stages:

   - Data gathering and preprocessing: Data is collected from diverse sources and cleaned, labeled, and tagged. This stage requires high-throughput storage networks and efficient data pipelines to ensure that large data sets can be ingested and prepared without bottlenecks.

   - Model selection and training: The curated data is used to train models, often requiring clusters of GPUs interconnected with high-bandwidth, low-latency fabrics. The network must support massive east–west traffic, parallel data transfers, and collective communication operations.

   - Deployment and monitoring: Trained models are deployed for inference, and their performance is monitored. This stage may involve both backend (training) and frontend (inference) networks, each with different latency, bandwidth, and reliability requirements.

2. These are the differences between ROD and RUD:

   - ROD: Each GPU in a server is connected to a separate leaf switch, forming "rails." This design minimizes intra-rail latency and maximizes bandwidth, as each GPU has a dedicated path to the network. It allows for efficient scaling by adding more rails (leaf switches) and supports high GPU counts per cluster. Faults are isolated to individual rails, limiting the impact of a switch failure.

   - RUD: Multiple GPUs from a server connect to the same leaf switch. This simplifies cabling and can reduce costs, but it increases the risk that a single leaf switch failure will isolate all GPUs in a server. Scaling is easier in terms of cabling but less optimal for performance and fault isolation compared to ROD.

   ROD is preferred for large-scale, high-performance clusters where minimizing latency and maximizing parallelism are critical. RUD may be chosen for smaller deployments or where cost and cabling simplicity are prioritized and when larger chassis-based systems are used (for example, a higher-end multi-linecard Ethernet switch instead of a 1RU ToR).

3. These are the key trade-offs:

    - Top of rack (ToR): Switches are placed at the top of each rack, minimizing intra-rack cable lengths and simplifying management. However, this design increases per-rack power and cooling requirements.

    - Middle of row (MoR): Switches are centralized in the middle of a row, reducing the number of switches but increasing cable lengths and complexity.

    - End of row (EoR): Switches are placed at the end of a row, further centralizing switching but requiring the longest cables and careful planning for airflow and power.

    ToR is best for high-density, high-performance clusters where minimizing latency and maximizing manageability are key. MoR and EoR can reduce switch count and cost but may complicate cabling and cooling. The choice depends on cluster size, density, and operational priorities.

4. The Clos topology uses multiple stages (leaf, spine, super spine) to create a non-blocking, highly parallel network. Each leaf connects to every spine, ensuring multiple equal-cost paths between any two endpoints. Clos can scale to tens of thousands of endpoints with the addition of more stages and higher-radix switches. At extreme scale, challenges include managing oversubscription, cabling complexity, and power/cooling and maintaining low-latency paths. As the number of GPUs increases, the number of required switch ports and interconnects grows rapidly. Multi-stage Clos (three-stage, five-stage, seven-stage) and chassis-based spines/super spines are used to manage this, but careful planning is needed to avoid bottlenecks and ensure efficient load balancing.

5. Dragonfly connects groups of switches in a mesh, reducing the number of hops and the network diameter. It offers lower latency and better scalability for certain traffic patterns but requires more complex routing and fault management.

    Torus connects nodes in a ring (1D), grid (2D), or cube (3D), providing multiple paths and high bisection bandwidth for nearest-neighbor communication. It is cost-effective and easy to scale but can suffer from higher average latency and less flexibility for arbitrary traffic patterns.

    Both topologies can complicate routing, require specialized hardware/software support, and may not be as flexible as Clos for mixed or unpredictable workloads.

6. Scheduled fabric splits packets into fixed-size cells, uses virtual output queueing (VOQ) to prevent head-of-line blocking, and schedules cell transmission across the fabric. This approach allows for fine-grained congestion management, efficient spraying of traffic across multiple links, and improved fairness.

    The key benefits of scheduled fabric are reducing latency, maximizing link utilization, and preventing congestion hot spots. Scheduled fabric is particularly effective for bursty, synchronized AI/ML workloads, where traditional packet-based switching may struggle. Scheduled fabric requires advanced switch hardware and careful configuration, and it may introduce additional complexity in troubleshooting and monitoring, as well as higher costs compared to a distributed lossless Ethernet fabric with shallow buffers.

7. Modern AI/ML servers (for example, DGX H100) can require up to 15 kW per server, with racks exceeding 60 kW. This necessitates advanced power distribution, redundant supplies, and high-capacity cooling (liquid, immersion, or advanced airflow). High-density racks may require distributed switches (for example, ToR) to minimize cable lengths and manage heat. Facility design must ensure adequate power delivery, cooling capacity, and airflow management to prevent hotspots and ensure reliability. Power and cooling are primary constraints in scaling AI/ML clusters, influencing rack placement, switch location, and overall data center architecture.

8. Deterministic path forwarding ensures that specific flows (for example, between GPUs in the same rail) follow predictable, optimized paths, reducing contention and improving performance. This is achieved through careful network configuration, use of deterministic routing protocols, and sometimes explicit path pinning.

   Traffic engineering involves dynamically adjusting routing and load balancing based on real-time network conditions, workload requirements, and failure scenarios. Techniques include ECMP, flowlet-based balancing, and policy-based routing. Such an approach improves reliability, reduces tail latency, and ensures that critical AI/ML jobs meet performance SLAs even as the network scales and workloads fluctuate.

Chapter 4: Optics and Cable Management

The following questions are designed to test your understanding of the content covered in Chapter 4. Following the questions, answers are provided so you can verify your conclusions.

Questions

1. Why are high-speed optics (200 Gbps/400 Gbps/800 Gbps/1.6 Tbps) critical for AI/ML data centers?
2. Explain the function of digital signal processors (DSPs) in optical transceivers.
3. Compare the use cases for multi-mode fiber (MMF) and single-mode fiber (SMF) in data centers.
4. What are the technical differences between the QSFP28, QSFP56, and QSFP-DD form factors?
5. How do modulation schemes like PAM4 enable higher bandwidth in optical links?
6. Describe the role and selection criteria for optical connectors (for example, LC, MPO/MTP) in high-density AI clusters.
7. What are the advantages and trade-offs of pluggable, linear-drive, and co-packaged optics?
8. How does cable management impact signal integrity and operational efficiency in AI data centers?

Answers

1. AI/ML clusters require massive bandwidth to move data between GPUs and servers. High-speed optics enable these data rates, reducing training time and supporting large-scale parallelism.

2. DSPs handle signal modulation, error correction, and equalization, compensating for signal degradation over long distances and enabling higher data rates with advanced modulation schemes like PAM4.

3. MMF is used for short-range connections within racks or rows (up to 150 m), while SMF supports long-range connections between buildings or data centers (up to 10 km or more). MMF and SMF require different transceivers and connectors.

4. QSFP28 supports 100 Gbps (4x25 Gbps), QSFP56 supports 200 Gbps (4x50G, PAM4), and QSFP-DD supports 400 Gbps/800 Gbps (8x50 Gbps/100 Gbps, PAM4), with increasing channel counts and backward compatibility for migration.

5. PAM4 encodes 2 bits per symbol (four amplitude levels), doubling the data rate per channel compared to NRZ (1 bit per symbol), enabling higher aggregate bandwidth over the same fiber.

6. LC connectors are used for single-mode, duplex connections; MPO/MTP connectors support multi-fiber, high-density connections (8, 12, 16, or 24 fibers), enabling efficient cabling for large-scale deployments.

7. Pluggable optics offer flexibility and easy replacement. Linear-drive optics reduce power and cost by moving DSP functions to the switch ASIC. Co-packaged optics integrate optics with the switch, increasing port density and efficiency but reducing flexibility.

8. Proper cable management minimizes signal loss, reduces crosstalk, and ensures efficient airflow for cooling. Poor management can lead to increased errors, downtime, and maintenance complexity.

Chapter 5: Thermal and Power Efficiency Considerations

The following questions are designed to test your understanding of the content covered in Chapter 5. Following the questions, answers are provided so you can verify your conclusions.

Questions

1. Why do AI/ML data centers have higher power and cooling requirements than traditional data centers?

2. What is power usage effectiveness (PUE), and how is it calculated?

3. Compare front-to-back, back-to-front, and bidirectional airflow cooling methods.
4. How does immersion cooling work, and what are its benefits and limitations?
5. Describe the cold plate liquid cooling method and its application in AI data centers.
6. What are the trade-offs between air and liquid cooling in high-density AI clusters?
7. How does rack design (height, width, and power budget) influence cooling strategy?
8. What is the impact of cooling system efficiency on overall data center sustainability?

Answers

1. AI/ML clusters use high-density GPU servers and high-speed switches, each consuming significant power and generating more heat per rack, necessitating advanced cooling and power distribution systems.
2. PUE = Total Facility Power / IT Equipment Power. A lower PUE indicates more efficient use of power for computing rather than cooling or overhead.
3. Front-to-back airflow cools optics first, and back-to-front airflow cools power supplies first. Bidirectional fans can be configured for either direction, offering flexibility but with higher cost and complexity.
4. Immersion cooling involves submerging equipment in a dielectric fluid, providing efficient heat removal and supporting higher power densities. It requires specialized equipment and facility design and may complicate maintenance.
5. Cold plate cooling involves circulating liquid directly to heat sinks attached to CPUs/GPUs, efficiently removing heat without submerging the entire system. It offers targeted cooling but requires custom plumbing and careful design.
6. Air cooling is simpler and less expensive but less effective at high densities. Liquid cooling (immersion, cold plate, spray) is more efficient but requires specialized infrastructure and higher upfront investment.
7. Rack dimensions and power density determine airflow requirements, cooling capacity, and the feasibility of different cooling methods. High-density racks may require liquid cooling or enhanced airflow management.
8. Efficient cooling reduces energy consumption, lowers operational costs, and minimizes environmental impact, contributing to more sustainable AI data center operations.

Chapter 6: Efficient Load Balancing

The following questions are designed to test your understanding of the content covered in Chapter 6. Following the questions, answers are provided so you can verify your conclusions.

Questions

1. What is the role of ECMP (equal-cost multipathing) in AI/ML data center fabrics, and how does it interact with flow hashing?

2. Why is static load balancing (SLB) often insufficient for AI/ML workloads, and what are its operational limitations?

3. Describe the operational modes of dynamic load balancing (DLB) and their impact on flow distribution.

4. How does flowlet-based load balancing address the challenges of bursty and synchronized AI/ML traffic?

5. What is global load balancing (GLB), and how does it enhance network-wide congestion management?

6. Explain the technical challenges and trade-offs of per-packet load balancing in RoCEv2-based AI fabrics.

7. How do load-balancing mechanisms interact with RoCEv2's low-entropy flow characteristics, and what enhancements are required?

8. Summarize the comparative strengths and weaknesses of SLB, DLB, GLB, and TE-LB (Traffic Engineering Load Balancing) in AI/ML data center networks.

Answers

1. ECMP enables the distribution of traffic across multiple network paths with equal cost, maximizing bandwidth utilization and redundancy. In AI/ML fabrics, ECMP relies on hash functions (typically using a 5-tuple: source/destination IP, source/destination port, protocol) to assign flows to specific paths. However, in RoCEv2-based AI clusters, low entropy in packet headers (due to similar source/destination pairs and UDP port 4791) can cause hash collisions, leading to uneven load distribution and potential congestion on certain links. Advanced ECMP implementations may incorporate additional fields (for example, RoCEv2 BTH QPAIR) to improve entropy and flow separation.

2. SLB assigns flows to paths based on a static hash, without considering real-time link utilization or flow size. In AI/ML clusters, where elephant flows dominate and flow entropy is low, SLB can result in persistent hot spots, underutilized links, and increased tail latency. SLB also lacks adaptability to dynamic traffic patterns, making it unsuitable for environments with bursty or synchronized workloads, which are typical of distributed training.

3. DLB improves upon SLB by considering real-time link and buffer utilization. Its modes include:

    - Assigned-flow mode: Each flow is pinned to a path for its lifetime. This is suitable for high-entropy, short-lived flows but can cause persistent congestion for long-lived elephant flows.

- Flowlet mode: Flows are divided into flowlets (bursts separated by idle periods). Flowlets can be reassigned to less congested paths to balance responsiveness and packet ordering.
- Per-packet mode: Each packet is independently assigned to the best path based on current link quality, maximizing utilization but requiring advanced NICs and software to handle packet reordering at the destination.

4. Flowlet-based DLB detects natural pauses in traffic (flowlets) and uses them as opportunities to reassign subsequent bursts to less congested paths. This approach balances the need for dynamic load distribution with the requirement to minimize packet reordering, making it well suited for AI/ML workloads that exhibit bursty, synchronized communication patterns (for example, gradient synchronization in distributed training).

5. GLB extends DLB by incorporating remote link quality metrics (for example, spine-to-leaf utilization) into path selection. Switches share link quality information, enabling more informed decisions that prevent bottlenecks at aggregation points. GLB is particularly effective in Clos and multi-stage topologies, where congestion can occur at intermediate layers. It reduces the risk of multiple flows converging on the same congested link, improving end-to-end bandwidth utilization and reducing tail latency.

6. Per-packet load balancing achieves nearly perfect link utilization by distributing packets across all available paths. However, it introduces packet reordering, which can degrade RDMA performance and increase CPU overhead for reassembly. Modern NICs (for example, Nvidia CX6/CX7) and DPUs can handle limited reordering for specific RDMA operations (for example, write opcodes), but excessive reordering can still impact throughput and latency. Selective per-packet spraying, enabled via ACLs and flow classification, allows administrators to balance efficiency and reliability based on workload characteristics.

7. RoCEv2 traffic often exhibits low entropy due to fixed UDP ports and similar source/destination pairs, making traditional hash-based load balancing less effective. Enhancements include incorporating RoCEv2 BTH QPair fields into the hash, using flowlet or per-packet modes, and deploying GLB to leverage remote link quality. These techniques increase flow separation, reduce collisions, and improve overall network utilization in AI/ML fabrics.

8. Strengths and weaknesses are as follows:
    - SLB: Simple and widely supported but static and prone to hot spots in low-entropy environments.
    - DLB: Adaptive, considers local link/buffer utilization, and supports flowlet/per-packet modes but may require hardware support and careful tuning.
    - GLB: Incorporates remote link quality and prevents aggregation bottlenecks but increases control-plane complexity and requires protocol enhancements.
    - TE-LB: Enables deterministic path selection and tenant isolation via policy-based routing but is complex to configure and maintain and may reduce path diversity, if overused.

The optimal choice depends on workload characteristics, hardware capabilities, and operational requirements.

Chapter 7: RoCEv2 Transport and Congestion Management

The following questions are designed to test your understanding of the content covered in Chapter 7. Following the questions, answers are provided so you can verify your conclusions.

Questions

1. What is RoCEv2, and how does it enable RDMA over Ethernet in AI/ML clusters?

2. Describe the main congestion points in RoCEv2-based AI data center networks and their impact on performance.

3. How does Explicit Congestion Notification (ECN) function in RoCEv2 fabrics, and what are its operational parameters?

4. Explain Priority Flow Control (PFC) and its limitations in lossless Ethernet fabrics for AI/ML.

5. What is Data Center Quantized Congestion Notification (DCQCN), and how does it combine ECN and PFC for end-to-end congestion control?

6. How does Source Flow Control (SFC) differ from traditional PFC, and what are its advantages in RoCEv2 fabrics?

7. Describe the role and operation of Congestion Signaling (CSIG) and in-band telemetry in RoCEv2-based AI fabrics.

8. Summarize the relationship between ECN, PFC, DCQCN, and the newer SFC in achieving lossless, high-performance RoCEv2 fabrics for AI/ML.

Answers

1. RoCEv2 (RDMA over Converged Ethernet version 2) encapsulates RDMA traffic in UDP/IP packets, enabling RDMA capabilities over standard Ethernet networks. It leverages lossless Ethernet features (for example, PFC, ECN) to provide low-latency, high-throughput, zero-copy data transfers between servers, bypassing the CPU and kernel. RoCEv2 is widely used in AI/ML clusters for distributed training, where rapid synchronization of large data volumes is required.

2. Congestion can occur at multiple points:

    - Local leaf link congestion: Multiple servers sending line-rate traffic to a local storage or compute node

    - Leaf-to-spine and spine-to-leaf congestion: Multiple flows converging on the same uplink/downlink, especially in Clos topologies

    - Leaf-to-server congestion: Oversubscription or bursty traffic exceeding NIC or server bandwidth

    - Spine-to-super spine congestion: Aggregation points in multi-stage fabrics

Congestion at any point can cause packet loss, increased latency, and degraded JCT, especially for synchronized AI/ML workloads.

3. ECN enables end-to-end congestion signaling by marking packets when switch buffer utilization exceeds a configurable threshold. Marked packets trigger the receiver to send a congestion notification packet (CNP) to the sender, which then reduces its transmission rate. ECN thresholds must be carefully tuned to balance responsiveness and avoid excessive packet drops. ECN is effective for early congestion detection but may be too slow for microbursts or rapid congestion events.

4. PFC is a link-layer mechanism that pauses traffic for specific classes when buffer thresholds are exceeded, preventing packet loss. It operates on a per-priority basis, using XOFF/XON frames to control flow. Limitations include head-of-line blocking (pausing all flows in a class), risk of PFC storms (cascading pauses), and unfairness (one flow can block others). PFC must be carefully configured to avoid deadlocks and ensure fairness in high-throughput AI/ML environments.

5. DCQCN is a hybrid congestion control protocol for RoCEv2, combining ECN (for early, end-to-end signaling) and PFC (for lossless link-layer flow control). DCQCN uses ECN marks to adjust sender rates via a quantized feedback loop, reducing transmission rates before PFC is triggered. If congestion persists, PFC provides immediate lossless backpressure. DCQCN requires NIC and switch support, and its parameters (for example, ECN/PFC thresholds, rate reduction factors) must be tuned for optimal performance.

6. SFC (Source Flow Control) is a new IETF standard that allows congested switches to send congestion signals directly to the source, bypassing hop-by-hop PFC propagation. SFC can trim packet payloads and reverse source/destination headers, enabling faster, flow-based congestion mitigation. Unlike PFC, which operates at the class level, SFC targets specific flows, reducing head-of-line blocking and improving fairness.

7. CSIG is an emerging mechanism that embeds multi-bit congestion signals in live data packets using in-band network telemetry (INT). Switches add CSIG tags indicating buffer occupancy, congestion stage, and device/link IDs. Receivers reflect this information to senders, enabling real-time, path-aware congestion management. CSIG supports fine-grained, low-overhead congestion detection and can inform adaptive routing and rate control algorithms.

8. ECN provides early, end-to-end congestion signaling, enabling proactive rate reduction. PFC ensures lossless transport at the link layer but can cause head-of-line blocking and PFC storms if overused. DCQCN integrates ECN and PFC, using quantized feedback to adjust sender rates and minimize PFC activation. SFC offers fast, flow-based congestion mitigation, reducing reliance on class-based PFC. Together, these mechanisms provide a layered approach to congestion management, balancing responsiveness, fairness, and lossless operation in high-throughput, synchronized AI/ML workloads.

Chapter 8: IP Routing for AI/ML Fabrics

The following questions are designed to test your understanding of the content covered in Chapter 8. Following the questions, answers are provided so you can verify your conclusions.

Questions

1. Why is BGP (Border Gateway Protocol) widely adopted for routing in large-scale AI data center fabrics, and what are its key configuration considerations?
2. How does BGP Deterministic Path Forwarding (BGP-DPF) enhance traffic engineering in AI/ML clusters?
3. What are the advantages and limitations of using RIFT (Routing in Fat Trees) as an IGP in AI data center backbones?
4. How does IS-IS with FlexAlgo support path diversity and workload isolation in AI fabrics?
5. What are the trade-offs between BGP, IS-IS, and RIFT for AI/ML data center routing?
6. How does segment routing (SR/SRv6) enable advanced traffic engineering in AI data centers?
7. What is the role of telemetry and real-time monitoring in adaptive routing for AI/ML fabrics?
8. How does multi-tenancy impact routing and segmentation in AI data center networks?

Answers

1. BGP is favored for its scalability, very advanced IP routing policy control, and ability to handle large numbers of prefixes in Clos and non-Clos topologies. In AI fabrics, eBGP is often used with unique ASN assignments per rack or switch, leveraging BGP unnumbered (RFC 5549) for simplified peering via IPv6 link-local addresses. Key considerations include ASN allocation to prevent routing loops, use of BGP add-path for multipath redundancy, and route policies for prefix advertisement and filtering. BGP's path-vector nature and loop prevention via AS_PATH attributes are critical for maintaining stable, deterministic routing in multi-tier, high-bandwidth environments. On the same eBGP session within the fabric, different types of services can be enabled, such as EVPN for multi-tenancy using EVPN RT5 (Route Type 5) for IP prefix isolation and L2 MAC-VRF services for the MAC@ advertisements. Peering from the ToR using BGP to the server is also possible using open-source BGP stack at the server level, which makes an end-to-end IP routing protocol implementation more consistent.

2. BGP-DPF enables logical partitioning of the physical fabric into multiple "colored" paths or logical fabrics. By associating specific flows (for example, based on GPU ID or QPair) with a logical fabric, deterministic path selection is achieved, isolating elephant flows and ensuring predictable latency and bandwidth. This is implemented via BGP community attributes and

session coloring, allowing for tenant isolation, SLA enforcement, and optimized resource utilization in multi-tenant or multi-workload environments.

3. RIFT is designed for large-scale, hierarchical fat-tree topologies. It offers fast convergence, automatic disaggregation on failure, and built-in support for wide ECMP and unequal-cost multipathing (UCMP). It uses northbound link-state and southbound distance-vector propagation, reducing FIB size on leaf nodes and supporting zero-touch provisioning. However, RIFT is less flexible for policy-based routing and less mature in multi-vendor environments compared to BGP.

4. IS-IS FlexAlgo allows the definition of multiple logical topologies (algorithms) with distinct constraints (for example, bandwidth, latency). Each FlexAlgo computes its own SPF tree, enabling traffic to be steered over different paths based on workload requirements. This supports isolation of critical AI flows, multi-tenancy, and traffic engineering without requiring MPLS or SRv6 encapsulation, making it suitable for pure IP fabrics.

5. BGP offers policy control, scalability, and multi-vendor support but slower convergence and more complex configuration. IS-IS provides fast convergence and FlexAlgo for path diversity. It is a link-state protocol, but it is less commonly used in data centers. RIFT is optimized for fat-tree topologies and offers fast convergence and automatic disaggregation, but it is newer and less widely supported. The choice depends on scale, required features, and operational familiarity.

6. Segment routing enables explicit path control by encoding a list of segments (nodes or links) in the packet header. SRv6 uses IPv6 extension headers to carry segment lists, enabling deterministic routing, bandwidth guarantees, and fast rerouting. This is valuable for pinning AI workloads to specific paths, isolating tenants, and optimizing resource usage, but it requires hardware support and careful management of segment lists to avoid MTU issues.

7. Telemetry provides real-time data on link utilization, latency, buffer occupancy, and congestion events. This information can be fed into routing protocols or controllers to dynamically adjust path selection, reroute around congestion, and optimize load balancing. Technologies like in-band network telemetry (INT) and streaming telemetry (gNMI/gRPC) are essential for closed-loop, adaptive routing in high-performance AI fabrics.

8. Multi-tenancy requires strict traffic isolation, often implemented via VRF instances, EVPN-VXLAN overlays, and routing policies. Routing protocols must support per-tenant segmentation, route leaking where appropriate, and scalable handling of overlapping address spaces. BGP-EVPN is commonly used for control-plane signaling, enabling flexible, scalable multi-tenant architectures with fine-grained policy enforcement.

Chapter 9: Storage Network Design and Technologies

The following questions are designed to test your understanding of the content covered in Chapter 9. Following the questions, answers are provided so you can verify your conclusions.

Appendix A

Questions

1. What are the primary storage network architectures used in AI data centers, and how do they differ in performance and scalability?

2. How does NVMe over Fabrics (NVMe-oF) work, and what are its protocol options?

3. What is GPUDirect Storage, and how does it accelerate AI/ML workloads?

4. Compare InfiniBand and Ethernet (RoCEv2) as storage network transports for AI clusters.

5. How do parallel file systems support large-scale distributed AI training?

6. What are the key design considerations for redundancy and path diversity in storage networks?

7. How does storage network design differ between training and inference phases in AI pipelines?

8. What are the challenges and solutions for integrating on-premises and cloud storage in hybrid AI data centers?

Answers

1. AI data centers use block storage (NVMe-oF), file storage (parallel file systems like Lustre, GPFS, and WekaFS), and object storage (S3-compatible storage). NVMe-oF provides low-latency, high-throughput block access over Ethernet (TCP or RDMA) or InfiniBand. Parallel file systems enable simultaneous, high-speed access to shared data sets by multiple nodes, which is essential for distributed training. Object storage is used for scalable, cost-effective archival and RAG workloads. Each architecture has trade-offs in latency, throughput, scalability, and management complexity.

2. NVMe-oF extends the NVMe protocol over network fabrics, allowing remote SSDs to be accessed as if they were local. Protocol options include NVMe-o-TCP (which runs over standard Ethernet and provides easier deployment and higher latency), NVMe-o-RDMA (which uses RoCEv2 or InfiniBand for ultra-low latency), and NVMe-o-FC (Fibre Channel). NVMe-oF uses submission and completion queues, with capsules and PDUs for command and data transfer, supporting high IOPS and parallelism.

3. GPUDirect Storage enables direct data transfers between GPU memory and NVMe storage, bypassing the CPU and system memory. This reduces data movement overhead, lowers latency, and increases throughput for training and inference workloads. GPUDirect Storage leverages RDMA and DMA engines, and it is supported by Nvidia's CUDA and compatible storage systems.

4. InfiniBand offers ultra-low latency (around 300 nanoseconds), lossless transport, and credit-based flow control, making it ideal for high-performance storage fabrics. Ethernet with RoCEv2 offers similar RDMA capabilities over standard Ethernet, enabling greater scalability

and vendor diversity; however, it requires careful tuning of PFC, ECN, and DCQCN for lossless operation. InfiniBand is often used in HPC and legacy AI clusters, while RoCEv2 is preferred for large-scale, cost-sensitive deployments.

5. Parallel file systems distribute both data and metadata across multiple storage nodes, enabling concurrent access by thousands of compute nodes. They support POSIX semantics, high aggregate bandwidth, and redundancy. Examples include Lustre, GPFS, BeeGFS, and WekaFS. These systems are optimized for large, sequential reads/writes and can integrate with object storage for tiered data management.

6. Redundancy is achieved through dual fabrics (A/B), multipath I/O, and RAID or erasure coding at the storage layer. Path diversity ensures that failure of a switch, link, or storage node does not disrupt access. Storage networks must be designed with non-blocking topologies, sufficient buffer space, and failover mechanisms to maintain high availability and performance.

7. Training requires high-throughput, low-latency access to large data sets, favoring NVMe-oF and parallel file systems. Inference often involves smaller, random-access workloads, where object storage or distributed file systems may be more appropriate. Storage architectures must be optimized for the specific I/O patterns and concurrency levels of each phase.

8. Hybrid architectures require seamless data movement between on-premises NVMe/parallel file systems and cloud object storage. Solutions include S3 gateways, data movers, and unified namespace file systems (for example, WekaFS with S3 tiering). Challenges include maintaining consistency, minimizing data transfer latency, and managing security and access control across domains.

Chapter 10: AI Network Performance KPIs

The following questions are designed to test your understanding of the content covered in Chapter 10. Following the questions, answers are provided so you can verify your conclusions.

Questions

1. What are the most critical KPIs for evaluating AI data center performance, and how are they measured?
2. How does MLCommons' MLPerf benchmark suite standardize AI performance evaluation?
3. Why is job completion time (JCT) a key metric for AI/ML clusters, and what factors influence it?
4. How do throughput and latency metrics differ in their significance for training versus inference workloads?
5. What is the role of power- and energy-efficiency metrics (for example, FLOPS/Watt) in AI data center benchmarking?

6. How does scalability (strong and weak scaling) affect AI data center design and KPI interpretation?

7. Why is reproducibility essential in AI benchmarking, and how is it enforced in MLPerf?

8. How can benchmarking results inform architectural and operational improvements in AI data centers?

Answers

1. Key KPIs include job completion time (JCT), throughput (FLOPS, IOPS), latency (per operation and tail), accuracy (model quality), power consumption (Watts, PUE), and scalability (speedup, efficiency). These are measured using standardized benchmarks (for example, MLPerf), telemetry data, and application-level metrics. Accurate measurement requires synchronized clocks, representative workloads, and consistent test environments.

2. MLPerf provides closed-division (fixed model/data set) and open-division (innovation allowed) benchmarks for training, inference, and storage. It specifies reference models, data sets, accuracy targets, and test harnesses, enabling fair, reproducible comparisons across hardware, software, and cloud services. Results are peer reviewed and published for transparency.

3. JCT measures the total time to train a model to a target accuracy. It is influenced by compute performance, network bandwidth and latency, storage throughput, parallelism efficiency, and tail latency. Reducing JCT accelerates model iteration and deployment, directly impacting business agility and research productivity.

4. Throughput (samples/sec, FLOPS) is critical for training, where large batches are processed in parallel. Latency (response time) is more important for inference, especially in real-time applications. Both metrics must be balanced to optimize resource utilization and user experience.

5. Power efficiency determines operational cost and sustainability. Metrics like FLOPS/Watt and PUE (power usage effectiveness) quantify how effectively hardware converts electrical power into useful computation. Energy-efficient designs reduce cooling requirements and environmental impact.

6. Strong scaling measures how performance improves as more resources are added for a fixed problem size; weak scaling measures performance as both resources and problem size increase proportionally. Poor scaling indicates bottlenecks in network, storage, or software, guiding optimization efforts.

7. Reproducibility ensures that results are reliable and comparable across systems and over time. MLPerf enforces this by requiring open-source code, fixed data sets, accuracy validation, and peer review. This builds trust in published results and drives industry progress.

8. Benchmarking identifies bottlenecks (for example, network congestion, storage latency), validates design choices, and guides investment in hardware/software upgrades. Continuous benchmarking enables data-driven decision-making for scaling, tuning, and evolving AI infrastructure.

Chapter 11: Monitoring and Telemetry

The following questions are designed to test your understanding of the content covered in Chapter 11. Following the questions, answers are provided so you can verify your conclusions.

Questions

1. What are the primary monitoring and telemetry tools used in AI data center networks, and what metrics do they collect?

2. How does in-band network telemetry (INT) provide granular visibility into AI/ML fabric performance?

3. What is the role of historical versus real-time monitoring in AI data center operations?

4. How do telemetry and monitoring systems support closed-loop automation in AI fabrics?

5. What are the challenges of monitoring tail latency and microbursts in high-speed AI networks?

6. How does correlation of server and switch telemetry enhance root cause analysis?

7. What is the function of in-band flow analyzers (IFAs) in AI data center fabrics?

8. How do monitoring and telemetry systems contribute to data center sustainability and efficiency?

Answers

1. Tools include SNMP (for polling interface, CPU, and memory stats), streaming telemetry (gNMI/gRPC for real-time metrics of the DCQCN), syslog (for event logging), sFlow/IPFIX (for flow-level traffic analysis), and agent-based probes (for active measurements). Metrics collected include link utilization, buffer occupancy, tail latency, packet drops, PFC/ECN events, and power/thermal data.

2. INT embeds metadata (for example, timestamps, queue depth, hop latency) directly into data packets as they traverse the network. This enables per-packet, per-hop visibility into latency, congestion, and path selection, supporting real-time troubleshooting and adaptive routing.

3. Historical monitoring enables trend analysis, capacity planning, and anomaly detection over days/weeks. Real-time monitoring supports immediate detection of congestion, failures, and performance degradation, enabling rapid response and automated remediation.

4. Telemetry feeds real-time data into controllers or orchestration platforms, which can automatically adjust routing, load balancing, or resource allocation in response to detected issues. This enables self-healing, adaptive networks that maintain SLA compliance under dynamic workloads.

5. Tail latency and microbursts can occur at microsecond time scales, requiring high-resolution telemetry and timestamping. Traditional SNMP polling is too slow; INT and hardware timestamping are needed to capture transient events that impact JCT and application performance.

6. Correlating metrics across layers (for example, GPU utilization, NIC queue depth, switch buffer occupancy) enables precise identification of bottlenecks, distinguishing between compute, network, and storage issues. This accelerates troubleshooting and targeted optimization.

7. IFA tags packets with metadata at ingress, collects per-hop data (for example, latency, queue ID, congestion), and aggregates the data at egress or collectors. This provides end-to-end flow visibility, supporting SLA monitoring, congestion localization, and performance tuning.

8. By tracking power, cooling, and resource utilization, telemetry enables dynamic adjustment of workloads, proactive maintenance, and optimization of energy consumption, supporting sustainability goals and reducing operational costs.

Chapter 12: Ultra Ethernet Consortium (UEC)

The following questions are designed to test your understanding of the content covered in Chapter 12. Following the questions, answers are provided so you can verify your conclusions.

Questions

1. What is Ultra Ethernet Consortium (UEC), and what are its primary objectives for AI data center and HPC networking?

2. How does the UEC protocol stack differ from traditional Ethernet and RoCEv2?

3. What are the new packet delivery modes defined by UEC, and how do they benefit AI workloads?

4. How does Credit-Based Flow Control (CBFC) in UEC improve upon Priority Flow Control (PFC)?

5. What is the role of In-Network Collectives (INC) and collective communication libraries (CCLs) in UEC?

6. How does UEC ensure interoperability and backward compatibility with existing Ethernet networks?

7. What are the key congestion management mechanisms in UEC, and how do they interact?

8. How does UEC address the scaling and performance challenges of next-generation AI clusters?

Answers

1. UEC is an industry group developing open standards for Ethernet optimized for AI, HPC, and cloud workloads. Its goals include ultra-high scalability (1 million or more endpoints), deterministic low latency, lossless transport, multi-vendor interoperability, and integration of advanced congestion management and collective communication features.

2. UEC introduces new transport and link-layer protocols (UET, CBFC, LLR), supports both UDP-based and raw IP encapsulation, and adds semantic and packet delivery sublayers (SES, PDS) for advanced flow control. It enables flexible packet delivery modes (ROD, RUD, RUDI, UUD), built-in security, and in-network collective operations, while maintaining backward compatibility with standard Ethernet.

3. ROD (reliable ordered delivery) ensures in-order, reliable delivery; RUD (reliable unordered delivery) allows out-of-order delivery with reliability; RUDI (reliable unordered delivery idempotent) supports idempotent operations for collective updates; and UUD (unreliable unordered delivery) is best-effort delivery. These modes enable fine-grained control over performance, reliability, and resource usage for diverse AI workloads.

4. CBFC provides per-priority, per-virtual-channel lossless transport, supporting more classes and better scheduling than PFC. It uses explicit credit exchange between sender and receiver, reducing head-of-line blocking and PFC storms, and enabling more granular congestion management.

5. INC enables switches to participate in collective operations (for example, AllReduce, Broadcast), offloading aggregation and synchronization from servers to the network. CCLs provide software APIs for collective operations, tightly integrated with AI frameworks. Together, they reduce latency, improve bandwidth utilization, and accelerate distributed training.

6. UEC supports dual-mode operation, allowing devices to communicate using either standard Ethernet or UEC protocols, based on negotiation. It maintains standard Ethernet framing, supports UDP/IP encapsulation, and provides compliance and certification frameworks for multi-vendor interoperability.

7. UEC uses end-to-end mechanisms (NSCC, RCCC) for congestion control, segment-level CBFC for lossless transport, and packet trimming for fast retransmission. NSCC uses window-based control with ECN feedback; RCCC uses receiver-managed credits. These mechanisms work together to minimize packet loss, reduce JCT, and maintain high throughput under heavy load.

8. UEC's protocol stack, collective communication features, and congestion management enable scaling to millions of endpoints, deterministic low latency, and more efficient resource utilization; for example, using packet trimming, the originator will re-send well-identified packets if any packet loss is observed. Its open, programmable architecture supports rapid innovation, multi-vendor ecosystems, and future-proofing for evolving AI/HPC workloads. The AI data center admin will be able to cover the backend and frontend as well as storage with the unified administration tooling.

APPENDIX B

Acronyms

Acronym	Acronym definition
AALC	Air Assisted Liquid Cooling – A cooling method using air and liquid for data center equipment.
ACC	Accelerator – Specialized hardware (e.g., GPU, TPU) designed to speed up AI/ML computations.
AEC	Active Electrical Cable – Copper cables with integrated electronics for high-speed data transfer.
AFH	AI Fabric Header – A protocol header used in Scale-Up Ethernet (SUE-T) for AI workloads.
AI	Artificial Intelligence – The simulation of human intelligence by machines.
AIC	AI Cluster – A group of interconnected servers for AI processing (context-dependent).
AOC	Active Optical Cable – Fiber optic cables with integrated transceivers for high-speed connections.
API	Application Programming Interface – A set of rules for software components to communicate.
ASIC	Application-Specific Integrated Circuit – A chip designed for a specific application, such as networking.
AXI	Advanced eXtensible Interface – A high-performance, on-chip communication protocol.
BCH	Bose–Chaudhuri–Hocquenghem – An error-correcting code used in digital communications.
BGP	Border Gateway Protocol – The main routing protocol for exchanging information between networks on the internet.
BMS	Bare Metal Server – A physical server dedicated to a single tenant, without virtualization.
BTH	Base Transport Header – A header used in InfiniBand and RoCEv2 protocols for RDMA.
CBFC	Credit-Based Flow Control – A congestion control mechanism using credits to manage data flow.
CCL	Collective Communication Library – Software for efficient data exchange in parallel computing (e.g., NCCL, RCCL).

Acronym	Acronym definition
CFP	C Form-factor Pluggable – A standard for optical transceivers used in high-speed networks.
CNP	Congestion Notification Packet – A packet used to signal network congestion in RDMA networks.
CPU	Central Processing Unit – The main processor in a computer, executing instructions.
CQ	Completion Queue – A queue that tracks completed operations in RDMA or storage systems.
CQE	Completion Queue Entry – An entry in a completion queue indicating a finished operation.
CXL	Compute Express Link – A high-speed CPU-to-device and CPU-to-memory interconnect.
DAC	Direct Attach Copper – Short-distance copper cables for direct server-to-switch connections.
DC	Data Center – A facility housing computer systems and networking equipment.
DCQCN	Data Center Quantized Congestion Notification – A congestion control protocol for RDMA over Ethernet.
DCR	Data Center Reach – An optical transceiver type for medium-range data center connections.
DFE	Decision Feedback Equalization – A technique to improve signal quality in high-speed data links.
DL	Data Link – The layer or protocol responsible for node-to-node data transfer (e.g., in UALink).
DLB	Dynamic Load Balancing – A method for distributing network or compute load dynamically.
DSP	Digital Signal Processor – A processor optimized for digital signal processing tasks.
DWDM	Dense Wavelength Division Multiplexing – A technology for increasing bandwidth over fiber by combining multiple wavelengths.
ECMP	Equal Cost Multi Path – A routing strategy that uses multiple paths with equal cost for load balancing.
ECN	Explicit Congestion Notification – A network feature for signaling congestion without dropping packets.
EDR	Enhanced Data Rate – A high-speed InfiniBand link rate.
EoR	End of Row – A data center rack design with switches at the end of a row.
ESUN	Ethernet Scale-Up Networking – An open framework for high-speed, low-latency Ethernet interconnects in scale-up AI systems.
EVPN	Ethernet Virtual Private Network – A technology for extending Layer 2 networks over Layer 3 infrastructure.
FAD	Flexible Algorithm Definition – A set of rules for flexible routing algorithms (e.g., in IS-IS).
FCT	Flow Completion Time – The time taken to complete a network flow or job.
FEC	Forward Error Correction – A method for detecting and correcting errors in data transmission.
FEP	Fabric Endpoint – A node (server or switch port) in a UEC network.
FIB	Forwarding Information Base – A table used by routers to determine packet forwarding.
FIFO	First-In, First-Out – A queueing method where the first element added is the first to be removed.
FLOPS	Floating Point Operations Per Second – A measure of computer performance, especially in scientific calculations.
FPGAs	Field Programmable Gate Arrays – Reconfigurable integrated circuits used for custom hardware acceleration.
FR	Far Reach – An optical transceiver type for longer-range connections.
GDS	GPU Direct Storage – Technology for direct data transfer between GPU memory and storage.
GLB	Global Load Balancing – A load-balancing method that considers global network state.

Acronym	Acronym definition
GPU	Graphics Processing Unit – A processor specialized for parallel computations, widely used in AI/ML.
GRH	Global Routing Header – A header in InfiniBand for routing packets between subnets.
HBM	High Bandwidth Memory – A type of fast, high-capacity memory used in GPUs and accelerators.
HPC	High Performance Computing – Computing at high speeds and large scales, often for scientific or engineering tasks.
IB	InfiniBand – A high-speed networking technology for data centers and HPC.
IBTA	InfiniBand Trade Association – The industry group that develops InfiniBand standards.
IFA	In-Band Flow Analyzer – A telemetry technology for monitoring network flows in real time.
INC	In-Network Collectives – Performing collective communication operations within the network switches.
INT	In-band Network Telemetry – Embedding telemetry data within live network traffic.
IP	Internet Protocol – The principal communications protocol for relaying packets across networks.
iSCSI	Internet Small Computer Systems Interface – A protocol for linking data storage over IP networks.
IS-IS	Intermediate System to Intermediate System – A routing protocol for moving information efficiently within a network.
JCT	Job Completion Time – The total time required to finish a computational job or task.
KPI	Key Performance Indicator – A measurable value that demonstrates how effectively objectives are being achieved.
LID	Local Identifier – An address used in InfiniBand networks.
LLH	Link Layer Header – The header at the link layer of a network protocol.
LLM	Large Language Model – An AI model trained on large text data sets for natural language processing.
LLR	Link Layer Retry – A mechanism for retransmitting lost packets at the link layer.
LR	Long Reach – An optical transceiver type for long-distance connections.
LRO	Linear Receive Optics – Optics with a linear receive path for improved performance.
MAC	Media Access Control – A sublayer that controls how devices on a network gain access to data.
MAC-VRF	MAC Virtual Routing and Forwarding – Virtualization of MAC address routing tables.
MAP	Mean Average Precision – A metric for evaluating accuracy in information retrieval and object detection.
MIG	Multi-Instance GPU – NVIDIA technology for partitioning a GPU into multiple instances.
MMF	Multi-Mode Fiber – An optical fiber designed to carry multiple light modes for short distances.
MoE	Mixture of Experts – An AI model architecture using multiple specialized sub-models.
MTID	Multi-Topology Identifier – An identifier for different topologies in routing protocols.
NCCL	NVIDIA Collective Communication Library – A library for multi-GPU and multi-node communication.
NDR	Next Data Rate – The latest high-speed InfiniBand link rate.
NIC	Network Interface Card – Hardware that connects a computer to a network.
NNH	Next-to-Next-Hop – A BGP attribute for advanced routing decisions.
NPA	Network Physical Address – A physical address in UALink scale-up systems.
NRZ	Non-Return-to-Zero – A binary signal modulation method.

Acronym	Acronym definition
NSCC	Network Signal Congestion Control – A UEC protocol for end-to-end congestion management.
NSPN	Network Sequence Packet Number – A sequence number for packets in SUE-T.
NVLink	NVIDIA proprietary GPU interconnect – A high-speed link for connecting NVIDIA GPUs.
NVMe	Non-Volatile Memory Express – A protocol for accessing high-speed storage media.
NVMe-oF	NVMe over Fabrics – Extending NVMe protocol over network fabrics.
NVMe-o-RDMA	NVMe over RDMA – NVMe protocol over RDMA networks.
NVMe-o-TCP	NVMe over TCP – NVMe protocol over TCP/IP networks.
NVSwitch	NVIDIA proprietary switch for GPU interconnect – A switch for connecting multiple NVIDIA GPUs.
OAM	Operations, Administration, and Maintenance – Functions for managing and monitoring networks.
OCP	Open Compute Project – An initiative for open-source hardware and data center designs.
OM1/2/3/4/5	Optical Multimode fiber types – Different grades of multimode optical fiber.
OSFP	Octal Small Form-factor Pluggable – A form factor for high-speed optical transceivers.
OSPF	Open Shortest Path First – A link-state routing protocol for IP networks.
PAM4	Pulse Amplitude Modulation with Four Levels – A modulation technique for high-speed data transmission.
PCS	Physical Coding Sublayer – A sublayer for encoding and decoding data on physical media.
PDC	Packet Delivery Context – A logical connection/session in UEC networks.
PDS	Packet Delivery Sublayer – A UEC protocol layer managing delivery mechanisms.
PDU	Protocol Data Unit – A unit of data specified in a protocol.
PFC	Priority Flow Control – A mechanism for pausing traffic on specific priorities to prevent data loss.
PGAS	Partitioned Global Address Space – A memory model for parallel programming.
PIDonFEP	Process ID on Fabric Endpoint – Identifies a process on a UEC fabric endpoint.
PMA	Physical Medium Attachment – A sublayer for connecting to physical transmission media.
POSIX	Portable Operating System Interface – A family of standards for maintaining compatibility between operating systems.
PUE	Power Usage Effectiveness – A metric for data center energy efficiency.
QAM	Quadrature Amplitude Modulation – A modulation method for transmitting data.
QDR	Quad Data Rate – A high-speed InfiniBand link rate.
QOS	Quality of Service – Techniques to manage network traffic and ensure performance.
QPAIR	Queue Pair – A pair of queues used in RDMA for send/receive operations.
QPS	Queries Per Second – A measure of system throughput.
QSFP-DD	Quad Small Form-factor Pluggable Double Density – A higher-density version of QSFP.
QSFP	Quad Small Form-factor Pluggable – A form factor for optical transceivers.
RAG	Retrieval-Augmented Generation – An AI technique combining retrieval and generation.
RCCC	Receiver Credit Congestion Control – A UEC protocol for receiver-based congestion management.
RCCL	ROCm Communication Collectives Library – AMD's library for collective communication.
RCF	Reliability Control Field – A field in SUE-T for reliability management.

Acronym	Acronym definition
RETH	RDMA Extended Transport Header – A header for RDMA operations.
RH	Reliability Header – A header in SUE-T for reliability information.
RIFT	Routing in Fat Trees – A routing protocol for large-scale data center networks.
RMA	Remote Memory Access – Accessing memory on a remote device directly.
RoCE	RDMA over Converged Ethernet – A protocol for RDMA over Ethernet networks.
RoCEv2	RDMA over Converged Ethernet version 2 – An updated version of RoCE using routable IP.
ROD	Reliable Ordered Delivery – A UEC packet delivery mode ensuring in-order delivery.
RODI	Reliable Ordered Delivery Idempotent – A UEC delivery mode for idempotent operations.
RUD	Reliable Unordered Delivery – A UEC packet delivery mode allowing out-of-order delivery.
RUD/ROD/RUDI/UUD	UEC packet delivery modes – Various reliability and ordering options in UEC.
RUD/UUD	Reliable/Unreliable Unordered Delivery – UEC packet delivery modes.
RUDI	Reliable Unordered Delivery Idempotent – A UEC delivery mode for idempotent, unordered operations.
S3	Simple Storage Service – Amazon's object storage service.
SAN	Storage Area Network – A dedicated network for data storage devices.
SC	Subscriber Connector – A type of fiber optic connector.
SDN	Software Defined Networking – Network management using software-based controllers.
SDR	Single Data Rate – An InfiniBand link rate.
SFC	Source Flow Control – A congestion control mechanism signaling directly from switch to source.
SHMEM	Shared Memory – A parallel programming model for sharing memory between processes.
SID	Segment Identifier – An identifier for segments in segment routing (SRv6).
SLB	Static Load Balancing – A load-balancing method using static rules.
SMF	Single Mode Fiber – An optical fiber for long-distance, single-mode light transmission.
SNMP	Simple Network Management Protocol – A protocol for monitoring and managing network devices.
SPA	System Physical Address – A physical address in UALink scale-up systems.
SR	Short Reach – An optical transceiver type for short distances.
SRv6	Segment Routing over IPv6 – A routing protocol using IPv6 segments.
SSD	Solid State Drive – A storage device using flash memory.
SUE	Scale-Up Ethernet – An Ethernet-based scale-up interconnect for accelerators.
SUE-T	Scale-Up Ethernet Transport – The protocol and transport layer for SUE.
SUPN	Super Spine – A high-level switch in multi-stage data center networks (context-dependent).
TCAM	Ternary Content Addressable Memory – A memory type used for high-speed searching in networking.
TCP	Transmission Control Protocol – A core protocol for reliable data transmission over IP networks.
TE-LB	Traffic Engineering Load Balancing – Load balancing using traffic engineering techniques.
TL	Transaction Layer – The protocol layer for transactions in UALink.
ToR	Top of Rack – A switch placed at the top of a server rack.
TPU	Tensor Processing Unit – A processor specialized for AI workloads, developed by Google.

Acronym	Acronym definition
UALink	Ultra Accelerator Link – An open standard for high-speed, low-latency accelerator interconnects.
UCIe	Universal Chiplet Interconnect Express – A standard for connecting chiplets within a package.
UEC	Ultra Ethernet Consortium – An industry group developing advanced Ethernet standards for AI/HPC.
UET	Ultra Ethernet Transport – The transport protocol defined by UEC for AI/HPC.
ULS	Ultra Link Switch – The switch used in UALink scale-up systems.
UUD	Unreliable Unordered Delivery – A UEC packet delivery mode with no reliability or ordering.
VAST	Vendor name, parallel file system – A high-performance file system for AI/data workloads.
VC	Virtual Channel – A logical channel for separating traffic on a physical link.
VNI	VXLAN Network Identifier – An identifier for VXLAN segments.
VOQ	Virtual Output Queue – A queueing method to prevent head-of-line blocking in switches.
VXLAN	Virtual Extensible LAN – A network virtualization technology for overlaying Layer 2 networks over Layer 3.
WDM	Wavelength Division Multiplexing – A technique for sending multiple signals over a single fiber.
WQE	Work Queue Element – A data structure for RDMA or storage operations.
ZR	Extended Reach – An optical transceiver type for very long distances.

Index

Numerics

400G ZR, 73
400G-SR8, 76

A

A100 server, 68
AALC (air-assisted liquid chromatography), 92. *See also* cooling systems
ACC (accelerator), 276–277, 279, 280. *See also* GPU/s; scale-up; xPU
accuracy, 223
acknowledgement packet, RoCEv2, 14–15
ACLs (access lists), 175
Adjacency SID, 180
AEC (active electrical cable), 79
AETH header, 14–15
AFH (AI Fabric Header), 281–282
agent-based network monitoring, 231
AI. *See also* models
  models, 1
  training, 1
AI data center/s. *See also* fabric; inference; training
  benchmarking for ML, 225–226
  burstiness, 23
congestion management, 24–25, 26–27, 156
  CSIG (Congestion Signaling), 137–139
  DCQCN (Data Center Quantized Congestion Notification), 27–28, 134–136
  ECN (Explicit Congestion Notification), 127–129
  orchestration, 268
  PFC (Priority Flow Control), 130–134
  SFC (Source Flow Control), 136–137
  super spine-to-spine link, 126
  in the UEC specification, 261–265
  UET (Ultra Ethernet Transport), 242–243
cooling systems, 88
  back-to-front airflow, 88–89
  bidirectional fans, 89
  choosing airflow direction, 89
  cold plate liquid cooling, 91–92
  front-to-back airflow, 88
  immersion liquid cooling, 90
  liquid cooling, 89–90
  rear-door heat exchanger liquid cooling, 92–93
  single-phase immersion cooling, 90
  sprayed liquid cooling, 93
  two-phase immersion cooling, 91

elephant flows, 24–25
Ethernet, 22. *See also* Ethernet
flowlets, 23
GPUs, 23
high-bandwidth flows, 23
inference, 3, 20, 33, 226
Infiniband, 21. *See also* IB (InfiniBand)
JCT (job completion time), 6–7, 24
KPIs (key performance indicators), 223
load balancing, 25–26. *See also* load balancing
   dynamic, 25
   global, 25
   IP ECMP, 24
   selective, 26
   static, 25
monitoring, 229, 231
   agent-based, 231
   collector software, 231–232
   corrective actions, 237–238
   IFA (In-band Flow Analyzer), 230, 234–237
   IPFIX, 231
   network utilization, 232–233
   real-time, 231, 233
   RPC query, 230
   sFlow, 231
   SNMP polling, 230
   SNMP traps, 230
   syslog, 230
   telemetry, 230, 232
performance benchmarking, 222
power consumption, 87, 301
rack design, 45, 48–49
   end-of-row, 47–48, 77
   middle-of-row, 47, 77
   thermal management, 88
   ToR (Top of Rack), 45–47
RDMA (remote direct memory access), 8. *See also* RDMA (remote direct memory access)
   data transfer, 9
   transport types, 9–10
   WQE (work queue element), 9
   RoCEv2 (RDMA over Converged Ethernet version 2), 11. *See also* RoCEv2 (RDMA over Converged Ethernet version 2)
   acknowledgement packet, 14–15
   header, 11
   low entropy, 22–23
   messages, 11–14
   sessions, 11
   ROD (rail-optimized design), 34–40
   storage, 32
   tail latency, 6–8
   training, 19–20, 33. *See also* training
   vendor interoperability, 300
AI training lifecycle, 209
   data preparation, 191
   data storage positioning, 192
   training and tuning phase, 192
algorithm/s, 1, 20
   Dijkstra, 144
   FEC (Forward Error Correction), 73
   job, 6
   link quality band, 103
all-gather/all-reduce, 4–5
AMD, Infinity Fabric, 67
AOC (active optical cable), 79
API, 243
   LibFabric, 241
   Verbs, 9
architecture, 76–77. *See also* scale-out; scale-up
   inference DC, 56–60
   rack design, 48–49
      end-of-row, 47–48
      middle-of-row, 47
      ToR (Top of Rack), 45–47
   scheduled fabric, 49–50
   training DC, 33
      GPU-to-leaf connectivity, 33–34
      ROD (rail-optimized design), 34–40, 300–301
      RUD (rail-unified design), 42
      servers, 33–34
ASIC, 98, 99, 101, 104–105
   INC agents, 268

Index

PFE, 70
    SerDes (serializer/deserializer), 71
ASNs (autonomous system numbers), 145–146, 149–151
assigned flow mode, DLB (dynamic load balancing), 104
AXI interface, SUE-T, 285

B

backend network, storage, 192
back-to-front airflow, 88–89
backward propagation, 3
bandwidth, 280
    data center, 68
    DLB, 99, 103–104
    ECMP, 97
    optics, 68–69
    UEC scaling, 260
BCH (Bose-Chaudhuri-Hocquenghem) codes, 73
benchmarking, 221–222
    for ML, 225–226
    suites, MLCommons, 224–225
BGP, 111, 143–144, 145
    ADD-PATH, 151–152
    ASNs (autonomous system numbers), 145–146, 149–151
    DPF (Deterministic Path Forwarding), 155–162
    Link Bandwidth Extended Community, 153–155
    minimum peers per IP prefix, 155
    NNHN (next-next-hop nodes), 108–110
    AS-PATH strip and replace, 152–153
    session establishment, 146–148
    unnumbered implementation, 145–149
bidirectional fans, 89
block, 38–39
block storage, 198, 199–201
BMSaaS (Bare Metal Server as a Service), 171
on-box agent, 162
brick, 38–39
BTH header, InfiniBand, 11
burstiness, 23

C

cabling
    fiber-optic. *See also* optics
        AOC (active optical cable), 79
        LC (Lucent Connector), 78
        MMF (multi-mode fiber), 74–75
        MPO, 78
        SMF (single-mode fiber), 75
        transceiver types, 76–77
    multiplanar architecture, 60
cache coherence, 291
CBFC (Credit-Based Flow Control), 242, 263–264
CCL (collective communication library), 3–4, 243, 246, 266–268
central controller, 162
certification, Ultra Ethernet Specification v1.0, 269
CFP2, 80
CFP4, 80, 81
clock data recovery, 73
Clos topology, 50, 52, 56. *See also* topology
clusters, 240. *See also* GPUs; server/s
    combining server- and network-level multi-tenancy, 175
    GPUaaS, 171
    GPUs, 36–40
    SR (Segment Routing), 183–184
    training, 33
CNP (congestion notification packet), 128
cold plate liquid cooling, 91–92
collapsed storage design, 196–197
compliance, Ultra Ethernet Specification v1.0, 269
Compliance working group, 243–244
congestion
    leaf-to-server link, 125
    leaf-to-spine link, 124
    local leaf link, 123–124
    spine-to-leaf link, 124–125
    spine-to-super spine link, 126
congestion management, 24–25, 26–27, 156
    CSIG (Congestion Signaling), 137–139
    DCQCN (Data Center Quantized Congestion Notification), 27–28, 134–136

ECN (Explicit Congestion Notification), 127
    CNPs, 128
    data transfer, 129
    ECN bits, 127–128
    ECN threshold, 129
    lossy queue, 129
    message flow, 128
    packet flow between servers, 128
orchestration, 268
PFC (Priority Flow Control)
    frames, 130
    packet flow, 131–132
    pause frames, 130
    storm, 133
    watchdog, 133–134
    XOFF/XON thresholds, 130–132
SFC (Source Flow Control), 136–137
super spine-to-spine link, 126
in the UEC specification, 261
    CBFC (Credit-Based Flow Control), 263–264
    NSCC (Network Signal Congestion Control), 261–262
    packet trimming, 264–265
    RCCC (Receiver Credit Congestion Control), 262
    UET (Ultra Ethernet Transport), 242–243
control plane, SR (Segment Routing), 180
control verbs, 292
controller-based fabric, 178–179
controller-based load balancing, 179–180
cooling systems, 88
    back-to-front airflow, 88–89
    bidirectional fans, 89
    choosing airflow direction, 89
    front-to-back airflow, 88
    liquid cooling, 89–90
        cold plate liquid cooling, 91–92
        immersion liquid cooling, 90
        rear-door heat exchanger liquid cooling, 92–93
        single-phase immersion cooling, 90
        sprayed liquid cooling, 93
        two-phase immersion cooling, 91

co-packaged optics, 82–83
CPAK, 80
CPO (co-packaged optics), 82
CPU, cold plate liquid cooling, 91–92
CRC (cyclic redundancy checking), 253–254
CSIG (Congestion Signaling), 137–139
CtlOS, 248
CUDA (Compute Unified Device Architecture), 213, 304
CXL (Compute Express Link), 67, 275

D

DAC (Direct Attach Copper), 78–79
data centers. *See* AI data centers
data gathering, 2
data link layer, UALink, 287
data parallelism, 4–5
data plane, SR (Segment Routing), 180
data preparation, 191
data tagging, 2
DCQCN (Data Center Quantized Congestion Notification), 27–28, 40, 108, 134–136, 240
DD-QSFP. *See* QSFP-DD (QSPF Double Density)
Dell'Oro report, 68–69
demultiplexers, 71
Dijkstra algorithm, 144
direct-to-chip liquid cooling, 91. *See also* liquid cooling
DLB (dynamic load balancing), 25, 99, 103–104, 156
    assigned flow mode, 104
    flowlet mode, 104–106
    per-packet mode, 116
DPF (Deterministic Path Forwarding). *See* BGP, DPF (Deterministic Path Forwarding)
Dragonfly, 50–52, 164–167, 246–247
DSP (Digital Signal Processor), 60, 71–72
    clock data recovery, 73
    equalization, 73
    error detection and correction, 73
    FEC (Forward Error Correction), 73
    modulation, 72–73

DWDM (dense wavelength division multiplexing), 73, 75
dynamic IP routing protocols. *See* IP routing protocols

E

eBGP underlay, 145
ECMP (equal cost multipathing), 97–99, 102, 153–155. *See also* load balancing
ECN (Explicit Congestion Notification), 24, 27–28, 127. *See also* DCQCN(Data Center Quantized Congestion Notification)
    CNPs, 128
    data transfer, 129
    ECN bits, 127–128
    ECN threshold, 129
    lossy queue, 129
    message flow, 128
    packet flow between servers, 128
EDR (Enhanced Data Rate), 15
efficiency, 223
elephant flows, 24–25, 106
encapsulation, 252
    UDP-based, 252–255
    UET over IP, 255–256
end-of-row design, 47–48, 77
entanglement, 304
equalization, 73
error detection and correction, 73
ESUN (Ethernet Scale-Up Networking), 276
Ethernet. *See also* RoCEv2 (RDMA over Converged Ethernet version 2); SUE-T (Scale-Up Ethernet Transport)
    advantages in AI training clusters, 22
    comparison with InfiniBand, 15–16
    and UEC, 246–247
extension header, SRv6, 182–183

F

FA (fabric address), 244–245
fabric, 32, 301. *See also* Ethernet; IB (InfiniBand); IP routing protocols; NVMe-oF (NVME overFabrics); scale-up; UEC (Ultra Ethernet Consortium)
    burstiness, 23
    controller-based, 178–179
    eBGP underlay, 145
    extending IP routing to the server, 177–178
    IGPs (interior gateway protocols), 162–163
    IP Clos, 143
        IS-IS, 168–171
        RIFT (Routing in Fat Trees), 163–168
    JCT (job completion time), 6–7
    scale-up, 276
    UEC IP, 246
    underlay, 156
fans
    back-to-front airflow, 88–89
    bidirectional, 89
    choosing airflow direction, 89
    front-to-back airflow, 88
FBF (filter-based forwarding), 161
FCoIP (Fibre Channel over IP), 194
FEC (Forward Error Correction), 73
FEP (Fabric Endpoint), 244–245, 249, 250–252
FFE (feed-forward equalization), 73
fiber-optic cables. *See* optics
FIFO interface, SUE-T, 285
file storage, 198
file systems, high-performance, 208–209
    VAST, 211
    WekaFS, 209–211
Flex Algo, 169–171
flit packing, 286–289
flood reduction, IS-IS, 168–169
flow pinning, 26
flow-based load balancing, 99–100
    DLB (dynamic load balancing), 99, 103–104, 156
        assigned flow mode, 104
        DLB flowlet mode, 104–106
    GLB (global load balancing), 99, 106–108
        NNHN (next-next-hop nodes), 108–110
    SLB (static load balancing), 99, 100–102
    TELB (traffic engineering load balancing), 99, 110–111

flowlet mode, DLB (dynamic load balancing), 104–106
flowlets, 23
forward propagation, 3
four-pod scale-up design, 278–279
frames, PFC, 130
front-to-back airflow, 88

G

GBP (group-based policy), 177
generative AI, 1
GLB (global load balancing), 25, 99, 106–110, 156, 300–301
GPT model, 302
GPUDirect Storage, 211–213
GPU/s, 23, 97–98, 104, 111, 280
    cluster, 35–37
    cold plate liquid cooling, 91
    job scheduler, 179
    -to-leaf connectivity, 33–34
    Multi-Instance, 173
    multiplanar architecture, 57
    NICs, 33, 68
    Nvidia, 67
    NVLink, 67
    optical interconnects, 304
    parallel processing, 3–4
    rails, 34
    -server, 24
    vendors, 302
gradients, 3

H

H100 server, 68
hardware coherence, 291
hash, 99
hash key, 101–102
HBM (high-bandwidth memory), 279
HCA (host channel adapter), 22
HDD
    network-connected, 190
    PCIe-connected, 190–191

HDR (Hundred Gigabit Data Rate), 15
header
    IFA (In-band Flow Analyzer), 235–237
    RoCEv2 (RDMA over Converged Ethernet version 2), 11
high-bandwidth flows, 23
higher-order modulation, 72
high-performance file systems
    VAST, 211
    WekaFS, 209–211
historical network monitoring, 231
home agents, 291
HPC (high-performance computing) systems, 19, 241
hybrid fabric storage, 196–197

I

IB (InfiniBand), 9, 15–16, 21
    advantages in AI training clusters, 21
    AETH header, 14–15
    BTH header, 11
    comparison with UEC, 270–271
    HCA (host channel adapter), 22
    for storage, 213–214
        LID (local identifier), 215–216
        typical designs, 214–215
    transport services, 21
idempotent, 259–260
IEEE 802.3bm, 79
IEEE 802.3bs, 79
IFA (In-band Flow Analyzer), 230, 234–235,237
    header, 235–237
    latency, 237
IGPs (interior gateway protocols), 143, 162–168. *See also* IP routing protocols
IM (INC Manager), 246
immersion liquid cooling, 90
    single-phase, 90
    two-phase, 91
inactivity timer, DLB (dynamic load balancing), 104–105
INC (In-Network Collectives), 243, 246, 266–268

inference, 3, 20, 33, 226
    DC architecture, 56–60
    fabric, 32
    multi-node, 56
    quality of data, 31
    requirements, 20
Intel, CXL (Compute Express Link), 67
interconnect points, 281–282
interoperability and backward compatibility, Ultra Ethernet Specification v1.0, 269
inter-rail communication, 36, 40
intra-rail communication, 36
IP ECMP load balancing, 24
IP routing protocols, 143, 144
    BGP, 143–144, 145
        ADD-PATH, 151–152
        ASNs (autonomous system numbers), 145–146, 149–151
        DPF (Deterministic Path Forwarding), 155–161
        Link Bandwidth Extended Community, 153–155
        minimum peers per IP prefix, 155
        AS-PATH strip and replace, 152–153
        session establishment, 146–148
        traffic-to-fabric color mapping, 161–162
        unnumbered implementation, 145–149
    IS-IS, 144
        Flex Algo, 169–171
        flood reduction, 168–169
    OSPF, 144
IPFIX, 231
IS-IS, 143
    Flex Algo, 169–171
    flood reduction, 168–169
    TLV (Type-Length-Value), 170–171
iteration, training, 4
ITU-T G.959.1, 79
iWARP (Internet Wide Area RDMA Protocol), 10

J-K

JCT (job completion time), 6–8, 24, 222
job, 6
job scheduler, 179
JobID, 245–246, 254
KPIs (key performance indicators), 221
    AI data center, 223
    model, 222

L

labeled data, 19
latency, 223
    IFA (In-band Flow Analyzer), 237
    NVLink, 275
    PCIe, 191, 275
    residence time, 237
    RUD (rail-unified design), 42
    storage network, 190
    tail, 120
LC (Lucent Connector), 78
LDPC (low-density parity-check), 73
leaf switch/node, 34–35, 146, 149, 151,152, 153–155, 161, 170, 173
    link congestion, 124
    top-of-rack, 45–47
leaf-to-server link congestion, 125
leaf-to-spine link congestion, 124
LibFabric, 241, 243
LID (local identifier), 215–216
life cycle, AI model, 2–3
Link Layer Working Group, 242
link-state protocols
    IS-IS, 144, 168–169
    OSFP, 144
liquid cooling, 89–90
    cold plate, 91–92
    immersion, 90
        single-phase, 90
        two-phase, 91
    rear-door heat exchanger, 92–93
    sprayed, 93
LLMs (large language models), 1, 189
LLR (Link-Layer Reliability), 242, 265–266
load balancing, 25, 97, 98–99
    controller-based, 179–180
    dynamic, 25

flow-based, 99–100
    DLB (dynamic load balancing), 99, 103–106, 156
    GLB (global load balancing), 99, 106–108
    SLB (static load balancing), 99, 100–102
    TE-LB (traffic engineering load balancing), 99
    TELB (traffic engineering load balancing), 110–111
global, 25, 300–301
hash key, 101–102
IP ECMP, 24
mechanism comparison, 117–118
per-packet, 115–116
    DLB, 116
    random spray, 116
resilient hashing, 101–102
selective, 26
selective packet spraying, 116–117
static, 25
LoadGen, 225
local leaf link congestion, 123–124
logical separation, storage network, 195–196
lossless queue, 130
lossy queue, 129
low entropy, RoCEv2 (RDMA over Converged Ethernet version 2), 22–23
LPO (Linear Pluggable Optics), 60, 82–83
LRO (Linear Receive Optics), 60, 82–83

M

MAC-VRF/RT5-VRF, 162
Management working group, 243–244
MCP (Model Context Protocol), 3
memory coherence, 291–292
micro-segment SRv6, 183
middle-of-row design, 47, 77
MIG (Multi-Instance GPU), 173
MLCommons, 223
    benchmarking suites, 224–225
    initiatives, 224
    objectives, 224
MLCube, 224
MLPerf, 224
MMF (multi-mode fiber), 74–75
model/s, 1, 33, 97. *See also* algorithms; training
    deployment, 31
    GPT, 302
    inference, 3
    KPIs (key performance indicators), 222
    life cycle, 2–3
    monitoring, 3
    optimization, 302–303
    parallelism, 5–6
    parameters, 302–303
    selection, 31
    training, 3
        backward propagation, 3
        collective communication, 4
        data parallelism, 4–5
        forward propagation, 3
        gradients, 3
        iteration, 4
        JCT (job completion time), 6–7
        model parallelism, 5–6
        parallelism, 4
modulation, 72–73
    higher-order, 72
    NRZ (Non-Return-to-Zero), 81
    PAM4, 72, 81
    quadrature amplitude, 72
MoE (Mixture of Experts), 277–278
monitoring, 229, 231
    agent-based, 231
    collector software, 231–232
    corrective actions, 237–238
    historical network, 231
    IFA (In-band Flow Analyzer), 230, 234–235, 237
        header, 235–237
        latency, 237
        nodes, 234
    IPFIX, 231
    real-time, 231, 233
    RPC query, 230
    sFlow, 231
    SNMP polling, 230

SNMP traps, 230
syslog, 230
telemetry, 230, 232
MPLS (Multiprotocol Label Switching), 180
MPO, 78
multi-node inference, 56
multiplanar architecture, 56–60, 281
multiplexors, 71
multi-tenancy
    combining server- and network-level, 175
    network-level, 171–173
    server-level, 173

N

NCCL (NVIDIA Collective Communication Library), 10, 266–267. *See also* RCCL (ROCm Communication Collectives Library)
NDR (Next Data Rate), 15
network-level multi-tenancy, 171–173, 175
NICs, 33, 68, 240
    in multiplanar architecture, 57
    storage network, 189–190
NNHN (next-next-hop nodes), 107, 108–110
Node SID, 180
NRZ (Non-Return-to-Zero), 72, 81
NSCC (Network Signal Congestion Control), 242, 247, 261–262
Nvidia
    A100 server, 68
    B300, 280
    CUDA (Compute Unified Device Architecture), 304
    GPUDirect Storage, 211–213
    GPUs, 67
    H100 server, 68
    H100/H200 servers, 155
    NVSwitch, 42
NVLink, 67, 275, 292–293
NVMe-oF (NVME over Fabrics), 190, 191, 199–201
NVMe-o-FC (NVMe over Fibre Channel), 200
NVMe-o-RDMA (NVMe over RDMA), 192, 200
NVMe-o-RDMA/RoCEv2 state machine, 206–208
NVMe-o-TCP (NVME over TCP), 123, 194, 200–201
NVMe-o-TCP state machine, 201–206
NVSwitch, 67

O

OAM (Ops/Admin/Maintenance), 107
object storage, 198
off-premises storage, 196–197
OIF-OSPF-1.0, 79
optics, 73–74
    400G-SR8, 76
    AOC (active optical cable), 79
    bandwidth, 68–69
    CFP4, 81
    co-packaged, 82–83
    DWDM (dense wavelength division multiplexing), 75
    industry challenges, 70
    LC (Lucent Connector), 78
    Linear Receive, 82–83
    MMF (multi-mode fiber), 74–75
    MPO, 78
    OSFP, 81–82
    QSFP (Quad Small Form-factor Pluggable), 80–82
    SMF (single-mode fiber), 75
    transceiver types, 76–77
orchestration, 268
OSFP (Octal Small-Form Factor Pluggable), 79, 81–82
OSPF (Open Shortest Path First), 144

P

packet delivery modes (UEC), 257–259, 260–261
    ROD (reliable ordered delivery), 259
    RUD (reliable unordered delivery), 259
    RUDI (reliable unordered delivery idempotent), 259–260
    UUD (unreliable unordered delivery), 260

packet flow
    demultiplexers and multiplexers, 71
    DSP (Digital Signal Processor), 71–72
        clock data recovery, 73
        equalization, 73
        error detection and correction, 73
        modulation, 72–73
packet spraying, selective, 116–117
packet trimming, 264–265
PAIR (People+AI Research), 224
PAM4, 72, 81
parallelism, 3–4
    data, 4–5
    model, 5–6
    pipeline, 5
    tensor, 5–6
parameters
    model, 302–303
    training, 2
path attributes, ADD-PATH, 151–152
AS-PATH strip and replace, 152–153
path-vector protocol, BGP, 145
pause frames, 130
PBR (policy-based routing), 111
PCIe (Peripheral Component Interconnect Express), 67, 189
    -connected HDD/SDD, 190–191
    latency, 275
PDC (Packet Delivery Context), 245
PDS (Packet Delivery Sublayer), 245, 248, 250–251
per-flow load balancing, 99–100
performance
    benchmarking, 221–222
    JCT (job completion time), 222
    KPIs (key performance indicators), 221
    network, monitoring, 232–233
    tail latency, 6–8
Performance and Debug working group, 243–244
per-packet load balancing, 115–116
    DLB (dynamic load balancing), 116
    random spray, 116

PFC (Priority Flow Control), 24, 27–28. *See also* DCQCN (Data Center Quantized Congestion Notification)
    frames, 130
    lossless queue, 130
    packet flow, 131–132
    pause frames, 130
    storm, 133
    watchdog, 133–134
    XOFF/XON thresholds, 130–132
PFE (packet forwarding engine), 99
PFE ASIC, 70, 71
physical layer (PHY), 247–248
Physical Layer working group, 243–244
physical separation, storage network, 194
PIDonFEP, 245–246, 254
pipeline parallelism, 5
ports, server, 34
POSIX (Portable Operating System Interface), 209–210
power consumption, data centers, 87, 301
preprocessing, workload, 31
PRI (Packet Rate Improvement), 242
profiles, UEC (Ultra Ethernet Consortium), 241
protocol stack, UEC, 247–248
    PDS (Packet Delivery Sublayer), 250–251
    physical layer (PHY), 247–248
    session establishment, 248–250
PSN (packet sequence number), 11, 258–259, 260, 265
PUE (power usage effectiveness), 88
PyTorch, 210–211

Q

QAM (quadrature amplitude modulation), 72
Qiskit SDK, 304
QML (quantum machine learning), 304
QoS, 216
QP (queue pair), 11
QSFP (Quad Small Form-factor Pluggable), 80–82
QSFP28, 79

QSFP56, 79, 80–81, 87
QSFP-DD (QSPF Double Density), 79, 80–82
quantum computing, 303–304

R

rack design, 48–49. *See also* cooling systems
    end-of-row, 47–48, 77
    middle-of-row, 47, 77
    scale-up, 276
    thermal management, 88
    ToR (Top of Rack), 45–47
RAG (retrieval-augmented generation), 3, 189
rail-only design, 33–34
rails, 34
random spray per-packet load balancing, 116
RCCC (Receiver Credit Congestion Control), 242, 262
RCCL (ROCm Communication Collectives Library), 10, 247
RDMA (remote direct memory access), 8, 301
    data transfer, 9
    message exchange, 11–14
    NVMe over, 200
    over Converged Ethernet (RoCE), 9–16. *See also* RoCEv2 (RDMA over Converged Ethernetversion 2)
    PSN (packet sequence number), 11
    QP (queue pair), 11
    transport types, 9–10
    Verbs API, 9
    WQE (work queue element), 9
real-time network monitoring, 231, 233
rear-door heat exchanger liquid cooling, 92–93
redundancy, storage network, 193–194
resilient hashing, 101–102
Resource Index, 245–246, 254
RH (Reliability Header), 282–283
RIFT (Routing in Fat Trees), 143, 163–168
RoCEv2 (RDMA over Converged Ethernet version 2), 11, 22, 99, 104,117, 123, 155, 194, 240, 247, 301
    acknowledgement packet, 14–15
    comparison with UEC, 270–271
    DCQCN (Data Center Quantized Congestion Notification), 40
    header, 11
    messages, 11–14
    sessions, 11
ROD (rail-optimized design), 33–40, 300–301
    BGP DPF, 156–159
    block, 38–39
    GPU scaling, 38–40
    inter-rail communication, 36, 40
    leaf switch, 34–35
    spine switch, 36–37
    super spine switch, 40
ROD (reliable ordered delivery), 245, 259
RPC query, 230
RUD (rail-unified design), 33–34, 42, 300–301
RUD (reliable unordered delivery), 245, 259
RUDI (reliable unordered delivery idempotent), 245, 259–260

S

scalability, 223
scale-out, 275, 276
scale-up, 1, 275, 293. *See also* SUE-T (Scale-Up Ethernet Transport)
    chassis, 278
    fabric interconnect points, 276
    four-pod design, 278–279
    memory coherence, 291–292
    multi-planar design, 281
    physical constraints, 276
    rack systems, 276, 280
    server, 276–277
    SUE-T (Scale-Up Ethernet Transport), 276, 280, 292–293
        AFH (AI Fabric Header), 281–282
        AXI interface, 285
        on-die memory, 285
        end-to-end protocol stack, 283–284
        FIFO interface, 285
        interconnect points, 281–282
        RH (Reliability Header), 282–283
        shared memory model, 284

systems comparison, 292–294
UALink, 286
    control verbs, 292
    data link layer, 287
    flit packing, 286–289
    PGAS (Partitioned Global Address Space), 292
    physical layer, 286–287
    shared memory semantics, 286–287
    transaction layer, 287, 288, 292
    UPLI (UALink Protocol Level Interface), 289–290
    virtual pod partitioning, 289
    xPU, 286
use cases, 277–278
xPU, 276–277, 279
    ACC (accelerator), 280
    bandwidth, 280
    HBM, 279
scaling, GPU cluster, 36–40
"Scaling Distributed Machine Learning with Gigabit Ethernet", 68
scheduled fabric, 49–50
sDLB (selective load balancing), 26
sectors, 288
selective packet spraying, 116–117
semi-supervised training, 2
SerDes (serializer/deserializer), 71, 286–287
server/s, 299
    A100, 68
    clusters, 239
    connectivity options, 75–76
    extending IP routing to the, 177–178
    H100, 68
    internal switch, 34
    -level multi-tenancy, 173
    multi-tenancy, 175
        combining server- and network-level, 175
        network-level, 171–173
        server-level, 173
    PCIe connection, 190
    ports, 34
    quantum, 304

scale-up, 276–277
topology, 67–68
training DC, 33–34
SES (Semantic Sublayer), 242–243, 245, 248, 250–251
session establishment, UEC, 248–250
SFC (Source Flow Control), 136–137
sFlow, 231
SID (SR identifier), 180
single-phase immersion cooling, 90
SLB (static load balancing), 25, 99, 100–102
SMF (single-mode fiber), 75
SNMP polling, 230
SNMP traps, 230
SNR (signal-to-noise ratio), 73
software coherence, 291–292
Software working group, 243
Source PFC. *See* SFC (Source Flow Control)
spine switch/node, 36–37, 146, 149, 152, 153–155, 170, 173
spine-to-leaf link congestion, 124–125
spine-to-super spine link congestion, 126
sprayed liquid cooling, 93
SR (Segment Routing), 180
    for AI/ML clusters, 183–184
    control plane, 180
    data plane, 180
    SID (SR identifier), 180
    SR domain, 180
SRv6
    -based traffic engineering, 182–183
    compressed SID, 183
    extension header, 182–183
    micro-segment, 183
SSD (solid-state drive), 189
    network-connected, 190–191
    PCIe-connected, 190–191
state machine
    NVMe-o-RDMA/RoCEv2, 206–208
    NVMe-o-TCP, 201–206
storage, 189
    block, 198
    file, 198
    GPUDirect Storage, 211–213

object, 198
    off-premises, 196–197
storage data center, 32
storage networks, 217
    AI training server connection, 192–193
    backend, 192
    IB (InfiniBand), 213–214
        LID (local identifier), 215–216
        typical designs, 214–215
        VLs (virtual lanes), 216
    latency, 190
    NICs, 189–190
    NVMe-oF for block-level access, 199–201
    speed, 192
    SSD/HDD storage, 189–191
    training
        collapsed storage design, 196–197
        hybrid fabric storage, 196–197
        inter-site redundancy, 194
        logical separation, 195–196
        node- and link-level redundancy, 193
        physical separation, 194
Storage working group, 243–244
structured data, 191
SUE-T (Scale-Up Ethernet Transport), 276, 280, 292–293
    AFH (AI Fabric Header), 281–282
    AXI interface, 285
    on-die memory, 285
    end-to-end protocol stack, 283–284
    FIFO interface, 285
    interconnect points, 281–282
    RH (Reliability Header), 282–283
    shared memory model, 284
super spine switch, 40
super spine-to-spine link congestion, 126
supervised training, 2
switches
    high-radix, 68
    internal, 34
    leaf, 34
    PFE (packet forwarding engine), 99
    rack design, 48–49
        end-of-row, 47–48

        middle-of-row, 47
        ToR (top-of-rack), 45–47
    server connectivity options, 75–76
    spine, 36–37
    super spine, 40
    VOQ (Virtual Output Queues), 50
syslog, 230

T

tagging, 2
tail latency, 6–8, 120
TCP, 126
TE-LB (traffic engineering load balancing), 99
TELB (traffic engineering load balancing), 110–111
telemetry, 230
tensor parallelism, 5–6
thermal management, rack systems, 88. *See also* cooling systems
thread execution, 6
throughput, 223
TLV (Type-Length-Value), 170–171
topologies, 50
    Clos, 50, 52, 56
    Dragonfly, 50–52
    middle-of-row, 47
    Torus, 53–55
topology. *See also* architecture; rack design
    rail-optimized, 34–40
    ROD (rail-optimized design)
        block, 38–39
        GPU scaling, 38–40
        inter-rail communication, 36, 40
        spine switches, 36–37
        super spine switch, 40
    RUD (rail-unified design), 42
    server, 67–68
ToR (Top of Rack) design, 45–47
Torus, 53–55, 246–247
traffic engineering, 110–111, 179, 182–183. *See also* TELB (traffic engineering load balancing)
traffic-to-fabric color mapping, 161–162
training, 2, 31. *See also* AI training lifecycle

architecture, 33. *See also* architecture; topology
   GPU-to-leaf connectivity, 33–34
   ROD (rail-optimized design), 34–40, 300–301
   RUD (rail-unified design), 42
   servers, 33–34
backward propagation, 3
clusters, 33, 240
data centers, 19–20
distributed, 226
fabric, 32
forward propagation, 3
gradients, 3
iteration, 4
JCT (job completion time), 6–7
labeled data, 19
parallelism, 3–4
   data, 4–5
   model, 5–6
semi-supervised, 2
storage, 189
storage network
   collapsed storage design, 196–197
   hybrid fabric storage, 196–197
   inter-site redundancy, 194
   logical separation, 195–196
   node- and link-level redundancy, 193
   physical separation, 194
supervised, 2
time requirements, 226, 302
unsupervised, 3
Transport working group, 242–243, 257–258
TSS (UET Transport Security Sublayer), 254, 256
two-phase immersion cooling, 91

U

UALink, 276, 280, 285, 286, 288
   control verbs, 292
   data link layer, 287
   flit packing, 286–289
   PGAS (Partitioned Global Address Space), 292
   physical layer, 286–287
   shared memory semantics, 286–287
   transaction layer, 287, 288, 292
   UPLI (UALink Protocol Level Interface), 289–290
   virtual pod partitioning, 289
   xPU, 286
UCIe (Universal Chiplet Interconnect Express), 67
UDP, 123
UDP-based encapsulation, 252–255
UEC (Ultra Ethernet Consortium)
   challenges and future directions, 269–270
   comparison with InfiniBand and RoCEv2, 270–271
   Compliance WG, 243–244
   congestion management, 261
      CBFC (Credit-Based Flow Control), 263–264
      NSCC (Network Signal Congestion Control), 261–262
      packet trimming, 264–265
      RCCC (Receiver Credit Congestion Control), 262
   existing Ethernet and, 246–247
   INC (In-Network Collectives), 266–268
   interoperability and backward compatibility, 269
   Link Layer WG, 242
   LLR (Link-Layer Reliability), 265–266
   Management WG, 243–244
   motivations for redesigning AI/ML fabrics, 240–241
   network architectures, 246
   orchestration, 268
   packet delivery modes, 257–259, 260–261
      ROD (reliable ordered delivery), 259
      RUD (reliable unordered delivery), 259
      RUDI (reliable unordered delivery idempotent), 259–260
      UUD (unreliable unordered delivery), 260
   Performance and Debug WG, 243–244
   Physical Layer WG, 243–244
   profiles, 241
   protocol stack, 247–248

PDS (Packet Delivery Sublayer), 250–251
    physical layer (PHY), 247–248
    session establishment, 248–250
  Software WG, 243
  Storage WG, 243–244
  Transport WG, 242–243, 257–258
  working groups, 241
UET (Ultra Ethernet Transport), 241, 242, 243, 246
  over IP, 255–256
  UDP-based encapsulation, 252–255
Ultra Ethernet, 239
underlay, eBGP, 145–149
unstructured data, 191
unsupervised training, 3
UPLI (UALink Protocol Level Interface), 289–290
use cases
  scale-up systems, 277–278
  UEC (Ultra Ethernet Consortium), 241
UUD (unreliable unordered delivery), 245, 260

V

VAST, 211
vendor interoperability, 300
Verbs API, 9
virtual pod partitioning, 289
VLs (virtual lanes), 216
VOQ (Virtual Output Queues), 50
VRF, 162

VXLAN, 145, 162, 171
  GBP (group-based policy), 177
  RT5, 173

W

watchdog, PFC, 133–134
WDM (wavelength division multiplexing), 74
weighted ECMP, 102, 153–154
WekaFS, 209–211
working groups, 241
  Compliance, 243–244
  Link Layer, 242
  Management, 243–244
  Performance and Debug, 243–244
  Physical Layer, 243–244
  Software, 243
  Storage, 243–244
  Transport, 242–243, 257–258
WQE (work queue element), 9

X-Y-Z

XOFF/XON thresholds, 130–132
xPU, 275, 276–277, 279. *See also* GPU/s
  ACC (accelerator), 280
  bandwidth, 280
  HBM (high-bandwidth memory), 279
  SPA (System Physical Address), 292
  UALink, 286

ZR (extended reach), 77

Register Your Product at informit.com/register

Access additional benefits and save up to 65%* on your next purchase

- Automatically receive a coupon for 35% off books, eBooks, and web editions and 65% off video courses, valid for 30 days. Look for your code in your InformIT cart or the Manage Codes section of your account page.
- Download available product updates.
- Access bonus material if available.**
- Check the box to hear from us and receive exclusive offers on new editions and related products.

InformIT—The Trusted Technology Learning Source

InformIT is the online home of information technology brands at Pearson, the world's leading learning company. At informit.com, you can

- Shop our books, eBooks, and video training. Most eBooks are DRM-Free and include PDF and EPUB files.
- Take advantage of our special offers and promotions (informit.com/promotions).
- Sign up for special offers and content newsletter (informit.com/newsletters).
- Access thousands of free chapters and video lessons.
- Enjoy free ground shipping on U.S. orders.*

* *Offers subject to change.*
** *Registration benefits vary by product. Benefits will be listed on your account page under Registered Products.*

Connect with InformIT—Visit informit.com/community

informIT

Addison-Wesley • Adobe Press • Cisco Press • Microsoft Press • Oracle Press • Peachpit Press • Pearson IT Certification • Que